Teaching Elementary Social Studies

Strategies, Standards, and Internet Resources

Third Edition

James A. Duplass
University of South Florida

WADSWORTH
CENGAGE Learning™

Australia • Brazil • Japan • Korea • Mexico • Singapore • Spain • United Kingdom • United States

WADSWORTH
CENGAGE Learning

Teaching Elementary Social Studies: Strategies, Standards, and Internet Resources, **Third Edition**

James A. Duplass

Education Editor: Christopher Shortt
Assistant Editor: Caitlin Cox
Editorial Assistant: Linda Stewart
Media Editor: Dennis Fitzgerald
Marketing Manager: Kara
Kindstrom-Parsons
Marketing Assistant: Dimitri Hagnéré
Marketing Communications Manager:
Martha Pfeiffer
Content Project Manager: Tanya Nigh
Creative Director: Rob Hugel
Art Director: Maria Epes
Print Buyer: Paula Vang
Rights Acquisitions Account Manager, Text:
Bob Kauser
Rights Acquisitions Account Manager, Image:
Leitha Etheridge-Sims
Production Service: Cadmus
Text Designer: Lisa Langhoff
Copy Editor: Kelly Horvath
Cover Designer: Lisa Langhoff
Cover Image: Gregor Schuster
Compositor: Cadmus

For product information and technology assistance, contact us at **Cengage Learning Customer & Sales Support, 1-800-354-9706**

For permission to use material from this text or product, submit all requests online at **www.cengage.com/permissions.** Further permissions questions can be emailed to **permissionrequest@cengage.com**

Library of Congress Control Number: 2009939396
ISBN-13: 978-0-495-81282-1
ISBN-10: 0-495-81282-X

Wadsworth
20 Davis Drive
Belmont, CA 94002-3098
USA

Cengage Learning is a leading provider of customized learning solutions with office locations around the globe, including Singapore, the United Kingdom, Australia, Mexico, Brazil, and Japan. Locate your local office at **www.cengage.com/global.**

Cengage Learning products are represented in Canada by Nelson Education, Ltd.

To learn more about Wadsworth, visit **www.cengage.com/wadsworth**
Purchase any of our products at your local college store or at our preferred online store **www.ichapters.com.**

Printed in the United States of America
1 2 3 4 5 6 7 13 12 11 10 09

Contents

Contents

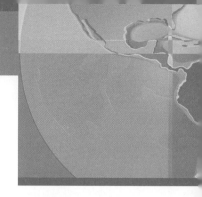

Premium Website

www.cengage.com/login

Premium Website Clickable Links

The Premium Website has the following clickable links listed by topic:

A The Websites cited in the textbook that appear in green.

B Bonus and updated Websites.

C ERIC Online full text documents.

D Annenberg's Learner.org on-demand, streaming videos.

E Thirteen.org's Concept to Classroom's on-demand, streaming videos.

Downloadable Elementary Grades Social Studies Textbook Excerpts for Use in Authentic Lesson Planning Activities

Houghton Mifflin K–6 Social Studies Series Readings

FIRST GRADE TEXT School and Family

Reading 1, Core Lesson 1	Learning About the Past	History
Reading 2, Core Lesson 2	The First Americans	History
Reading 3, Core Lesson 1	Our Earth	Geography
Reading 4, Core Lesson 1	Needs and Wants	Economics
Reading 5, Core Lesson 5	Symbols of our Country	Government
Reading 6, Core Lesson 2	In Your Classroom	Civic Values

THIRD GRADE TEXT Communities

Reading 7, Core Lesson 1	Coming to America	History
Reading 8, Core Lesson 2	Our Country's Geography	Geography
Reading 9, Core Lesson 1	Using Money	Economics
Reading 10, Core Lesson 1	Local Government	Government
Reading 11, Core Lesson 3	Community Resources	Civic Values

TeachSource Videos

Video#	Title	Related Book Topic
1	*Teaching as a Profession: Collaboration with Colleagues*	(Topics 5 & 50)
5	*Cooperative Learning in the Elementary Grades: Jigsaw Model*	(Topic 43)
7	*Inclusion: Grouping Strategies for Inclusive Classrooms*	(Topic 9)
13	*Assessment in the Elementary Grades: Formal and Informal Literary Assessment*	(Topic 13)
16	*Portfolio Assessment: Elementary Classroom*	(Topic 14)
18	*Elementary Reading Instruction: A Balanced Literacy Program*	(Topic 16)
20	*Elementary Writing Instruction: Process Writing*	(Topic 27)
27	*Multiple Intelligences: Elementary School Instruction*	(Topic 9 & Bonus Topic C)
29	*Metacognition: Helping Students Become Strategic Learners*	(Topics 23 & 38 & Bonus Topic C)
33	*Diversity: Teaching in a Multiethnic Classroom*	(Topic 7 & Bonus Topic A)
36	*Inclusion: Classroom Implications for the General and Special Educator*	(Topic 9)
41	Academic Diversity: Differentiated Instruction	(Topic 32 & Bonus Topic A)

Premium Website

Graphic Organizers

Twenty-two downloadable graphic organizers.

Lesson Planning Templates and Examples to Provide a Format and Tools for Authentic Lesson Planning Assignments

Lesson Plan Statement of Goals Template

Lesson Plan Class Notes Template

Lewis and Clark Lesson Statement of Goals

Lewis and Clark Lesson Class Notes

Employment Portfolio and Résumé Templates to Assist Students in Their Transition into Their First Teaching Positions

Bonus Topics

A   Teaching Diverse Populations

B   Temperament and Ideology

C   Learning Practices and Theories

D   Classroom Organization

E   Classroom Management

F   Parent-Teacher Relations

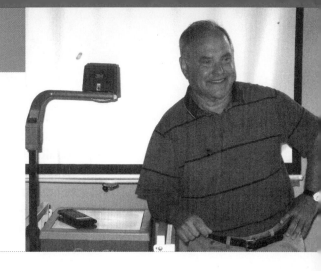

Professor's Preface

Dear Colleague:

I am pleased that ***Teaching Elementary Social Studies: Strategies, Standards, and Internet Resources*** was selected for a third edition by Cengage after its acquisition of the Houghton Mifflin College Division. The decision to launch a third edition reflects the confidence Cengage has in this kind of 21st-century textbook that is fully integrated with digital technology and reflects the continued increase in adoptions since the first edition. I want to thank the more than 20 college professors and elementary school teachers who have reviewed the book since its inception to help me ensure that it stays current with practice while maintaining the attributes that has resulted in so many adoptions.

Why Will This Book Make My Teaching More Effective?

This text and the extensive website resources for professor and students alike will facilitate your teaching in many ways.

1. An introduction to the individual **social studies disciplines** and **standards** is presented to expand students' understanding of social studies. Many students may only have a cursory background in the modes of reasoning used in the social studies disciplines.
2. The straightforward, easily readable, concise text is organized into **compact topics** (rather than dense chapters of text), with the result that students are more inclined to actually read their textbook.
3. To facilitate documentation for **accreditation** and state program approval, a variety of assignments are tied to the Interstate New Teacher Assessment and Support Consortium (INTASC), which can accommodate

almost any state's and National Council for Accreditation of Teacher Education's (NCATE) 2008 critical tasks documentation regime. The intent is to provide a menu of assignments from which you can select and modify those that will make your documentation work easier that would otherwise be possible and that will be most beneficial to your students.

4. **Elementary social studies textbook chapters** are offered in PDF form at the Premium Website from Houghton Mifflin's K–6 series and Doubleday's Core Knowledge series for you and your students to use in applying instructional approaches to content.

5. Through this book's **Premium Website,** you and your students can access all the websites and teaching materials cited in this text. The Premium Website has continuously updated, clickable practical and scholarly resources from sites such as ERIC, Gateway to Educational Materials, Marcopolo, and Edsitement and social studies gateway websites such as National Geographic and EconoED.

6. **Online videos** have been incorporated into the text either for students to view at home or on campus on an independent study basis, as part of an online course or for in-class broadcasts. The online, on-demand, streaming videos are drawn from the award-winning Houghton Mifflin video cases (see the table of contents "TeachSource") as well as from the Annenberg library at Learner.org, Thirteen.org's (New York City's Public Broadcasting station) Concept to Classroom workshops, YouTube, and TeacherTube.

7. At the **Premium Website,** you will also find:

   a. A complete set of **PowerPoint** files for each topic is available for download as a compacted file to your computer. These files have been created for you to download to your computer and modify. You can use them in class to engage students with a mixture of discussion, lecture, demonstration, out-of-class assignments, and in-class activities. The files include content from the textbook and additional content to support active learning at the college level.

   b. An **Instructor's Guide** with suggestions for using and integrating various elements of the book and website resources.

   c. A **Final Exam Item Databank** that contains true-false and multiple-choice questions should you use this kind of final exam in addition to the other assignments available in the book.

   d. A **Sample Syllabus** for a 16-week, one-day-a-week class.

   e. A **Sample Grade Book** in Microsoft Excel format 3.

   f. **Examples and Templates** for lesson- and unit-planning activities.

   g. **Bonus Topics** in PDF form for downloading.

Through strategic use of online resources, posed questions, assignments, and text boxes of Teacher's Tips and key ideas in the form of famous quotes, students are called upon to reflect and be actively engaged in the construction of their pedagogical content knowledge of social studies.

What Is the Same from the Prior Editions?

The second edition of this book has been enhanced with a particular emphasis on examples of both upper and lower elementary education approaches (see next section) while keeping the following underlying approach and principles.

1. A vision of social studies as central to citizenship and character education
2. A narrative comprised of relatively short, easy-to-read, research-based topics
3. A comprehensive introduction to the social studies disciplines and the standards of professional organizations and learned societies
4. Numerous pragmatic tips and thought-provoking quotes and questions
5. Emphasis on literacy, basic skills, and multiple methods of instruction
6. A website for professors with PowerPoints for each topic, sample exam, syllabus, and other features
7. A **Premium Website** for students and professors with clickable links to almost 1,000 resources, including the websites and ERIC online documents mentioned in the text
8. Authentic, performance-based assignments tied to NCATE and INTASC standards that can be used in the accreditation or state program approval process
9. Handy graphic organizers that are downloadable from the Premium Website

Teacher's Tip

WebCT® and **Blackboard®** users: The PDF versions of basal textbook chapters, as well as Internet links, assignments, grade book, sample syllabus, and other Premium Website resources, may be downloaded and transferred to your WebCT or Blackboard course (or another comparable system) during the semesters in which you adopt the book.

What Is New in This Edition?

Among the more significant changes are:

1. The new National Council for the Social Studies (NCSS) statements, *Expectations of Excellence: Curriculum Standards for Social Studies* and *Powerful and Purposeful Teaching in Elementary School Social Studies,* are introduced to reflect the most current thinking of the goals and scope of social studies.
2. Basic skills approaches are now based on the newly announced collaboration of the NCSS and the Partnership for 21st Century Skills.
3. The new 2008 NCATE Standards are integrated into the new and revised assignments for purposes of meeting NCATE teacher education standards.
4. "Close reading" strategies are used to expand the unit on reading strategies.
5. Topics on Character and Values education are expanded to create a clearer link to the role of the teacher in school settings.
6. Topics on Citizenship education and Government include a more extensive narrative about the historical origins of human's approach to society formation.

7. Discovery learning, Service learning, Role Playing and Differentiated Instruction have expanded treatments.
8. The almost 1000 Internet links have been updated and with the new additions, insure that students have the newest Internet resources.
9. More than 80 post-2005 citations reflecting the most recent scholarship have been incorporated into the textbook.
10. New **on-demand online videos** from TeachSourse (the former Houghton Mifflin videos), Annenberg's Learner.org, WNET Thirteen.org's Ed Online, YouTube and TeacherTube for broadcast in the classroom or for student to view outside of class. Each TeachSource video case is a 4- to 6-minute module consisting of video files presenting actual classroom scenarios that depict the complex problems and opportunities teachers face every day. The video clips are accompanied by reflection pedagogy and "artifacts" to provide background information and allow preservice teachers to experience true classroom dilemmas in their multiple dimensions. These cases provide shared field experiences demonstrations, and models of best practices.

How Does This Book Support the Professor's Documentation in a Standards-Based Teacher Education Program?

The Interstate New Teacher Assessment and Support Consortium (INTASC) is an association organized by chief state school officers from nearly 40 states and professional organizations that sets standards for **initial licensure** of teachers for member states. The National Council for Accreditation of Teacher Education (NCATE) is the professional accrediting body for teacher education programs and sets certification standards for its voluntary member colleges.

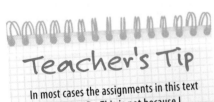

Teacher's Tip

In most cases the assignments in this text are very specific. This is not because I believe my ideas are best, but because I believe it is easier for you to modify detailed assignments than assignments that are too generic.

About 500 of the 1,200 teacher education programs are seeking NCATE accreditation. In addition, and although not the focus of this text, the National Board of Professional Teacher Standards has identified standards for in-service teachers' professional development.

INTASC and NCATE share a common construct (see Table P.1) that is being adopted by teacher education programs to qualify their students for certification and licensure through their states. Through the No Child Left Behind legislation, states are required to adopt a standard under what is known as the High Objective Uniform State Standard of Evaluation (HOUSSE) so that teachers can demonstrate competency in content areas. The assignments included in *Teaching Elementary Social Studies: Strategies, Standards, and Internet Resources* were developed to help professors and teacher education programs demonstrate their compliance with the NCATE and INTASC.

Table P.1   NCATE (2008) and INTASC Standards (See List of Assignments, page 411)

NCATE Standards for Accreditation/Certification	INTASC Core Standards for Licensing
Content Knowledge for Teacher Candidates. Teacher candidates have in-depth knowledge of the subject matter that they plan to teach as described in professional, state, and institutional standards. They demonstrate their knowledge through inquiry, critical analysis, and synthesis of the subject. All program completers pass the academic content examinations in states that require examinations for licensure.	**Principle 1: Subject Matter Expertise.** The teacher understands the central concepts, tools of inquiry, and structures of the discipline(s) he or she teaches and can create learning experiences that make these aspects of subject matter meaningful for students.
Pedagogical Content Knowledge for Teacher Candidates. Teacher candidates reflect a thorough understanding of pedagogical content knowledge delineated in professional, state, and institutional standards. They have in-depth understanding of the subject matter that they plan to teach, allowing them to provide multiple explanations and instructional strategies so that all students learn. They present the content to students in challenging, clear, and compelling ways and integrate technology appropriately.	**Principle 4: Multiple Instructional Strategies.** The teacher understands and uses a variety of instructional strategies to encourage students' development of critical thinking, problem solving, and performance skills. **Principle 6: Communication Skills.** The teacher uses knowledge of effective verbal, nonverbal, and media communication techniques to foster active inquiry, collaboration, and supportive interaction in the classroom. **Principle 7: Instructional Planning.** The teacher plans instruction based upon knowledge of subject matter, students, the community, and curriculum goals.
Professional and Pedagogical Knowledge and Skills for Teacher Candidates. Teacher candidates reflect a thorough understanding of professional and pedagogical knowledge and skills delineated in professional, state, and institutional standards. They develop meaningful learning experiences to facilitate learning for all students. They reflect on their practice and make necessary adjustments to enhance student learning. They know how students learn and how to make ideas accessible to them. They consider school, family, and community contexts in connecting concepts to students' prior experience and applying the ideas to real world problems.	**Principle 3: Diverse Learners.** The teacher understands how students differ in their approaches to learning and creates instructional opportunities that are adapted to diverse learners. **Principle 5: Motivation and Classroom Management.** The teacher uses an understanding of individual and group motivation and behavior to create a learning environment that encourages positive social interaction, active engagement in learning, and self-motivation.
Student Learning for Teacher Candidates. Teacher candidates focus on student learning and study the effects of their work. They assess and analyze student learning, make appropriate adjustments to instruction, monitor student learning, and have a positive effect on learning for all students. They collaborate with other professionals to identify and design strategies and interventions that support student learning.	**Principle 2: Learning and Development.** The teacher understands how children learn and develop, and can provide learning opportunities that support their intellectual, social, and personal development. **Principle 8: Assessment.** The teacher understands and uses formal and informal assessment strategies to evaluate and ensure the continuous intellectual, social, and physical development of the learner.
Professional Disposition for All Candidates. Candidates work with students, families, colleagues, and communities in ways that reflect the professional dispositions expected of professional educators as delineated in professional, state, and institutional standards. Candidates demonstrate classroom behaviors that create caring and supportive learning environments and encourage self-directed learning by all students. Candidates recognize when their own professional dispositions may need to be adjusted and are able to develop plans to do so.	**Principle 9: Professional Commitment & Responsibility.** The teacher is a reflective practitioner who continually evaluates the effects of his or her choices and actions on others (students, parents, and other professionals in the learning community) and who actively seeks out opportunities to grow professionally. **Principle 10: Partnerships.** The teacher fosters relationships with school colleagues, parents, and agencies in the larger community to support students' learning and well-being.

Acknowledgments

I would like to acknowledge the continuing support of my colleagues: Dr. Barbara Cruz and, of course, my wife Anne, who makes so much of the life I enjoy possible. I also wish to thank the learned societies/professional organizations for granting permission to reprint many of their documents in this text and the Houghton Mifflin School Division and the Core Knowledge Foundation for allowing the reprinting of the content from their elementary school book series.

Grateful acknowledgment goes to the many reviewers who made constructive suggestions and provided thoughtful reactions during the development of the manuscript. Reviewers of this edition included Myra Zarnowski, CUNY, Queens College; Caroline Sheffield, University of South Florida; Barbara Levandowski, North Park University; Linda L. Reiten, University of Montana Western; Lynn E. Nielsen, University of Northern Iowa; and Gayle Mindes, Depaul University. In addition, I would like to thank Sue Pulvermacher-Alt, who believed in this new kind of text from the beginning, Mary Finch, and Lisa Mafrici, who developed both the first and second editions, and Caitlin Cox and Chris Shortt of Cengage for their assistance with this third edition. Thanks also to the production staff who supported a contemporary design for this integrated book and website offerings. Thank you all.

Professors,
To adopt this text, please order it through your bookstore or contact your sales representative. Please use ISBN 111111742X to order the book with the free Premium Website and Educator's Guides or ISBN 111111465X to order just the book with the free Premium Website.

To logon to the Professor's Website, please go to www.cengage.com/login and register. If you have any difficulties, please call 1-800-354-9706.

By adopting one of these ISBN numbers your students will receive free access to the Premium Website for a semester with the purchase of a new book. Students who might buy used editions should be directed to visit www.cengage.com/iChapters to purchase access to the website.

Student's Introduction

Teaching Is a Challenge

Teaching in an elementary school is a challenge. A recent graduate was asked what surprised her most upon becoming a third grade teacher. Her answer bears repeating: "I was surprised at how easy it is to get by as a mediocre teacher and how hard the job is if you want to be a really good teacher."

Some elementary education majors experienced excellent social studies instruction while they were in elementary school, but most students seem to be able to better recall high school social studies. For many, a popular joke reflects their last memory of social studies.

What is the first name of every social studies teacher in the United States? Coach.

Sure, there are excellent teachers who also coach, but jokes are funny because they have just enough truth to create a tension that tickles our funny bone. The implication of this joke, of course, is that anyone can teach social studies.

Teaching social studies with organization, enthusiasm, accuracy, and precision is every bit as much of a challenge as teaching math or science. Excellence in teaching is hard to define, but most of us know it when we see it. For an elementary school teacher, learning the content and pedagogy for each discipline is no easy task. Thomas Edison was fond of pointing out that his success came from 99 percent perspiration and only 1 percent inspiration. The inspiration grows out of the hard work that precedes it. The purpose of this book is to provide you the social studies **pedagogical content knowledge** and resources on the Internet that will allow you to inspire your students to personal growth and productive citizenship. Becoming a great teacher of social studies will require both inspiration and perspiration if you are to be successful in the standards-based education environment.

> *Of course there's a lot of knowledge in universities: the freshmen bring a little in; the seniors don't take much away, so knowledge sort of accumulates.*
>
> Anonymous

Standards-Based Teacher Training?

Standards-based teacher training is a relatively new, nationwide movement that has come to the forefront during the last 10 years at the same time as standards-based education for the K–12 system. The **Interstate New Teacher Assessment and Support Consortium** (INTASC) and the **National Council for Accreditation of Teacher Education** (NCATE) are the national organizations that, in consultation with colleges, have established the commonly used standards for teacher preparation programs. The 10 INTASC standards are listed in the "Professor's Preface" (see Table P.1), and you should review them so that you better understand what is expected of novice teachers.

Whenever you see a word or phrase in green, such as INTASC and NCATE above in the text, it means that there is a clickable link at the Premium Website that will bring you to the website for the organization or document referenced.

How to Use *Teaching Elementary Social Studies: Strategies, Standards, and Internet Resources*

Unlike traditional textbooks, which may require only a passive reading prior to class, this book expects you to *interact* with the text, the Internet, the professor, clinical faculty members, and your fellow students as you construct your knowledge about teaching social studies. *Teaching Elementary Social Studies: Strategies, Standards, and Internet Resources* achieves this with a number of strategies and features described here.

Special Features of This Text and Website

Students' responses to this text have consistently carried the theme that the layout of bulleted points, large print, and text boxes made the ideas easy to understand and that it is the kind of text they would keep as a reference once they were full-time teachers. The following are some tips on how to best use the book and its Premium Website.

Assignments

The purpose of the assignments in this textbook is for you to think about a concept, reconstruct your understanding of it, and apply your knowledge. Many of the assignments are practical and pragmatic (referred to in the professional literature as **authentic assessments**), such as lesson plans that will be expected of you as a teacher. Some of the assignments create opportunities for you to interact with clinical faculty in what are known as **early field** or **clinical experiences** as part of **field-based teacher preparation programs,** and others are designed to have you reflect on your future practices as a teacher. Each assignment is tied to an **INTASC standard** (see Table P.1 in the "Professor's Preface") so that it can be demonstrated by your college that you have met a specific standard.

Questions

Questions will appear throughout the text to help you reflect on what you are learning. The symbol (?) will be your cue to consider the idea that is presented and develop an answer to a question. You should be prepared to respond to these questions during class.

Teacher's Tips

In addition to the narrative, you will see a significant number of **Teacher's Tips**—practical ideas that you can use in the classroom.

Quotations and Reflections

Notable quotes, key concepts, and thought-provoking ideas will be highlighted in the margins of the text. These are intended to give you insights that you might not easily recognize about a topic and to support your development as a reflective practitioner. You should be prepared to discuss these ideas in class.

References

Traditional references (in contrast to online "Full Text" ERIC documents) appear as citations in the text and are listed in the "References" section at the end of the book so that you can further investigate the topics covered in this textbook.

Internet Resources

At the **Premium Website, www.cengage.com/login,** you will find

1. Downloadable PDF copies of **elementary social studies textbook chapters** that are used in schools today so that you can create lesson plans with authentic materials.
2. Live links to **websites, materials, lesson plans,** and **downloadable ERIC documents** that appear in the text. In addition, there are **bonus links** not included in the book totaling more than 500 in all.

One of the similarities between college and secondary-school teachers is that we are both expected to address state standards.

J. Duplass

A question that intrigues historians is whether the personal computer and the Internet will, 200 years from now, be judged as inventions that transformed the world.

3. **Lesson planning templates and examples** to provide a format and tools for authentic lesson planning.
4. **Bonus topics** on key concepts such as "Classroom Management" and "Parent-Teacher Relations" and templates for developing an employment portfolio (see Table of Contents).
5. **On-demand online video cases** from TeachSource and **video lessons** from Annenberg's Learner.org and WNET Thirteen.org's EdOnline for you to use in assignments and learn on a self-directed basis. These cases provide shared field experiences, demonstrations, and models of best practices.

[This technology] is designed to revolutionize our education system and . . . in a few years it will supplant largely, if not entirely, the use of textbooks.

Thomas Edison on the invention of film, 1922

Use of the Internet

Because the Internet is now an essential tool for teachers, its use has been extensively integrated into this text. In addition to accessing this book's Premium Website, you will use the Internet in two ways.

1. **General Internet searches.** Searches for content and lesson plan ideas can be conducted using general searchers in any browser, such as *Google, Look Smart, Copernic,* or *Lycos*.
2. **Site-specific searches** for social studies resources. The Internet has made an extensive number of resources related to elementary education and social studies available to teachers. With this book, you will become familiar with the major multidiscipline websites, such as *ERIC (Educational Resources Information Center)* and the *Gateway to Educational Materials (GEM)*. In addition, you will be expected to use a number of social studies discipline-specific websites, such as the ones sponsored by *EconEd* and *National Geographic*.

Teacher's Tip

You can enter this book's website for students at college[Catlin, please provide address]. You will need the passkey provided in new copies of the text to access all the website resources. Be sure to save this page as one of your favorites because you will be using it frequently in this class and, in all likelihood, during the remainder of your education.

Editorial: Become an Independent Thinker

To greater or lesser degrees, all books reflect an author's experiences and opinions. In many cases I raise issues for your consideration, and in others I make specific recommendations. Professors are expected to "profess" what they believe to be the wisest approach to their field of study. Not all professors will agree with my opinions. However, there is nothing more important to academia and a free society than the free exchange of ideas. If you read something in this book that you don't agree with, I suspect nothing would please your professor more than for you to raise the topic in class and provide a thoughtful analysis and some good examples of why you disagree.

I wish you the very best and the greatest success as a teacher.

Students,

To access the Premium Website, use the access card included in your book to register at www.cengage.com/login.

If you have a textbook that did not include an access card, it can be purchased at www.cengage.com/ichapters. If you have any difficulties, please call 1-800-354-9706.

Unit One

Introduction to Social Studies
Fundamental Goals

"MY MOM SAYS SHE HOPES I HAVE KIDS LIKE ME . . .
BUT I DON'T LIKE THE WAY SHE SAYS IT."

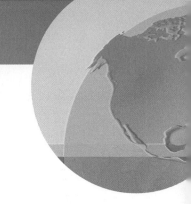

Topic 1

What Is Social Studies Education?

Educare, the Latin root for the English word "education," means to "bring out." So instead of using a passive and, perhaps, boring, strategy (see Topic 32), in which the professor tells you what social studies is and "brings out" very little, let's use a more engaging, active, participatory, questioning process that uses your prior knowledge to develop a more sophisticated understanding of what social studies is.

Teacher's Tip

*New teachers often mistakenly believe that they don't have to plan and prepare a diagram of what they will write on a chalkboard (also called **boardwork**) during a lecture or discussion; they think they can just wing it. The best practice entails developing a model set of questions and answers, anticipating what students might say, developing a drawing of the final boardwork you want the students to see, and leading the students to that end.*

The List, Group, and Label Method

Hilda Taba's **list, group, and label method** (Taba et al., 1971; Costa & Loveall, 2002) is considered a best practice and is recommended for use in social studies classrooms because it expects students to construct new social studies information under a teacher's guidance. The teacher leads the whole class or smaller groups of students in developing a list, guides them through dialogue to group social studies information knowledge into logical categories, and then labels the categories. Assignments 1.1 and 1.2 apply this teaching approach. This emphasis on construction and organization of knowledge is based on the constructivist theory of learning. (See Jean Piaget's theories for more information about constructivist theories.)

Assignment 1.1

INTASC Standards 2, 4, 7, and 9

What Is Social Studies?

The Data Organizer graphic organizer at the book's Premium Website should be used for this activity.

1. List what comes to mind when someone says "social studies." Be creative; don't limit yourself to the obvious.

2. When you're finished, convert the list into a table. In the top row above each column, organize the list into categories based on their commonality and then label the columns. You may want to label columns *and* rows. By analogy (see Topic 41), this is like being asked to name the food items you like to eat, then organizing them into such categories as vegetables and meats and the time you eat them (breakfast, lunch, or dinner).

3. Be prepared to share your concept of social studies in class.

Assignment 1.2

INTASC Standards 1, 2, 3, 4, 5, 7, and 8

Apply the List, Group, and Label Method to Symbols

Now let's apply the same **list, group, and label method** in this assignment by pretending you are preparing a lesson for your first grade class on "U.S. Symbols."

1. Go to the book's Premium Website and download the elementary textbook selection Houghton Mifflin Reading 5, "Symbols of Our Country," to preview the content on symbols. Assume that students have not read the passage.

2. Start with what your students might know about symbols to create a context and analogy. Assume you will start the lesson with a question: "Does anyone know what a symbol is?" In advance of the lesson, hypothesize and create a list of what you think third grade students *might* say based on their personal experiences with symbols. Their examples might include the school's symbol, street signs, etc. Using a Data Organizer from the Premium Website, fill in the cells based on how you want your students to come to understand the concept *symbols*.

(Continued)

Assignment 1.2

You will use this list and organizer as your notes in class and as a bridge from what they know to what they don't know by first introducing them to the concept *symbols*. Although you have a list to work from in case they have difficulty coming up with examples, the list and organizer on the chalkboard should reflect both yours and the students' answers.

Teacher's Tip

*This is an **authentic assignment**, a simulation of what teachers do in preparing for class. But it is also an example of how to choreograph instruction and create a context or schema—(see the book's Premium Website Topic C, "Learning Practices and Theories") for students to acquire **procedural** and **information knowledge** (see Topic 2 for more about these two crucial concepts).*

3. Create a second Data Organizer in preparation for your lesson on U.S. symbols based on the content of the basal text and other information you can find on the Web about U.S. symbols. This Data Organizer should have more information and categories than those provided in Reading 5. Your first question would be: "Can someone think of a U.S. symbol?" You could use images from the Internet as you progress through questions about just one of the symbols and provide students the additional information you gleaned from the Internet while you write it on the board. Next, you could give students a blank organizer and have them complete it by forming groups and finding as much information about each symbol as they can by reading the passage. Once they have finished, debrief the students by filling in the remaining cells of the organizer and expanding on each symbol with information not found in the text.

4. Finally, as a culminating activity, ask the students to create a postcard for a symbol, explain the symbol with some facts (perhaps from a search on the Internet), and have them address the card and mail it to one of their classmates. You may want to teach them about zip codes as well.

🌐 WEBSITE RESOURCES • Social Studies Assessment

Websites	Websites that are cited in the text narrative (designated by the green color) and those listed in "Website Resources" at the end of most topics (see Topic 2, as an example) are available as clickable links at www.cengage.com/login for ease of access. These links will be updated periodically to reflect changes and new resources as they become available.

Topic 2

Social Studies Knowledge

"Social studies" means different things to different people, and your vision of social studies and its goals will determine how and what you teach. *Learning* and *knowledge* are sometimes defined too narrowly. If "learning" is defined as teachers imparting facts and concepts, it fails to capture the essence of a social studies education, which is the development of the more objective, reflective, analytical, and logical disposition that prepares a person to be a lifelong acquirer and evaluator of social studies knowledge so that he or she can fulfill his or her potential as a human being and be a productive citizen. We want students to not only to see new things, but also to see things differently.

Teachers need a practical framework for organizing their thoughts about what is important to teach and eventually what is the most effective way for students to learn social studies knowledge. These decisions are made during lesson planning, when standards, goals, objectives, strategies, and knowledge are developed and choreographed. The following sections in this topic explain a number of interrelated terms and concepts that should help you define what you will teach when you teach social studies. Although these terms and concepts are presented as discrete categories, the nature of knowledge and the various ways in which terms are used in the professional literature make such categories somewhat artificial.

NCSS Goals Statement

The National Council for the Social Studies (NCSS) provides leadership in the development of principles and practices for elementary, middle, and high school social studies. Planned for release in 2009, is the revised (from 1984) NCSS position statement on social studies for young learners (NCSS, 2008b). The entire position statement will be available, along with a number of position statements on teaching social studies, at the NCSS Website. The following is excerpted from the revised, draft statement.

Teacher's Tip

Don't make the mistake of thinking that your job is to teach the social studies basal textbook supplied to you by your school. Your job is to:

1. Evaluate the book in terms of how it will help you achieve your objectives.
2. Design lesson plans that choreograph the book and other resources.
3. Focus on big ideas, procedural knowledge, and basic skills.
4. Use the information knowledge from the text and other resources to achieve your objectives.

The purpose of elementary school social studies is to establish a learning environment and instruction to enable each student to understand, participate, and make informed decisions about their world. Social studies explains students' relationships to other people, to institutions, and to the environment. It equips them with the knowledge and understanding of the past necessary for coping with the present and planning for the future. It provides them with the skills for productive problem solving and decision making, as well as for assessing issues and making thoughtful value judgments. Above all, it integrates these skills and understandings into a framework for responsible citizen participation, whether in the school, the community, or the world.

Social Studies Knowledge: Concepts and Vocabulary

The terms **social studies** and **social sciences** are often used interchangeably and at times can create confusion. "Social studies" is the preferred term in part because it is more inclusive. While "social sciences" typically refers only to the academic disciplines of sociology, psychology, and sometimes anthropology, social studies also includes history, economics, geography, the humanities, and philosophy. At the elementary level, social studies typically integrates all of these fields of study.

There are many different models or ways of organizing your thoughts about what social studies is at the elementary school level. This book uses the following terms and organizing scheme.

Information Knowledge

Information knowledge (sometimes referred to in the academic literature as "propositional knowledge," "declarative knowledge," or just plain "content") typically includes the facts, concepts, and generalizations that students acquire in social studies. Many students remember only the drudgery of memorization or the boredom of long lectures, because the teacher failed to focus explicitly on the **procedural knowledge** and **big ideas** (see Topic 8) or to allow the students to grapple with concepts and generalizations.

> **Could you share a memory of social studies from when you were an elementary student? Is it a good or bad memory?**

Facts

Facts serve multiple purposes in social studies. They should be used as (1) building blocks to a concept (such as cars, plans, and trains are all types of transportation), and (2) examples of a concept (such as the American, French, and Russian revolutions are examples of people demanding greater rights).

Facts are used to acquire concepts and generalizations that last a lifetime, long after the specific facts themselves have been forgotten. They also serve another purpose. According to E. D. Hirsch (1987, 2001), information knowledge is central to a shared culture. For example, envision some U.S. citizens having lunch in a café in the Middle East when one of them suddenly realizes that it is July 4th. What would come into their minds would be a shared memory of parades, fireworks, baseball games, and barbecues, and also an appreciation of their ancestors' struggle for freedom and democracy. These affective responses to a date on the calendar that would be meaningless to their Middle Eastern colleagues are the glue that binds people to a culture. This concept is collectively referred to as **cultural literacy**. The Battle of Waterloo has a cultural meaning for the British, as does *Cinco de Mayo* for Mexicans. Items like dates, events, places, people, music, and art contribute to the shared culture of a people and provide a sense of being connected to other human beings. A common vocabulary is the foundation upon which individuals can easily communicate shared values.

> *Everyone is entitled to his own opinion, but not to his own facts*
>
> Daniel Patrick Moynihan

Another unique attribute of facts in social studies is that social studies has both *definite information*, such as George Washington was the first president, and *indefinite information*, such as when two definitive facts seem to contradict each other, where not all facts are known, or where multiple facts must be synthesized (see Topic 29 for how charts can be deceiving). Definite information can be taught in a similar fashion to other subjects such as mathematics, as an example, but indefinite information is subject to personal interpretation and prior existing opinion. Every student has a right to the conclusion s/he has reached. When working with indefinite information, the teacher's role is to develop the disposition in students to consider all the facts and examine an issue as objectively as possible.

Of great concern to elementary school teachers, development of reading comprehension skills requires the tiered accumulation of information knowledge: The more information knowledge you know, the easier it is to comprehend what you read (Willingham, 2006). For all of these reasons, students should be expected to have a command of facts, knowing full well that many of the facts will be forgotten long term. The enlightened approach is to require the mastery of facts as part of an engaging lesson about a Big Idea, rather than by rote memorizing. Additional ideas associated with cultural literacy can be found at the Core Knowledge Website.

Concepts

Concepts are mental labels, abstractions. The simplest of concepts are often the ideas expressed in *terms* like "congress," "Indian" (the preferred term now is "First American"), "supply," "equality," "prime minister," and "longitude." Tony Blair was the prime minister of Britain. In this example, Tony Blair is the fact associated with the concept *prime minister*, just like an amoeba and a protozoan are factual representations of the concept *one-celled organisms*. *Prime minister* along with *president* and *chancellor* can be elevated to a **universal concept** of *state leader* (Erickson, 2002). Concepts are defined by their attributes. The more attributes a concept has, the more complex and difficult it is to define a universal meaning. The concept of *democracy* or *equal rights* has many different interpretations; *1776* is ordinarily a date, but in U.S. culture it is laden with affective attributes of freedom and other associations, giving it concept-like attributes.

From a teacher's perspective, the focus of instruction should be concepts, generalizations, and Big Ideas (see Topic 8) and with facts used to teach to this level (Erickson, 2002). As an example, the concept of revolution as a means to secure more rights can be developed by using facts from the American Revolution, French Revolution, the Spartacus revolt, and the like (this is known as the **comparable entities approach**). A teacher can craft lessons to turn what may be thought of as mundane facts into an engaging discussion of, "When is it alright to revolt?" or "When would it be alright to disobey parents?" Such a big idea as the *right to freedom* or *willingness to give up one's life for a belief is* what Brophy and Alleman (2002) refer to as **cultural universals**. Such concepts, if they are the focus of teaching, can bridge age, gender, and cultural differences. They enable a teacher to present social studies content in a way that engages students in higher-order thinking and provides a framework to remember facts (Lattimer, 2008).

Generalizations

Generalizations express relationships between and among facts and concepts. As an example, in a lesson a teacher might compare the reasons why people in Mexico invented sombreros and people in Russia wear fur "diplomat hats" with ear flaps. The generalization that students should come to know is that climate is a major determinant of local dress. Generalizations are often referred to as "principles," "theories," "laws," and "conclusions." In the area of social studies, careless use of generalizations can lead to unintended passing on of teacher biases and dangerous **stereotypes**. *Generalizations*, as opposed to *stereotypical concepts*, are open to change with new information and are based on clues rather than assumptions (Cortes, 2000).

"An alligator ripped all three men apart" is a factual statement with an implicit generalization: "Alligators are dangerous." This kind of statement appeals to our affective domain and creates vivid images in our mind's eye. A less melodramatic statement would be an explicit generalization: "Crocodilian reptiles are carnivorous." If your intent were to communicate to students a fear of alligators, the first statement would make your point. If you were teaching about reptiles, the latter would be more appropriate, although you might use the former if it is a headline in the newspaper and you want an attention-getter to start your **instructional sequence** (see Topic 9).

> Can you think of an occasion when one of your teachers was biased and presented her or his generalization as a fact?

Generalizations are powerful because they convey a great deal of information in a brief, summary form. In addition to being sometimes too simplistic (Starnes, 2004), generalizations can be dangerous if the teacher unintentionally or intentionally leaves out some information that may be essential to students' understanding. Telling students a *nonfact-based* generalization like, "President Johnson was a great president," has a very different learning objective than a *fact-based* statement like, "President Johnson passed more civil rights legislation than any other president," or "President Johnson increased the United States' involvement in the Vietnam War." With generalizations, teachers should expect to also provide students with **evidence** (as a modeling strategy, see Topic 38) by elaborating on the related concepts and their underlying facts with additional clarification.

Teacher's Tip

Nonfact-based generalizations are a necessary part of age-appropriate instruction and textbooks. But teachers should use them either to teach children how to read (see "Close Reading" in Topic 23) social studies content critically (i.e., is this generalization supported with facts?) or to serve as a launching pad for a lesson on how to develop facts around a generalization.

A rich vocabulary (see Topic 24) is crucial to learning knowledge. Social studies information knowledge provides vocabulary (**information knowledge vocabulary**) that must be used both to understand one topic and to apply it as a universal concept. As an example, *bicameral legislature* is important to understand the topic of U.S. government, but it also should be retained for learning about other types of government at a later time. In addition, social studies **procedural knowledge vocabulary**, such as *multiple causation* or *cultural diffusion,* represents universal concepts about how to think about information knowledge.

Basic Skills Knowledge

Generic basic skills are the foundation upon which social studies knowledge rests. Without math skills, students cannot understand economics or calculate distances. Reading, verbal communication, and writing are essential to all social studies knowledge acquisition (see Unit 5). The awareness that some U.S. citizens do not have the skills required to function in society has led to an emphasis on a back-to-basics approach and so-called "high-stakes testing." Social studies teachers are expected to integrate the development and practice of generic basic skills into social studies as part of schoolwide efforts to upgrade the abilities of U.S. citizens.

From a different perspective, in 2008, the NCSS and the Partnership for 21st Century Skills collaborated to define and integrate 21st century skills into social studies instruction at every grade level (Nagel, 2008). The broad categories are of these skills are:

- Creativity and innovation;
- Critical thinking and problem solving;
- Communication;
- Collaboration;
- Information literacy;
- Media literacy;

- Information and communication technologies literacy;
- Flexibility and adaptability;
- Initiative and self-direction;
- Social and cross-cultural skills;
- Productivity and accountability; and
- Leadership and responsibility.

For ideas on how to integrate these 21st century skills into social studies at the elementary level go to the 21st Century Skills Website.

Social studies basic skills are difficult to define because, as an example drawing a timeline is "basic" to a high school student, but not for a first grader. The NCSS has taken the approach of defining "essential skills." Many of these social studies essential skills can be found in Topic 17 as part of the NCSS (2008a) revised curriculum standards. This however, is where it gets a little confusing because many of these essential skills will appear to be what we define as procedural knowledge in the following section. The definitions and classifications of knowledge and skills in education are not black and white and reflect a significant but diverse set of perspectives drawing on psychology, philosophy, anthropology, and other disciplines to bring some uniformity to the field of education.

Procedural Knowledge

Dewey (1916) made the distinction between a *record of knowledge* (information knowledge) and *knowledge* (both information knowledge and procedural knowledge). In history, for example, to know the dates of important battles in the Civil War is very different from being able to explain how the chronology and outcomes of each battle influenced the outcome of the war (see Van Sledright [2004] for teaching about historical thinking). Information knowledge is knowing *what;* procedural knowledge is knowing *how* (i.e., how to make sense of information knowledge).

The purpose of procedural knowledge in social studies education is to empower people to set aside bias and subjectivity in order to engage in impartial analysis of new knowledge for the sake of more objective ideas. By doing so, students not only acquire a more unbiased knowledge set but also gain new insights into themselves and can become better human beings and effective citizens.

Generic Procedural Knowledge

The terms **thinking skills** and **critical thinking** (see Topic 35) are often used to describe generic procedural knowledge that can be used in all disciplines, whereas **modes of reasoning** (see the following section) are typically ways of thinking or working with information knowledge within a specific *domain* (social studies) or *discipline* (history, geography, etc. [Johnson, 2002]). You might want to review the article on schoolwide approaches to developing thinking skills at ERIC Online, ED447084, "Theory into Practice: Best Practices for a School-Wide Approach to Critical Thinking Instruction" (Kassem, 2000).

The kinds of procedural knowledge that cut across the domains are outlined in Bloom's *Taxonomy of Educational Objectives* (1956). *Evaluation, synthesis, analysis, application,* (these first four are by definition critical thinking skills; see Topic 35) *understanding,* and *knowledge* are the six categories. Each of the six domains or skills can be applied to a subject area. If you type "Bloom's Taxonomy" and "social studies" into a Web search engine, you will find a number of sites that explain the taxonomy and show how it may be applied to social studies. For another approach, the Critical Thinking Community has a list of the "35 Dimensions of Critical Thought." These generic thinking skills become a *disposition* (see later in this chapter) that can be used with all disciplines and are used extensively in the social studies disciplines. Planned opportunities for critical thinking, through discovery learning, discussion, problem solving, and decision making (see Unit 6) are essential components of social studies lessons, as opposed to the rote, lecture method that too many students still associate with social studies education.

Social Studies Procedural Knowledge

Thinking skills at the domain and discipline levels are often referred to as "modes of reasoning," "executive processes," and "habits of mind." Knowing how to draw inferences and conclusions from a primary document is a mode of reasoning in history, determining climate based on location is an executive process in geography, and examining a chart relating crime and age for author bias is a habit of mind. The focus of instruction in social studies at all grade levels is on transferring to students the executive processes that allow them to be lifelong learners with social studies content.

Give a man a fish, you've fed him for a day. Teach a man to fish, you've fed him for a lifetime.

Source unknown

Procedural knowledge requires one to:

1. Decide on the nature of the problem.
2. Create a mental image of the problem.
3. Develop a strategy to employ basic skills and executive processes to understand the problem (Grigorenko & Sternberg, 2000).

In social studies instruction, information knowledge and procedural knowledge cannot be separated (Resnick & Klopfer, 1989). By analogy, if information knowledge is the cake's ingredients, then procedural knowledge makes up the directions to be followed and the skills needed to make the cake. When they have mastered both these types of knowledge, students should be able to bake any cake by themselves in the future.

Did you find this analogy helpful in understanding this concept? If so, see Topic 41, "Analogies."

The National Council for Social Studies represents the interests of social studies on the national education stage. The 10 primary themes of social studies (NCSS, 1994) listed in Topic 17 may be thought of as types of modes of reasoning in the social studies; some states are basing their state standards (see Topic 16) on the NCSS themes, and it is possible that they will be the basis of high-stakes testing in social studies. You will note that the NCSS themes do not specify which content should be taught. Assignment 2.1 is an excellent example of another kind of social studies procedural knowledge that a teacher could use with different social studies information knowledge. Note the emphasis would be on teaching cause and effect; which content, whether the American Revolution or the Great Depression, would be the information knowledge and not the primary focus of teaching.

Assignment 2.1

INTASC Standards 1, 2, 3, 4, 5, 7, and 8

Text Structures

An example of modes of reasoning is Devine's (1987) six text structures, or organizing schemes that historians use to organize and explain events.
1. Generalization supported by examples
2. Enumeration (lists of items)
3. Time patterns (items or events placed in chronological order)

(Continued)

Unit One Introduction to Social Studies Fundamental Goals

4. Climax patterns (items arranged from least important to most important, worst to best, or smallest to largest)
5. Compare-and-contrast patterns
6. Cause-and-effect patterns

Download Houghton Mifflin's Reading 9, "Using Money," from the Premium Website. Assume you are preparing a lesson based on this content and have as one of your goals to explicitly teach students these six modes of reasoning. Identify examples from the reading material or make up your own examples based on the content. Be prepared to discuss your results in class and submit the paper to your professor.

Conceptualizations

A **conceptualization** is a thought or initial opinion that a person formulates on the basis of his or her unique accumulation of basic skills knowledge, information knowledge, and procedural knowledge. Students come to the classroom with ideas and beliefs, and the goal of the teacher is to model, teach, and encourage the integrated use of basic skills knowledge, information knowledge, and procedural knowledge so students can formulate ideas and beliefs in a more detached, analytical fashion than they may be used to.

Ideas

Ideas may be correct or incorrect; all ideas are only partially formed and, therefore, imperfect. Adults regularly say, "The sun always rises in the east" because that's how it looks from our point of view, but at one time this was also taken as scientifically correct. Today we know this idea is not correct: The sun doesn't rise; rather, the earth rotates. Similarly, children's versions of ideas are not as well formed as adults', but that does not make them incorrect: We often refer to these as "naïve ideas" or "theories" (Brophy & Allerman (2006). Some ideas, however, are incorrect. The teacher, through dialogue with students, can convert both erroneous ideas and naïve ideas into more advanced, sophisticated understanding.

Ideas may be thought of as propositions communicated with the expectation that others will reflect on them and consider adopting them into their personal schemas. In a classroom, however, everyone brings his or her unique ideas based on unique personal experiences. We usually assume that when students say something they believe it, but sometimes children state ideas in social studies to get attention, to challenge a teacher's authority, to persuade others to adopt the idea, or to check their own thinking about a tentative belief. To some extent, we all have naïve ideas or theories our entire lives; our job as teachers is to provide grade-appropriate, well-reasoned ideas to our students for them to reflect on.

Beliefs

A **belief** is an idea that is transformed because we embrace it, value it, and think it to be correct (Fenstermacher, 1994; Richardson, 1996). Beliefs become part of our persona and can be difficult to dislodge because we need to have a sufficient ego to be open to new ideas that might challenge existing beliefs. Giving up a belief can be agonizing, but it is made easier if teachers can (1) provide a bridge from one belief to another potential belief by introducing alternative ideas, and (2) demonstrate through their personal behavior and openness to new ideas and tolerance for different beliefs and ambiguity.

Racism and sexism are undemocratic beliefs, yet some of your students may come to school affirming them having inherited their parents' beliefs. How is a teacher to reconcile the conflict between family belief systems and those of a democratic society if they are different?

Big Ideas

The big ideas approach is really a lesson planning strategy (see Topic 8), but ends up as a conceptualization for each student. Big ideas are powerful, long-lasting ideas (concepts or generalizations) or beliefs, that you can organize facts around when you prepare lessons (Erickson, 2002). In geography, it might be how to use latitude and longitude or the effect of location on the foods we eat and the clothes we wear. For the American Revolution it might be what patriotism is, whether the bravery of the founders is an admirable quality and what its limits are, and whether the British practiced fairness toward the colonists. You could ask your students whether there are two sides to every story, or what it would take for someone to revolt against his or her country today? In economics, it could be how advertising might affect demand and sales.

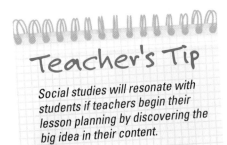

Teacher's Tip

Social studies will resonate with students if teachers begin their lesson planning by discovering the big idea in their content.

Academic Disposition

If procedural knowledge is *how* to think more like an expert in a domain or discipline, an **academic disposition** is the *instinct* to use procedural knowledge and the *expertise* to use the appropriate type of procedural knowledge.

Dispositions are composed of four elements: (1) *abilities:* the capabilities and skills required to carry through on the behavior; (2) *motivations:*

the capacity to make the decision to be engaged; (3) *sensitivities:* alertness to appropriate occasions for exhibiting the behavior; and (4) *inclinations:* tendency to actually behave in a certain way (Ritchhart, 2002). We each have a **conative** style, or a preferred method of putting thought into action. Kolbe (1990) identifies four conative modes.

1. **Fact finder:** instincts to probe, refine, and simplify
2. **Follow through:** instincts to organize, reform, and adapt
3. **Quick start:** instincts to improvise, revise, and stabilize
4. **Implementer:** instincts to construct, renovate, and envision

Learners must activate these instincts each time they encounter new information. Students acquire this habit by seeing teachers model it and by completing teacher-assigned tasks (Ritchhart, 2002). For example, you could teach students the cause-and-effect pattern using the specific events of the American Revolution as factual examples. The primary purpose would be to impart the procedural knowledge that most immediate causes of any war can be better understood by organizing the precipitating events into a sequence. A student reading about the Vietnam War who instinctively applies a cause-and-effect pattern to those facts has acquired an academic disposition. The development of an academic disposition to employ procedural knowledge comes with the recognition that such tools are essential to understanding information in the domain or discipline. Part of what makes historians, anthropologists, and geographers, as examples, so good at what they do is that they have a command of procedural knowledge, wealth of information knowledge, and the academic disposition to be insightful when they apply their craft. Arguably, procedural knowledge should be the focus of the classroom experience because it needs to be taught and is used to make sense of information knowledge; whereas, information knowledge can be gleaned by students on their own from sources, such as an online encyclopedia (i.e. Wikipedia). Your elementary students should be introduced to grade-appropriate procedural knowledge so that they can begin the journey to becoming independent learners and productive members of society.

What Is an Education—A Big Idea?

Based on what you have read so far, you have likely started formulating beliefs about the goals of social studies education for your classroom. One of the most important academic dispositions to encourage in all students is openness to new ideas, and, hopefully, the focus on procedural knowledge will enable you to formulate your personal vision of social studies education. Social studies teachers have a duty to encourage, cajole, and jolt students into constantly reevaluating their ideas. The use of **primary documents** and **realia** (see Topic 28) is one of the more interesting ways to entice students to appreciate history and culture and consider new ideas. There are

The real voyage of discovery consists not of seeking new landscapes, but of seeing through new eyes.

Marcel Proust

more than 7 million primary source documents at the American Memory Website of the Library of Congress. The following primary document offers you the opportunity to consider what a Native American in 1744 saw as being important about education. A response from Conassatego, of the Iroquois nation, to the Virginia legislature's offer to educate six youths at the College of William and Mary, should encourage you to rethink your idea of education. Plan to share your thoughts in class.

> *We know you highly esteem the kind of learning taught in these colleges, and the maintenance of our young men, while with you, would be very expensive to you. We are convinced, therefore, that you mean to do us good by your proposal; and we thank you heartily. But you who are so wise must know that different Nations have different conceptions of things; and you will not therefore take it amiss, if our ideas of this kind of education happen not to be the same as yours. We have some experience of it. Several of our young people were formally brought up in the colleges of the Northern Provinces; they were instructed in all your sciences; but, when they came back to us, they were bad runners, ignorant of every means of living in the woods, unable to bear either the cold or hunger, knew neither how to build a cabin, take a deer, or kill an enemy, spoke our language imperfectly, were therefore neither fit for hunters, warriors, nor counselors; they were totally good for nothing. We are however not the less obliged for your kind offer, tho' we decline accepting it; and to show our grateful sense of it, if the gentlemen of Virginia shall send us a dozen of their sons, we will take care of their education, instruct them in all we know, and make men of them.*

Langer (1996)

How would you characterize an education, given Conassatego's view?

Assignment 2.2

INTASC Standards 1, 4, 7, and 8

Web of Social Studies Education

Webs, like all concept organizers, are an important part of teaching at all levels because they allow people to create mental maps. Draw a web depicting your understanding of the structure of social studies education using the major terms from this topic. Be prepared to turn in the web and to share your ideas with the class. The web should be attractive enough to put in your portfolio.

Video	*Learner.org* Creating Effective Citizens explains how social studies concepts are necessary for effective citizens and democracy.
Essay	**ERIC Online** *EJ718743*, Debunking the Myth: The Social Studies and Rigor *(2005)*. *ED475583*, Content That Counts: Educating for Informed, Effective, and Responsible Citizenship *(2001)*. *Education Excellence.com* Where Did Social Studies Go Wrong? *(2003)*.
	All websites (designated by the green color) and those listed in the "Website Resources" boxes in each topics are available as clickable links at www.cengage.com/login for ease of access. These links will be updated periodically to reflect changes and new resources as they become available.

Topic 3

Character Education

In the final analysis, unlike mathematics or science education (as examples) which provide skills for careers or lead to the advancement of science, the purpose of social studies education is to facilitate the enlightenment of the individual so that she or he can fulfill his or her human potential and become a productive member of society (Duplass, 2008). It is for this reason, that this and the next topic are central to social studies education. It is what gives meaning to learning about history, geography, economics, and the like. Or put another way, why learn any social studies if the end is not to be a better person living among other human beings?

Character education is also referred to as "values education" or "moral education." Character education requires a teacher to promote an often ambiguous and fluid set of societal expectations referred to as "values" and "virtues." Fundamentally it is how personal judgments about right and wrong are to be thought of and acted upon. Through social studies we share with students the accumulated examples and ideas of civilization (both good and bad) so that they can become wiser and better understand themselves and their duties to others. Through the culture of the classroom created by the teacher, students are exposed to democratic principles such as compassion, hard work, self-reliance, patience, etc. Through character education, adults seek to help children develop the ideas and habits to reconcile internal challenges with those that come from being a part of a larger community (Stallones, 2004).

> *The unexamined life is not worth living.*
>
> Socrates

The Roots of Character Education

Character education has its roots in Western philosophical traditions dating back to Greek antiquity (Huitt, 2004). Plato and his mentor, Socrates (c. 469–399 B.C.E.), concluded that knowledge is our best hope for knowing the right thing to do, but having knowledge is no guarantee that someone will do the right thing. Some people have a great deal of knowledge but still make poor choices. And some people with little education seem to do the right things instinctively. Socrates distinguished between *true opinion*, which may come to people instinctively or by mimicking others, and *knowledge*, which he defined as not only knowing the right thing but also having *reasoned* why the alternatives are not right. Knowledge is our best hope for becoming wise and then acting wisely. When we choose to do the right thing, we enjoy what philosophers call the "good life." By this term philosophers do not refer to a wealthy lifestyle but rather to a satisfying state of mind and being, the knowledge that we are fulfilling our potential as honest human beings.

> *All modern philosophy is a footnote to Plato.*
>
> Alfred North Whitehead

> What do you think of someone in front of you in the "seven items or less line" at the supermarket who is buying nine items?

Virtues and Values

Virtue is a character trait. We can say that a person is virtuous or acts virtuously. The term **values** is a sociological concept. When we say people have good values, we mean they are virtuous. Values are part of the changing, normative system of a culture. Children often assimilate the culture's norms (values) into their beliefs without reflection, as if their familial and community values were the *only* way to think and behave. Parents, communities, and peers are the greatest influence on both the values and virtuous behavior that children bring to their schools (Trumbull et al., 2001). Doing something we know to be wrong is often referred to as a dichotomy between *conceived values* (what we know to be virtuous) and *operational values* (how we act). As an example, most children understand that they must do their homework (conceived value) but not all do their homework (operational value) because it is more fun to watch television or play with friends. The importance or value their parents place on homework shapes the conceived value (for better or worse!) and operational value of your students.

Aristotle (384–322 B.C.E.) provided an extraordinary insight into virtuous behavior for his time and place. He believed that virtues are character traits that regulate desire and that they lie at a mean (in the middle) between more extreme character traits. For example, the virtue of courage lies at the mean between the excessive extreme of rashness and the deficient extreme of cowardice. A fearful child needs to develop the virtuous character trait of courage. A child who curbs fear too much is rash, which is a vice, and a child who curbs fear too little may be judged as cowardly, which is also a vice. Aristotle's concept is not unique to Western civilization. Buddha (563–483 B.C.E.) espoused a view that is similar to Aristotle's, known as the "Middle Way." These may be thought of as *personal virtues* in contrast with equal opportunity and freedom of speech, which may be thought of as *civic values* Religions have also influenced the concept of virtues. In part, based on the Greek philosophical tradition, the Roman Catholic Church adopted the "Seven virtues" as a tool to teach members what values are important to achieving eternal salvation and the Muslim religion has the "99 Names of Allah," virtues that the Koran attributes to God and that all Muslims should aspire to. The goal of character and citizenship education is to shape students' characters by having them adopt productive personal virtues and civic values.

Socialization

The **socialization** that takes place in the elementary school setting is a crucial component of character and citizenship education (Epstein & Shiller, 2005). Because they come to school from dissimilar families and communities based on diverse cultures, communities, experiences, and **socioeconomic status**, socialization transforms students by allowing them to adopt and act on personal virtues and civic values that are important to individual growth and citizenship as well as virtuous behavior beyond the values they bring with them. These differences create what Bourdieu (1986) called "cultural capital," which affects how students adjust and adapt to the socialization process as well as the learning process. U.S. schools have always been thought of as great equalizers for disadvantaged students because they provide equal opportunities. Elementary schools are first and foremost seats of learning, thus making the socialization of children into a *culture of learning* a primary goal. This is particularly important to a democracy that needs a highly literate citizenry to function.

Students' characters are tested by the academic and socialization challenges of schools, just as their adult characters will be challenged as members of their societies. Parents, to differing degrees, prepare their children academically and socially for the school experience. Teachers are expected to reinforce the productive behaviors that children bring to school and discourage unproductive behaviors. It is, arguably, the most fundamental democratic principle at work, to say that each child must learn to give up some preferred behaviors (doing what they want when they want to, etc.) for the common good of the classroom members so that learning can proceed in an orderly fashion (Stanley, 2005). In this sense, classrooms are the potential training ground where students develop the character traits to be effective members of a democratic society. Many students who are not prepared for the rigors and structure of school will need their teacher to provide an entirely new way of thinking about their school experience and their duties to their classroom society.

Social emotional learning (SEL) is the process by which children come to learn to recognize and manage their emotions so that their behaviors and choices can reflect a balancing of self-interest and the public good (Elias et al., 1997, 2003). Emotions and intellect are inseparable (McCombs, 2001) and they come to the forefront when teaching social studies. The Collaborative for

Academic, Social and Emotional Learning (CASEL) defines these five core SEL competencies (2003), as:

1. *Self-Awareness:* Recognizing feelings as they occur; having a realistic assessment of one's own abilities and a well-grounded sense of self-confidence.
2. *Social Awareness:* Sensing what others are feeling; being able to take their perspective; appreciating and interacting positively with diverse groups.
3. *Self-Management:* Handling emotions so they facilitate rather than interfere with the task at hand; delaying gratification to pursue goals; persevering in the face of setbacks.
4. *Relationship Skills:* Handling emotions in relationships effectively; establishing and maintaining healthy and rewarding relationships based on cooperation; negotiating solutions to conflict; seeking help when needed.
5. *Responsible Decision Making:* Accurately assessing risks; making decisions based on a consideration of all relevant factors and the likely consequences of alternative courses of actions; respecting others; taking personal responsibility for one's decisions.

The NCSS (2009) also has developed a number of social studies goals related to character and citizenship education under the heading, "Personal Interaction & Civic Engagement Strategies." As a teacher you should promote these character traits through lesson plans, modeling, and classroom management practices.

Personal Interaction and Civic Engagement

PERSONAL
- Exhibit honesty and integrity.
- Convey creativity and ingenuity.
- Communicate personal beliefs, feelings, and convictions.
- Demonstrate self-direction when working toward and accomplishing personal goals.
- Demonstrate flexibility as goals and situations change.
- Adjust personal behavior to fit the dynamics of various groups and situations.
- Respect and be tolerant of other's beliefs, feelings, and convictions.

COLLABORATIVE
- Contribute to the development of a supportive climate in a group.
- Participate in making rules and guidelines for group activities.

- Assist in setting, working towards, and accomplishing common goals for a group.
- Participate in delegating duties, organizing, planning, making decisions, and taking action in group setting.
- Participate in persuading, compromising, debating, and negotiating in the resolution of conflicts and differences.
- Use diverse perspectives and skills to accomplish common goal.

Developing Children's Internal Locus of Control

If you bungle raising your children, I don't think whatever else you do well matters very much.

Jacqueline Kennedy Onassis

For socialization and personal development to take place, children must develop self-discipline and their ability to delay gratification to have a high-functioning **internal locus of control (ILC)**. ILC is the ability of children to see themselves as responsible for the outcomes of their own actions. Teachers can influence these character traits by the way they structure lessons and use their interpersonal skills to motivate individual students. Apathy, poor performance, avoidance behavior, and aggression are symptomatic of children who are rebelling against accepting responsibility for their actions (Peck, 1997), and their negative behavior creates more problems for them.

We have evidence of what works with most children who don't bring to the school setting the cultural capital and/or ILC to succeed as they first enter the classroom door (see KIPP schools; Will, 2008). Research was conducted with 15 schools in which different levels of teacher and school interventions were compared with schools with more typical interventions. By age 27 years, the former elementary school children who were in the school with high holistic interventions were leading more successful lives than those who did not (Hawkins, et al., 2008). The interventions included: Teachers were given training in classroom management; children were taught impulse control, how to get what they want without aggressive behavior, how to recognize the feelings of other people, and how to stay out of trouble and still have a good time; and parents were taught how to involve children in setting family rules, how to use positive reinforcement, and how to effectively monitor their children.

The greatest discovery of my generation is that a human being can alter his life by altering his attitudes of mind.

William James

Problems or Challenges

Teachers must turn the problems of learning and being participating members of their class into challenges that students can overcome. There are few substitutes for success, and achievement leads to ILC. For student achievement, teachers need to create doable tasks and segment the tasks into achievable steps. However, there are two parts to every problem: the challenge itself (the *substantive problem*) and the emotional pain (suffering) that accompanies every problem (the *corollary problem*; see Figure 3.1). Most of us have

Figure 3.1 The Cycle of Challenges

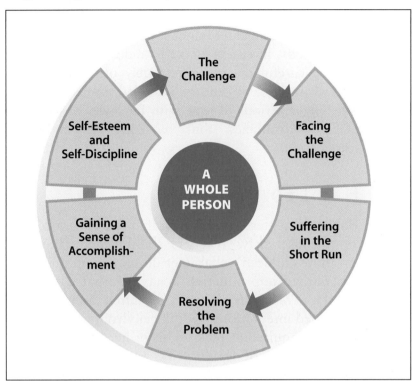

witnessed a crying child who gets emotionally worked up but can't remember what precipitated the hysteria. In such a case the problem has dissipated, but the emotional unhappiness lingers. Through their planning of stimulating learning activities and interpersonal communications, elementary school teachers are expected to inspire students to take up the challenges of learning and to deal with the emotional distress that accompanies every challenge.

What we do to our children our children will do to our society.

Pliny the Elder of Rome

Self-Discipline and Delayed Gratification

Self-discipline is learned and requires courage because it entails a degree of suffering. Teachers can impose discipline, which may result in students' mimicking self-disciplined behavior, but real self-discipline involves a cognitive choice on the part of the student. Taking up the problems of school requires one to suffer in the short run and to delay gratification for long-term gains. In **delayed gratification**, one decides to engage in an activity even though the rewards are not immediate. As an example, learning in school is the primary problem that society imposes on children with few rewards that are meaningful to them. The advantages of

Teacher's Tip

Don't tell your students a task is easy. Affirm that it is hard but that you are there to assist them and that you are confident they can succeed. If it were easy, would it be worth doing?

education are usually not obvious to elementary school students in industrialized societies. Children in preliterate societies knew that what they learned had an immediate and practical outcome. As an example, an elder might say, "Always step well over a log in the woods, in case a snake is underneath." The benefits of stepping carefully were immediately obvious. For success or survival in the 21st century, knowledge must be accumulated over longer periods of time with far fewer observable and immediate advantages, thus requiring the ability to delay gratification.

Habit Formation

Habits are patterns of behavior that can be formed consciously or unconsciously. Teachers should encourage habits that promote children's character development, and they should discourage unproductive behaviors that can become bad habits. *Serendipitous habit formation* occurs as a result of random, unplanned interactions with the environment: As an example, a child who is not required to pick up his or her toys after playing will soon develop the habit of leaving toys scattered around the room. *Affirmative habit formation* is purposeful and planned, and it can be self-initiated or structured by another person. Using the same example, a parent can start the formation of the habit of picking up toys by helping the child perform this task; eventually the child will adopt the habit, and parental intervention will be unnecessary.

An Example

Parents face the problem of getting children to begin brushing their teeth as early as 2 years of age. Scenario 1 is the shared process in which children brush their teeth standing next to their parent each day as part of a routine. The parent sets aside time for doing the activity with the child. If articulated with enthusiasm as a shared activity, the parent often finds little resistance and the habit is formed in the child even though the child initially is not intrinsically motivated and has not made a cognitive choice to brush his or her teeth. This is a very different process from Scenario 2, in which the parent mandates tooth brushing as a requirement, constantly badgers the child to brush his or her teeth, or gives the child rewards for doing so. In both scenarios, the child will eventually come to value clean teeth more than using the time to play or do other things and will adopt the behavior. The first scenario requires sacrifice by the parent, which is often why it is not chosen. But that sacrifice allows the child to develop a sense of self-determination, to gain competence, and to experience delayed gratification while being comforted through the suffering with companionship. Scenario 2 leads to confrontation and alienation, or learning to do things only if there is an external reward.

Teacher's Tip

Encourage students to keep daily or weekly **dialogue journals** in which they write about things that are important to them and you give personal advice or ask questions as feedback. This provides the teacher with insights into the unique needs of the child and often illuminates potential classroom management problems. At the same time the diary provides opportunities for children to develop their thinking, reflecting, and writing skills.

The important thing is this: To be able at any moment to sacrifice what we are for what we could become.

Charles Dubois

Teacher's Tip

Writing a famous quote on the board every day and debriefing it is an excellent strategy to get children to consider their goals and obligations. Quotes may be found at the *LibrarySpot*.

The principles of affirmative habit formation apply to the elementary school classroom as well as to the home. Teachers not only establish goals and work alongside students to help them develop the habits they need in order to succeed, but they also orchestrate environments that encourage good habits. As an example, teachers who provide time and require students to arrange their desk and materials neatly at the end of the day are using an affirmative habit formation approach. And like parents, they must set boundaries and empathize with their students who have difficulty making the adjustments needed to succeed in the classroom. Holding students accountable for deadlines and assignments is also a form of affirmative habit formation.

If there is no struggle, there is no progress.

Frederick Douglass

> Can you think of some more examples of teachers' affirmative habit formation practices?

Approaches to Character Education

George Washington felt civility was such an important character trait that he recorded and tried to live his life by 110 rules of courtesy and decent behavior. Today, many critics contend that civility is lacking in our political discourse and our everyday interactions with our fellow human beings because of a lack of character education. According to a 1996 U.S. News/Bozell poll, 89 percent of U.S. citizens long for more civility. But the Jerry Springer show has been on TV for over 15 years! Civility is crucial to a democratic society, but not everyone agrees on the role that teachers and schools should play in character education (Halverson, 2004).

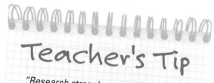

Teacher's Tip

"Research strongly suggests that 80 to 90% of all children respond well to simple, schoolwide discipline policies that emphasize good behavior" (Cortese, 2007).

It is axiomatic that values cannot not be taught. A teacher who says to his or her first grade class, "Please, children, let's take turns," is teaching a virtue. The teacher's own manifestation of virtuous behavior communicates values to students. How well you are prepared for class, how you interact with students, and how you insist students interact with each other all establish a classroom culture in which the challenging tasks of learning can take place. How a teacher regulates the interactions of children with each other and how they are expected to care for the classroom and school are part of the socialization process. These kinds of often subtle messages about values and behaviors are always perceived by children and are referred to as the **hidden curriculum**.

Civility is more than just being nice. The underlying principle is that people should care about others, be open to hearing and adopting their ideas, and respect them even if they disagree with others' beliefs. The culture you create in your classroom by having high expectations for students to be civil offers a unique opportunity for students to learn civility.

Explicit Teaching of Character

The role of the teacher in character education can be profound, and starts with a culture of care that is created in the classroom. The creation of a classroom where students understand that the teacher has their best interest at heart, even though his/her decisions and mandates may cause suffering (as defined in Figure 3.1) starts with the teacher being willing to suffer through the challenges with the students. This concept is epitomized in the works of Nel Noddings (1984, 1995). Referred to as **relational ethics**, it emphasizes the importance of "ethical caring" which is the conscious decision to act in a caring way for another even though you too will experience pain of suffering along with your student. This ethical caring is substantially different from the kind of "natural caring" which is an act of love for a friend, as an example. As teachers, one can argue, we are called to a profession that demands relational ethics.

The Character Counts movement is one of a number of organizations promoting schoolwide and classroom teaching of character (see the websites at the end of this topic for lesson plan ideas). This group has proposed six character education goals that teachers should include in their social studies planning.

The Six Pillars of Character

1. Caring
2. Citizenship
3. Fairness
4. Respect
5. Responsibility
6. Trustworthiness

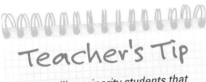

Teacher's Tip

Just telling minority students that their intelligence is under their control improves their effort on schoolwork. (Nisbett, 2009)

In addition, the NCSS "Essentials Skills of Social Studies Education–Interpersonal Relationships and Social Participation" can be found in Topic 17. It is an excellent list of character education behaviors that we should help students acquire.

One of the dominant approaches to character education at the lower elementary grade level is to share with students such stories as "The Fable of George Washington and the Cherry Tree" from *The Life of Washington*, by Mason Locke Weems, 1809 (see the Premium Website for online link at the University of Virginia). This kind of folklore is intended to portray acts of virtue and to encourage students to also act virtuously. At YouTube, one can find the Disney cartoon, the *Three Little Pigs* an excellent study in the virtue, prudence. Classic stories of virtue can be found in *The Book of Virtues: A Treasury of Great Moral Stories* by William J. Bennett (1996), many of the books listed in the *NCSS Notable Children's Books,* and online versions of children's classics that promote virtues at American Folklore. While such stories are also effective for all lower elementary school students, at the upper elementary grade levels students can begin to investigate current issues like those found at Public Agenda. Crucial to both approaches is the debriefing, as the teacher allows students to share their thinking and examples from their own lives and probes each student's thinking by posing alternative perspectives (see Topic 37, "Steps in Value Analysis").

Best Practices for Developing Children's Character

Teachers can make a difference by

- Creating rigorous and meaningful learning experiences
- Creating a classroom climate for students to develop productive habits
- Encouraging the right priorities
- Limiting and ordering learning tasks so that students have a great prospect of success
- Empathizing with each student's suffering during the task
- Encouraging delayed gratification
- Requiring homework
- Modeling and requiring habits of being organized, doing required work, paying attention, listening, neatness, and timeliness
- Using literature and historical examples to expose students to considerations of the concepts of right and wrong
- Offering service learning opportunities (See Topic 48)

Teacher's Tip

Having students think about what kind of life they would like to have, what difficulties they anticipate, how they would deal with them, and how they think others may help, resulted in improvements on standardized tests. (Nisbett, 2009)

Assignment 3.1

INTASC Standards 2, 3, and 5

Self-Discipline Interview

Using the Field Interview Graphic Organizer from the Premium Website, contact an elementary teacher and record his or her responses to the following questions. Be prepared to submit the completed organizer to the professor and to share your interview with the class.

1. Have you ever had a student who refused to do work in class or at home? What did you do?
2. What was your worst discipline problem, and how did it get resolved?
3. How do you deal with the diversity of ability in your class?

Assignment 3.2

INTASC Standards 1, 2, 3, 4, 5, 7, and 8

Character Education: YouTube Lesson Plan

Using the Disney cartoon, *The Tree Little Pigs*, from YouTube create a set of questions (see Topic 40) and information on analogies in Topic 41, that you would use with students to promote their consideration of the virtues found in the video..

WEBSITE RESOURCES • Character Education

Essay	**ERIC Online** *ED497054, Character Education. What Works Clearinghouse Topic Report (2007).* *EJ718739, Facing the Challenge of Character Education (2005).* *ED469279, Applying Cognitive-Behavioral Techniques to Social Skills Instruction (2002).* *ED440911, Building Good Citizens: Character Education Resource Guide (2000).* *ED424190, Using Stories about Heroes to Teach Values (1998).*
NCSS Position Statement	Fostering Civic Virtue: Character Education in the Social Studies.
Websites	*Good Character* *Character Counts* *Random Acts of Kindness Foundation* *Teaching Tolerance* *Conflict Resolution Activities for K–12*
Lesson Plan: Upper Elementary	*Read/Write/Think* A Bad Case of Bullying: Using Literature Response Groups with Students. The book, A Bad Case of Stripes, allows for a personal reflection of acceptable behaviors; ways to prevent bullying in the classroom and school are also discussed.

Bonus Topics	Topic A: *Teaching Diverse Populations*
	Topic B: *Temperament*
	Topic C: *Learning Theories and Practices*
	Topic D: *Classroom Organization*
	Topic E: *Classroom Management*
	Topic F: *Parent-Teacher Relations*
	Topic G: *Advice for the First-Year Teacher*
	All linked websites (designated by the green color) and those listed here are available as clickable links at the book's Premium Website, www.cengage.com/login, for ease of access. These links will be updated periodically to reflect changes and new resources as they become available.

Topic 4

Citizenship Education

At first glance, Topic 21, "Government, Standards, and Internet Resources," and this topic might seem to cover the same material. Although they are closely related, **citizenship education** (also known as *civics education*) has a different purpose than just learning about government(s) and its structure, processes, and history. Particularly at the elementary school level, citizenship education is intended to instill in the next generation an appreciation of democratic ideals and civic virtues. At its core, civic virtue is the necessity to place the public good above private interest. Such *civic* virtue is different from *personal* virtue (refer to the preceding topic on character education), although without personal virtue, the kind of communal civic virtue is, arguably, unrealizable. The U.S. classroom serves as a unique gathering place for students of dissimilar beliefs to engage with others, where students of low socioeconomic and culturally diverse backgrounds that come from families that may feel disenfranchised from citizenship participation are welcomed and nurtured (McGuire & Cole, 2005), and where citizenship lessons encourage civic virtues and democratic ideology (see Topic 21 for an explanation of ideology.)

Unlike the subject field mathematics, in which everyone agrees that 3 + 3 = 6, the social studies concepts in citizenship education allow two people to disagree about the conclusions they reach and both to believe their positions are appropriate, if not correct. As examples, we still debate the merits of capital punishment and abortion, the bombing of Hiroshima, and the impeachment of President Bill Clinton. These kinds of disagreements about the right or wrong of public policy can result from individuals' having incorrect facts, having correct but different sets of facts, or having the same agreed-upon facts but interpreting them differently or assigning different levels of importance to the facts. Other ideas may defy logical analysis because of their emotional underpinnings. As an example, someone who lost a family member in the Iraq war may have a very different idea and belief about the need for the war, as opposed to those who have not suffered the loss of a loved one during the war.

Paul Hanna (1937) characterized the shortcomings of teaching social studies as it was taught in the first half of the century (and, many would argue, is still being taught today) as follows.

With all our reciting of the facts that Columbus, an Italian, discovered America in 1492 and that the Pilgrims, from England, landed at Plymouth in 1620 we go on hating foreigners as much as if we hadn't learned the historic fact that most of us are originally from foreign shores. With all of our "book learning" of the structure of city and state government we still have corruption in high places and indifference among our citizens. With all our geographic fact teaching we face increasing national insecurity because geography has not taught us to conserve our soil, forests, and other natural resources. Nor have we much evidence that through social studies we have aided in promoting happier family relations, bettering juvenile social behavior, obtaining higher standards of living, or generally in solving the vast number of problems that plague our culture.

A man's country is not a certain area of land, of mountains, rivers, and woods, but it is a principle and patriotism is loyalty to that principle.

George William Curtis

Key Citizenship Education Concepts

The goal of citizenship education is for students to mature into productive, wise citizens of their country and the world (see Topic 5). Citizenship education draws on history, government, economics, geography, current events, and the social sciences, and it uses a variety of methods including service learning, simulations, group discussions of controversial issues, literature about heroic citizens, and mock trials. The following key citizenship education concepts can serve as a basis for your approach to developing lesson plans for your students on the duties, rights, and obligations of citizenship.

Civics in the United States

When one looks at other nations, there are two concepts worth considering that, arguably, makes civics more important to sustaining the United States.

My country, right or wrong. When right, to be kept right, when wrong, to be put right.

John Paul Jones

Peopling of North America

Unlike many other nations, the land in which the United States government is sitting was repopulated with its "discovery" in 1492. Since then, people chose to leave their birthplaces to come here from all over the world. The United States has seen waves of immigrants from all the European, Asian, African, and Latin American regions. The United States is the most culturally diverse country in the world and in the history of the world. Consider this, in the United States, the pilgrims, George Washington, Ellis Island, and the Betsy

Ross stories are all used to promote a national identity. But in the United States, we may have Black children playing the role of George Washington in a school play, a Pakistani girl playing Betsy Ross, and a White child playing Pocahontas. Arguably, U.S. citizens' identity is not shaped in the same way as that of the people of France, England, or Japan where ancestry and class played a greater role in determining the current citizens' national identity.

National Identity

Unlike the European countries whose "bond" is typically forged out of a common ancestry, U.S. citizens are so diverse that what holds them together is not first and foremost ethnic, cultural, or religious bonds, but something very different from that found in other countries. One can be of Pakistani origin, born in London and, thus, a citizen of the British Empire living in England, yet one would not necessarily be considered "English." Conversely, the United States seems to use a different prism to view its citizens. To be a U.S. citizen, is not based on historical ethnic, cultural, or country-of-origin connotations as is the case in most other societies (MacMillan, 2009). In Britain, one would not hear, "he is an Italian Englishman" as an example, but such an expression as "he is an Italian American" or "he is an African American" is commonplace in the United States. For U.S. citizens, it is argued that the bond that holds the people of the United States together is an unspoken recognition that we share a system of beliefs, such as the ideas of liberty, rule of law, and rights, etc. as embodied in the Constitution. Arguably, U.S citizens are U.S. citizens because of what they believe.

Western Civilization

Teleology is from the Greek *telos*, meaning end or purpose. Teleology holds that all things have a purpose and are directed toward a final result. This concept holds true whether you believe a god is the director of life or not. In Western civilization, it can be argued that most people see the ascent of humankind to a higher ethical plane as the final result of their teleology and is evidenced by its history of increasingly more humane treatment of fellow humans on the planet. This is so fundamental to Western ideology that it is rarely spoken of. As examples, another person's gender, sexual orientation, ethnicity, or culture should have no bearing on his or her treatment by others or the state, and religious beliefs, while they may shape individuals' ideology, are subservient to such broader democratic notions. So, the status of women, child labor, health care, etc. in a country becomes, for most people in the Western world, one of the measures of humankind's advancement as a species. The tension created between countries based on the differences between ideologies is both a source of conflict and alliances among nations. The current "war on terrorism" can be viewed as a war about ideology, where U.S. citizens point to Middle Eastern cultures as too undemocratic and oppressive of their people and Middle Eastern cultures point to the United States as decadent and too secular.

The history of the human species ascent since the time of recorded history is unmistakable, however. While there have been peaks (Gandhi's nonviolent revolution, King's civil rights success, an American civil war that ended slavery, the American revolution that established the principle of equality, etc.) and valleys (the imposition of Christianity on the peoples of South America, the mistreatment of the First Americans as Europeans repopulated North America, Nanking [where the Japanese army slaughtered thousands of Chinese women and children], the Jewish Holocaust, etc.) the overall trajectory of our species is to a more humane world. And, Westerners tend to measure this ascent by the diffusion of human rights, education, health, technology, and wealth to those areas of the planet that are not as advanced as Western countries and advancements in human treatment within countries with rich traditions of protection of less-well-off populations and minorities.

History of Nations

Government evolved starting with hunter-gatherer bands of humans and was believed to be generally kinship-oriented and egalitarian, meaning the group would have a high level of equality among its members. The governance of such "preliterate" (this term is preferred over "primitive") communities likely relied on a process not unlike direct democracy in which small bands of people would have made decisions around campfires based on consensus and a shared wisdom passed on from elders who could draw on personal experiences. Within these communities, individuals would rise to leadership of the group by consent of the members based on the many of the same attributes we look for in leaders today. These **tribal societies** introduced chieftains, the predecessors of monarchs, in response to the growing complexity of governance. Ordaining children of monarchs as successors insured stability and some knowledge of governance. The originally kinship-oriented, egalitarian societies evolved into stratified societies that were less egalitarian and that valued wealth or status more than kinship. These **societies** evolved into complex social hierarchies organized with institutional governments in various geographic regions throughout the world. To insure that their common values were sustained and adopted, they defined desirable and undesirable behaviors by codifying laws to reflect their belief systems. Such codifications communicated the expected behavior and the desirable virtues to members of the group. Strategies (treaties, war, fortifications, standing armies, etc.) were used to buttress the benefits of the **society** from non-members who threatened its stability. By about 5000 B.C., we have evidence of well-formed governments to support these societies, most notably Sumar (present day Iraq). By the year 3000 B.C., the better-known Egyptian civilization has a society, relatively speaking, with many at-tributes of today's nations. It was out of these early societies that the concept of nations and nationalism evolved into what we have today, that nations have a right to rule themselves on a defined piece of geography regardless of the mix of cultures, religions, etc. that are present within the specified geographic region (MacMillan, 2009), As an example, in the United States it is the practice to have one judicial system and laws for all based on secular notions of justice. But the practice in some Middle Eastern nations was to allow different cultures to handle legal matters within their communities based on their traditions. So members of a Jewish community across the street from a Muslim community might impose one form of justice on its members that is different from the Muslims across the street. One of the inherent problems created by this kind of system was the conflict and resolution over offenses that occurred between cultures. One of the challenges with the U.S. system (as most nations today) is that for it to work, it must be and be perceived as impartial and equitable, regardless of culture, "race," etc.

Common Citizenship Concepts

Regardless of which nation one happens to born into or immigrates to, there are concepts about national identity and citizenship which are shared across the planet.

Patriotism is love of and devotion to one's country. It is essential to the functioning of nations. U.S. elementary-level students, as are students in other countries, are given the opportunity to express their patriotism through reciting the Pledge of Allegiance, singing patriotic songs, dramatizing events like the signing of the Declaration of Independence, and learning about and celebrating national holidays. In the United States, but not in all countries, two people in a democratic society can hold contrary opinions and positions on their government's policy, but both can be patriotic. Regrettably, people are sometimes accused of being unpatriotic if they hold unpopular views.

At the Premium Website, download the Core Knowledge Reading 22, "Give Me Liberty or Give Me Death." Can you think of a way you could use this reading in your classroom?

In less democratic societies, patriotism and civil dissent are seen as contradictory and "blind" patriotism is promoted as a higher goal than deliberate, thoughtful decision making. Children's inclination to converting ideas into black-and-white choices makes it difficult for them to appreciate that patriotism and social criticism are complementary. Focusing on helping children gather facts and allowing them to discuss issues is one of the best ways to appreciate the balance between social criticism and patriotism.

Social criticism is intimately tied to free speech, a right many U.S. citizens take for granted. Teachers should encourage social criticism but demand and ensure that students base that criticism on facts and logical argument and create a civility in the classroom that communicates to students the importance of listening as well as talking. Combined with passions, these strongly held beliefs lead to social activism.

Social activism is also essential to a democratic state, and students should be given opportunities to act on their beliefs and values in constructive ways. Service learning (see Topic 48) is one vehicle and includes such things as a cleanup day at the school, in a park, or on a playground and collections for needy families, that the class could take on. However, it only becomes a social studies lesson (as opposed to a feel-good activity), if students receive a thorough grounding in an issue or public policy.

Civil disobedience requires not only knowing the right thing to do and doing it, but also being willing to suffer the consequences of your beliefs. Mohammed Ali was prohibited from boxing for three years because he refused induction into the army during the Vietnam War; as a consequence, he lost millions of dollars and ran the double risks of never being allowed to box again and going to jail. The signers of the Declaration of Independence were, on the whole, members of the upper class, and their decision to rebel against their country was considered treason in Britain. Not only could they have lost their earthly possessions; they also could have lost their lives. Martin Luther King, Jr., did more than change the landscape for civil rights and lose his life for the cause; he brought the practice of peaceful civil disobedience to the Americas. Such examples of courage from history prepare students for their citizenship duties.

Can you think of a current-day example of an unpopular but patriotic view? How would you develop this example as a lesson on the topic in the classroom?

Teaching Citizenship's Values—Two Potential Pitfalls

Anthropologists usually define "culture" as all learned patterns of thought and behavior that are characteristic of a population or society. **Enculturation** (also *acculturation* or *cultural transmission*) is the process by which a culture and its civic values are transmitted from one generation to the next. The United States has a more diverse culture than do many other nations. That fact and the ubiquity of television, films, the Internet, global communication, and a comprehensive public school system (compared with 50 or even 25 years ago) means that students are exposed to more and different ideas and behaviors than those limited to just their families, universal education, and immediate communities.

Teacher's Tip

A social studies teacher's job is not to teach students **what** to think, but **how** to think.

Schools and teachers are major players in this cultural transmission. In the area of civic virtues (also called *public values* and *democratic ideals*), we use social studies to try to pass on the democratic beliefs and behaviors that our culture has deemed desirable or widely accepted (Gagnon, 2003; Wineburg, 2001). Deciding what those public values are is no easy matter, but the National Council for Social Studies (NCSS) has authored a position statement, "Democratic Beliefs and Values," on what democratic ideals should be taught (see Topic 17 for the full statement), and the NCSS (2008a), in an effort to not only promote the knowledge of citizenship, but to promote **civic engagement** proposes the following:

"I must study politics and war that my sons may have liberty to study mathematics and philosophy."

John Adams

- Understand the fundamental processes of democracy;
- Identify and understand public and community issues;
- Dialogue with others who have different perspectives;
- Participate in their communities through organizations working to address an array of cultural, social, political, and religious interests and beliefs;
- Act politically to accomplish public purposes through group problem solving, public speaking, petitioning and protesting, and voting; and
- Exhibit moral and civic virtues, such as concern for the rights and welfare of others, social responsibility, tolerance and respect, and belief in the capacity to make a difference.

Teachers' Ideology and Indoctrination

Teachers' personal values and political orientation may differ from those of their students, their students' parents, or the community's culture. It is crucial for teachers to recognize their own personal values and **political ideology** (political perspective, whether liberal, conservative, or other) so as not to promote their personal political agenda, which would be **indoctrination** (Hess, 2004). We know a teacher's personal political persuasion, when not the same as a particular student, can even lead to the unfair grading of students of the other persuasion (Shores & Weseley, 2007).

It is easy to influence children in a classroom setting because teachers are authority figures and children expect that what they hear from adults is in their best interest. Elementary school–aged children accept ideas without the kind of healthy skepticism that is acquired as they mature into adulthood. Part of citizenship education is to teach students the disposition that they have an obligation to be well informed before forming an opinion, have a healthy skepticism about ideas from so-called authorities, be open to new ideas, and use social studies modes of reasoning to inform themselves. In fields like mathematics, it is usually a question of the teacher's having a greater degree of expertise. In social studies, the difference can be expertise (better command of the modes of reasoning and the facts and concepts) or it can be merely the teacher's values versus the student's values.

Kelley (1986) identifies various examples of ways that teachers may intentionally or unintentionally indoctrinate students to their way of thinking and the options to avoid indoctrination. One of the ways to *enculturate*, rather than *indoctrinate*, in teaching elementary school children is to withhold your personal opinions on matters requiring decisions about personal and public values and focus on the procedural knowledge, thus forcing students to think through the issues for themselves rather than trying to please the teacher or simply mimic their parents' perspective. Once students have had an opportunity to analyze the issues in terms of their personal values, the teacher can introduce different, more democratic perspectives for the children to consider.

> *Children have never been very good at listening to their elders, but they have never failed to imitate them.*
>
> James Baldwin

Have you ever been indoctrinated?
Have you ever been enculturated?
What do you think are the critical attributes of each process?
From your answers to these questions, can you hypothesize the critical attributes of a democratic classroom (see Assignment 4.1)?
Should you permit students to say anything they want?

A Democratic Classroom and Classroom Management

It is essential for teachers to distinguish between a thoughtful democratic classroom and an undisciplined classroom. You must establish order through classroom rules, rewards, and penalties to make it possible for students to learn—and learn to be responsible citizens (see Bonus Topic E, "Classroom Management" at the book's Premium Website). One of the rules that you may establish might be that students cannot use curse words or words that make other people feel bad. This rule is based on the Right to Dignity, which is one of the NCSS's Democratic Beliefs and Values (see Topic 17).

For example, if the class is learning about Susan B. Anthony and the suffrage movement and a male student says, "Girls are stupid; they shouldn't be allowed to vote," what would you do? This statement would produce a visceral response from the teacher and other students, and we refer to such statements as "undemocratic beliefs."

The student who said, "Girls are stupid" has articulated an *idea* that is incorrect, but it is also undemocratic and contrary to the ideas we believe are necessary for the general good of a democratic society. We certainly do not want other students to adopt the idea, and we can't be sure that this student really *believes* what he has said.

As another example, suppose a student uses a racial epithet in class, it may reflect unhealthy democratic ideology, but it is also a classroom management problem. Although it would certainly be a **teachable moment**, you should handle the classroom management problem immediately by

1. Reminding the student of the classroom rule prohibiting such statements and words.
2. Asking him or her to repeat the rule for the benefit of the class.
3. Reminding all students that people sometimes say things in a way they regret.
4. Possibly asking the student if he or she regrets using the term.
5. Apologizing to affected minority students (looking each one in the eye) by saying, "I am sorry that you had to hear that word, and I apologize and hope you never have to hear it again."

By taking this no-nonsense approach, you will have modeled a thoughtful, reflective, caring teacher that students should want to emulate and, we hope, defused a potential problem. Then immediately return to teaching as if the episode had never happened! For the next day, come prepared to teach a lesson dealing with human intelligence and the origins of the concept *race* (see Cruz and Duplass, 2009).

Fundamental Approaches to Citizenship Education

While all students have a right to their beliefs (and the teacher does as well), your goal is not to teach them your beliefs. Our duty as teachers is not only to provide elementary school students with examples of democratic ideals, but also to teach them the modes of reasoning to think about the issue and their duty to themselves and others. We are also expected to exemplify (model) the thoughtful, deliberate, and open (to new ideas) disposition needed to be a productive citizen. As an example, at times a teacher must intervene and demonstrate the democratic value of civility by giving a student who misspoke or overstated an argument the chance to correct the statement. On other occasions, the teacher must serve as a "devil's advocate" to promote a more democratic idea or defend a student whose belief is under attack. We hope (and believe, although there is no guarantee) that from this knowledge and modeling they will develop beliefs that are compatible with a democratic ideology (Parker, 2001).

There are at least two characteristics of civics that make teaching civics unique, as compared to mathematics, reading, science, etc. These pedagogical bedrocks are as necessary to civics education as the concepts of varying exceptionalities and differentiated instruction are to special education.

Freedom of Thought and Conscience

In Topic 2, the point was made that because social studies includes indefinite information (unlike mathematics where we all agree that 2 +2 = 4) conclusions reached by two people may both be correct. It is also true that two people can have the same exact facts (definitive information) in social studies and still reach different conclusions and be correct. The decision to go to war in Iraq had ingredients of both of these possibilities. In such cases it is the dialogue that becomes paramount as a teaching strategy.

For this reason, teachers of social studies must *not* emphasize *their* opinions or conclusions and must create an environment where students will not be intimidated by other students. Their goal is to create an environment and process where students are expected to be full participants in a dialogue that is in search of each student's personal truth by expecting students to consider their own biases, share their ideas in a thoughtful way, justify their positions with logic and facts, and demonstrate a willingness to consider others' ideas. The teacher's role is to structure lessons that focus on the critical attributes of an issue, and serve as an interlocutor, "devil's advocate," introducer of facts, and clarifier of opinions while engaging all the students.

Fallacies of Thinking

Statements made in discussions can detract from the search for greater understanding. Thus, it is important for teachers to spot fallacious arguments and reveal them as untruths. **Fallacies of thinking** are deceptive arguments that are sometimes used to assert a claim (Zeidler & Duplass, 2000). The teacher should reveal the erroneous argument for what it is by carefully questioning the student who voices it. Teachers should introduce facts to assert alternative ideas with an openness that promotes the search for truth.

Table 4.1 lists the most common rhetorical devices used to evade truth finding. Note that offensive gender-based and race-based stereotypes appear in the table only to clearly convey the prejudice of the fallacies.

People demand freedom of speech to make up for the freedom of thought which they avoid.

Søren Kierkegaard

Table 4.1 Fallacies of Thinking

Argument/Fallacy	Explanation	Example
The Dramatic Instance	Overgeneralization.	"Blacks can make it in this country just as Whites can. I know a Black businessman who is rich. He even has a boat."
Retrospective Determinism	What happened in the past could not have worked out any other way.	"There have always been people who are hungry, it is human nature, and we need to take the good with the bad."
Misplaced Concreteness	Society caused the problem, not the people.	"It's the government's fault we have hungry people in the United States."
Personal Attack	Diverts the dialogue in the absence of facts.	"Poor people are lazy." "You're as lazy as they are."
Appeal to Prejudice	A subtle attack on a group or class of people.	"I fight poverty, I work."
Circular Reasoning	Conclusions are used to validate assumptions that are used to create the conclusions.	"Chicanos hold menial jobs because they are not smart. They can't hold jobs that require you to be smart because they are only good at menial jobs."
Fallacy of Authority	Almost everything we know is based on acceptance of another's perceived authority or expertise of another.	"Michael J. Fox said that there isn't enough funding for Parkinson's disease. He should know, he has it."
Fallacy of Composition	What is true for the part is true for the whole.	"If my uncle can find work, everyone can."
The Non Sequitur	It does not (necessarily) follow.	"Data show that the amount of welfare payments by state governments has increased dramatically during the administration of Democratic presidents."

Adapted from Zeidler & Duplass, 2000.

Social Emotional Learning and Detached Objectivity

Since Socrates, the call for reason over emotion has been the beacon for the advancement of civilization. As an example, someone who lost a family member to a drunken driver may have great difficulty being objective about a discussion of DUI laws, as would someone whose parent who, on one occasion consumed alcohol, was convicted and jailed for a DUI offense.

The kinds of social and emotional learning (SEL) skills proposed by the Collaborative for Academic, Social and Emotional Learning explained in Topic 3 should be pursued as a school-wide program to have the greatest impact. But they also frame the second bedrock approach to teaching social studies, that is, the emphasis on thoughtful, considerate, detached, objective analysis and discussion of history, cultures, current events, etc. so that children can develop their SEL skills. The appropriate role of passion is to stimulate us to inquiry and to act after the objective inquiry and analysis is complete. This disposition is believed to be acquired in the school setting through the academic learning process itself, interaction in "thoughtful" classrooms that social studies teachers cultivate, and the demeanor of the teacher who exhibits the qualities that come to be perceived by students as the appropriate disposition they should have in the search for the truth (DeVries & Zan, 1994; Zins, et al., 2001, 2003).

> **Teacher's Tip**
>
> A "class meetings" approach on a weekly basis, in which discussions of the class culture and issues are voiced in a constructive fashion is an excellent approach to encouraging a greater degree of social emotional intelligence (Angell 2004).

Discussion Strategy

Communicating with words is our most fundamental way of examining complex issues and clarifying the beliefs needed for a democratic state to operate. In social studies, discussion as a fundamental approach, as contrasted with telling students what they need to think, is required in social studies to set a tone of collaboration and thoughtfulness in which everyone's perspective deserves to be aired and examined (Edwards-Groves 2001). Teachers face four challenges in engaging students in a discussion about beliefs.

> *If you are not part of the solution, you are part of the problem.*
>
> Eldridge Cleaver

1. They must maintain their own and other students' empathy for a child who poses an unpopular or undemocratic notion.
2. They must create a climate—a *democratic classroom*—that helps students develop an ego that allows them to be open to new or more sophisticated ideas.
3. They must promote a democratic ideology while also permitting undemocratic and unpopular ideas to be voiced and examined in the hope that students will reject undemocratic ideas.
4. They must strive for efficiency, because of limited amounts of time for instruction, to overcome students' limited attention spans and intellectual capacity.

Often discussion turns into a debate, which commonly degenerates into less than a shared dialogue in search of greater understanding. By a thoughtful, deliberate analysis of facts and concepts, teachers should lead discussions with students to ensure they understand that any issue has multiple perspectives that they should thoughtfully consider.

Critical Attributes Strategy

Critical attributes is a teaching strategy that focuses on transmitting the procedural knowledge of identifying the essential elements of a concept so that students do not form inaccurate concepts and ultimately inadequate ideas and insufficient beliefs that are necessary to be affective citizens. Every issue or topic has *critical*, as opposed to *noncritical* attributes. The use of the fallacies of thinking is a good example of how noncritical attributes can distract teachers and students during a discussion from the search for the truth. Teaching children to distinguish the noncritical and critical attributes is a systematic strategy that leads to the most accurate conceptualization and sound decision making. When questions of civic values, such as "Why are some people homeless?" arise, this strategy allows students to focus on the essential elements of a complex issue so that they can adopt a belief that is based on a rational and systematic analysis of relevant information. For a non-values–based example, with first grade students a teacher developing a lesson on landforms would use the critical attributes method to present the concept *peninsula*—a body of land surrounded by water on three sides. To understand how this strategy can be used, you should complete Assignment 4.1.

Assignment 4.1

INTASC Standards 1, 2, 4, 7, and 8

Islands' Critical Attributes

What are the critical and noncritical attributes of an island? Complete the Critical Attributes Organizer found at the Premium Website. Students whose last names start with A to M should pretend to be first graders who live in Florida. Students whose last names start with N to Z should pretend to be first graders who live in Alaska. Complete the form by correctly defining the critical attributes. For the noncritical attributes, list examples from the perspective of first graders from the state you are pretending to live in. You may want to look up the dictionary definitions of "island." Be prepared to turn in the assignment to your professor and to discuss your results in class.

Can you apply this critical attributes strategy to the concepts *indoctrination* and *enculturation*?
Can you apply this strategy to the concept *hero*?

Best Practices to Create a Democratic Classroom

Based in part on ideas from Newmann (1988) and Kelley (1986), the following strategies should be used as a guide for students to create a **democratic classroom**.

1. The teacher models the characteristics of a thoughtful person by showing interest in students' ideas and their suggestions for solving problems, by modeling problem-solving processes rather than just giving answers, and by acknowledging the difficulties involved in gaining a clear understanding of problematic topics.

2. The teacher ensures that classroom interactions focus on sustained examination of a few topics rather than on superficial coverage of many.

3. The teacher poses questions rather than promoting answers.

4. The teacher suggests more democratic ideas that may be beyond students' experiences.

5. The teacher is silent about his or her own beliefs. When students do not know where the teacher stands, they are forced to rely more on their own critical intelligence.

6. The teacher presses students to clarify or justify their assertions rather than merely accepting and reinforcing them indiscriminately.

7. Students are given sufficient time to think before being required to answer questions.

8. Students are encouraged to generate original, unpopular, and unconventional ideas in the course of the interaction.

They came first for the Communists, but I didn't speak up because I wasn't a Communist. Then they came for the Jews, but I didn't speak up because I wasn't a Jew. Then they came for the Unionists, but I didn't speak up because I wasn't a Unionist. Then they came for the Catholics, but I didn't speak up because I was a Protestant. Then they came for me, and by that time there was no one left to speak up for me.

The Reverend Martin Niemoller, a Lutheran minister, commenting on events in Germany from 1933 to 1939

Can you conceptualize how you might use this famous statement by the Reverend Niemoller in a lesson?

Assignment 4.2

INTASC Standards 1, 2, 3, 4, 5, 7, and 8

Citizenship Education Lesson Plan: Internet Lesson Plan

Download the elementary textbook selection Houghton Mifflin Reading 6, "In Your Classroom," from the Premium Website and review the content in the chapter. Conduct a search for an Internet lesson or activity that can be used to build upon the chapter and bring it to class to turn in to your professor. Be prepared to discuss your results in class and submit the Internet material to your professor.

WEBSITE RESOURCES • Citizenship Education

Video	*Learner.org* Exploring Unity and Diversity: Because themes of unity and diversity surface within both academic content and classroom climate, this session focuses on strategies for teaching provocative issues in social studies as well as methods of addressing a diversity of learners. The onscreen teachers examine national documents for themes of unity and diversity, explore Howard Gardner's theory of multiple intelligences, and develop a minilesson on immigration and citizenship. *Learner.org,* Caring for the Community: The lesson focuses on the concept of community and explores how students can help make a difference in each other's lives.
Essay	***ERIC Online*** *ED49669,* The Nation's Report Card[TM]: Civics 2006—National Assessment of Educational Progress at Grades 4, 8, and 12 (NCES 2007). *EJ718720,* It Is Democratic Citizens We Are After: The Possibilities and the Expectations for the Social Studies (2004). *ED475617,* Helping Your Child Become a Responsible Citizen (2003). *ED475582,* Fostering Democratic Discussions in the Classroom: An Examination of Tensions in Civic Education, Contemporary Schools, and Teacher Education (2003).

NCSS Position Statement	Creating Effective Citizens
Lesson Plans	*American Heritage Foundation*. This website has multiple high-quality lesson plans.
Website	*Education World,* Teaching Citizenship's Five Themes National Alliance for Civic Education
	All linked websites (designated by the green color) and those listed here are available as clickable links at the book's Premium Website, www.cengage.com/login, for ease of access. These links will be updated periodically to reflect changes and new resources as they become available.

Topic 5

Multicultural and Global Education

The diverse cultures found in the United States' elementary schools and the freedoms and traditions established by the U.S. Constitution and our founders provide children a unique opportunity to learn about, and come to appreciate, the contributions that *all* people and cultures have made to the advancement of humankind. This is the special focus of multicultural education and global education.

Multicultural Education

J. A. Banks identifies three attributes of **multicultural education**.

> *Multicultural education is at least three things: an idea or concept, an educational reform movement, and a process. Multicultural education incorporates the idea that all students—regardless of their gender and social class and their ethnic, racial, or cultural characteristics—should have an equal opportunity to learn in school . . . [It] is also a reform movement that is trying to change the school and other educational institutions so that students from all social class, gender, racial, and cultural groups will have an equal opportunity to learn . . . Multicultural education is also a process whose goals will never be fully realized. Educational equality, like liberty and justice, are ideals toward which human beings work but never fully attain.*

(Banks, 1997)

Goals of Multicultural Education

The National Council for the Social Studies (NCSS) prepared the following statement on multicultural education, which serves as a theoretical basis for teachers of social studies and also identifies the three main reasons that multicultural education is necessary.

> *People are socialized within families and in communities where they learn the values, perspectives, attitudes, and behaviors of their primordial culture. Community culture enables people to survive. It also, however, restricts their freedom and their ability to make critical choices and to reform their society. Multicultural education helps students understand and affirm their community cultures and helps to free them from cultural boundaries, allowing them to create and maintain a civic community that works for the common good. Multicultural education seeks to actualize the idea of* e pluribus unum *within our nation and to create a society that recognizes and respects the cultures of its diverse people, people united within a framework of overarching democratic values. A unified and cohesive democratic society can be created only when the rights of its diverse people are reflected in its institutions, within its national culture, and within its schools, colleges, and universities. A national culture or school curriculum that does not reflect the voices, struggles, hopes, and dreams of its many peoples is neither democratic nor cohesive. Divisiveness within a nation-state occurs when important segments within its society are structurally excluded and marginalized.*
>
> *Three major factors make multicultural education a necessity: (1) ethnic pluralism is a growing societal reality that influences the lives of young people; (2) in one way or another, individuals acquire knowledge or beliefs, sometimes invalid, about ethnic and cultural groups; and (3) beliefs and knowledge about ethnic and cultural groups limit the perspectives of many and make a difference, often a negative difference, in the opportunities and options available to members of ethnic and cultural groups.*

> *Rather than a melting pot, America should be thought of as a salad bowl.*
>
> Source Unknown

Adopted 1976 by NCSS Board of Directors, revised 1991, available at the NCSS Website.

Multiculturalism and Cultural Literacy

In what is known as the "culture wars," **multicultural education** and **cultural literacy** are depicted in the education literature as opposing forces in the fight for the minds and hearts of U.S. youth and the future of civilization (for more on this topic, see "The language police: How pressure groups restrict what students learn" (Ravitch, 2003a) and the online article "Toward a Centrist Curriculum: Two Kinds of Multiculturalism in Elementary School" [2005] at the Core Knowledge Website. In the extreme, advocates of cultural literacy are depicted as promoting the superiority of Western civilization and U.S. culture in much the same way Hitler promoted German superiority. In the extreme, multiculturalists are portrayed as moral relativists who fail to appreciate the unique advancements in civilization brought about by the democratic and intellectual traditions of the West that are reflected in U.S. culture today.

Both multicultural education and cultural literacy are vital to the character and citizenship development of elementary students and to your success as a social studies teacher. Both provide insights into the shared human experience and encourage people to develop the wisdom necessary to the common task of providing for the common welfare of the inhabitants of our planet. Your students should come to appreciate the values, traditions, and history of the United States, with its rich evolving multicultural and intellectual traditions. It is difficult to imagine teaching social studies without this kind of academic disposition.

Multicultural Education and Children's Development

Children seek autonomy and identity. Regrettably, some people feel powerful when they deride the ethnicity or culture traits of others. Teachers can create a classroom climate that supports multiculturalism by being good role models as people who appreciate differences and who view them as learning opportunities for themselves and their students (Banks et al., 2005).

Appreciation of the uniqueness of other people and of oneself is at the heart of multiculturalism. Alex de Tocqueville traveled the United States in the 1800s chronicling the unique temperament and habits of "these people who call themselves Americans," and in *Ciao, America: An Italian Discovers the U.S.,* Beppe Severgnini (2002) humorously points out numerous characteristics of contemporary U.S. citizens that make us different, unique, and odd to other cultures. Such insights come from an academic disposition of objectivity that leads to self-reflection. It can be learned during social studies instruction and is crucial to civility.

Multiculturalism is not just appreciation by the many of the few or appreciation of what is different (Meyer & Rhoades, 2006). It is also giving a voice to children who are not in the majority. Whether children are recent immigrants or their families have lived in the United States over a longer period, every student in your class has something special to offer from his or her family heritage. All students have unique stories to share. Their developing self-image is based, in part, in their family's culture and history. Your students' lives can be turned into lessons in which appreciation of other cultures is the big idea, and students find that the attributes that make them different also make them unique. Children from other cultures can give their classmates a greater understanding of life outside their family, immediate community, and experience. Encouraging students to share stories, language, traditions, food, intellectual contributions, and religious customs can be more powerful than the textbooks and literature that are intended to introduce them to other cultures.

Although multicultural education is typically articulated as a philosophy, teaching strategy, or a curriculum theme within the United States' borders and its educational system, it is inexplicably linked to world ideologies that have come to the United States as a result of our open society. If the teacher does not take great care, multicultural education can imply that all political ideologies are equal. Feudalism of the Middle Ages and Nazism of the mid-20th century are not equal to democracy's support for individual autonomy and worth. Ideologies that come to the U.S. typically come as part of a culture, and while children should be encouraged to appreciate various attributes of cultures, undemocratic ideologies that accompany those cultures should be examined in light of democratic ideals.

> *We do not understand the ideals of other cultures better by mis understanding our own, or adequately enrich an intercultural synthesis by offering to it anything less than the best we have.*
>
> A. E. Murphy

Global Education

A greater understanding of other countries' cultures and ideologies and approaches to government is crucial to the continuing advancement of society in the U.S. and the world. However, children need to understand the difference between ideology and culture, even though the two are intertwined. As an example, one can decry the lack of rights of women in some cultures as an uninformed ideology and failure of government, while still admiring other attributes of the culture. Teachers in the United States have an obligation to promote democratic beliefs while encouraging understanding other people's cultural traditions in other countries. You have an obligation to help your students appreciate their own and other cultures, but you also must promote their responsibility to work for all people to have the democratic rights they enjoy and perhaps even take for granted.

The NCSS International Activities Committee constructed the following definition of **global education**.

> *Global education refers to efforts to cultivate in young people a perspective of the world that emphasizes the interconnections among cultures, species, and the planet. The purpose of global education is to develop in youth the knowledge, skills, and attitudes needed to live effectively in a world possessing limited natural resources and characterized by ethnic diversity, cultural pluralism, and increasing interdependence . . .*
>
> *Social studies should assume a major role in providing students with opportunities (1) to learn to perceive and understand the world as a global system, and (2) to see themselves as participants in that system, recognizing the benefits, costs, rights, and responsibilities inherent in such participation.*

> Approved by NCSS Board of Directors (1981), available at the NCSS Website.

The Content of Global Education

Kneip (1987) defined the topics that are developed in a global education lesson as follows.

- The study of diverse human values that transcend our differences
- The study of global systems: economic, political, ecological, and technological
- The study of global issues and problems: peace, security, development, environment, and human rights
- The study of global history to better understand contemporary issues and problems

The love of one's country is a splendid thing. But why should love stop at the border?

Pablo Casals

Such U.S. political principles as equality under the law, freedom of speech and religion, human rights, and tolerance have largely been endorsed by the 1948 Universal Declaration of Human Rights of the United Nations, which can be found at the United Nations Website. In some nations, cultural traditions perpetuate undemocratic behaviors and treatment of some people. You can further children's development as U.S. citizens who "think globally" by

- Encouraging children to think of themselves as unique individuals and members of the human race as a whole. Being born into one culture or another is secondary to our connection to all humankind. Loyalty to ethnic, religious, and/or secular groups can sometimes lead to strife.
- Sharing the history of civilization, including the unique emphasis on democratic principles of Western civilization and the fact that many cultures helped advance humankind, thus allowing students to learn from different cultures.
- Helping children appreciate different cultures regardless of their societies' current status on human rights. The examples listed in the following section may be helpful in this regard.

Multicultural and Global Instructional Learning Experiences

Limiting the scope of multicultural or global education to fostering appreciation of the qualities and diversity of cultures would be contrary to the very goals of these educational philosophies. In addition, almost any lesson in social studies has some aspect of culture at its core. The promotion of cultural awareness is often selected as the goal of a lesson plan because the information knowledge lends itself to this kind of objective.

Mary Merryfield (2004) recommends a number of approaches and goals that teachers should pursue as global educators, some of which are presented here.

- Teach students to recognize and understand underlying assumptions and values in their own perspectives and those of others and how they change over time.
- Identify stereotypes students bring to class and address stereotypes directly.
- Teach students to recognize how "exotica" (the out of the ordinary) may interfere with cultural understanding.
- Aim for a balance between cultural differences and commonalities and teach students to examine cultural universals.
- Teach about prejudice and discrimination within and across diverse world regions.
- Teach the dynamic nature of cultural change and diffusion.
- Help students understand how cultural norms change over time in real people's lives.

Approaches to elementary instruction that focus on multicultural education and appreciation include:

1. Exhibitions, presentations, and guest speakers representing various cultures;
2. Historical accounts of contributions of world cultures, civilizations, and regions; and
3. Children's literature (see Topic 26) used as an effective means of transmitting cultural appreciation and improving basic skills. For example, the Michigan State University Library provides a "gateway site" (meaning the site has multiple listing and links) to multicultural literature resources for teachers at the elementary school level.

O, yes. I think it would be a good idea.

Mahatma Gandhi, when asked what he thought of Western civilization

Because holidays and languages have cross-cultural commonalities as well as qualities that are unique to each culture, the following two examples are excellent springboards to lessons on cultural appreciation.

1. Holidays and festivals are the outcome of cultures celebrating seasonal changes in fall, winter, spring, and summer with observances, festivals, and holidays. Many of these celebrations have become formalized into religious and cultural traditions. Children are generally unaware of the holidays and festivals of other regions of this country and across the world. Depending on your own religion, education, and experience, you may need to learn more about world religions and festivals before you can use this kind of multicultural lesson to teach big ideas. Three websites that can serve as gateways to information are the Earth Calendar, Holidays, and Virtual Religion Index.

2. Language is also a gateway to multicultural appreciation. Encouraging students to learn phrases in the home languages of other students and relying on bilingual students to model perfect accents create a culturally nurturing class environment. The languages themselves provide root words for insights into the culture. *Baton Rouge*, the capital of Louisiana, means "red stick," and the city got its name because Native Americans gave the French explorer who "discovered" the area a ceremonial red baton. *Barbecue* is an Arawak word (from one of the indigenous tribes of the Caribbean). Two websites that can help you develop a lesson around languages and words are: the Say Hello to the World Project, which includes a listing of many activities and information on how to say "hello" in multiple languages, and the Internet Public Library where you can learn about word origins and expressions of cultural origins.

Can you share a tradition, story, or unique expression or word from your family's culture? What would the big idea be?

Assignment 5.1

INTASC Standards 1, 2, 3, 4, 5, 7, and 8

Multicultural Perspectives: Resources for a Lesson Plan

Download the elementary textbook selection Houghton Mifflin's Third Grade Reading 7, "Coming to America," from the Premium Website and review the topics in the chapter. Assume you are preparing a lesson based on all or part of the content. Conduct a search on the Internet for at least five resources (maps, primary documents, timelines, background information for the teacher, images, etc.). Prepare a one-page summary of your idea for the lesson and how you would use the five resources. Attach a copy of at least the first page of each resource. Be prepared to discuss your results in class and submit the paper to your professor.

Video	*TeachSource,* Culturally Responsive Teaching: A Multicultural Lesson for Elementary Students demonstrates how to connect multicultural themes to the lives of students with a writing assignment. *TeachSource,* Diversity: Teaching in a Multiethnic Classroom uses a creative and unique approach to reading in a class in which English is the second language for half the students. *Learner.org,* Celebrations of Light: A lower elementary thematic lesson on holiday celebrations combines a read-aloud and learning stations in math, writing, and drawing located throughout the classroom.
YouTube	*Schoolhouse Rock - The Great American Melting Pot* by School House Rock
Essay	**ERIC Online** *EJ719893,* Our Multicultural Classroom (2005). *ED477609,* Exploring the Function of Heroes and Heroines in Children's Literature from around the World (2003). *ED469428,* Making Diversity Awareness Part of Your Teaching (2001). *ED458186,* Developing Political Tolerance (2001).
Websites	**NCSS** *Notable Trade Books* *Edchange Multicultural Pavillion* is a gateway Website with resources that support multicultural education including songs, expressions, activities, etc. *Awesome Library of* multicultural education resources. *Peace Corps:* Kids World.
Lesson Plan	*EdWeb* We Hold These Truths to Be Self-Evident explores diversity.
	All linked websites (designated by the green color) and those listed here are available as clickable links at the book's Premium Website, www.cengage.com/login, for ease of access. These links will be updated periodically to reflect changes and new resources as they become available.

Unit Two

Planning Social Studies Instruction

Topic 6

Expanding Communities and Core Knowledge Frameworks

What and when you teach have traditionally been known as "curriculum," "scope and sequence," or **framework**. The past decade has also seen the increased use of the words "standards" (see the next topic) and "benchmarks" to refer to the curriculum. How you teach is usually called "pedagogy," "approaches," "methods," "strategies," or "instruction" and is the focus of this textbook and its Premium Website.

Unlike some nations, the United States does not have a nationally mandated scope and sequence or content or curriculum standards for social studies. As a result, each state decides what and when social studies should be taught. However, the **expanding communities approach** (see later in this topic) has provided some consistency in the last 50 years, although not without criticism. The National Council for the Social Studies (NCSS), in 2006, formed a task force to consider the issues of scope and sequence. In their 2008 draft, "Expectations of Excellence: Curriculum Standards for Social Studies" (see NCSS Website), the task force has not defined or recommended a grade-level by grade-level curriculum of information knowledge, procedural knowledge or basic skills, but instead identified "themes, learning expectations, and essential skills" that should be used to shape a social studies curriculum.

"Standards-based education" is now the dominant approach to defining the curriculum in most subject fields by the individual states. No doubt "Expectations of Excellence: Curriculum Standards for Social Studies," which is expected to be approved in late 2009, will begin to influence the way state boards of education think about their social studies curriculum. The closest curriculum model available with a grade-by-grade content orientation is the **core knowledge approach** (see later in this topic).

Social studies content standards are more controversial among educators than approaches to instruction (Nash, Crabtree, & Dunn, 1997; Symconx, 2002). For example, when the National Center for History in the Schools published its *National Standards for History* in 1996 (see Topic 18), some educators charged that these standards elevated relatively minor historical figures and events for the sake of diversity, losing accurate proportionality based on roles of individuals or events in history for the sake of political correctness. Others claimed that some groups, individuals, and events were omitted altogether or were not given adequate coverage because of bias, due to U.S. Eurocentrism, or ethnocentrism (see Gitlin, 1995; Leming, Ellington, & Porter, 2003; Ravitch 2003a, 2003b). Depending on local traditions, history, and ideology, each state has adopted various components of standards published by the different national organizations (see Unit 4). So even though there is no official U.S. curriculum, the national organizations bring a degree of consistency to the scope and sequence.

Would you expect Florida, Texas, and California to have different standards than Wisconsin, Maine, and Missouri?

The state in which you teach will have standards that are intended to govern general educational and social studies expectations for your classroom. Typically, for reasons of economics the national textbook companies design books that address the needs of the states with the largest populations and generalize the books to be usable by many states (Finn & Ravitch, 2004). As a result, your textbook is unlikely to be precisely linked to your state's standards. However, two approaches (or a combination of the two) can be found in textbooks to accommodate the most typical scope and sequence of the individual 50 states: the expanding communities approach and the core knowledge approach.

A Historical Perspective

Prior to the early 1900s, "social studies" did not exist as a term. The curriculum focus was on history that integrated geography, government, and folklore (see Topic 18). History was a core subject at every grade level and provided students with a rich knowledge of history and civic values associated with U.S. democratic traditions. By the mid-1900s, the social efficiency and activities-based movements along with the growing specialization of the relatively new social studies disciplines led to the evolution of the history curriculum as it had been formerly taught into only one of many subjects, and socialization and citizenship education became a major feature of activities-based classrooms. See ERIC Online ED 481631, *Where Did Social Studies Go Wrong*, 2003 for a critique of social studies education and Topic 34 for the activities-versus-active learning approaches to learning.

Expanding Communities Approach

In the early 1940s, Paul Hanna (1965) articulated **expanding communities** as the scope and sequence for elementary social studies. By the 1960s the approach had become widely accepted by school systems and textbook publishers, and it is still the de facto scope and sequence of social studies (Welton, 2002). For the most part, Hanna's model has been characterized as a series of concentric circles with the individual at the center (the starting point of social studies instruction), progressing from self to the family, school, neighborhood, state, nation, and international community (LeRiche, 1987; Stallones, 2004). The former curriculum, a sequential treatment of history with government and geography infused, became shorter vignettes mixed with life experience topics intended to be more relevant to the child's world as he or she was experiencing it (see Table 6.1). As a result, the expanding communities' textbooks do not typically present a comprehensive, chronological development of world or U.S. history until the upper elementary grades.

Table 6.1 Elementary Grades Expanding Communities Scope and Sequence

Grade Level	Expanding Communities	Houghton Mifflin Text Topics[*]	(Scope and Sequence)
Kindergarten	Self	**My World:** Our Family Comes from around the World; Our Big Home; Time Places; America Is ...	
Grade 1	Family	**School and Family:** People Everywhere; Where We Live; World of Work; Everything Changes; Good Citizens	
Grade 2	School	**Neighborhoods:** People and Places; Places Near and Far; Ways of Living; People at Work; America's Past; America's Government	
Grade 3	Neighborhood	**Communities:** Community and Geography; America's Early Communities; People Move from Place to Place; Community Government; Making Economic Choices; Celebrating People and Cultures	
Grade 4	Local Community	**States and Regions:** People and Places; Places Near and Far; Ways of Living; People at Work; America's Past; America's Government	
Grade 5	State Community	**United States History:** Geography and First Peoples through Present	

*The publishers Macmillan/McGraw-Hill and Silver, Burdett & Ginn offer a comparable national sequence based, in part, on the expanding communities approach.

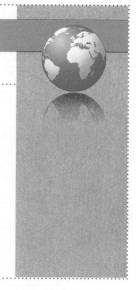

INTASC Standards 1, 2, 7, and 9

State Standards Comparison

You can find most states' standards at **Education Standards**. Using Table 6.1 as a model, record your state's scope and sequence for each grade level. Select a parent's, relative's, or friend's state and compare its scope and sequence with your state's. Be prepared to turn in the assignment to your professor and to discuss your analysis in class.

Often overlooked by educators and publishers was Hanna's **thematic approach**, which is reflected in the new NCSS themes (see Table 6.2).

Assignment 6.2

INTASC Standards 1, 2, 7, and 9

State Scope and Sequence

Determine whether your state is using the NCSS themes or another approach in its standards. Using Table 6.2 as a model, identify which themes, if any, appear in the elementary social studies curriculum; record them in the last column of the table. Be prepared to turn in the assignment to your professor and discuss your results in class.

Core Knowledge Approach

E. D. Hirsch's (1987) concept of **core knowledge** has been presented as an alternative to Hanna's scope and sequence model. Doubleday's seven-book series *What Every American Should Know* for kindergarten through sixth grade takes the core knowledge approach and provides a more sequential treatment of history with infused government and geography and no contemporary topics as found in expanding communities. Table 6.3 compares the two approaches. The core knowledge books contain world and U.S. history, government, and geography at ascending degrees of complexity; they promote citizenship and character education through folklore and traditional children's literature that focuses on values.

Table 6.2 NCSS Themes of Learning

Expanding Communities Themes (1965)	NCSS Themes (1994)	Your State's Themes
	Culture	
	Time, Continuity, and Change	
Protecting and Conserving Environments	People, Places, and Resources	
Producing	Production, Distribution, and Consumption	
Governing	Power, Authority, and Governance	
	Civic Ideals	
	Individuals, Groups, and Institutions	
Creating	Science, Technology, and Society	
Transporting	Global Connections	
Expressing (spiritual)	Individual Development and Identity	
Educating		
Recreating		
Communicating		

Table 6.3 Comparison of Expanding Communities and Core Knowledge Curricula

Grade Level	Houghton Mifflin Expanding Communities Text Topics (Hanna Approach)	Doubleday Text Topics Core Knowledge (Hirsch) Approach
Kindergarten	**My World:** Our Family Comes from around the World; Our Big Home; Time Places; America Is . . .	World History by Continents American History and Geography American Leaders Democracy's Beginning Great Works: *Aesop's Fables, Humpty Dumpty, The Three Little Pigs, Look Before You Leap,* etc.
Grade 1	**School and Family:** People Everywhere; Where We Live; World of Work; Everything Changes; Good Citizens	Ancient History and Great Religions American History: Land Bridge through 1776 and Great Americans of the Revolution Great Works: *Aesop's Fables, Brer Rabbit, Pinocchio,* etc.
Grade 2	**Neighborhoods:** People and Places; Places Near and Far; Ways of Living; People at Work; America's Past; America's Government	World Geography World Civilization: Babylon through Alexander, Africa and China American Civilization The New Republic to Lincoln, Major Events and Persons, and Civil Rights Great Works: Ancient Mythologies
Grade 3	**Communities:** Community and Geography; America's Early Communities; People Move from Place to Place; Community Government; Making Economic Choices; Celebrating People and Cultures	Geography Americas and Early Explorers World Civilization Rome and Islamic Civilization American Civilization First Americans to the Revolution Ourselves Great Works: Norse Mythologies, *Arabian Nights, William Tell, Give Me Liberty,* etc.

(Continued)

Grade Level	Houghton Mifflin Expanding Communities Text Topics (Hanna Approach)	Doubleday Text Topics Core Knowledge (Hirsch) Approach
Grade 4	**States and Regions:** People and Places; Places Near and Far; Ways of Living; People at Work; America's Past; America's Government	Geography by Regions World Civilization Middle Ages, Islam, China Through the End of Byzantium American Civilization Revolution to the Civil War Great Works: Frederick Douglass, Sojourner Truth, *Robinson Crusoe,* etc.
Grade 5	**U.S. History:** Geography and First Peoples through Present	World Civilization American Indian Civilizations, European Explorers, The Renaissance, the Enlightenment, and French Revolution American Civilization Civil War through Spanish American War Great Works: *Tom Sawyer, Iliad* and *Odyssey, Casey at the Bat,* etc.

Both approaches have been criticized (Gitlin, 1995; Nash, Crabtree, & Dunn, 1997; Ravitch, 2003a, 2003b; Duplass, 2007). Hanna's model is viewed as inadequate by detractors because it is based on a theory of the learning sequence that is no longer valid, because the treatment of U.S. and world history is disjointed, because topics like street signage are trite, and because topics such as what a family is and what a neighborhood is would be learned vicariously. Hirsch is criticized for proposing content that is too Eurocentric and, therefore, not sufficiently diverse, advocating a body of knowledge that every U.S. citizen should know, lacking relevance to lives of children, and overemphasizing information knowledge.

Hanna first began to articulate his ideas in the 1940s; Hirsch's ideas gained wider acceptance in the 1990s. Put your sociology cap on and hypothesize about how the United States differed in the 1940s and the 1990s. What societal forces or events might have had an influence on these models?

Assignment 6.3

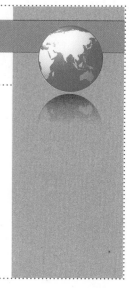

INTASC Standards 1, 4, 7, and 8

Hanna or Hirsch?

Print out the Venn Diagram Graphic Organizer from the book's Premium Website and bring it to class. Hypothesize about why Hanna's and Hirsch's concepts are so different based on the time periods when they were proposed. Consider the types of communities, the technology, and the sociology of the 1940s and 1990s as potential critical attributes. Be prepared to work with another student and discuss your results in class and turn the assignment in to your professor.

Given the choice between Hanna's and Hirsch's lists of topics in Table 6.3, which would you prefer to teach? As a parent, which would you prefer your children to learn?

 WEBSITE RESOURCES

Check the Premium Website, **www.cengage.com/login**, for additional links and links that are periodically updated to reflect new resources as they become available.

Topic 7

Instructional Models

Whether your school uses expanding communities, core knowledge or a mixture of the two curricula, as part of the planning process you will want to use a number of different **instructional models**. The five most common models in social studies education are single discipline teaching, interdisciplinary teaching, thematic teaching, infusion, and extensions.

The Single Discipline Teaching Model

As a novice teacher, you will likely need to start your teaching career using the **single-discipline teaching approach** because it is the simplest and most straightforward. In this approach you focus on either history (the American Revolution) or geography (North American land forms) as examples, and limit yourself to modes of reasoning and content in that discipline. You will probably select your goals based on your state's standards. For example, if your state mandates that students should learn about other cultures based on the National Council for the Social Studies (NCSS) theme, "Cultures" or about North America's geography based on the NCSS theme, "People, Places, and Environments" (see Topic 17), you can decide to use content from the social studies basal text (like those at the book's Premium Website) or you can develop your own information knowledge with children's books, Internet resources, or CD-based encyclopedias.

The **comparable entities approach** is a powerful method in social studies because it allows students to learn the *critical attributes* of and *information knowledge* about two or more entities at one time. For example, if you are using the single-discipline approach to teach the U.S. revolt against Britain, comparing and contrasting it with Australia's or India's movement away from British rule

Teacher's Tip

When developing content for the **comparable entities approach**, teachers should draw on their unique backgrounds and those of students. If a teacher has had the good fortune to travel to Japan, comparing Japanese and U.S. landforms can be enriched by firsthand knowledge. Conversely, if there are many students from Mexico in a teacher's class, a comparison of U.S. and Mexican governments would make instruction more engaging.

enhances the ease with which students develop concepts about revolutions. Using the comparable entities approach, there are two possibilities that come to mind in, as an example, a lesson on Australia.

1. Present Australia as the primary source of the information knowledge, with comparisons made to the United States as the second source.
2. Present the same information knowledge (examples of landforms, government titles, currency, etc.), but with the goal of having students see what is similar between the two countries in order to grasp the concepts that the two comparable entities share.

It is reasonable to start your career with this traditional, cautious single-discipline approach. By the end of your second or third year, it is just as reasonable to become more eclectic. A variety of interdisciplinary, thematic, infusion, and extension lesson plans should be your longer-term goal.

Interdisciplinary Teaching Model

Teaching students to organize historical events in a chronological sequence using the facts from the American Revolution requires only a procedural knowledge approach from the discipline of history. But to teach about the Aztec, Greek, or Roman civilizations, or the Middle Ages, or a social science topic like poverty or immigration, an interdisciplinary approach drawing on all the social studies fields is more appropriate (see ERIC Online ED 476500, *The Best of Both Worlds: Blending History and Geography in the K–12 Curriculum* [2003] for an example of interdisciplinary teaching).

Interdisciplinary instruction uses some or many of the social studies disciplines to build a more profound understanding of a subject by using multiple social studies modes of reasoning (see Figure 7.1). For example, to understand crime, political scientists look at government policy and laws, economists

Figure 7.1   Web of Interdisciplinary Social Studies

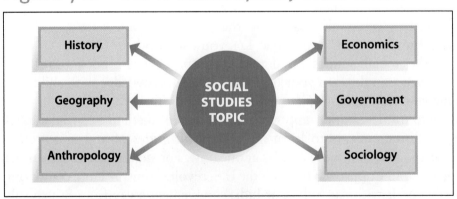

examine the financial status of criminals and victims, geographers analyze places and movements, historians examine personal histories and history of government policies, and sociologists and anthropologists look at family and cultural influences. Similarly, students will better understand Australia, as an example, if the lesson plan includes a history of its colonization; its unique geographic features; its seasons and its location in the Southern Hemisphere; the cultures of its indigenous peoples and settlers; its money system and natural resources; its parliamentary government and legal system; and the contemporary culture and population demographics.

The Thematic Teaching Model

For the purposes of this text, "interdisciplinary teaching" is defined as integrating the social studies disciplines. **Thematic teaching** adds other disciplines, such as language arts, math, science, physical education, art, music, and dance (see Figure 7.2). However, you should note that searching the Internet for the terms "interdisciplinary" or "integrated units" will often produce the same results as "thematic lesson." Regardless of the terms, this approach can be exceptionally powerful because it allows children to engage in learning that is connected and placed in a context (Pappas, Keefer, & Levstik, 2005).

Planning for thematic teaching is complex, but it provides teachers with an excellent opportunity to be creative and collaborate with other teachers. One of the best approaches is for teachers at the same grade level to cooperate in developing a theme, with each taking a component. The first step is to select the theme. Teachers often select a social studies topic rather than one from science or math because social studies is, by nature, integrative and based in the real world, so it is more proximate to students' experiences and prior knowledge. Themes can be drawn from the NCSS themes, historical periods, and social issues. Examples are the Renaissance, technology, communications, success, the westward movement, rain forests, energy, medicine, a country like France or Australia, and money, among others.

Figure 7.2   Web of Thematic Teaching

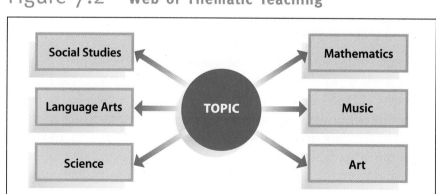

Teachers should ask the following questions as they develop a thematic unit.

1. Do we have or can we acquire the materials needed to support each component and build a quality experience?
2. Are the students ready for thematic learning; do they have prerequisite and dispositional skills?
3. Will students learn the subject field's knowledge better using a thematic approach?
4. Can the learning be made relevant and meaningful to students' current interests and lives?
5. Is the theme important?

The following website resources exemplify the power of the Internet in constructing a lesson, as an example, on Australia.

WEBSITE RESOURCES • Teaching about Australia	
Lesson Plan	*Edsitement* Australian Aboriginal Art and Storytelling for language arts
Activity	*GEM* The Stick That Comes Back: A physical education activity
Websites	*GEM* Who Am I? Australian Mammal, *Australian National Botanical Gardens* has plants of Australia and *Australian Animals* is organized by birds, mammals, etc. with pictures, habitat, and other information for science
	National Geographic downunder for geography on Australia *CIA Fact Book for Australian Government and Economics* *Australian Aboriginal Links* is a gateway with over 162 links about Aborigines. *Southern Cross University* has samples and history of Aboriginal Music. *The National Museum of Australia* has a virtual tour of Aboriginal habitats.

Infusion Teaching Model

Unlike thematic teaching, which might be viewed as the ideal instructional model for social studies at the elementary level, the **infusion approach** is the product of necessity (Hinde, 2005).

As an elementary school teacher, you will feel significant pressure to focus on basic skills because they are the building blocks of all learning and have particular importance to your state's high-stakes testing. In addition, advocates will insist that more of your social studies time should be dedicated to geography rather than to history or economics, or vice versa. Others will campaign for inclusion of focused topics like the ones in Topic 22. You will almost certainly come to think of social studies as competing with science, music, physical education, and art for the time left after math, reading, and language arts have been covered.

The emphasis on basic skills has reduced the time dedicated to teaching social studies in any model in the elementary school classroom and teachers view of its importance given the demands of high-stakes testing (Passe, 2006; Rothman, 2005; Zhao & Hoge, 2005). Since 2001, there has been a 36 percent reduction in time dedicated to teaching social studies in elementary school classrooms (Center for Instruction Policy, 2008).

Infusion can be the incorporation of social studies into reading, writing, math, science, physical education, music, and art lessons as a way to meet the needs of future citizens while developing the basic skills required through the *No Child Left Behind* legislation (see Topics 16 & 17). It is often used in place of a distinct social studies lesson so that students at least get the most basic introduction to social studies. In a classroom using the infusion approach, a teacher would offer, for example, primary documents from U.S. or world history for reading activities, U.S. census data for mathematics instruction, and newspaper and magazine articles on world or U.S. social issues for students to write stories or essays.

Most CD-based or Internet encyclopedias like Wikipedia are a great resource for historical information that can be infused into a lesson. The invention of the numeral zero; the development of calendars, days of the week, and months; the creation of the thermometer; time zones; the history of children's games; the history of musical instruments; and alphabets are examples of content in the other disciplines that can be developed as history lessons. The histories of non–social studies topics allow students to see the uses of history.

The language arts bloc consumes the greatest part of the instructional time in most elementary classrooms, but the reading materials are typically narrative, generic, story-based, standalone genres as opposed to **informational text** (see Topic 23). Information text like that found in social studies textbooks makes up less than 20 percent of the typical reading program (Moss & Newton, 2002). Yet the development of comprehension, as opposed to mere decoding, of text requires immersion in a social studies topic (such as the American Revolution) so that social studies concepts can be scaffold. One of the best ways to do that is to plan to use your social studies textbook (see the Core Knowledge series examples, Readings 21, 23, and 25, at the Premium Website) for the language arts bloc and supplement the lesson with related primary documents, charts, etc. in the social studies bloc (Hirsch, 2006).

The Extension Teaching Model

Extensions are used to relate and integrate a social studies lesson plan to another discipline or basic skill. In some ways, extensions are the other side of the infusion coin: Instead of infusing social studies into other subjects, the other subjects become extensions of social studies. For example, if a social studies lesson is about banking, a math extension would have students simulating purchases and making change. If populations are being studied in social studies, the population numbers could be used for a math activity. An art extension of a lesson on Betsy Ross would have students make a five-pointed star and flag of the United States.

For an excellent example of an extension linking geography and writing for third grade, go to Thirteen.org's lesson plan, "Community Treasures (Rivers and Trees): An Integrated Curriculum Unit." For excellent writing extensions, go to the Read/Write/Think Website.

TEACHSOURCE VIDEO CASE ASSIGNMENT 7.1

INTASC Standards 1, 2, 3, 4, 5, 7, 8, and 9

Thematic and Interdisciplinary Instructional Models: Group Activity

Cooperation with other teachers is the key to creating interdisciplinary and thematic units. For this assignment, view the TeachSource Video Case "Teaching as a Profession: Collaboration with Colleagues" to see how new teachers can benefit from working with other teachers. Then form a group of four with your peers and select a country, continent, or period in history (the Middle Ages, etc.). Research the Internet for resources (lesson plans, activities, or materials) that you could use in teaching the topic from a thematic perspective. Each member of the group should prepare a list of at least five resources from the Internet. Be prepared to submit your individual list and a copy of a page from the Internet for each resource to your professor and to discuss your results in class.

	WEBSITE RESOURCES • Instructional Models
Video	*Learner.org's* Celebrations of Light. *Concept to Classroom* Interdisciplinary Learning in Your Classroom.
Lesson Plans	*Core Knowledge* has the most extensive and detailed single discipline lesson plans on the Internet..
Website	*TeAchnology* has a large number of Interdisciplinary lesson plans.
	All linked websites (designated by the green color) and those listed here are available as clickable links at the book's Premium Website, www.cengage.com/login, for ease of access. These links will be updated periodically to reflect changes and new resources as they become available.

Topic 8

Lesson Planning & Differentiated Instruction

At first, planning to cover all of the subjects an elementary school teacher must teach to 20, 25 or 30 individuals can seem overwhelming. There are so many ways to teach, so much content, so little time, and the students are so diverse! And then there are the unexpected institutional interruptions and the inherent unpredictability of the dynamic classroom environment (Slavco, 2008). Planning is essential to overcome these barriers and those associated with widening variations in skills that students bring to your classroom. Your planning does not have to be complicated, but it does require a great deal of thought, organization, inspiration, and judgment. The purpose of this topic is to propose an outline and process for orchestrating your strategies and types of knowledge (procedural knowledge, information knowledge, and basic skills knowledge), critical thinking opportunities, and big ideas.

> *Organizing is what you do before you do something, so that when you do it, it's not all mixed up.*
>
> Christopher Robin, in
> A. A. Milne, Winnie the Pooh

Focus and Clarity

Whether your aim in a social studies lesson falls under the heading of social studies knowledge, citizenship education, or character education, you can focus your lesson plan by identifying the big idea(s) and planning to make the big idea explicitly known to your students. Such planning requires that you find the big idea, because it will be highly unlikely that it will be identified in your basal textbook, although it is sometimes found in standards and benchmarks.

Big Ideas

Big Ideas, as explained in Topic 2, are powerful, long-lasting ideas and beliefs that you can organize facts around when you prepare lessons (Erickson, 2002). Students who are challenged with big ideas are more likely to become engaged in the learning process and they will consider the new ideas and examine their beliefs. Basic skills knowledge, procedural knowledge, information knowledge and critical thinking should be structured under the umbrella of a big idea(s). Although big ideas are all around us, planned teaching of big ideas requires insight from teachers. For example, when you are planning a lesson on the American Revolution, think about what you want elementary students to get out of it. There are some facts and chronologies to add to their cultural literacy, the cause-and-effect and chronology patterns are important procedural knowledge, and a timeline would be appropriate basic skills knowledge. But what big idea should they take away from a lesson on the American Revolution? As explained in Topic 2, the big ideas of loyalty, patriotism, fairness, cowardice, and their limits excite students and would require critical thinking to analyze these concepts. When they are emotionally engaged, information knowledge, basic skills knowledge, and procedural knowledge have greater meaning and purpose.

How would you use Houghton Mifflin's Reading 22, "Give Me Liberty or Give Me Death" from the Premium Website to enhance a lesson on the American Revolution?

Explicit Teaching

Explicit teaching (also referred to as *concepts-based teaching*, Erickson, 2002) takes place when teachers overtly plan to teach big ideas and procedural knowledge using information knowledge as a foundation. By contrast, many teachers make the mistake of beginning their lesson planning by selecting key facts from the textbook that they will cover. Your basal text's or state's standards will suggest a topic and provide some content, but the topic and facts will fail to resonate with students and will be easily forgotten unless you explicitly find and promote the big idea through a creative lesson. You can make students aware—by explanation, modeling, or active learning experiences—that they are being empowered with the skills of procedural knowledge. For example, begin by teaching about causes and effects using an analogy from daily life ("If I am not organized in the morning, I will be late"); require students to know the term "cause-and-effect pattern", and expect them to use the term with social studies content. Then, challenge students to consider the implications, concepts, and assumptions inherent in this kind of big idea. Big ideas can be procedural knowledge as well, such as an idea drawn from content such as the American Revolution.

For an excellent example of how to shape a lesson around three big ideas and explicitly teach it, go to Learner.org's online video lesson *Explorers in North America*, a lesson on the theme of exploration in North America in which the teacher organizes the entire lesson around three big ideas, or as the teacher puts it, "themes."

Planning Efficient Instruction

The process recommended in this and following topics should serve as a starting point for new teachers with the expectation that as you mature into your role, you will adopt a planning processes and format that best fit your disposition and the needs of your students. But this is a good way to start!

The Importance of Planning

Planning requires setting priorities among mathematics, science, social studies, and other fields and, in the case of social studies, selecting the social studies information knowledge you will use to teach basic skills knowledge, procedural knowledge, critical thinking and the big idea. Your school may require detailed daily, weekly, monthly, semester, and year-long planning as part of a formal monitoring and evaluation process for a new teacher.

One of the most common observations that students majoring in elementary education make after watching a class in session is that experienced elementary school teachers' plans are not as detailed as those proposed by the models and examples in this or other textbooks. This is often true, and after a number of years of experience you may not need as detailed a road map, either. Because you are a student, your professor may require a specific format and a great deal more detail because your lesson plan assignments are not just for your use with students. Typically, the plans are also used for accreditation or to have a state-approved program, which requires you to demonstrate your **pedagogical content knowledge** to your college. As a new teacher, you will be expected to provide your supervisor with clearly articulated lesson plans so that you can assure your elementary school that you are meeting state standards. As a result, what you prepare as a lesson plan now, as a student, should have much more detail and be more formal in its presentation than an experienced teacher's lesson plan.

There are two main schools of thought about planning:

- Alternative 1 is deciding what students should know based on standards, selecting the strategies by which students will learn, and deciding on the assessment.
- Alternative 2 is deciding what students should know based on standards, designing the assessment, and selecting the strategies by which students will learn.

Teacher's Tip

You can always have too much planned, but classroom management problems start when teachers underplan and find themselves without meaningful experiences for students in the afternoon.

Teacher's Tip

The Premium Website provides two Bonus Topics, "Classroom Organization" and "Classroom Management." Both provide ideas that will help make your planning and teaching more effective.

Which alternative do you prefer? Why? Do you think both are equally effective?

Planning is crucial for a novice teacher because plans:

1. Define the big ideas, procedural knowledge, information knowledge, tasks (basic skills knowledge and critical thinking), strategies, and the sequence of events.
2. Require you to think through what you plan to do and have your students do, which becomes your plan of **choreographed instruction** (see Topic 9).
3. Act as a road map that will keep you headed in the right direction and your students on task.
4. Structure the process of developing, selecting, and organizing your materials to support your choreographed instruction.
5. Ensure that the instructional time is meaningful, productive, and rigorous so that you make the best use of the limited amount of time you have with students.
6. Integrate assessment into instruction as seamlessly as possible.
7. Focus assessment on providing remediation rather than grades.

Teaching the Textbook: A Word of Caution

Regrettably, many teachers believe that they should "teach the textbook," or they plan their instruction based solely on the publisher-provided material or ideas (Martin-Hansen, 2004).

Some teachers resort to teaching the textbook because the task of developing lesson plans for multiple subjects is daunting. The textbook should be used to provide an accurate and well-conceived presentation of information knowledge, but typically the teacher must introduce the big ideas, critical thinking, procedural knowledge, and basic skills knowledge. The elementary social studies textbook chapters provided to you at the Premium Website should be viewed as (1) an example and beginning point of possible content you may use to develop a lesson plan, (2) a resource to develop reading skills, and (3) just one of many resources for a lesson plan.

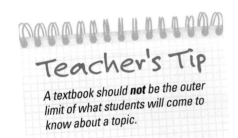

Teacher's Tip

A textbook should **not** be the outer limit of what students will come to know about a topic.

Instructional Efficiency

As a professional, you decide how to teach and what to teach and how much time to allocate to each topic in each subject field. Accurately gauging and planning the amount of time and number of days it will take to complete a lesson is difficult at best. For that reason, it is wise to start planning by thinking in terms of taking as much time as needed for students to gain the knowledge you plan for them to learn. Lesson planning should begin after asking the question, "How do I want them to think differently at the end of the lesson?" Your lesson should then be structured to produce that result (Bearman et al., 2003).

One of the key planning decisions that affects efficiency is determining (a) what should be covered in class, and (b) what knowledge or tasks should be allocated to homework, so that students can either practice what you have taught them or come to class with a **baseline of information** which can make your instruction more efficient (see Topic 25). Once this decision is made, efficient use of the instructional time becomes paramount and will depend on your planning skills, your classroom management skills, your instructional delivery skills, and your approach to classroom organization (WestEd, 2001).

Differentiated Instruction

The proportion of U.S. elementary students from diverse cultural backgrounds and with special needs will continue to grow, according to the National Center for Education Statistics. In addition, in urban environments children with special needs disproportionately come from families with lower socioeconomic status (Karlin, 2005). Creating a classroom culture that supports all students as individuals is a first step toward effective instruction. Identifying a particular practice or strategy as most relevant to one population or another can be misleading. Excellent instructional practices can meet the needs of all students.

The goal of **differentiated instruction**, one of the primary vehicles for responding to students' various degrees of readiness, diverse interests, and diverse learning styles is to modify—while planning—learning experiences that will create a higher likelihood of success of each unique student, while keeping the class as a whole moving forward (Cox, 2008; Smutny, 2003; Tomlinson, 1999, 2001). In using this approach, teachers plan their instruction with the following goals in mind:

> *The sources of inequality of educational opportunity appear to lie first in the home itself, and the cultural influences immediately surrounding the home. Then they lie in the schools' ineffectiveness to free achievement from the impact of the home.*
>
> James S. Coleman

1. To give students choices about how to express what they have learned.
2. To use reading materials with different levels of readability.
3. To plan to present ideas both visually and verbally.
4. To meet with small groups to reteach key concepts.
5. To pair students of lesser and stronger reading ability.
6. To vary the length of time for students to complete projects so struggling students can succeed.
7. To provide for individual work as well as collaborative work.
8. To tie instruction to assessment.
9. To use flexible grouping like readiness and mixed-readiness groups, same and different interest groups, and random groups.
10. To carefully organize and explain classroom routines (like where to put assignments), directions, and objectives.

Teacher's Tip

For an example of how a teacher incorporates **multiple intelligences theory** into an elementary school classroom, see the video, **Multiple Intelligences: Elementary School Instruction** at the Premium Website.

For additional information on strategies that should be used in planning to accommodate ethnic minority students, linguistic and culturally diverse students, "at-risk" students, mainstreamed "special needs" students, and "gifted and talented" students, please download the bonus topic, Topic A, "Teaching Diverse Populations" from the Premium Website.

Teacher's Tip

Those unexpected, periodic detours that take you away from your planned trip can often lead to excellent learning experiences if used judiciously. These are what are known in the literature as "teachable moments."

Types of Lesson Plans

Expectations for the amount and detail of lesson planning vary greatly among schools and districts. Planning requires progressing from yearlong plans to semester (multiple months and weeks) plans to daily lesson plans for each one of your preparations (see Figure 8.1).

Figure 8.1 Lesson Planning

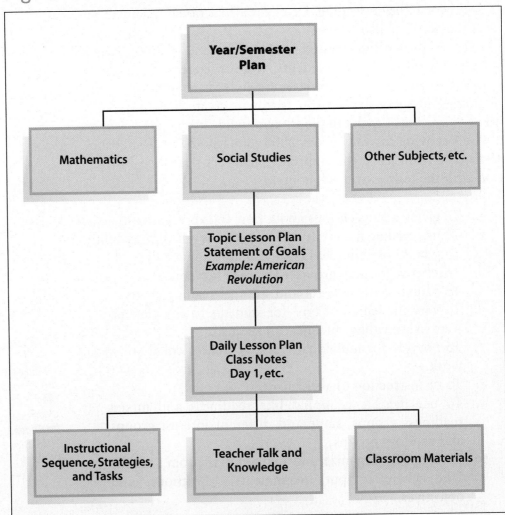

There are many kinds of lesson plan formats, and you should eventually create a format that best meets your needs. At the book's Premium Website, you can download templates for a **lesson plan** as well as a sample of a lesson plan based on the U.S. history topic, "The Lewis and Clark Expedition." The lesson plan and templates, in a Word file format, consist of a **statement of goals** and daily **class notes**. These materials can be useful to you as a new teacher until you settle on your own preferred formats. The MS Word "Calendar Wizard" can be used to create your semester-long and year-long plans.

The Planning Process

Planning a lesson is a creative endeavor that combines pedagogical knowledge with information knowledge and procedural knowledge to engage students and forge new thinking on their part (Brandt & Perkins, 2000). This is known as **pedagogical content knowledge**, "the ways of representing and formulating the subject that make it comprehensible to others" (Shulman, 1986, p. 9), which this book is dedicated to helping you acquire.

Key Planning Questions for the Teacher

1. What is the goal or standard? You begin by considering state or national standards, but then you should also think about how you plan to assess the students (see Unit 4).
2. Do I have the background knowledge to teach this topic? If not, where and how can I get up to speed, fast? Today, your best resource will often be the Internet.
3. How much time am I going to have to commit to learning the content to teach it well? What resources are available to teach it well? Are there resources for the students so that this can be an active learning experience?
4. What is the big idea in the topic?
5. Is there procedural knowledge that can be the focus of the lesson? If not, are there basic skills that could be the focus? Are there both?
6. How can I make the topic relevant to students' lives?
7. How much time will I give to my instruction and practice (the application of concepts)?
8. What tasks can I have students complete to ensure that they reconstruct the knowledge?
9. What instructional approaches should I use to ensure that I am accommodating individual differences among the students and using a variety of methods?
10. Will this change the way students think in the future (create a new academic disposition)?

Can you think of some additional questions you should ask?

The Seven-Step Lesson Planning Process

The following process model should be helpful to a first-year teacher. However, the planning process in not as linear as it appears in the following sequence; it is more interactive and divergent. For example, resources change as goals change, and goals change as you discover more resources; or you may initially think you will lecture but then change to a group activity.

Macro Planning: Year-long, Semester-long, and Week-long Plans

1. *Identify* the state standards for social studies.
2. *Evaluate* the basal textbook, the publisher's ancillary materials, and other resources (like the Internet) both for background knowledge for your personal benefit and for materials that you could use, such as graphic organizers, didactic materials, readings, primary documents, simulations, activities, sample lesson plans, and so on.
3. *Draft a year-long, semester-long, and week-long plan* based on topics you will cover to achieve the state standards. For a novice teacher, the textbook is a valuable asset because it defines the broad topics and the usual sequence of the content.

Micro Planning: Topic Statement of Goals and Class Notes Plan

1. *Conceptualize* the big ideas, identify procedural knowledge and information knowledge related to the state standards, and identify the basic skills, critical thinking, and academic disposition that can be developed using the information knowledge you will teach.
2. *Identify and collect your* specific *resources*, such as maps, primary documents, other teachers' lesson plans, the textbook's ancillary materials, manipulatives, and so on. The availability of resources over the Internet has dramatically changed this step of lesson planning. Prior to the World Wide Web, material for lesson plans was limited primarily to ideas from colleagues at your school and your publisher's ancillary materials that accompanied the textbook. Now, teachers no longer have to start by conceptualizing their topic but can use field-tested lesson plans, materials, and activities as their starting point and modify them.
3. *Create a topic lesson plan*, which consists of two major components: (a) a statement of goals for the entire topic or unit, and (b) a set of class notes that detail the choreography of each class session you decide to dedicate to the topic.

a. *The statement of goals* should include the following for the entire plan (that is, all the class sessions needed to complete the plan):

- **Topic lesson plan title** (often the same as the topic).
- **Resources.**
- **Big idea(s).**
- **Standards** (national if not state). Some professors and school districts prefer that teachers write behavioral objectives rather than goals or include behavioral objectives in the class notes section.
- **Basic skills development.**
- **Information knowledge.**
- **Procedural knowledge.**
- The **academic disposition** you want students to acquire during or as an outcome of the lesson.
- **Assessment.** Decide how you will know they have learned what you have taught; that is, what the forms of evaluation will be.

b. *Class notes* (see Topic 9 for a three-column class notes approach and the Lewis and Clark example at the Premium Website). It is wise to complete one set of notes, but segment it into days based on your initial (but imperfect) assessment of how long the lesson will take and your students' attention spans. The class notes evolve from the statement of goals for the lesson and are sequentially organized. They link together what you will say, what the students will do, and the resources you will use by drawing on the following components of the **instructional sequence** (see Topic 9):

- Homework due
- Attention-getter
- Statement of objectives for the daily lesson
- Review
- Content presentation(s)
- Guided practice(s)
- Independent practice or homework
- Evaluation(s)

As you develop your thinking about the attention-getter, content presentations, practice sessions, homework assignments, and evaluations, you draw upon your pedagogical knowledge to employ a variety of methods and strategies (see Units 5, 6, and 7) that appeal to different temperaments and that accommodate diversity.

Teacher's Tip

For lower elementary students in particular, a trade book with a social studies theme, such as tolerance, is often the source of a lesson. The postreading activity in the form of a debriefing can comprise the largest part of the lesson plan. At the National Council for the Social Studies Website, you can find hundreds of notable social studies children's books to develop a lesson that meets your state standards.

4. Prepare the materials (graphic organizers, supplemental readings, visual images, handouts, didactic materials, quizzes, rubrics, etc.) needed to choreograph the lesson.

The lesson may be longer or shorter than you planned; this is not unusual even for experienced teachers. You should always overprepare and plan on doing the lesson right, even if it takes a long time—but within reason!

Assignment 8.1

INTASC Standards 7, 9

Download Lesson Planning Templates and Models

At the Premium Website, download the following documents and bring them to class for use in tandem with this textbook.

1. Lesson Plan Statement of Goals Template
2. Lesson Plan Class Notes Template
3. Lewis and Clark Statement of Goals Example
4. Lewis and Clark Class Notes Example

WEBSITE RESOURCES • Lesson Planning & Differentiated Instruction

Video	*TeachSource* Academic Diversity: Differentiated Instruction *Concept to Classroom*, Teaching to the Academic Standards
Essay	**ERIC Online** *ED493953,* Differentiating Instruction in Inclusive Classrooms: Myth or Reality? (2006). *ED491580,* Differentiated Instruction: Principles and Techniques for the Elementary Grades (2006). *ED486626,* High-Needs Schools—What Does It Take To Beat The Odds? (2005).
	All linked websites (designated by the green color) and those listed here are available as clickable links at the book's Premium Website, www.cengage.com/login, for ease of access. These links will be updated periodically to reflect changes and new resources as they become available.

Topic 9

Choreography of Instruction

In Topic 8, you were introduced to the concept of a *statement of goals*. This statement can take many forms but is intended to define scope and sequence of the entire unit or lesson plan. It includes:

- Topic lesson plan title
- Resources
- Big Idea(s)
- Standards
- Basic skills development
- Information knowledge
- Procedural knowledge
- Critical thinking
- Academic disposition
- Assessment

This topic provides an in-depth look at the choreography of *daily* instruction based on your statement of goals by explaining:

1. The typical components of the **instructional sequence**, the sequential steps of instruction that would be taken during a typical class session.
2. **Class notes** as a strategy for organizing the lesson into a written format the teacher can use as a script in the classroom.

Instructional Sequence

You will probably be exposed to many **instructional sequences** in a methods course, including Madeline Hunter's *Mastery Learning* method (Hunter, 1984); Robert Gagné's *Nine Events of Instruction*

Teacher's Tip

The challenge of teaching to a diverse population is not unique to social studies, but because social studies content is more familiar than that of some other subjects, it can often serve to motivate students' overall interest. (See Bonus Topic A, "Teaching Diverse Populations" at the Premium Website and the Website resources at the end of this topic.)

You may learn from books at home; but the detail, the color, the tone, the air, the life which makes it live in us, you must catch all these from those in whom it lives already.

John Henry Newman

model (Gagné, 1965; Gagné et al., 1992); David Merrill's *First Principles of Instruction* (Merrill, 2002); and George Gagnon and Michelle Collay's *Designing for Learning: Six Elements in Constructivist Classrooms* (Gagnon & Collay, 2001), to name a few. The steps listed in Table 9.1 are generally accepted as the most common elements of an effective instructional sequence.

Table 9.1 Instructional Sequence

Instructional Sequence Steps	Examples of Strategies and Tasks
Attention-Getter	Show an image, picture, map, or chart. Begin with a question, "What do you think . . . ?"
Statement of Objective	Draw from standards. Explain lesson objectives. Describe what students will learn. Provide written objectives. Demonstrate the actual performance that is expected. Provide a model of the task's outcome.
Review/Debriefing	Pretest for existing skills or knowledge. Use graphic organizers to show current conceptions and misconceptions about topic. Dialogue with students about prerequisite knowledge and skills, other issues. Debrief homework.
Content Presentation (CP)	Present Information and Procedural Knowledge through a variety of methods: **Reading** (in class or for homework prior to discussion of the topic) Basal text Primary documents Other texts **Active Learning** Simulation Problem solving Group activity Decision making Lecture Cooperative learning Projects Internet Discussions Graphic organizers Case study Others **Debriefing** Ask questions. Circulate among groups to give feedback. *Since many lessons have multiple CPs, the content can be subdivided into smaller and incremental segments.*
Practice (in groups or independently) or Homework	Students demonstrate skill or apply knowledge during class, often in groups, with teacher guiding by assigning tasks. Students create relevant graphic organizers, write essays, solve problems, calculate formulas, role-play, etc. Students perform the tasks as homework.
Evaluation	Observe students. Give traditional tests of new knowledge and skills. Use authentic assessment products. Evaluate students' presentations and other activities.

The *practice* and *evaluation* segments of the instructional sequence underscore a basic principle in elementary education: It is not enough for a teacher to be able to demonstrate that something was taught; teachers are expected to have students demonstrate that they have learned the new knowledge. This sequence is a framework for choreographing your instruction using a variety of methods that are either **direct instruction approaches** or **indirect instruction** (see Topic 32).

Plans are only good intentions unless they immediately degenerate into hard work.

Peter Drucker

Class Notes

A teacher's class notes are, as they say, "where the rubber meets the road." First and foremost, they constitute the teacher's choreographed script that helps move students through the instructional sequence. Class notes are what you have on your desk or in your hand as you move down the learning path. They should include:

1. What you will say (teacher talk) and do;
2. What you expect the students to do (tasks) and know; and
3. All the classroom materials, AKA teaching resources (images, supplemental readings, handouts, transparencies, etc.) identified that you need to teach the class.

The design of your class notes may vary, and you should develop a style that meets your needs.

The **three-column class notes system** (see Table 9.2) developed by the author can be used not only to organize your instruction but also to serve as a way to catalog your lesson plans on your computer so that the lesson plan and resources can be easily identified and retrieved in future years (Cruz & Duplass, 2006; Duplass, 2006).

The three columns are used as follows.

A lesson is not the activity or task, nor is it the texts or resources we use . . . or even the groups we arrange or the product of the activity. Clearly the partnership between teaching and learning and teacher and learner is forged by the talk of the classroom.

Christine J. Edwards-Groves (2001)

COLUMN 1: INSTRUCTIONAL SEQUENCE, STRATEGIES, METHODS, AND TASKS

- **Instructional sequence** typically includes such items as an attention-getter, review, content presentation, practice, and evaluation and can be subdivided into days or sessions.
- **Strategies** and **methods** are the instructional approaches drawn from what you have learned in you courses and field experiences. This includes different kinds of lectures, cooperative learning, learning centers, reading, debriefing, and so on.
- **Tasks** are what you want the students to do. They are written into the class notes in the sequence in which you will explain them during teacher talk. Tasks can be *processes*, such as directions for students to move into certain kinds of groups, or *products* students are to produce, such as a timeline.

COLUMN 2: TEACHER TALK AND KNOWLEDGE

- **Teacher talk** is also known in the literature as "instructional explanations," "lesson talk," "classroom talk," and "scripts." Teacher talk is the script: the planned and purposeful part of a teacher's verbal communication. It is intended to convey knowledge through a variety of verbal strategies, such as explanation and questioning, or to explain the tasks through which students will acquire or demonstrate their knowledge. It is *your* script of what you will say to teach efficiently and is likely to be more detailed for a preservice teacher than for an experienced teacher. Teacher talk is not limited to what you will say; it also includes what statements or answers to questions you anticipate from students that you need to move the lesson through the instructional sequence. No matter how complicated we may try to make it, the craft of teaching basically involves choreographing teacher talk, reading materials, visuals and manipulatives, and tasks so that students will internalize and then generalize content.
- **Knowledge** is information knowledge (vocabulary, facts, and generalizations), procedural knowledge, and big ideas.

COLUMN 3: CLASSROOM MATERIALS

- These **resources** can be Internet based, PC based (because you have saved them on your computer), or hard-copy materials, such as a world globe, textbook, or manipulatives.

Table 9.2 Three-Column Class Notes

Class Notes		
Topic		
Grand Level		
Teacher Background Resources		
Big Idea	Needed only if a statement of goals is not prepared as part of the planning process	
Standards		
Objectives		
Instructional Sequence, Strategies, Methods & Tasks	Teacher Talk & Information Knowledge (Vocabulary/ Facts/ Concepts/), Big Ideas & Procedural Knowledge	Classroom Materials
Attention Getter		
Homework Due		
Review/Debriefing		
Content Presentation		
Practice		
Assessment		

Unit Two Planning Social Studies Instruction

Using both your statement of goals and class notes in planning ensures that you as a new teacher will pass through the kind of comprehensive thinking process needed to guard against inefficient or ineffective instruction. The class notes by themselves might be just as effective for a more experienced teacher, for shorter lessons, or for adapting lesson plans and activities found on the Internet (see Topics 11 and 12).

Your class notes document (and statement of goals document) should be saved to your hard drive, in your *Social Studies* folder, based on a subfolder category such as *American History*, as an example, and perhaps the subfolder topic (i.e., *American Revolution*) as Word documents, perhaps *American Revolution CN.doc* (where CN stands for "class notes"). Develop a consistent pattern in which the topic is first (see the example in Topic 11 for Lewis and Clark); all classroom materials documents appear alphabetically and grouped together by name within your *Social Studies* folder on your computer for easy retrieval, and your class notes serve as your catalog of resources as well as your lesson plan notes. This three-column class notes format and cataloging nomenclature can easily be adjusted to suit your personal preferences for organization and style.

The following TeachSource video cases, available at the book's Premium Website, can help you understand how to differentiate instruction, use grouping strategies, include special education students, and apply multiple intelligence theories to lesson planning.

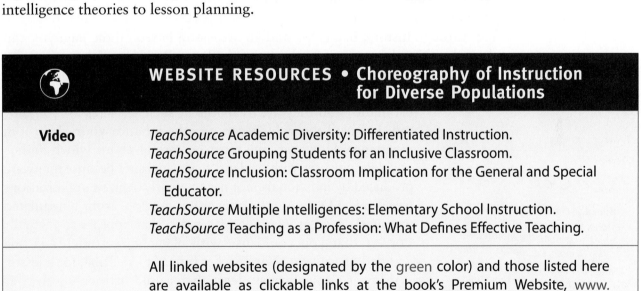

Teacher's Tip

When you are a novice teacher, scripting your lesson reduces anxiety and increases the likelihood of success during your first weeks and months.

	WEBSITE RESOURCES • Choreography of Instruction for Diverse Populations
Video	*TeachSource* Academic Diversity: Differentiated Instruction. *TeachSource* Grouping Students for an Inclusive Classroom. *TeachSource* Inclusion: Classroom Implication for the General and Special Educator. *TeachSource* Multiple Intelligences: Elementary School Instruction. *TeachSource* Teaching as a Profession: What Defines Effective Teaching.
	All linked websites (designated by the green color) and those listed here are available as clickable links at the book's Premium Website, www.cengage.com/login, for ease of access. These links will be updated periodically to reflect changes and new resources as they become available.

Topic 10

Internet Resources, Sources, and Safety

The Internet is a remarkable resource for teachers. And social studies, arguably, has benefited more than most disciplines because social studies content such as that found in museums, archives, and historical sites is readymade for conversion to Internet access. As an example, if you were preparing a lower elementary education lesson on the U.S. flag, at just one website—the Betsy Ross site, sponsored by the Betsy Ross Historical Association in Philadelphia, you can learn about the history of the U.S. flag's creation, see images of all the flags through history, flag rules, and an art lesson based on the flag; you can also take your class on a virtual tour of the Betsy Ross House historical site. Ten years ago, none of this would have been possible! More recently, there has been an explosion of Podcasts (includes Vodcast, i.e. video as opposed to just audio) and they are available at such websites as YouTube and TeacherTube, which can greatly enhance your classroom experience. However, one must be careful about which audios or videos one uses with students from such sites because many are produced by individuals, not nationally recognized organizations (see Topic 11's cautions about using material from unregulated websites). A great example of a video that appears to factually correct that you could use with elementary students is one entitled "Sacagawea" at TeacherTube. At YouTube, for a lesson for lower elementary students that would be focused on character education, one can find the Disney cartoon Who's Afraid of the Big Bad Wolf.

Advantages of the Internet

In fall 2005, nearly 100 percent of public schools in the United States had access to the Internet, compared with 35 percent in 1994. And, 42 percent of 5 to 9-year-old children and 69 percent of 10 to 14-year-old children use the

Internet (U.S. Department of Education, 2007). With that level of access and familiarity with the Internet, the potential for you to improve the learning experiences of your students in social studies through the Internet is greatly enhanced.

Prior to the blossoming of the Internet, teachers relied heavily on textbook packages (a textbook, teacher edition, and ancillary materials, such as worksheets, transparencies, etc.) and stand-alone commercial teacher materials that teachers would purchase at their own expense to plan their teaching. New thinking about teaching by experts and sample lesson plans developed by other practicing teachers were published in journals only found at universities. Thus, teachers were required to travel to academic libraries, commonly at great inconvenience, to have access to new ideas and resources. Teachers used the textbook chapters as the primary source of information on what should be taught in the subject fields at each grade level, and so textbooks often became the outer boundary of instruction rather than just one resource. Rarely were comprehensive lesson plans included with the ancillary materials of the basal textbook. The best source for a lesson plan and its materials was often just what a colleague might have been willing to share with you.

> *I do not fear computers.*
> *I fear the lack of them.*
>
> Isaac Asimov

Today, the Internet can be used to overcome all of these shortcomings and, indeed, may be a necessity. Current lesson planning needs to be driven by state standards in each subject field, not by a textbook. The new digital resources, such as lesson plans and digital teaching materials, need to be electronically saved, cataloged, and organized (Cruz & Duplass, 2006). Instruction can be greatly improved by learning from collaborating with your fellow teachers, and now you can access plans from teachers all over the United States (and anywhere in the world). And the most reputable resources can be retrieved conveniently from your classroom or home. Many Internet resources have been peer reviewed (meaning other experts have vouched for their authenticity and quality) or were developed by teams interested in advancing the quality of instruction at the elementary school level.

Primary Types of Assets on the Internet

Types of Resources

Five primary types of resources for teachers can be found on the Internet.

1. **Content background information sites** where you can learn more about a topic before you plan a lesson and teach it. The reading level would be appropriate for adults, not children, but as a teacher you could also use the content to write grade-appropriate social studies reading materials for your students.

2. **Lesson plans,** such as those at the Core Knowledge, MarcoPolo, and National Endowment for the Humanities Websites that are presented as sample resources in Unit 4 and elsewhere in this book.

3. **Activities** that are, for the purposes of this text, different from lesson plans. Internet activities are typically short in duration and usually are not developed by the author as part of a comprehensive lesson plan with the equivalent of a statement of goals and other elements. These may stand alone for a relatively short and focused segment of instruction on a social studies topic. As an example, at the Gateway to Educational Materials (GEM) Website you can find a lower elementary, grade-appropriate, stand-alone reading activity about courage based on George Washington's life, "America's Heritage: An Adventure in Liberty (Elementary Edition), Pt. 7: George Washington—Our First President," or, alternatively, "Peacelympics" for an outdoor activity covering peace education and environmental awareness objectives. These kinds of limited Internet activities can be integrated into a comprehensive lesson. As an example, "Cut a Star in One Snip" at the Betsy Ross site would be an excellent art extension to a social studies citizenship lesson or "Sample Scavenger Hunt—Select a Decade" at GEM could be used to structure independent learning activities that cover history over the decades.

4. **Class materials** (maps, primary documents, graphic organizers, tests, etc.), such as the 15 coloring pages at The Crayon House providing images associated with Thanksgiving that you could use during the holidays for lower elementary education. YouTube and TeacherTube provide podcasts that teachers can use for background information and for use in the classroom.

5. **Children's sites** to use in the classroom on a PC or whole class monitor, or in the school's library or resource center while children are using individual PCs. A good example is the interactive U.S. map.

Multiple examples of each are provided throughout this textbook as a guide in formulating how and what you will teach in your classroom.

Searching the Internet

There are two primary approaches to finding resources on the Internet, **general searches** and **site-specific searches**.

General Search

With any search engine like Google or MSN, you can conduct detailed searches by using quotes and **booleans** such as "AND," "OR," and "NOT." As an example, if you insert "'George Washington' AND 'lesson plan'" into a Google search box, you will generate a list of over 68,000 websites. Then it is largely a matter of sifting through each site and assessing its quality and fit with your needs. The results of a *general search* of the Internet (as opposed to a *site-specific search*) require greater scrutiny because they may not be from a credible or known source. The U.S. government, state agencies, national and state professional teacher organizations, textbook publishers, school districts and universities, and nonprofit organizations offer a degree of credibility, quality, and durability that teachers can usually rely on because the lesson plan has typically undergone peer review. Commercial websites, such as Educationworld, and personal websites (for example, by a teacher who created some materials and posted them on the Web) offer many fine materials or lesson plans, but these resources may not have undergone any third-party review, and thus they cannot be assumed to have the same level of credibility as those that do.

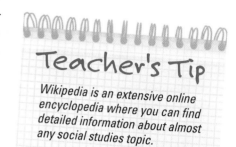

Teacher's Tip

Wikipedia is an extensive online encyclopedia where you can find detailed information about almost any social studies topic.

Site-Specific Search

A number of sites are dedicated to a specific field of social studies instruction, and these have been listed in Unit 4's topics for each discipline. Three examples are:

- *National Geographic*
- *EconEdlink*
- *Civics OnLine*

(Remember that all words in green in this textbook are available as clickable links for your convenience at the Premium Website.)

In addition, there are multidiscipline sites that cover elementary education and social studies and three sites managed by the federal government. These sites are described in the next two sections and should become part of the resources you rely on.

Multidiscipline Sites for Teaching Resources

Multidiscipline sites are not limited to any one teaching field and are usually organized with a search box and/or listings by subject field, grade level, or type of material (lesson plan, rubrics, etc.). The following are some of the best sites because they have extensive collections, and typically the nonprofit organizations' resources are of a high quality.

MarcoPolo	A nonprofit consortium of premier national and international education organizations that catalogs many of the lesson plans and materials from other sites listed in this table.
Core Knowledge	Extensive lesson plans for all grade levels in all the subject fields.
American Heritage Education Foundation	Focuses on social studies and character education.
Edsitement	The National Endowment for the Humanities maintains the website with assets for all the humanities.
Critical Thinking Community	Dedicated to helping teachers convert typically low-level thinking lessons to critical thinking lessons.
Character Education	Lesson plans on character education.
Beacon Learning Center	Has comprehensive social studies and other discipline unit plans.
Learner.org	By the Annenberg Foundation. You can select the discipline, subject, and grade level for videos of exemplary teaching.
Thirteen Ed Online	New York's public television's Web service for teachers.
Smithsonian	Resources span the humanities through the sciences and has both a teachers' and a kids' section.
MiddleWeb.com	Dedicated to middle education but has many resources adaptable to elementary education.
PBS	Offers multiple types of resources based on many of their educational programs.

Discovery School	Allows you to select for materials by subject field and grade level.
Lessons Plans Page	Over 2,500 activities, many very brief but could be effective if redeveloped into a real lesson plan.
Education World	Comprehensive, with information on classroom rules, learning games, lesson plans, and more.
Awsomelibrary	A large number of reviewed lesson plans gleaned from multiple sites are organized by subject field and grade level.
Sites for Teachers	Hundreds of Websites for teachers rated by popularity.
Gateway to Educational Materials	Has thousands of teaching resources.
ERIC	Over 1 million documents, such as essays and books, from academic journals and conferences, many of which are downloadable in PDF format.
What Works Clearinghouse	Houses publications about education; a major difference, however from ERIC, is that it limits its publications to reviews of scientific evidence for the effectiveness of replicable education strategies.
TeacherTube	Podcasts in social studies and other subjects that can be used in the classroom
	All linked websites (designated by the green color) and those listed here are available as clickable links at the book's Premium Website, www.cengage.com/login, for ease of access. These links will be updated periodically to reflect changes and new resources as they become available.

Social studies–specific Websites will be cited throughout this textbook and, in particular, in Unit 4.

Internet Safety

Safety is a significant consideration for teachers who have their students use the Internet in school. It is always better to err on the side of caution.

Teachers need to follow three key practices in their classroom use of the Internet:

1. When using the Internet in presentations with children, the teacher should preview the site(s).
2. When students are doing an activity designed by the teacher, the teacher should preview and limit the sites to be used by the students.
3. When students are expected to search the Internet, the teacher must state the objectives for going to sites that are appropriate to the goal of the lesson and should monitor students throughout the activity.

Assignment 10.1

INTASC Standards 1, 4, 7, and 8

Search a Multidiscipline Website

Download Houghton Mifflin's Reading 3, "Our Earth," from the Premium Website and review the content. Conduct an Internet search on either YouTube or TeacherTube for a podcast that can be used to build upon the reading and submit a description to your professor that includes how it will be used. Be prepared to discuss your results in class and submit the Internet material to your professor.

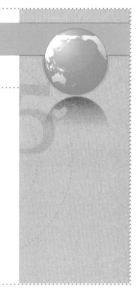

Assignment 10.2

INTASC Standards 1, 2, 3, 4, 5, 7, and 8

Internet Resources: General Search

Download either Reading 21, 23, or 25 from the Doubleday Core Knowledge Chapters at the Premium Website and review the content. Identify a person, place, thing, and event from the reading and conduct an Internet search for a resource that could be used in a lesson. Prepare a paper citing each source and how it could be used and print out a page of each resource to be submitted to your professor. Be prepared to discuss how you might use the results in a lesson plan

Check the book's Premium Website, www.cengage.com/login, for additional links and links that are periodically updated to reflect new resources as they become available.

Topic 11

Creating Lesson Plans Using Internet Resources

The purpose of this topic is to provide you with a concrete example of how to create a lesson, "from scratch," if you will. The next topic will focus on how to adapt **Internet lesson plans** to your classroom. In both cases, the capacity to make judgments about what subject matter within social studies to teach and the approach to use in developing a lesson plan that integrates resources from the Internet and elsewhere, is an essential skill for today's elementary school teacher. In addition to the Internet, social studies teachers have traditionally found such items as classroom wall maps, beach ball globes, realia (see Topic 28), and didactic materials essential to their lessons. In addition, CDs such as Microsoft's Encarta encyclopedia and videos (see Topic 49) are also powerful resources. Before selecting resources, you should first consider the criteria you should use in selecting materials from the Internet.

Criteria for Selecting Internet Resources

A primary consideration is the validity of a website and its assets. Anyone can create a website. Some websites are inaccurate, biased, and purposefully misleading. This makes websites different from textbooks issued by a national publisher, professional organization, or the government, which have typically undergone review and editing to ensure accuracy and a balanced presentation.

You can minimize the risks of invalid or inaccurate information or faulty strategies by focusing on websites sponsored by recognized and reputable institutions, such as museums, school districts, universities, libraries, and national organizations for teachers. Extensions identify types of institutions: *.com* (dot-com) indicates the sites of commercial enterprises, whose content is unregulated. The websites of educational institutions (*.edu*), nonprofit organizations (*.org*), and government institutions (*.gov*) are generally more reliable. The following questions are those you should ask yourself when you select resources from the Internet.

Questions to Ask in Evaluating a Website

1. Are the goals and motives of the author and sponsor stated and clear?
2. Is the sponsor of the website known and credible?
3. Is the author of the materials on the website credible or an expert?
4. Do the aesthetics, graphics, content details, spelling, grammar, and other elements indicate that site has been thoughtfully organized and published?
5. Is the site dated?
6. Are the content and materials accurate, up to date, and usable?
7. Are the resources grade appropriate?
8. Is advertising clearly labeled as such?
9. Is there a way for you to respond to the sponsor or author?
10. Can you count on the website to exist in the future?

These are the questions I asked myself as I searched the Internet for the resources in this book that would be most helpful to you.

Conceptualizing your Goals and Class Notes

The topic of the Lewis and Clark Expedition will be used to share with you the thinking process that a teacher would use in developing his or her goals for a lesson and the class notes to teach the lesson with. If you have not already done so, you should download the following documents from the Premium Website and refer to them as you read through this topic.

- *Lewis and Clark—Statement of Goals Example*
- *Lewis and Clark—Class Notes Example*
- Houghton Mifflin's Reading 17, "The Nation Grows"

Key Questions in Deciding What Topics to Teach

1. How much do I know about this topic?
2. How much more am I going to have to learn to teach it well?
3. What resources are available so that I can quickly get up to speed on the topic?
4. Can I find a big idea in the topic?
5. Is there procedural knowledge that can be the focus of the lesson? If not, are there basic skills that could be the focus?
6. Are there resources for students to make this an active learning experience?
7. Will this change the way students think in the future (a new academic disposition)? The planning process is not as linear as it appears in the

following sequence, but it is more interactive. For example, resources change as goals change, and goals change as you discover more resources; you may initially think you will lecture but instead do a group activity.

8. Is the content mandated by your state?

Developing a Lesson Plan: The Lewis and Clark Example

The crafting of a lesson plan begins when a teacher picks a topic and then conceptualizes a lesson. That involves originating an idea, clarifying your goals, and identifying resources. After you have the initial concept in mind, detailed planning can begin based on the framework you provide in the statement of goals and the class notes you will create.

Let's follow step by step the process of conceptualizing a lesson plan about the Lewis and Clark expedition.

Why Teach the Lewis and Clark Expedition?

For the purpose of this simulation, let's start with the assumption you are a fifth grade teacher in Florida and your textbook is Houghton Mifflin's *United States History* fifth-grade text. And let's say you are at a point in the year where you have covered the American Revolution and the early period of the republic. Imagine yourself sitting at your kitchen table with a copy of the Sunshine State Standards for Florida Grade 5 History. There are a series of **benchmarks** listed that you are expected to achieve as a fifth grade teacher:

Benchmark	Descriptor	Standard
SS.5.A.1.1	Use primary and secondary sources to understand	Historical Inquiry and Analysis
SS.5.A.1.2	Use timelines to identify and discuss U.S. history time periods	Historical Inquiry and Analysis
SS.5.A.6.1	Describe the causes and effects of the Louisiana Purchase.	Growth and Westward Expansion
SS.5.A.6.2	Identify roles and contributions of significant people during the period of westward expansion.	Growth and Westward Expansion
SS.5.A.6.4	Explain the importance of the explorations west of the Mississippi River.	Growth and Westward Expansion

By the way the "descriptor" is written, you should note that all five benchmarks are focused on procedural knowledge. These are the tools, the "modes of reasoning" used by historians to make sense out of historical facts and if taught effectively, can be used by students again when they encounter content that is different from the "Growth and Westward Expansion" information knowledge. In fact, the first two may have been achieved earlier with some other content.

Assume, you also have your textbook in front of you, which has a section on the Lewis and Clark Expedition, which is part of the "Growth and Westward Expansion" period in U.S. history. Go to the Premium Website and download Reading 17, Houghton Mifflin's Core Lesson 2, "The Nation Grows," so you can see how much of a the Lewis and Clark Expedition is presented in a typical U.S. history textbook for fifth grade.

Now, consider the options you, as an elementary school teacher, would have given the state has mandated through its standards that you must cover the above topics.

1. You could decide to use the topic and the *single-discipline* or *interdisciplinary* teaching model (see Topic 7) to meet a standard and to develop a big idea (see Topics 2, 8 and 9), and you dedicate three or four hours to it. You could emphasize the geography, the history or folklore around Sacagawea, reasons why people explore, the dangers and difficulties of the expedition, and so on.

2. You could decide to give Lewis and Clark a "glancing blow" as part of the larger topic of the general growth of the nation or as a follow-up to the Louisiana Purchase.

3. You could use the *extension* teaching model, to integrate it into a language arts lesson.

4. You could decide, in spite of the mandate, that there is not enough time in your schedule for students to learn about Lewis and Clark because you need more time for other subjects or other social studies topics you feel are more important. In this case, you might only require students to read the book and remember the historical events based solely on their reading. Regrettably, because of the emphasis on basic skills high-stakes testing and "grading" of schools, there is considerable evidence that teachers are under so much pressure to focus exclusively on mathematics, reading, and writing basic skills, that such benchmarks in disciplines like social studies are not a priority and they may not even require students to read their social studies textbook (Passe, 2006). Rothman's (2005) survey of 33 states found that in 16 states social studies instructional time had been reduced.

These potential scenarios are important to appreciate because you will probably not be able to cover all the content suggested by what is in your textbook even if you believe deeply in the importance of social studies. If social studies becomes included (or is included in your states high-stakes testing regimen), you will likely have a school district that will insist on your completing them. In any case, a large part of a teacher's job is to make judgments about what to teach. Given that all the content can never be known, it is wise to select the topics you will cover based on the procedural knowledge, basic skills, cultural literacy (CL), and big ideas that you can teach with one topic. For the purposes of this simulation, we will take option 1 and teach about Lewis and Clark and achieve the five benchmarks.

The National Standards Alternative

Although it is preferable to use your state standards, the following are drawn from the national National Council for the Social Studies (NCSS) themes (see Topic 17), which can serve as national standards, and this example will also be based on achieving the following national themes.

1. *NCSS Culture*
   - Explore and describe similarities and differences in the way groups, societies, and cultures address similar human needs and concerns.
   - Give examples of how experiences may be interpreted differently by people from diverse cultural perspectives and frames of reference.
2. *NCSS Time, Continuity, and Change*
   - Demonstrate an understanding that different people may describe the same event or situation in diverse ways, citing reasons for the difference in views.

Can you identify a standard or benchmark for your state that could be achieved using the topic of the Lewis and Clark expedition?

The basal textbook chapter that you downloaded on Lewis and Clark can help you achieve your standards. By planning to have students read the content as a homework assignment or in class, you can also improve their reading skills. *Remember,* however, that your job is not to teach the textbook or just the content that appears in the text. Your job is to incorporate the reading material found in the textbook into your lesson as a baseline of information to facilitate what you will teach—which will go beyond the content in the book.

A **baseline of information** is knowledge acquired before teaching begins, for example, when teachers require students to read content prior to instruction and hold the students accountable for the reading information knowledge by bellwork (see Topic 23, Teacher's Tip) or a test prior to teaching the lesson. This method enables the teacher to tier the instruction starting at a shared knowledge point where students have a greater command of the vocabulary and facts than would otherwise be the case and focus on procedural knowledge, critical thinking and the big idea.

Finding a Big Idea

A big idea in a history lesson often comes out of the imagination and creativity of the teacher. Some teachers are more creative than others; some teachers make up for a lack of innate ideas through their training and exposure to the creative strategies of others. When I was planning a lesson on the Lewis and Clark expedition, I decided to introduce a big idea about cultural appreciation and cultural prejudice. This may sound like a leap, but it really isn't. Social scientists have long realized that a person who comes across a different kind of person, group, or society may either appreciate the differences or be disdainful of them. People tend to be judgmental. Children can be encouraged to learn more about a new classmate with an accent or different skin color and thus learn more about themselves, or they can learn to choose not to like the new kid because he or she is different. I found the meeting of Lewis and Clark with Native Americans from the Great Plains to be an entrée to this big idea that will allow me to make it relevant to the students' lives.

Creativity is essentially a lonely art. An even lonelier struggle. To some a blessing. To others a curse. It is in reality the ability to reach inside yourself and drag forth from your very soul an idea.

Lou Dorfsman

Resources

A general search of the Internet using Google produced more than 29,000 websites on Lewis and Clark. Gateway to Educational Materials had 53 items appropriate for fifth grade and Edsitement had 151, many of which were cataloged from the National Geographic Website. These resources included primary documents (such as diary entries and the treaty to purchase the Louisiana territory), maps from the period and recent maps, timelines, images of Lewis and Clark, lesson plans, and folklore. (See Lewis and Clark statement of goals and class notes at the Premium Website for examples.) At Teacher-Tube, you can find a 3 minute clip of the PBS series on Lewis and Clark. These are the kinds of easily accessible resources that you should consider an essential part of lesson planning in an Internet environment.

Information Knowledge

Information knowledge begins with vocabulary and includes content-specific facts, concepts, and generalizations.

You would include the following vocabulary in anticipation that students' cultural literacy would be improved.

Key Facts	Key Concepts/Generalizations
Thomas Jefferson, President	Cultural bias and appreciation
Louisiana Purchase 1803	Explorers
Meriwether Lewis	First Americans
Mississippi River	Map legend
New Orleans	Presidential constitutional authority
Napoleon	Primary documents

William Clark
Sacagawea
Saint Louis Gateway Arch
   Significant states, rivers,
   and landforms of the
   Louisiana Territory

Rain dance/religious observance
Treaty
Cardinal directions, longitude
   and latitude, and scale
   and distance

Procedural Knowledge

The following procedural knowledge applications are drawn from the NCSS themes: the modes of reasoning for history, social sciences, and geography (see Unit 4 for sources).

Social studies procedural knowledge applications include:

1. Interpreting primary documents such as Jefferson's letter commissioning the expedition (this can be found at the Thomas Jefferson Digital Archives);
2. Comparing and contrasting differing accounts of the same event using the example of an "Indian" rain dance;
3. Considering the effects of location on food, human traits, race/ethnicity, shelter, clothing, and so on when considering the differences between First Americans and the explorers;
4. Analyzing the interests and values of the various people involved when discussing Sacagawea's role as guide and translator;
5. Learning how to use navigation with cardinal directions, longitude and latitude, and scale and distance; interpreting legends and making maps when tracing the journey from Saint Louis to the Pacific Ocean;
6. Interpreting maps in tracing the journey from Saint Louis to the Pacific Ocean; and
7. Using the timeline to recognize the cause-and-effect sequence of events leading up to the expedition.

Generic procedural knowledge applications include:

1. Synthesizing the idea of a rain dance with their own religious traditions; and
2. Analyzing the discrepancy between the constitution provisions on buying land and Jefferson's decision to purchase the Louisiana Territory.

Basic Skills Knowledge

A number of basic skills will be developed during this lesson (see Topic 17 for one source). Students will:

1. Read the basal text to create a baseline of information;
2. Read primary documents related to the expedition;

3. Use mathematics and drawing skills when creating a map of the expedition; and

4. Use communication skills during participation in discussion of rain dance.

At this stage, the teacher has completed the goal-setting phase. Another teacher may take a different tack, perhaps emphasizing more geography, integrating a book such as a biography of Sacagawea, or expanding the lesson into comparisons of western and eastern First Americans (a.k.a. *Indians*). The possibilities and variations are endless, but each teacher draws on his or her own knowledge, experience, and preferences. No matter what the plan, however, the teacher needs to get the content right, achieve one or more state standards, focus on procedural knowledge, and use a variety of instructional approaches. Once you have defined your goals, your focus turns to your class notes.

Class Notes for the Lewis and Clark Lesson

The Lewis and Clark class notes from the Premium Website present the choreography of instruction using the three-column class notes approach explained in Topics 8 and 9. The example is based on the preceding goals.

Strategies, Methods, and Tasks

Based on earlier topics and sections of this topic and the example you downloaded from the Premium Website, you should have a solid grasp of how to set your goals and select content, find resources to enrich your teaching, and articulate them in a set of class notes. To a great degree, the rest of this book introduces the strategies you should learn to use in teaching social studies. You should think of Units 3, 4, 5, 6, and 7 as a menu or palette from which you can select strategies to create lessons with a variety of approaches that appeal to the learning styles of all of your students. As you prepare lesson plans, you should use terms from the book to demonstrate that you are well versed in the language of your **community of practice**.

In the Lewis and Clark class notes example you are likely to see some familiar and not so familiar strategies. Each strategy can be found in this book and some are also listed in Table 11.1. In Table 11.1, I have identified which topics the strategies came from that appear in the Lewis and Clark class notes as a way of helping you understand the importance of using proven methods and a variety of them.

Table 11.1 Applications of Instructional Approaches

Strategies	Topic	Explanation
Homework	44 25	A form of practice used to facilitate another strategy known as a *baseline of information*
Debriefing	23	One of six possible *postreading strategies*
Boardwork of Timeline	42 31	Falls under the general heading of graphic organizers; you can learn the correct way to create a timeline in Topic 31
Attention-Getter: Questioning	9 40	Uses images and questioning to gain students' interest
Chronological Lecture Chronological and Pause Procedure Lecture	39	One of more than 12 types of lectures; combined, these two lectures are grade appropriate and efficient
Breakout Group with Concept Organizer	43 42	Adds variety to the lesson by putting students in groups to read a teacher-created, grade-appropriate biography of Lewis and Clark and create a Who, what, when where, why how (WWWWWH) chart

Teacher's Tip

One of the marks of a professional is the ability to use the language of one's profession, or community of practice, as it is sometimes referred to.

Assignment 11.1

INTASC Standards 1, 2, 3, 4, 5, 7, and 8

Strategies for the Lewis and Clark Lesson Plan

Using this book's index, find the remaining instructional approaches in the Lewis and Clark class notes and record them in a chart with information similar to that shown in Table 11.1. Be prepared to turn in the document to your professor and share your ideas with the class.

Check the book's Premium Website, www.cengage.com/login, for additional links and links that are periodically updated to reflect new resources as they become available.

Adapting Internet Lesson Plans and Resources to Your Classroom

In the last topic, we discussed how to create a lesson plan, and the Lewis and Clark example made good use of Internet resources. The purpose of this topic is to focus on the use of **Internet lesson plans, Activity plans,** and other kinds of resources that can be found on the Internet.

In the three-column class notes approach discussed in previous topics, the last column, "Classroom Materials" would include a variety of resources. For the Lewis and Clark class notes example, almost all are were taken from the Internet. When you are choreographing a teacher-created lesson plan, you can find various kinds of resources such as graphic organizers, primary documents, games, exams, "worksheets," virtual tours, child-appropriate readings, art projects, music activities and the like at multiple websites on the Internet that can enrich the learning experience. The Internet also has what are sometimes classified as "lessons" or "lesson plans," but should more appropriately be called *activity plans*. These activities are not classroom materials, like graphic organizers or documents. Substantive *Internet lesson plans* would be more similar to the teacher-created Lewis and Clark goals and class notes examples proposed in Topic 11. For an example of a substantive Internet lesson plan, visit the Core Knowledge Website, which has some of the most comprehensive, well-thought-out lesson plans on the Web.

To start, we will consider these Internet resources first.

When I took office, only high energy physicists had ever heard of what is called the World Wide Web . . . Now even my cat has its own page.

Bill Clinton

How to Use Internet Activity Plans

The **activity plans approach** is particularly well suited for many of the topics and limited time allocated for lower elementary social studies. They tend to be of short duration, perhaps a morning, which works well for an activity for something like Flag Day. Or they would be planned as, perhaps a half-hour segment of a multiday lesson plan. They are typically much more limited in scope than lesson plans, have few attached resources, and provide limited background knowledge, context and detail for the teacher. These activities can be very effective by themselves or they can serve as an excellent ingredient for a teacher-created lesson plan or an Internet lesson plan (ILP). The following are some examples.

- Teaching About Tolerance Through Music at Education World is a music activity to foster the virtue of tolerance that could be taught at anytime as a stand-alone lesson.
- Thanksgiving Day Placemats at Kids National Geographic is an activity for Thanksgiving where kinds make placemats for the dinner table as a history/art project, but has not social studies content.
- The Nation's Motto at the American Heritage Foundation is a resource that is a very brief, lower-elementary activity that introduces students to "In God We Trust." It is not the kind of substantive resource that could be called an Internet lesson, but it is an important lesson that could be taught as a stand-alone activity.
- King Tut's Treasures at National Geographic is a very specialized activity. Although it has many of the attributes of a great lesson plan, it would need to be part of a larger lesson on the ancient world and Egypt in particular—which is missing, and thus would need to be supplied by the teacher to give this activity context. Therefore, it would more likely be used as a resource and activity that you would include in your teacher-made lesson plan.
- State Geography Game at Gateway to educational Materials (GEM) is a schoolyard game requiring students to name a state using clues. It is an excellent culminating activity for either an Internet or teacher-created lesson plan on U.S. geography.
- YouTube has a graphically rich video that explains why we experience seasons on earth, the actor Sam Waterston reciting the "Gettysburg Address," a scene from the movie "Glory" depicting the bravery of the all black 54th Massachusetts regime, and School House Rock's "The Preamble" and "Stock Market."
- Multicultural Calendar at Lesson Plans Page is an that activity requires students to research and create multicultural calendars. It is a great idea for a world geography lesson but needs context and doesn't have the kind of detail, such as a link to standards, specified content, etc. required of a full-fledged lesson plan.

Here are some additional examples of activities that could be added to a lesson plan that you create or could serve as a starting point for developing a lesson plan that uses the activity. These kinds of activities can often be used to turn a potentially boring and uninspired lesson into one that actively engages students. This can also be used as a culminating activity.

For both upper and lower elementary students, you will likely find that your planning will include a mix of activity lessons and more detailed, multiday, and

Sample High-Quality Internet Activities

Lower Elementary	*Education World Geography:* Our Changing Community has students analyze their local community with an active learning strategy.
	Education World Geography: Finding Captain Hook's Treasure uses the story of Peter Pan to set up a treasure map activity.
Upper Elementary	*GEM History:* First American Board Game has students create and play a board game like Monopoly after learning about First Americans.
	Discovery School History (Egyptian History): Wheel of Pharaoh has students create and then play the wheel of fortune game based on what they learned about Egypt.

comprehensive Internet lesson plans or teacher-made lesson plans that require sustained learning and concept development.

Adapting Internet Lesson Plans to Your Classroom

Why reinvent the wheel? The Internet has made it so easy for teachers and professional organizations to share substantive lesson plans, you should take full advantage of their expertise and modify their plans to meet your students' needs. In Topic 10 are a number of websites that are recommended as a source for substantive Internet lesson plans, and Unit 4 will provide you websites related to each of the social studies disciplines. Once you have determined that a lesson plan contains most of the components you need (or that you can bring it up to speed), you will likely still need to link its objectives to your state standards and introduce modifications that match your students' abilities. One of the best ways to do this is to prepare a statement of goals and class notes based on the Internet lesson. The Internet lesson plan would be one of a number of resources listed in your statement of goals.

Criteria for Selecting High-Quality Internet Lesson Plans

The extent to which something on the Internet that is called a "lesson plan" actually is a *lesson plan*—rather than an *activity plan or a resource*—is based largely on how many of the following six components are found in the plan.

Teacher's Tip

Even the best Internet plans should be modified to meet your students' needs and your state's standards!

The degree to which a lesson plan is evaluated as excellent depends on the quality of the components. Lesson plans on the Internet may also vary based on whether they are selected through either general searches or site-specific searches; within those two categories are further wide variations in quality. There are a number of indicators of a well-developed Internet lesson plan that you should also consider.

The criteria and questions you should use for selecting Internet lesson plans are the following.

1. **Standards:** Is the plan tied to national or state standards?
2. **Instructional Sequence:** Is there a clear and detailed explanation of the sequence of instruction?
3. **Rigor:** Does the plan challenge students with tasks and activities that require critical thinking and self-discipline?
4. **Creativity:** Does the plan creatively engage the students with
   a. opportunities to further develop basic skills;
   b. a variety of strategies; and
   c. meaningful, grade-appropriate content?
5. **Resources:** Are there resources, such as well-crafted handouts or links to other high-quality websites?
6. **Evaluation:** Is there an evaluation component?

The following are examples of substantive Internet lessons (also see those cited in Unit 4)

 WEBSITE RESOURCES • Internet Lessons

Sample High-Quality Internet Activities

Lower Elementary	*American Heritage Citizenship:* America the Beautiful: Students find out about the background and creation of the nation's "unofficial" anthem, "America the Beautiful." Education Foundation.
	EconEd Economics: If You Give a Mouse a Cookie, the children's book, is used as the basis of an economics lesson using the postreading strategy for the development of concepts.
Upper Elementary	*GEM History and Government:* Separating Church and State explores constitutional issues and the history of persecution of religious groups.
	Core Knowledge Geography: Where in the Latitude Are You? A Longitude Here is an exceptionally detailed and complete plan for teaching longitude and latitude.

Assignment 12.1

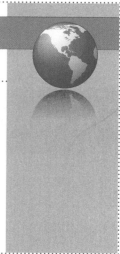

INTASC Standards 1, 2, 3, 4, 5, 7, and 8

Lesson Planning Based on an Internet Activity

Select a reading from Houghton Mifflin's Fifth Grade Readings 12–16 at the Premium Website and download the class notes template or use a format preferred by your professor. Find an Internet activity that you could use to enrich your students' understanding of the basal text content. Prepare your class notes for submission to your professor and be prepared to present your ideas to the class.

Assignment 12.2

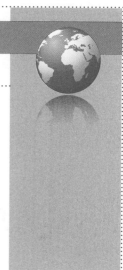

INTASC Standards 1, 2, 3, 4, 5, 7, and 8

Lesson Planning Based on an Internet Lesson

Select a reading from Houghton Mifflin's Fifth Grade Readings 12–16 at the Premium Website and download the statement of goals template or use a format preferred by your professor. Find an Internet lesson plan that you could use to teach all or a segment of the topic of the basal text content. Prepare your statement of goals based on the Internet lesson plan and content for submission to your professor and be prepared to present your ideas to the class.

Check the Premium Website, www.cengage.com/login, for additional links and links that are periodically updated to reflect new resources as they become available.

Unit Three

Assessing Student Learning in Social Studies

"I WOULD HAVE GOTTEN AWAY WITH IT IF ONLY I HADN'T SIGNED THE REPORT CARD, 'MOMMY.'"

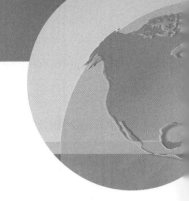

Topic 13

Assessment

To begin this unit, we should first clarify and define a few key terms about assessment that are often confused. **Assessment** is the collection of data such as tests, assignments, and tasks that indicate student performance (Weber, 1999). **Evaluations** are made based on the assessments we have for a student. **Grades** reflect a teacher's evaluation of the student. The term **alternative assessment** (see Topic 14) is often used to refer to the full range of approaches that may be used in the assessment process, whereas **traditional assessment** (see Topic 15) typically refers to objective or essay paper-and-pencil tests.

Your approach to assessment should, and likely will, grow out of your philosophical approach to instruction. Teachers who believe that assessments should take place after they finish telling students what they need to know usually prefer objective paper-and-pencil tests given at one point in time. However, if your philosophy is that students learn in increments, learn by doing and by being required to think, and can demonstrate their learning in a multiplicity of ways, then you will want to use a variety of alternative and traditional assessment approaches at different times throughout the year.

Assessment can be *informal*, such as the daily questions teachers ask to check for understanding, or *formal*, those that are planned and administered. In social studies as in the other disciplines, we should be measuring both procedural knowledge and information knowledge. It is relatively easy to measure information knowledge (e.g., who was the first president?), but more challenging to measure procedural knowledge (e.g., why do toys cost more when there are fewer of them in stores and what terms do we use to explain this?).

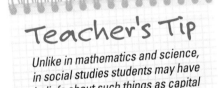

Teacher's Tip

Unlike in mathematics and science, in social studies students may have beliefs about such things as capital punishment, poverty, and the like for which there is no right answer but many answers. In such cases, students' beliefs should be measured by their ability to support their belief by logic or facts that express why one conclusion is better than another. Essays and discussions are often the best way to evaluate beliefs.

> How does one measure patriotism or a person's concept of fairness, arguably both legitimate goals of social studies? Can they be measured, at all?

Just as excellent teachers accommodate diverse learners by using a variety of teaching strategies (see Units 5, 6, and 7 and Bonus Topic A, "Teaching Diverse Populations"), teachers need to provide a variety of vehicles for students to demonstrate their knowledge. A paper-and-pencil test on the American Revolution could pose particular problems for English language learner students, for example, while a product assessment (see Topic 14) in which they can express their understanding of the American Revolution offers a different avenue to success (Snowman & Biehler, 2006).

Ordinary talent is measurable, uncommon talent is difficult to measure and genius not at all.

Brothers Grimm, quoted by Karl Jaspers

Purposes of Social Studies Assessment

The National Council for Social Studies (NCSS, 1990) has called for frequent, challenging, and consistent assessment of social studies instruction; assessment of progress in knowledge, thinking skills, valuing, and social participation; and a variety of methods of assessment. In 1991, the NCSS adopted a set of principles on testing and evaluation that can be retrieved at the NCSS Website: see "Position Statements." The following purposes are drawn from this position paper. Evaluation instruments should

1. Focus on stated curriculum goals and objectives.
2. Be used to improve curriculum and instruction.
3. Measure both content and process.
4. Be chosen for instructional, diagnostic, and prescriptive purposes.
5. Reflect a high degree of fairness to all people and groups.
6. Involve a variety of instruments and approaches to measure students' knowledge, skills, and attitudes.
7. Measure long-term effects of social studies instruction.

State-Mandated Testing

State-mandated tests at various grade levels (or **high-stakes testing**), is a relatively new procedure being used by most states to meet the mandates of the No Child Left Behind Act of 2001 (see Topic 16). One major disadvantage of high-stakes testing is that teachers feel compelled to "teach to the test" rather than creating engaging lessons and allowing the assessments to measure students' knowledge (Grant, 2007; Vogler & Virtue, 2007).

State-mandated testing almost exclusively involves paper-and-pencil tests and assessment of knowledge that can be demonstrated in that form. The normative data gathered from statewide testing is being used not only as assessment information about students' progress, but also as a way to "grade" schools, draw inferences about teachers, and provide incentive systems. Combined with the tests' typical one-attempt approach, the term, "high stakes" has taken on a particularly onerous meaning.

Not all of these tests include all subjects. They tend to focus on reading, writing, and calculating skills, and, as a result, high-stakes testing is believed to be a main reason why instruction in social studies has declined in elementary schools (Rothman, 2005; Passe, 2006). As of 2004, only 10 states included social studies in their high-stakes testing (Grant, 2007). Some have argued for social studies high-stakes testing to be included in the No Child Left Behind regimen as a way of restoring its importance in the curriculum (Dolinski, 2006; Green, 2007). Others have argued that social studies' long-term goals of character and citizenship values cannot be measured and that any attempt at measurement while in school would lead social studies back into a regimen of mind-numbing facts (Duplass, 2008).

> *Education is what survives when what has been learned has been forgotten.*
>
> Denis Diderot

Does your state test for social studies? Why do you think many states do not?

High-stakes testing will not be the focus of this unit because this book focuses on options that are directly under your control.

Classroom Assessment

It is easy to lose sight of the purpose of assessment, which is primarily a way for the teacher to get feedback on how well the student is learning and to improve instructional practices. This is typically called "formative assessment" (Carol, 2002)

Over the last 20 years, as teachers have moved away from traditional paper-and-pencil tests alone, legitimate concerns about the subjectivity of a teacher's evaluations have been raised. In addition, because parents and school districts demand "proof" beyond teachers' honest evaluations and common sense findings, there is a greater emphasis on finding ways to substantiate assessments. This has led to what sometimes is referred to as "defensive testing," in which teachers test to document students' failures rather than to remedy them.

Use of models and rubrics are effective strategies that reduce subjectivity and can insulate a teacher from accusations of favoritism or prejudice against a student. Teachers have to guard against the subtler problem of the *halo effect*, which occurs when teachers—often unknowingly—tend to grade some students' work product more favorably than is warranted. The opposite *Golem effect* can also work against students who have traditionally done poorly or have behavior problems (Rowe & O'Brien, 2002).

Teacher's Tip

Subjective tests can be unfair! In one study, elementary school teachers were given the identical essay to evaluate but with four different names for the student author: David, Michael, Elmer, and Herbert. The teachers consistently graded the essays by Elmer and Herbert lower.

(Harari & McDavid, 1973)

The Importance of Feedback

Feedback is the centerpiece of assessment because it leads to intervention and reduction of future learning deficiencies (Brookhart, 2008). Just telling students what their performance level is—that is, giving them their grades—does not necessarily lead to change and improvement. For this reason, teachers should carefully distinguish between assessment and grading.

In addition to providing feedback to students, **parent-teacher conferences** play an important role in developing the partnership needed to improve students' success. At the Premium Website you can read Topic F, "Parent-Teacher Relations" for additional ideas on how to build a collaborative approach with parents. Also there are two TeachSource videos worth watching: *Home-School Communication: The Parent Teacher Conference*, which demonstrates how an experienced teacher leads the conference with a concerned parent, and *Communicating with Parents: Tips and Strategies for Future Teachers*.

The following section describes types of feedback that should be helpful in communicating about performance to children and their parents. How you approach assessment will have an impact, for better or worse, on the democratic climate of your classroom.

> **Teacher's Tip**
>
> Student-led conferencing is an effective strategy that allows children to take charge of their education. Even kindergartners can prepare PowerPoint presentations!
>
> *(Young & Behounek, 2006)*

Rubrics

Rubrics identify the teacher's expectation of what students will learn from the experience that is about to take place. Rubrics restructure the learning assessment process from one in which students learn and are then evaluated to one in which learning and evaluation are seamless (see the next topic for a more detailed explanation of rubrics).

Practice Tests

Practice tests can be used to teach test-taking skills. They also give students a heads-up alert about important material. Like rubrics, practice tests can occur prior to the instructional process. Practice tests tell teachers about students' prior knowledge and needs so that feedback of a remedial nature is less likely to be required.

Assessment Progress Reports

Assessment progress reports allow students to receive feedback as they progress through a project. Students should also be expected to monitor and report their own progress. Using a rubric and progress reports, the teacher can give feedback and guide students to take responsibility for the quality and pace of their work. Typically, students are given a form that requires them to report the time spent on the project each day, problems encountered, and important benchmarks (e.g., read the passage, created an outline, drafted the report).

Informal Feedback

Informal feedback is part of the daily routine. It can be as simple as a "thumbs up," a low-key admonition, quiet questioning of an individual student about his or her performance, or a word of praise. If a student is not doing well, depending on the frequency of his or her poor performance, the teacher will need more formal documentation of the reasons for the failure because it might be necessary to support additional intervention efforts involving school personnel or parents.

Discussion

Whole-class, teacher-centered **discussion** is crucial to social studies assessment because it allows the teacher the opportunity to evaluate students' ability to apply logic to issues and to support value decisions based on a coherent structure of facts and concepts. As explained in Topics 42 and 43, participation in questioning and discussion should be a requirement for all students, even the shy or reticent active learner.

Written Assessments

Written assessments by teachers are the norm. They need to be carefully crafted to direct the student to reflection and intervention. This is different from subtracting or tallying points or marking right and wrong answers. Students who have done well receive statements of encouragement, while students who have not done well receive suggestions about how to improve. The student can be required to perform tasks to remediate knowledge (look up the wrong answers, further explain the answers), or the teacher can provide a prompt about behaviors (e.g., "If you pay more attention in class, I am sure your understanding will improve").

Interviews

Interviews with students are important to the evaluation process. As a general rule, it is best to ask open-ended questions that focus on the learning experience and that allow students to freely articulate their strengths and shortcomings.

1. For alternative assessment, interviews can be the assessment. They could include questions like these:
   - What did you like about the project?
   - What part did you find the most difficult?
   - What would you do differently?

2. For traditional assessment, questions while reviewing a test might include the following:
   - What was it about finding the longitude that gave you a problem, do you think?
   - Do you think you could find a longitude now?
   - Why did this question give you a problem?

These kinds of questions put students at ease and provide the teacher with diagnostic information to help them improve. Interviews are very efficient, as long as other students are occupied with other work, and they provide an opportunity for promoting remedies in a very pleasant way.

> *Honest criticism is hard to take, particularly from a relative, a friend, an acquaintance, or a stranger.*
>
> Franklin P. Jones

Peer Assessment

Peer assessment can be used in either alternative or traditional testing. Students should not be asked to score other students' work, nor should they record grades. Peer assessment is most effective when it is integrated into the learning experience as part of the drafting and rewriting process, rather than simply being tacked on to the end of a project. It should include verbal and written feedback, usually by pairs of students. Peer assessment is authentic because it is what takes place in the real world when adults help other adults succeed. The teacher needs to create an environment of trust so that peer reviews are a positive socialization process for students.

> **Have you ever participated in peer assessment? How did you feel about other students correcting your work?**

Self-Assessment

Self-assessment can be particularly effective for student presentations, particularly if they are videotaped. Rating scales for voice projection, mannerisms, eye contact, and other relevant factors can encourage objectivity and self-reflection and can provide a structured form for constructive feedback. In writing assignments, self-assessment is as difficult for children as for adults; we tend not to see our own grammatical and spelling errors and logical inconsistencies. If assessment rubrics are given out at the beginning of the task, students can be expected to check off required components as a self-assessment and to turn them in when that task is completed.

Class Review

Class review should be conducted after an assessment by reteaching items that all students did poorly on. Involving the whole class in a teacher-led review is one strategy, and putting students into groups to review mistakes is another approach.

Grading and Reporting

Establishing and communicating your grading system to students and parents should be a top priority. As an elementary school teacher, you will need to compile separate grades for multiple subjects and a second set of grades for dispositions like behavior and attentiveness. Some schools refer to this second set as "citizenship," and at one time it was called "conduct." Although a student's behaviors and academic progress are reported separately, the two are usually related in terms of the student's development. However, some students do very well in school while disrupting others, and some placid students perform poorly.

Best Practices for Grading and Reporting

The following are ways to score and report grades. You may want to communicate some of them to parents in your introductory letter and at an open house.

1. Establish a grading scale, such as A = 90–100, F = 60–69, and so on.
2. Establish categories and their weights for each subject during a grading period: for example, 100 total points for participation; 100 points for correct answers from questioning; 200 points for tests; and 200 points for the authentic assessment project.
3. Announce the scale, categories, and weights of the assessments in writing to parents and students at the beginning of the marking period.
4. Provide for dropping the lowest grade or two as an alternative to makeup tests for absences, in order to avoid having students make up more than one test and the additional scoring.
5. Vary the value of questions based on Bloom's *Taxonomy*, with greatest weight to higher-level abilities.
6. Grade all assignments within two days of receipt, and return them on the third day.
7. Reduce favorable and unfavorable bias by not looking at the names on the paper before or during your scoring.
8. Shuffle the papers before scoring to avoid bias by always grading students in a certain order.
9. Always score all the assignments once in pencil, and place A papers in one stack, B papers in another, and so on. Then score one stack at a time, to ensure comparability of your assessment of As, Bs, and so on.
10. Record the grades on the back of the assignment in ink, so students do not know what other students' grades are, unless they deliberately share them.
11. Record the numeric grades in a software package or gradebook.
12. Post correct answers on the board for students to review and record on their papers.
13. After returning assignments, go over items on which all students generally did less well than expected, and answer students' questions about other items.

14. As a self-assessment, have students write reasons why questions were not answered correctly on their papers.
15. Require parents to sign all assessments below a C grade.
16. Encourage comments from parents.
17. Have students maintain a file folder in a set location in the classroom with all their assessments.
18. If you make a mistake in scoring, admit it, and change the grade. Otherwise, do not change grades.
19. Call the parent of a student who has done poorly in two consecutive assessments; do not wait until a conference.
20. Do not give extra work as optional assignments to help students improve poor grades (this is not the same thing as giving all students the opportunity to redo or resubmit an assignment). Extra credit is contrary to the basic principle that you know what they need to know, you teach what they need to know, and you assess them on what they need to know.

Teacher's Tip

Assessment is one of the most sensitive issues teachers must communicate to parents. Building bridges to families is essential. You can learn a number of strategies at Concept to Classroom's video workshop, **Making Family and Community Connections**.

Assignment 13.1

INTASC Standards 1, 2, 3, 4, 7, and 8

Grading Plan

Tensions over grades can be particularly disruptive to teacher-student and teacher-parent relationships. A well-thought-out grading scheme and clear communication about grading is essential. Contact a practicing teacher. Interview the teacher and obtain copies of his or her grading scheme and communications with parents. Develop a letter to parents explaining your approach to grading. Be prepared to turn in the assignment to your professor and share your ideas with the class.

TEACHSOURCE VIDEO CASE ASSIGNMENT 13.2

INTASC Standards 1, 2, 3, 4, 5, 7, and 8

Directed Reading Activity Observation Guide

View the TeachSource video case, *Assessment in the Elementary Grades: Formal and Informal Literary Assessment* at the book's Premium Website. Then click on "Classroom Artifacts" to find a three-page directed reading activity (DRA) observation guide that was completed by teacher Chris Quinn. Using this as an example, create your own DRA observation guide for Houghton Mifflin Reading 3, "Our Earth," also found at the Premium Website. Be prepared to turn in your observation guide to your professor and to discuss this reading and assessment strategy in class.

	WEBSITE RESOURCES • Social Studies Assessment
Video	*Concept to Classroom,* Assessment, Evaluation, and Curriculum Design
Essay	**ERIC Online** *ED470206,* The Concept of Formative Assessment (2002) *ED459522,* Meeting the Challenges of High-Stakes Testing (2001) *ED373010,* Measuring Student Performance: Assessment in the Social Studies (1993)
Websites	*TeAchnology* for Online Crossword Puzzle maker, worksheets, rubrics, etc.
	All linked websites (designated by the green color) and those listed here are available as clickable links at the book's Premium Website www.cengage.com/login, for ease of access. These links will be updated periodically to reflect changes and new resources as they become available.

Topic 14

Alternative Assessment

Alternative assessments include authentic, product, and performance assessment, and the terms are frequently used interchangeably. **Authentic assessment** usually requires students to demonstrate knowledge and skills the way they might be used in the real world outside the classroom, as in writing a letter to a congressman. When an education major creates a lesson plan, it is an authentic assessment, but a quiz would not be an authentic assessment.

Teacher's Tip

Harold Gardner's theory of multiple intelligences is an excellent framework for teachers who want to infuse their instruction with alternative assessments to conceptualize their assessments within. Go to Concept to Classroom's Video Workshop, "Tapping into Multiple Intelligences," for ideas.

    Product assessment, such as creating a Venn diagram comparing the branches of government, results in a tangible product that can be assessed as opposed to a paper-and-pencil test (Pappas, 2007). **Performance assessment**, for the purpose of this book, evaluates the demonstration of skills during a process, such as a presentation rather than some kind of tangible end product. Performance and product assessments may or may not be authentic, but authentic assessments are almost always either performance or product assessments.

The Importance of Rubrics

Rubrics are an important part of the alternative assessment approach. The use of rubrics is one of the best ways to help students succeed at tasks and master content (see the sources at the end of this topic). Rubrics can be powerful because they transfer responsibility for learning to students by creating a process that requires them to think critically. A rubric clearly identifies what students need to do by defining the required components of a task, the performance standards they should meet, and the point values that will be used to evaluate their performance (Boston, 2002; Kist, 2001). **Analytic rubrics** communicate a level of performance for each criterion, whereas **holistic rubrics** articulate a level of performance for the entire assignment. The level of performance is defined by

descriptors that determine the assessment and grade. As an example, a timeline assignment requires dates, and the reading material may have 10 dates. The rubric's descriptors would say that there would be 1–3 dates for "Poor"; 4–6 dates for "Good"; and 6–10 dates for "Excellent."

A rubric usually includes a description of a task, such as a letter to a senator on an issue; the components (a salutation, address, analysis, recommendation, closing); the standards (neat, logical, correct spelling); and the scale (complete, partially complete, incomplete). Often the items are assigned a point value: The address is worth 2 points, the salutation 5, and so on. For an excellent example of a rubric and a checklist used with a comprehensive social studies lesson plan, go to the Read/Write/Think Website for *Escaping Slavery:* "Sweet Clara and the Freedom Quilt."

A **checklist** is often less detailed than a rubric. The teacher may give checklists to students before an assignment to foster self-evaluation, or the teacher may use them to score a product or performance with a greater degree of consistency. A **model** or **sample** can be substituted for rubrics and checklists. The disadvantage of models is that students tend to duplicate what they see, thus reducing individual creativity and initiative. With these kinds of tools, the degree of subjectivity that is part of all nonobjective testing should be reduced and teachers should be able to demonstrate to parents and administrators the standards that the children were expected to attain with the project.

Teacher's Tip

Teachers should tell students what the rubrics are in advance of the assignment so that there is little disagreement about expectations.

Authentic Assessments

Authentic assessment relies on products created by students as an integral part of the learning experience. Essays, maps, timelines, and graphic organizers are products that are unlikely to be authentic unless they are created in a real-world context, such as writing a letter to a student in Rome, writing directions for a trip, creating a family timeline as part of creating a family biography, or simulating a situation in which a student presents a new rule to an elected official. The following characteristics are associated with authentic assessment.

1. The assessment simulates a real-world activity, such as giving a verbal presentation or newscast, creating a written proposal, planning a trip, interviewing a historical figure, or flowcharting a set of events.
2. The assessment is preceded by relevant instruction on content and form. If students are asked to flowchart the way an idea becomes a law, instruction about flowchart symbols and how a bill becomes law precedes the assessment.
3. The assessment is both an assessment and a learning experience. Students developing a presentation are learning both during the preparation stage and during the presentation.

4. Students are expected to develop the information necessary for the assessment activity with a minimum of teacher supervision. Students planning a newscast simulation would work independently and in collaboration with other students, gathering information and authoring the script, while the teacher ensures that they stay on task.

5. Students progress at different rates to produce high-quality results. If 10 pairs of students are preparing for a simulation of an interview with a historical figure, one pair may finish the work more quickly than another, and that is acceptable within reason.

6. Scoring of the product or performance is consistent, but it allows for individual differences and creativity. One student might present the Gettysburg Address, while another might decide to do a simulation of Lee and Grant meeting at Appomattox.

7. Feedback addresses strengths and weaknesses. Students who give a presentation should receive feedback on both public speaking skills and content, and the feedback should identify the strengths and weaknesses of both.

Product Assessment

The elementary classroom should be weighted toward authentic and **product assessment**, but not to the exclusion of traditional paper-and-pencil tests. While traditional and standardized paper-and-pencil tests create anxiety, focus on point-in-time mastery, and typically provide for only one format and results, product assessment is integrated into the learning process, usually has multiple and sequential opportunities for feedback, and may have multiple acceptable responses. Well-designed product assessment can ensure the same mastery of information knowledge as a paper-and-pencil test, but a paper-and-pencil test can rarely be designed to achieve the outcome of a product assessment. The capacity of product assessments to accommodate individual differences and intelligences facilitates the development of the whole person and allows the teacher to model the kind of acknowledgment of individual differences important to a democratic society.

In lieu of a paper-and-pencil test, students could create the following kinds of products.

1. **Portfolios:** These are collections of students' work that provide a cumulative record of their development. A portfolio is not the same thing as a folder in the classroom into which students place their completed assignments. The best practice is to set an expectation that students will create and maintain a portfolio from materials that reflect their successes and that it will include both materials from the classroom folder and original work they choose to add (artwork, poetry, short stories, ideas, etc.). Students can be expected to rank the items in importance, and upper elementary students can be expected to write comments about each item

and how it could have been improved. Teachers might encourage more reflective reporting by asking why the student selected the item and where he or she got the idea. Students should be given responsibility for their portfolios to demonstrate what they know and what they can do. For additional tips on portfolio assessment, view the TeachSource video at the Premium Website, *Portfolio Assessment: Elementary Classroom.*

2. **Poster boards and collages:** These can be created of states, countries, presidents, and so on.

3. **Fact finding:** The students first decide what facts to gather and then gather them. Fact-finding can be done about such topics as crime and population.

4. **Response journals and chalkboard journals:** These require students to write their thoughts and feelings about events in history, such as a story about Anne Frank. Students contribute ideas from their personal journals to be recorded on the chalkboard.

5. **Letter writing:** A student can write a letter by taking on the persona of a slave at the time of the Civil War or a Native American who just met the explorer Hernando de Soto.

6. **Word webs:** Students take one word from a lesson (like "bravery" from a lesson on the American Revolution) and create a web of ideas, such as Paul Revere and his midnight ride to warn the Minutemen and Lexington, where the colonists first confronted the British.

7. **Dialogues:** Writing a dialogue places the student in a historical context where, for example, Jefferson Davis and Abraham Lincoln debate or discuss an issue.

8. **Idea lists:** After a lesson students list the main ideas and their reasons for selecting them.

9. **Headlines and newspaper articles:** Lower elementary students create catchy headlines about an event in history, like "Oops, Hello!" for Alexander Graham Bell's discovery of the telephone. Upper elementary students can create newspaper articles about historical events, particularly events that predate newspapers.

10. **Word or picture cards:** Creating cards using social studies vocabulary, events, or concepts requires students to organize, sort, or sequence them based on relationships rather than on simple matching.

Performance Assessment

Two of the most common methods used for **performance assessment** in the elementary school setting are questioning and observation. Teacher questioning should be an ongoing, systematic activity; it should include feedback; and the teacher should award and record points for participation and accuracy of student responses.

Observation is used extensively in elementary education to determine a student's progress. Behaviors as well as demonstration of knowledge are observed and recorded as part of the daily routine, during group discussions, and as students work on assignments. It is unrealistic to think that a teacher can evaluate every student every day using product or traditional assessments, but the teacher can plan a rotation of students to be observed. Five students may be the focus of the teacher's particular attention one day, and five other students the next day. A checkoff list of desired behaviors and thinking should be used.

TEACHSOURCE VIDEO CASE ASSIGNMENT 14.1

INTASC Standards 1, 2, 3, 4, 5, 7, and 8

Portfolio Assessment

View the TeachSource Video Case, "Portfolio Assessment: Elementary Classroom," at the Premium Website. You should then answer the viewing questions and prepare a short paper explaining how you would apply this approach to a portfolio of social studies products. Be prepared to discuss this strategy in class and turn in the assignment to your professor.

Assignment 14.2

INTASC Standards 1, 2, 3, 4, 7, and 8

Create a Product and an Assessment Rubric

Download one of the three Doubleday Core Knowledge K–6 Series chapters (Reading 21, 23, or 25) from the Premium Website. Assume you are preparing a lesson based on all or part of the content. Develop a sample of a product (Topic 27 has a number of examples) you want the students to make based on the reading topic you chose and prepare a rubric for the product. Tip: You may want to use RubiStar, a free online rubric generator. Be prepared to share your ideas with your classmates and turn the assignment in to your professor.

Video	*Concept to Classroom,* Tapping into Multiple Intelligences
Essay	**ERIC Online** *ED369389,* Performance-Based Assessment (1994) *ED443880,* The Role of Classroom Assessment in Teaching and Learning (2000)
Rubrics	*Chicago Public Schools,* Prentice-Hall

Sample High-Quality Internet Lessons or Activities That Use Rubrics

Lower Elementary	*Read/Write/Think* the Way West: A Duet of Plays has students explore the pioneers' and settlers' ways of life through drama, games, role-play, written text, and songs.
Upper Elementary	*Read/Write/Think* Learning about Research and Writing Using the American Revolution requires students to conduct research on a historical figure using a variety of resources and to write an acrostic poem.
	All linked websites (designated by the green color) and those listed here are available as clickable links at the book's Premium Website, www.cengage.com/login, for ease of access. These links will be updated periodically to reflect changes and new resources as they become available.

Topic 15

Traditional Assessment

Traditional assessment refers to quizzes and tests that are often objective—that is, examinations in which each question has one discrete answer (e.g., "When did Columbus discover America? In 1492"). The traditional essay (or in the case of lower elementary, sentence or paragraph) tests tend to be less objective, but teachers typically expect students to include information knowledge and demonstrate procedural knowledge skills in their writing.

Traditional assessments often fall into the trap of only measuring information knowledge rather than concepts or procedural knowledge. Their popularity has a great deal to do with the ease with which they can be scored and the ease of comparing the quantitative, relatively objective scores across a class. Not knowing factual information is often a good indication that a student has not learned concepts and procedural knowledge. It can be argued that alternative assessment provides an opportunity to demonstrate all forms of knowledge, concepts, and skills far better than traditional assessment. Teachers usually find it appropriate to use both forms of assessment.

> *Surely (an average) grade of 33 in 100 on the simplest and most obvious facts of American history is not a record which any high school can take pride in.*

Sam Wineburg of History News Service, June 2002, about a test of 668 Texas students in 1917, when less than 10 percent of school-aged children went to high school

Alternatives to Traditional Tests

The following approaches are neither alternative assessments nor traditional paper-and-pencil tests. These alternative forms of testing add variety to a teacher's testing palette and can be used to accommodate student differences.

Oral Exams

Oral exams, in which the teacher calls on students one at a time and asks questions (perhaps at the teacher's desk), quickly determine students' knowledge. Oral exams are effective because they individualize the test to the student by varying the pace and phrasing, and because the student has a chance to explain his or her thinking. Students with less developed writing skills often feel more comfortable with oral tests.

Teachers can allow students to choose a verbal quiz while others complete a paper-and-pencil assessment, but they also should require all students to select the oral exam option a couple of times a semester. Oral exams should be documented with a checklist, or the teacher can use a paper-and-pencil test to guide the questions asked. Engaging students one on one is a powerful experience; the student gets a chance to interact with the teacher in a more personal way, and the teacher learns more about the student's thinking processes and personality.

Classroom Jeopardy

Classroom Jeopardy simulates the television program, *Jeopardy*. When all students have the opportunity to be contestants, it can serve as a test rather than as a review. Students often enjoy this kind of assessment so much that they don't think of it as a test.

Pupil-Produced Tests

In **pupil-produced tests** students construct test items that make up the pool of questions from which the teacher constructs the actual test. This approach gives students a sense of control over the test because they helped create it.

Take-Home Tests

Take-home tests often set a higher standard than in-class tests because the amount of time is relatively unlimited. An honor system must accompany such tests, and parents as well as other students must be excluded from helping. The advantage of this kind of test is that it doesn't compete with important instructional time.

Word Scrambles

In **word scrambles** letters of the word are scrambled, and students must study the definition and reorder the letters to figure out the word. Like classroom Jeopardy and crossword puzzles (see below), word scrambles are less stressful because of their game-like qualities.

Teacher's Tip

Black students perform better on "tests" when they are presented as a puzzle.

(Nisbett, 2009)

Crossword Puzzles

Crossword puzzles usually are effective in testing facts, definitions, and vocabulary, but they can also be created to test relationships between concepts and facts. Puzzlemaker is an excellent tool for creating crossword puzzles and word scrambles.

Alphabet Tests

Alphabet tests require students to find key words from a lesson by starting with a keyword that begins with "A" and systematically proceeding through the alphabet, skipping letters when no word can be found.

Traditional Tests

Teacher-made tests can evaluate the kinds of thinking that we associate with Bloom's *Taxonomy of Educational Objectives* (1956). Bloom's *Taxonomy* can be used when creating the traditional tests by structuring questions that draw from all six levels. When using traditional tests, teachers should emphasize items that focus on the higher levels of evaluation, synthesis, analysis, and application as well as the lower levels of knowledge and comprehension. Teachers often give fewer points for knowledge and comprehension questions and more points for evaluation, synthesis, analysis, and application questions. The emphasis on evaluating higher-level thinking is crucial to procedural knowledge and the kind of critical thinking needed in a democracy.

Most of the following types of tests will be familiar to you as a student. As a teacher, you will need to consider the implications and nuances of the structure of each test.

Essay and Short-Answer Exams

Essay and **short-answer exams** can be used with upper elementary students. Lower elementary students may need fill-in-the-blank test questions instead.

- *Advantages:* Such exams are usually easy to construct, eliminate guessing, require recall of knowledge, and support a teacher's language arts goals by letting students organize information knowledge and express it in a unique form.
- *Disadvantages:* They take more time to score, are more subjective, and usually take more time to administer than true-false tests.
- *Advice:*
  1. Create a rubric of expected correct answers or components of answers to reduce subjectivity.
  2. Score one question at a time for all students rather than all questions for one student.
  3. Take off points for errors in spelling, handwriting, and grammar; give positive points for correct content.
  4. Require all students to answer some questions and provide other questions from which students can select, but do not offer optional or bonus questions.

Teacher's Tip

Remember that the ideal situation is for all students to do well. Providing students with the topics for a test or with a comprehensive list of possible test questions or vocabulary can promote greater success because students will review the test material based on the information they were provided.

Two variations on the short-answer test item are the **lead phrase approach** and the **mixed vocabulary approach**.

Lead Phrase Approach

One way to approach higher-order traditional testing is to provide a **lead phrase** for students to complete. Having taught the American Revolution, a teacher may provide leads for students to expand upon that are based on Bloom's *Taxonomy*. **Evaluation leads** would be phrases like, "The best event was . . . ," to which one answer might be, "Washington crossing the Delaware because . . ." and "The worst event was . . . ," to which an answer might be, "Bunker Hill because . . ." **Synthesis leads** would be phrases like, "What if" and "I wonder."

    Analysis leads would be phrases like, "It's like," "compared to," and "Why would." **Application leads** would be words like "Based on," "If . . . then," and "another example of."

Mixed Vocabulary Approach

In the **mixed vocabulary approach** the teacher provides perhaps 10 vocabulary words in alphabetical order, and students are expected to weave a story out of them. Upper elementary students are asked to create an essay, and lower elementary students are asked to create sentences.

Fill-in-the-Blank and Completion Test Items

Fill-in-the-blank and **completion** items typically require simple recall.

- *Advantages:* They are usually easy to construct, eliminate guessing, require recall of knowledge, and support spelling skills.
- *Disadvantages:* They take more time to administer and to score than do true-false tests.
- *Advice:*
  1. Create a rubric of correct answers.
  2. When testing for definitions, put the term in the question and require students to supply the definition.
  3. There should be no more than two blanks per question.
  4. Take points off for spelling and handwriting errors, and give positive points for correct content.
  5. Do not take sentences directly from the textbook.

True-False Tests

True-false tests may be the most widely used tests in elementary schools because they are so easy to construct and grade.

- *Advantages:* They can cover a lot of material in a short period of time, are easy to score, and provide quantitative comparative scores for students.
- *Disadvantages:* They encourage guessing, can be poorly phrased and confusing, tend to focus on facts (although higher-level true-false questions can be created), and there is little recall because key terms must be used in the item.
- *Advice:*
  1. Have no more than one concept in a question.
  2. For some questions, also require additional written elaboration (this is a modified true-false item).
  3. Because most students guess "true," make more than half the questions false.
  4. Avoid clue words like "all," "never," and "only."
  5. Avoid double negatives.
  6. Avoid complex and compound sentences.
  7. Avoid giving clues in the choice of grammar.
  8. Avoid the trivial.
  9. Don't take wording directly from the text.
  10. Make the test an application by providing a reading, diagram, graph, or image, and having students answer true or false based on their procedural knowledge.

Multiple-Choice Tests

Multiple-choice tests have a distinct advantage over true-false tests because they require judgments among multiple answers.

- *Advantages:* Advantages are the same as for true-false and they work well for concepts with closely related potential correct answers, reduce guessing possibilities, and can be constructed to require the choice of the best answer as well as the only correct answer.
- *Disadvantages:* They require little recall because key terms are included as options, time and skill are needed to construct plausible wrong answers, and they tend to focus on facts, although higher-order multiple-choice test items can be created.
- *Advice:*
  1. Stems (the phrases before the possible answers) should be either questions or incomplete statements.
  2. Make sure there is only one correct answer.

3. All options should be plausible.
4. Do not use "all of the above" or "none of the above."
5. An approximately equal number of correct answers should appear in each position (a test of 20 stems with four answers each should have five correct answers in the first position, and so on).
6. Four possible answers per question is a good amount. They should consist of parts of speech such as nouns and verb phrases.
7. Make the test an application by providing a reading, graph, diagram, or image and by having students make choices based on their procedural knowledge.

Matching Tests

Matching tests have a problem column and a response column. They can consist of terms and definitions, causes and effects, dates or people and events, and problems and solutions.

- *Advantages:* Advantages are the same as for true-false and they focus students on key ideas, reduce guessing possibilities, can be constructed to require choice of best answer as well as the only correct answer, and require less paper.
- *Disadvantages:* They require no recall and developing homogeneous columns (columns with all like items, such as names on the left and what the people did on the right) takes time and skill.
- *Advice:*
  1. Place like items in one column (like terms or people) and their matching definitions or events in the other column.
  2. Number the left column and use letters for the right column.
  3. Make sure there is only one correct answer.
  4. Provide more items in the response column than in the problem column.
  5. Keep the test to one page, with 15 or fewer items.
  6. Disperse responses throughout the list.
  7. Arrange responses in alphabetical or some other logical order.
  8. Keep responses short.
  9. Make the test an application by providing a reading, graph, diagram, or image and by having students answer based on their procedural knowledge.

Assignment 15.1

INTASC Standards 1, 2, 3, 7, and 8

Create a Traditional Test

Select and download one of three chapters (Reading 21, 23, or 25) of the Doubleday Core Knowledge K–6 Series found at the Premium Website. Assume you are preparing a lesson based on all or part of the content. Create a grade-appropriate traditional test with no fewer than 15 items and with at least one question for each of Bloom's categories. Identify the categories you have used. Be prepared to share your test with the class and turn in the assignment to the professor.

Check the Premium Website, www.cengage.com/login, for additional links and links that are periodically updated to reflect new resources as they become available.

Unit Four

Social Studies Disciplines, Standards and Internet Resources

Cartoon by Don Addis, Copyright St. Petersburg Times 1997

Topic 16

National and State Standards

Now that you have a sense of what social studies is, of how to plan and evaluate your instruction, and how to use Internet resources to create high-quality lesson plans, this unit will provide information on evolving national standards and the disciplines of social studies (history, economics, etc.) with an emphasis on modes of reasoning, standards, and Internet resources. In this topic, we will begin by discussing the standards-based reform movement.

Standards-Based Reform

School reform has been a constant feature of education since the founding of the country in 1776 (Johnston, 2004, quoted in Duplass, 2006). Those reforms have taken the shape of changes to the curriculum, methods of instruction, and the training of teachers (see "Professor's Preface"). Because you will typically be teaching multiple subjects as an elementary school teacher, you must balance the various and often conflicting expectations of state school boards standards for each discipline to cover the curriculum. The definition of those expectations comes in the form of **standards** or **benchmarks**.

Standards-based education is a relatively new phenomenon in education. It has many goals, not the least of which is to develop more uniform expectations about what each student in the United States must learn and to measure in some uniform way each student's success as he or she progresses through the public school system. Although the standards movement predates President George W. Bush's January 8, 2002 signing into law of the No Child Left Behind Act (NCLB) of 2001, the NCLB places the movement in a national context with a national impetus. As a new teacher, you are entering the profession at the beginning of a new "teacher accountability" and "standards-based" movement in U.S. education.

If there is anything that education does not lack today, it is critics.

Nathan M. Pusey

Developing National Standards

The 1983 report of the National Commission on Excellence in Education labeled schools and their lack of rigor as the "rising tide of mediocrity" and expressed concern about the adverse impact this lack of rigor was having on general and subject area literacy. And the 1998 *Nation Still at Risk: An Educational Manifesto* published by the Center for Educational Reform found no improvement in the 15 years since 1983. Hirsch (1996, 2001), an advocate of a more uniform and structured curriculum, believes that the current standards-based reform movement is a response to the "curricular chaos" that has existed in schools, particularly since what he calls the "child-centered progressive movement" of the 1960s. Because the U.S. Constitution left public education to the individual states, the United States is one of the few industrialized nations that does not have a mandated nationwide curriculum.

No Child Left Behind

The NCLB Act of 2001 redefines the federal role in K–12 education and is intended to close the achievement gap between traditionally low-achieving student groups and their peers. It is based on four basic principles:

1. Stronger accountability for results;
2. Increased flexibility and local control;
3. Expanded options for parents; and
4. An emphasis on teaching methods that have been proven to work.

You can learn more details about the act by reviewing the following online resources at the Premium Website.

- The federal government's Ed.gov Website (see Figure 16.1 for the NCLB homepage)
- EJ815733, *The Impact of State Intervention on "Underperforming" Schools in Massachusetts: Implications for Policy and Practice* (2008)
- ED 478248, *The Mandate to Help Low-Performing Schools* (2003)
- ED 477723, *Implications of the No Child Left Behind Act of 2001 for Teacher Education* (2002)

Accountability Standards

The **accountability standards** of the NCLB act have received the most attention. For the first time, there is a nationwide requirement that states must demonstrate students' "adequate yearly progress," and the government has required states to report students in five major ethnic categories, students with low socioeconomic status, disabled students, and students of limited English proficiency in order to comply and maintain their federal funding. The mandate to

Figure 16.1

report *disaggregated* data, as opposed to reporting only overall averages (as has been done traditionally), focuses the standards on the students who have usually been "left behind." Most of the states are adopting **high-stakes testing** (typically a point-in-time, paper-and-pencil test given to all students in a school district or the state) as the primary assessment tool of progress (Van Patten, 2002). As a consequence of these standards, you will find a new focus on basic skills (see Unit 5) and a need to be more attentive to individual students and their families to keep them from being "left behind" (Linn, 2002). Reading, writing, and math skills are the focus of accountability, and thus all teachers—regardless of the subject matter they may be teaching—will be expected to support the schoolwide goal of meeting the new standards by including more instruction and practice of basic skills in their practice.

Opportunities in Social Studies

Because social studies has not been mandated to be tested as part of NCLB, many states are not testing students' knowledge of social studies in their high-stakes testing regimen. As a result, some teachers and even school districts are deemphasizing social studies in the curriculum and classroom in favor of basic skills subjects that will be tested: writing, reading, and arithmetic (see Passe, 2006). Rothman (2005) found that in 16 of 33 states surveyed, social studies instructional time had been reduced. However, teachers should not perceive these new mandates to be forcing an "either-or" choice, to teach either social studies or basic skills (see Unit 5). For example, social studies subjects like economics and geography can be used to teach math skills. As for reading skills, social studies textbooks as well as children's books and folklore can be used to engage students' imagination to motivate them to become better readers during the language arts bloc. Also, projects like creating biographies or the ABC report (see Topic 27) are excellent for improving students' writing skills. These and many other strategies can be found in this text to assist you in integrating basic skills into your social studies content and using social studies to teach basic skills.

> **What have you heard about NCLB, and how do you think it is affecting what goes on in classrooms?**

Literacy and Basic Skills

Because of NCLB, talk of **literacy** and **basic skills** has escalated. The term "literacy" can be confusing because it is used in so many different ways. The following explanation should be helpful in this regard.

General Literacy

The terms "literacy" and "basic skills" are commonly used interchangeably in an effort to define what students should, at a minimum, be able to do and know, usually by a certain age or grade level. **Traditional literacy**, in its simplest form, is defined in terms of the ability to read and write. Today, reading cannot be defined just in terms of books, however. Film-based and digital media provide alternative means of communication. Teachers must prepare students to be literate in all forms of information, including television, video, computers, and the Internet (Moje et al., 2000). **Basic skills** is the broader of the two terms; it usually includes the ability to use mathematics (**numeracy**) and is commonly expanded to include such things as oral communication, study skills, and computer skills. **Thoughtful literacy** is defined by Allington and Johnston (2000) as the "ability to read, write, and think in the complex and critical ways needed in a postindustrial democratic society." It is thoughtful literacy that is the particular interest of U.S. society and schools (see Wood & Dickinson, 2000). The Partnership for 21st Century Skills (2008) is advocating a comprehensive spectrum of skills needed by students to be adopted by states and school boards and has divided those into four areas:

1. Core Subjects and 21st Century Themes,
2. Learning and Innovation Skills
3. Information, Media and Technology Skills
4. Life and Career Skills

For more information on this approach, go the Partnership for 21st Century Skills Website.

Subject Area Literacy

The NCLB is relying on learned societies to articulate standards for each subject field and is also relying on organizations of school administrators such as the American Association of School Administrators to suggest how to reconcile the competing demands for time in the curriculum among disciplines. The standards of the learned societies take on different levels of detail, and there are often multiple societies and agencies within a field recommending their own set of standards. For example, the *National Geography Standards* are much more detailed than the standards recommended by the umbrella organization for social studies, the *National Council for the Social Studies (NCSS)*. In the end, however, it is local or state school boards or legislatures that mandate the curriculum and requirements based on regulations emanating from NCLB.

Only 12 states have elementary school standards in history and social studies that are "clear, specific and grounded in content" (Education Week, 2006). How do you think this will affect your allocation of time to teaching social studies?

Shamos (1995), in writing about scientific literacy, identified three levels of literacy that epitomize thinking about literacy that is specific to subject fields.

1. **Cultural literacy:** The person knows numerous terms and definitions of any discipline.
2. **Functional literacy:** The person can coherently converse, read, and write using these terms and definitions of the field of study.
3. **True literacy:** The person knows something of the "enterprise and conceptual schemes" (referred to previously in this text as "modes of reasoning," "procedural knowledge," etc.) of the discipline. In all subject fields, the highest standard appears to be that all students should be able to *do* a subject, such as social studies (true literacy), as opposed to just *knowing about* social studies (cultural and functional literacy).

Assignment 16.1

INTASC Standards 1, 7, 8 and 9

State Standards

Go to the Education Standards Website maintained by the Wappinger's Central School District in New York State to find your state's standards for social studies education. You should print out the standards for social studies or one of the social studies disciplines for the grade level you are assigned by your professor. Be prepared to discuss your state's standards and those of the NCSS or one of the other learned societies.

Video	*TeachSource* Elementary Reading Instruction: A Balanced Literacy Program *TeachSource* Foundations: Aligning Instruction with Federal Legislation *Concept to Classrooms* Teaching to the Academic Standards
	All linked websites (designated by the green color) and those listed here are available as clickable links at the book's Premium Website, www.cengage.com/login, for ease of access. These links will be updated periodically to reflect changes and new resources as they become available.

Topic 17

Social Studies, Standards, and Internet Resources

The purpose of Topics 17–22 is to provide you with information and insights regarding:

1. National standards from the social studies learned societies for history, geography, etc.;
2. The body of knowledge of social studies and its procedural knowledge that can be developed at the elementary school level;
3. Underlying modes of reasoning that are most important for an elementary school teacher to know;
4. Exemplary Internet resources that teachers can use for background knowledge and to teach elementary students; and
5. Suggested lesson plan topics.

The Nature of Social Studies Knowledge

The Renaissance (1260–1700 c.e.) and the Enlightenment (1700–1800 c.e.) mark the beginning of the specialized fields that make up today's social studies. During these two periods in European history, Greek philosophy's emphasis on logic was rediscovered, and scholars infused a new, higher degree of objectivity and observation into understanding the world. Western civilization shifted away from the medieval ideology of reliance on faith and religious institutions toward reason and proof as the basis of inquiry and understanding.

Most social studies knowledge stems from the academic disciplines of history, political science, psychology, sociology, anthropology, economics, and geography. Central to these disciplines is the systematic, detached logic employed by historians, geographers, social scientists, and economists to better understand the world. In addition, social studies educators have simplified what are often thought of as highly complex schemes of thinking so that we can assist elementary students in acquiring the skills and dispositions inherent in these modes of reasoning. Much of what elementary school–aged students should come to know has been defined by the National Council for Social Studies (NCSS).

National Council for the Social Studies

The National Council for the Social Studies (NCSS) is one of many learned societies that promote learning and knowledge in the social studies, but serves as an umbrella organization for all the social studies. Most people who are interested in social studies education consider the NCSS to be the primary national organization that articulates the goals and objectives of social studies education in U.S. schools. You should visit the **NCSS Website** with particular attention to the resources identified here.

WEBSITE RESOURCES • Social Studies Standards	
Video	*Learner.org,* A Standards (NCSS) Overview: Provides an explanation and overview of the standards.
	Learner.org, Applying Themes and Disciplines: Working from the NCSS themes and standards, the onscreen teachers identify approaches to integrating disciplines while teaching social studies content.
Websites	*NCSS*
	NCSS Standards
	NCSS Position Papers
	NCSS Teacher Resource and Lesson Plan Ideas
	NCSS Social Studies and the Young Learner
	NCSS Expectations of Excellence: Curriculum Standards for the Social Studies (1994, 2008)

The NCSS Ten Primary Themes

In 1994, NCSS published Expectations of Excellence: Curriculum Standards for Social Studies. It has been updated in 2008: see NCSS (2008a). Citing the need to promote civic ideals and principles for life in the 21st century, the standards consist of 10 interdisciplinary **themes** and **strands** that guide the development of the social studies curriculum. This was a significant departure from the past, when the framework was defined in terms of individual disciplines such as history, civics, and geography.

Please note, that these strands are heavily weighted toward procedural knowledge as opposed to information knowledge. For example, look at the theme of culture and strand D, "Compare ways in which people from different cultures think about and deal with their physical environment and social conditions." As an approach to instruction, the strand offers excellent guidance to teachers on how to emphasize procedural knowledge and big ideas in their lessons. Conversely, these themes and strands offer little guidance on what content to use when developing a theme: The strand does not mention any one culture, which would require NCSS to define the information knowledge they feel is important. What information knowledge to use is left up to the states or book publishers; the teacher; or, in the case of the theoretician, E. D Hirsch (1987), a list of terms for cultural literacy. Under this new framework and this strand, procedural knowledge could be used to teach elementary school children about prehistoric humans, ethnic neighborhoods in the United States, early civilizations, regionalization of the U.S. colonies, contemporary comparisons of people in northern and southern climates, and so on.

The Ten Primary Themes of Social Studies NCSS, 1994, 2008

CULTURE—*Social Studies programs should include experiences that provide for the study of culture and cultural diversity, so that the learner can:*

A. Explore and describe similarities and differences in the ways groups, societies, and cultures address similar human needs and concerns;

B. Give examples of how experiences may be interpreted differently by people from diverse cultural perspectives and frames of reference;

C. Describe ways in which language, stories, folktales, music, and artistic creations serve as expressions of culture and influence behavior of people living in a particular culture;

D. Compare ways in which people from different cultures think about and deal with their physical environment and social conditions;

E. Give examples and describe the importance of cultural unity and diversity within and across groups.

TIME, CONTINUITY, AND CHANGE—*Social Studies programs should include experiences that provide for the study of the ways human beings view themselves in and over time, so that the learner can:*

A. Demonstrate an understanding that different people may describe the same event or situation in diverse ways, citing reasons for the differences in views;

B. Demonstrate an ability to use correct vocabulary associated with time such as past, present, future, and long ago; read and construct simple timelines; identify examples of change; and recognize examples of cause and effect relationships;

C. Compare and contrast different stories or accounts about past events, people, places, or situations, identifying how they contribute to our understanding of the past;

D. Identify and use various sources for reconstructing the past, such as documents, letters, diaries, maps, textbooks, photos, and others;
E. Demonstrate an understanding that people in different times and places view the world differently;
F. Use knowledge of facts and concepts, drawn from history, along with elements of historical inquiry, to inform decision making about and action taking on public issues.

PEOPLE, PLACES, AND ENVIRONMENTS—Social Studies programs should include experiences that provide for the study of people, places, and environments, so that the learner can:
A. Construct and use mental maps of locales, regions, and the world that demonstrate understanding of relative location, direction, size, and shape;
B. Interpret, use, and distinguish various representations of the earth, such as maps, globes, and photographs;
C. Use appropriate resources, data sources, and geographic tools such as atlases, databases, grid systems, charts, graphs, and maps to generate, manipulate, and interpret information;
D. Estimate distance and calculate scale;
E. Locate and distinguish among varying landforms and features, such as mountains, plateaus, islands, and oceans;
F. Describe and speculate about physical system changes such as seasons, climate and weather, and the water cycle;
G. Describe how people create places that reflect ideas, personality, culture, and wants and needs as they design homes, playgrounds, classrooms, and the like;
H. Examine the interaction of human beings and their physical environment, the use of land, building of cities, and ecosystem changes in selected locales and regions;
I. Explore ways that the earth's physical features have changed over time in the local region and beyond and how these changes may be connected to one another;
J. Observe and speculate about social and economic effects of environmental changes and crises resulting from phenomena such as floods, storms, and drought;
K. Consider existing uses and propose and evaluate alternative uses of resources and land in the home, the school, the community, the region, and beyond.

INDIVIDUAL DEVELOPMENT AND IDENTITY—Social Studies programs should include experiences that provide for the study of individual development and identity, so that the learner can:
A. Describe personal changes over time such as those related to physical development and personal interests;

B. Describe personal connections to place—especially place as associated with immediate surroundings;

C. Describe the unique features of one's nuclear and extended families;

D. Show how learning and physical development affect behavior;

E. Identify and describe ways family, groups, and community influence the individual's daily life and personal choices;

F. Explore factors that contribute to one's personal identity such as interests, capabilities, and perceptions;

G. Analyze a particular event to identify reasons individuals might respond to it in different ways;

H. Work independently and cooperatively to accomplish goals.

INDIVIDUALS, GROUPS, AND INSTITUTIONS—*Social Studies programs should include experiences that provide for the study of interactions among individuals, groups, and institutions, so that the learner can:*

A. Identify roles as learned behavior patterns in group situations such as student, family member, peer playgroup member, or club member;

B. Give examples of and explain group and institutional influences such as religious beliefs, laws, and peer pressure, on people, events, and elements of culture;

C. Identify examples of institutions and describe the interactions of people with institutions;

D. Identify and describe examples of tensions between and among individuals, groups, or institutions, and how belonging to more than one group can cause internal conflicts;

E. Identify and describe examples of tension between an individual's beliefs and government policies and laws;

F. Give examples of the role of institutions in furthering both continuity and change;

G. Show how groups and institutions work to meet individual needs and promote the common good and identify examples where they fail to do so.

POWER, AUTHORITY, AND GOVERNANCE—*Social Studies programs should include experiences that provide for the study of how people create and change structures of power, authority, and governance, so that the learner can:*

A. Examine the rights and responsibilities of the individual in relation to his or her social group such as family, peer group, and school class;

B. Explain the purpose of government;

C. Give examples of how government does or does not provide for needs and wants of people, establish order and security, and manage conflict;

D. Recognize how groups and organizations encourage unity and deal with diversity to maintain order and security;

E. Distinguish among local, state, and national governments and identify representative leaders at these levels such as mayor, governor, and president;

F. Identify and describe factors that contribute to cooperation and cause disputes within and among groups and nations;

G. Explore the role of technology in communications, transportation, information processing, weapons development, or other areas as it contributes to or helps resolve conflicts;

H. Recognize and give examples of the tensions between the wants and needs of individuals and groups, and concepts such as fairness, equity, and justice.

PRODUCTION, DISTRIBUTION, AND CONSUMPTION—*Social Studies programs should include experiences that provide for the study of how people organize for the production, distribution, and consumption of goods and services, so that the learner can:*

A. Give examples that show how scarcity and choice govern our economic decisions;

B. Distinguish between needs and wants;

C. Identify examples of private and public goods and services;

D. Give examples of the various institutions that make up economic systems such as families, workers, banks, labor unions, government agencies, small businesses, and large corporations;

E. Describe how we depend upon workers with specialized jobs and the ways in which they contribute to the production and exchange of goods and services;

F. Describe the influence of incentives, values, traditions, and habits on economic decisions;

G. Explain and demonstrate the role of money in everyday life;

H. Describe the relationship of price to supply and demand;

I. Use economic concepts such as supply, demand, and price to help explain events in the community and nation;

J. Apply knowledge of economic concepts in developing a response to a current local economic issue such as how to reduce the flow of trash into a rapidly filling landfill.

SCIENCE, TECHNOLOGY, AND SOCIETY—*Social Studies programs should include experiences that provide for the study of relationships among science, technology, and society, so that the learner can:*

A. Identify and describe examples in which science and technology have changed the lives of people, such as in homemaking, child care, work, transportation, and communication;

B. Identify and describe examples in which science and technology have led to changes in the physical environment, such as the building of dams and levees, offshore oil drilling, medicine from rain forests, and loss of rain forests due to extraction of resources or alternative uses;

C. Describe instances in which changes in values, beliefs, and attitudes have resulted from new scientific and technological knowledge, such as conservation of resources and awareness of chemicals harmful to life and the environment;

D. Identify examples of laws and policies that govern scientific and technological applications, such as the Endangered Species Act and environmental protection policies;

E. Suggest ways to monitor science and technology in order to protect the physical environment, individual rights, and the common good.

GLOBAL CONNECTIONS—*Social Studies programs should include experiences that provide for the study of global connections and interdependence, so that the learner can:*

A. Explore ways that language, art, music, belief systems, and other cultural elements may facilitate global understanding or lead to misunderstanding;

B. Give examples of conflict, cooperation, and interdependence among individuals, groups, and nations;

C. Examine the effects of changing technologies on the global community;

D. Explore causes, consequences, and possible solutions to persistent, contemporary, and emerging global issues, such as pollution and endangered species;

E. Examine the relationships and tensions between personal wants and needs and various global concerns, such as use of imported oil, land use, and environmental protection;

F. Investigate concerns, issues, standards, and conflicts related to universal human rights, such as the treatment of children and religious groups and the effects of war.

CIVIC IDEALS AND PRACTICES—*Social Studies programs should include experiences that provide for the study of the ideals, principles, and practices of citizenship in a democratic republic, so that the learner can:*

A. Identify key ideals of the United States' democratic republican form of government, such as individual human dignity, liberty, justice, equality, and the rule of law, and discuss their application in specific situations;

B. Identify examples of rights and responsibilities of citizens;

C. Locate, access, organize, and apply information about an issue of public concern from multiple points of view;

D. Identify and practice selected forms of civic discussion and participation consistent with the ideals of citizens in a democratic republic;

E. Explain actions citizens can take to influence public policy decisions;

F. Recognize that a variety of formal and informal factors influence and shape public policy;

G. Examine the influence of public opinion on personal decision making and government policy on public issues;

H. Explain how public policies and citizen behaviors may or may not reflect the stated ideals of a democratic republican form of government;

I. Describe how public policies are used to address issues of public concern; recognize and interpret how the "common good" can be strengthened through various forms of citizen action.

The NCSS themes are related to the traditional academic disciplines, as depicted in Table 17.1.

Table 17.1   NCSS Themes and the Academic Disciplines

NCSS Theme	Primary Academic Discipline(s) (Most Related)
Culture	Anthropology and Geography
Time, Continuity, and Change	History
People, Places, and Environments	Geography and Anthropology
Individual Development and Identity	Sociology and Psychology
Individuals, Groups, and Institutions	Political Science, Sociology, and Anthropology
Power, Authority, and Governance	Political Science
Production, Distribution, and Consumption	Economics
Science, Technology, and Society	History, Anthropology, and Political Science
Global Connections	Geography, Anthropology, and Political Science
Civic Ideals and Practices	Political Science and History

NCSS Expectations of Excellence: Curriculum Standards for Social Studies

This new 2008 document elaborates on the 1994 document and provides additional information on social studies knowledge that goes beyond the original themes and that can be very valuable to teachers of social studies.

Themes

For each of the 10 themes, the document used the following format and provides example of each:

Teacher's Tip

Just as you might decide to develop a lesson on the American Revolution, it is equally valid to develop a lesson plan to "evaluate sources of information" and "place (events) in proper sequence."

- *Key Questions*—a source for Big Ideas
- *Knowledge*—a source for key Information Knowledge's concepts
- *Processes*—a source for Procedural Knowledge
- *Products*—a source for assessment tools.

These serve as a way of offering additional guidance to teachers of social studies. The following is an excerpt for the NCSS theme, "Culture," that is listed in the preceding section.

NCSS "Learning Expectations" Example

- For the theme, "Culture," the document provides the following:

Purposes:

The learner will understand how human beings create, learn, and adapt to culture. They will understand how multiple perspectives derive from different cultural vantage points in order to better relate to and interact with people in this and other nations. This information will help learners make informed decisions in an increasingly interconnected world.

Questions for Exploration:
- What is culture?
- How are groups of people alike and different?
- How do the beliefs, values and behaviors of a group of people help the group meet its needs and solve problems?
- How does culture unify a group of people?
- What is cultural diversity and how does diversity develop both within and across cultures?

Knowledge—The learner will understand:
- That "culture" refers to the behaviors, beliefs, values, traditions, institutions, and ways of living together of a group of people;
- Concepts, such as similarities, differences, values, cohesion, and diversity;
- How cultural beliefs and behaviors allow human groups to solve the problems of daily living and how these may change in response to changing needs and concerns;
- How individuals learn the elements of their culture through interactions with other members of the culture group; and
- How people from different cultures develop different values and ways of interpreting experience.

Processes—The learner will be able to:
- Explore and describe similarities and differences in the ways different social groups meet similar needs and concerns;
- Give examples of how information and experiences may be interpreted differently by people from different cultural groups;
- Describe the value of cultural unity, as well as diversity, within and across groups; and
- Demonstrate how holding different values and beliefs can contribute or pose obstacles to understanding between people and groups.

Products—Learners demonstrate understanding by:
- Interviewing and observing, developing a description of a subculture to which they belong or have access (e.g., friends, school, and neighborhood);
- Selecting a social group and investigating the commonly held beliefs, values, behaviors, and traditions which characterize the culture of that group;
- Presenting a comparison and contrast chart demonstrating the similarities and differences between two or more social groups in given cultural categories (such as food, shelter, language, religion, arts, and beliefs); and

- Showing ways in which cultural differences between two or more groups can cause conflict and can contribute to solving problems.

For a small investment, you can acquire a copy of the document and it can be very helpful as you shift your focus away from the mundane teaching of facts to procedural knowledge and big ideas.

Essential Skills

In addition, this 2008 NCSS document on curriculum also provides a listing of "Essential Social Studies Skills and Strategies." The following are some of particular importance for elementary school teachers of social studies and should be a target of their lesson plans. You should note that some of the literacy skills and all of the critical thinking skills are what you have come to appreciate as procedural knowledge, although not all are grade-appropriate to young learners.

Essential Social Studies Skills and Strategies

LITERACY SKILLS FOR SOCIAL STUDIES
- Arrange events in chronological sequence.
- Analyze cause and effect relationships.
- Describe people, places, events, and the connections between and among them.
- Explore and/or observe, identify, and analyze how individuals and/or institutions relate to one another.
- Solve problems by analyzing conflicts and persistent issues.
- Develop an ability to use and apply abstract principles.
- Differentiate between and among various options.
- Explore complex patterns, interactions, and relationships.
- Articulate and construct reasoned arguments from diverse perspectives and frames of reference.
- Define and apply discipline-based conceptual vocabulary.
- Investigate, interpret, and analyze multiple historical and contemporary sources and viewpoints.
- Locate, analyze, critique, and use appropriate resources and data.
- Use a wide variety of media to access, analyze, evaluate and create messages and reports.
- Evaluate sources for validity and credibility and to detect propaganda, censorship, and bias.
- Differentiate fact from opinion.
- Determine an author's purpose.

CRITICAL THINKING SKILLS
Interpret Information
- State relationships between categories of information.
- Draw inferences from factual material.
- Predict likely outcomes based on factual information.
- Recognize and interpret different points of view.
- Recognize instances in which more than one interpretation is valid.
- Transfer knowledge into new contexts.

Analyze Information
- Form a simple organization of key ideas related to a topic.
- Separate a topic into major components according to appropriate criteria.
- Examine critically the relationships between and among elements of a topic.
- Detect bias in data presented in various forms.
- Compare and contrast credibility of differing ideas, elements, or accounts.

Synthesize Information
- Propose a new plan of operation, system, or scheme based on available data.
- Reinterpret events by relating knowledge from several disciplines.
- Present information extracted from one format in a different format, e.g., from print to visual.
- Communicate concisely orally and in writing.

Evaluate Information
- Determine whether or not sources are valid and credible.
- Estimate the adequacy of the information.
- Test the validity of the information, using such criteria as source, objectivity, technical correctness, and currency.
- Understand legal and ethical issues related to access and use of information.

RESEARCH, INFORMATION, AND TECHNOLOGY SKILLS
Locate Information
- Use library, online, or other search tools to locate sources.
- Use key words, tables, indexes, and bibliographies to locate information.
- Use sources of information in the community.

Explore Information
- Use various parts of a text, document, visual, electronic, or audio source.
- Conduct interviews of individuals in the community.
- Evaluate sources of information—print, visual, electronic, and audio.
- Use maps, globes, graphic representations and tools, and geographic information systems.
- Interpret social and political messages of cartoons.
- Interpret history through artifacts.

ORGANIZE INFORMATION IN USABLE FORMS INCLUDING OUTLINES, SUMMARIES, BIBLIOGRAPHIES, AND OTHER PRODUCTS

Use Computer-Based Technology and Media and Communication Technology
- Operate input devices.
- Operate other media and communication technology.
- Operate appropriate multimedia sources for directed and independent learning activities.

Use Internet-Based Information Networks
- Use tools and resources to manage and communicate information including correspondence, finances, data, charts, and graphics.
- Use online information resources and communities to meet the need for collaboration, research, publications, and communication.
- Use tools for research, information analysis, problem-solving, and decision making in learning.

NCSS Democratic Beliefs and Values

In 1990, NCSS approved a statement on beliefs and values as a guide for what teachers should be including in their planning of social studies instruction. These kinds of beliefs and values, serve as the foundation for *citizenship and character education*. For example, the American Civil War could be a lesson on the big idea of the right to liberty, and the civil rights movement of the 1960s could be a lesson in the big idea of the need to protect dissenting minorities. Beliefs such as the right to dignity and tolerance promote civic virtues that also provide a sound footing for your classroom management practices.

Beliefs and Values

Rights of the Individual

Right to life   Right to equality of opportunity
Right to liberty   Right to justice
Right to dignity   Right to privacy
Right to security   Right to private ownership of property

Freedoms of the Individual

Freedom to participate   Freedom of conscience
in the political process   Freedom of assembly
Freedom of worship   Freedom of inquiry
Freedom of thought   Freedom of expression

Responsibilities of the Individual

To respect human life
To respect the rights of
others
To be tolerant
To be honest
To be compassionate

To demonstrate self-control
To participate in the democratic
process
To work for the common good
To respect the property of others

Beliefs Concerning Societal Conditions and Governmental Responsibilities

Societies need laws that are accepted by the majority of the people.
Dissenting minorities are protected.
Government is elected by the people.
Government respects and protects individual rights.
Government respects and protects individual freedoms.
Government guarantees civil liberties.
Government works for the common good.

What Should Elementary Students Know?

Variations of this heading will be used throughout this unit, but it can be misleading because people generally think in terms of content knowledge when they see the term "know." In the sense used here, *knowing* involves not only information, but also *how* to do or think and the adoption of a way of thinking. In other words, it includes differing degrees of information knowledge, procedural knowledge, basic skills, big ideas, and an academic disposition.

Fundamental Social Studies Modes of Reasoning

During social studies instruction, students should come to adopt an academic disposition that leads to the use of the following modes of reasoning.

- **Openness to new information.** Students (adults, too, for that matter) often resist the reassessment of ideas and beliefs when confronted with new information because of the human desire to maintain stability. Because knowledge should always be thought of as tentative—because it is always changing—the teacher must model enthusiasm for the discovery of new facts and ideas and openness to changing personal beliefs. For example, lower elementary students are often taught the grade-appropriate idea that Lincoln's Emancipation Proclamation "freed the slaves," and Lincoln is placed on a pedestal (rightly deserved for reasons too lengthy to go into here). Later they must learn that the Emancipation Proclamation was actually a political, tactical maneuver that did not free slaves in the Union states and freed only slaves in parts of the Confederate states not yet under Union army control.

- **Cautious reliance on experts.** In contemporary cultures, the vast amount of knowledge has produced specialization and multiple sources ranging from the unregulated Internet to such extraordinary scholarly books such as 1491 (Mann, 2005). Accepting that we can know only so much about any topic also forces us to choose among the opinions of experts. Students must learn to question what they read and look for bias. Teachers are also viewed as authorities by students, and it is a positive sign if your students even question a statement you make! As an example, some teachers feel very strongly about saving the rain forests or perhaps the construction of a Wal-Mart because of its impact on a community. It is essential that you present a balanced perspective and give the students the tools to make up their own minds about the issue.

- **Recognition of subjectivity.** Excellent social studies professionals feel a duty to report facts and applications of concepts as distinct and separate from their conclusions and generalizations so that others can better evaluate any intentional or unintentional bias. There are typically four kinds of bias that students should learn about.

  1. Bias based on sources: All knowledge has one or more sources. Observers and participants left conflicting accounts of Charlemagne's coronation and the Boston Massacre. Recognizing the bias of sources is critical to forming accurate concepts.
  2. *Bias based on method:* Lack of attention to detail can create inaccurate concepts. When teaching about the American Revolution's rallying cry of "Taxation without representation," many teachers fail to explain that Great Britain's members of Parliament were expected to represent the interests of the entire British Empire, not just of a specific district or region, so the colonies were arguably as well represented as all other segments of the British Empire.
  3. *Bias based on prior knowledge:* People evaluate each new fragment of information in the context of their existing ideas and beliefs. People have both emotional and intellectual attachments to beliefs and ideas that can cause them to be less than objective. When a teacher is presenting a legal education lesson on driving under the influence (DUI), the thinking and concept formation of a student whose relative was killed by a drunken driver will be challenged to consider new ideas very differently than those of a student whose relative is in prison for a DUI conviction.
  4. Bias based on secondhand information: Most of what we know we learn secondhand. You learn about the Magna Carta, but you weren't

there at its creation. You learn about Australia, but you probably have not visited the continent, although you may have read about it or seen it on TV. Your parents tell you not to play with matches in the hope that you won't learn about fire the hard way. Reasoned trust in secondhand information is essential; skepticism, however, is an equally important virtue. Each step away from the original information portrayed in the flowchart in Figure 17.1 is a point at which inaccuracies can appear.

Figure 17.1 Secondhand Information

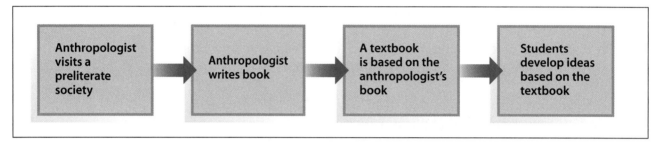

Three Social Studies Procedural Knowledge Strategies

The following are three examples of procedural knowledge and how they can be applied to information knowledge. As stated previously, the focus of the teacher is to teach procedural knowledge using information knowledge.

Organizing, Classifying, and Defining

By organizing, classifying, and defining information knowledge, students come to know fact and concepts. More important, however, they learn that by organizing, classifying, and defining they can draw logical conclusions about what we know and make informed decisions about what we want to do as citizens and personally. By pursuing this approach in a classroom setting, students learn others' perspectives and can work to resolve conflicts among their personal ideas or beliefs and those of others and the collective community.

You may be most familiar with a system from high school biology in which humans are classified as genus *Homo* and species *sapiens*. This classification system is derived from the work of Aristotle and later the scientist Linnaeus in *Systema Naturae* (System of Nature) published in 1735. It is a 12-level hierarchical system with five kingdoms at the top, followed by phyla, and ending with the most specific classifications, genus and species. The Linnaean system is still used in biology to classify organisms, although it is not the only system. Piaget's psychological description of classification, assimilation, and accommodation also has its origins in this same approach to the organization of knowledge and it is the process that lies at the center of philosophical inquiry.

As a teacher of social studies, you need to model and have students adopt this disposition of organizing, classifying, and defining. The following are two examples of how this would work in an elementary school classroom.

Example without Values Considerations

An example of a lower elementary grade topic that is not loaded with value considerations would be asking students to classify kinds of transportation like boats, planes, cars, and bicycles. When conceptualized by a teacher for a lesson, the process of teaching students to classify such items might be based on types of vehicles by location—(used in) the air, land, or sea—and then examples by time periods and the like. Modeling or putting students into groups to figure out the critical attributes would be part of a lesson on the history and impact of different types of transportation on our lives. Such information is one part of a lifelong building-block approach to beliefs and ideas that will be important to their role as citizens when making decisions about legislation on auto emissions, funding for transportation systems, purchase of a car, and other issues. The disposition to organize, classify, and define should be transferable to a classroom topic like classifying president, governor, mayor, and so on. However, the disposition toward organizing, classifying, and defining that is developed by the consistent use of the approach would be just as important to the analysis of all kinds of social studies content in the future as they build a larger, more mature knowledge base for decision making on a range of topics.

Teacher's Tip

For Internet materials on teaching a topic such as transportation, the Gateway to Educational Materials can serve as a entry to a number of resources including songs, lesson plans, and printable materials. As an example, by searching for "transportation" I was directed to 6 lesson plans at ALFY.com.

Example with Values Considerations

Leading a discussion about the characteristics of a good president before a presidential election requires a decision about what is "good." This is substantially different from the first example because the classification of transportation systems does not require value analysis and it deals with definitive information. Value-laden concepts have greater ambiguity because they deal with indefinite information; there may not be one correct answer, and all parties may not agree with the classification. One person's good might be another's bad or irrelevant. By focusing the lesson

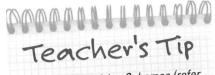

Teacher's Tip

The Six Organizing Schemes (refer to Assignment 2.1 from Topic 2) would be a fourth kind of procedural knowledge in social studies.

on the *criteria* for classifying presidents, we provide a framework for students to form a consensus on the criteria by applying a concept to examples. Together the teacher and the students refine the definition, criteria, caveats, and context by scrutinizing examples. This allows students to then apply the criteria to the candidates and support their decisions based on a deliberate thoughtful process modeled by the teacher. This process is, arguably, more important than the outcome.

Five General Types of Questions

Engle and Ochoa (1988) identified five forms of questions that can be used to engage students.

1. **Definitional questions:** In the simplest form, you are asking for a coherent definition, such as, "Can you define a rural community?" Definition questions should be asked and followed up on to ensure that only the *critical attributes* are being used. A question like, "Can you define, 'refugee'?" might take on ideological nonattributes if it is answered by someone who thinks there are "too many" refugees.

2. **Evidential questions:** What evidence can students cite to support their answers? "Can you give some examples of prejudice?"

3. **Policy questions:** What should be done about social problems? "What do you think would be the best policy for dealing with people who don't pay their taxes?"

4. **Value questions:** What values underlie suggested solutions to policy questions? "Why do you think it is wrong for dog owners not to keep their dogs on a leash?"

5. **Speculative questions:** What might have happened if things developed or were done differently? "What do you think life would be like if there were no television?"

The Who, What, When, Where, Why, How Method

Another approach students and teachers can use to investigate, collect, and organize information is the **WWWWWH method.** Begin with any person (for example, Susan B. Anthony or Alexander the Great), event (the Trojan War or the American Revolution), or document (the Magna Carta or the Declaration of Independence), and have students complete the remainder of the information based on research, a reading assignment, or during a lecture.

A two-column approach (such as the one in the WWWWWH Organizer at the Premium Website) or one-column approach can be used for this procedure.

Assignment 17.1

INTASC Standards 1, 2, 3, 4, 5, 7, and 8

Needs and Wants: Classifying

Download Houghton Mifflin's Reading 5, "Needs and Wants," from the Premium Website and review the content in the chapter. In a one-page paper, answer the following questions.

1. What procedural knowledge could you teach using this content?
2. What big idea could you teach using this content?
3. Brainstorm and report how this content might be extended to teach a values lesson.

Be prepared to discuss your results in class and submit the paper to your professor. Then apply the classification approach to the content by producing a diagram you would use as a transparency with an overhead projector in class.

Assignment 17.2

INTASC Standards 1, 2, 3, 4, 5, 7, and 8

Five Types of Questions: Modern History

Download Houghton Mifflin's Reading 15, "The Twenty-First Century Begins," from the Premium Website and review the topics in the chapter. Using all or part of the content, prepare an example and answer for each of the five types of questions. Be prepared to discuss your results in class and submit the one-page assignment to your professor.

Assignment 17.3

INTASC Standards 1, 2, 3, 4, 5, 7, and 8

The WWWWWH Method: Lincoln-Douglas Debates

Go to the Illinois Civil War site and the Lincoln/Net Website (or search the Internet for "Lincoln-Douglas debates"). Based on these resources, complete a two-column WWWWWH Organizer found at the Graphic Organizer section of the book's Premium Website that you would use as an overhead transparency titled, "The Lincoln-Douglas Debates" with a fifth grade class. Be prepared to share your organizer with the class and to submit the assignment to the professor.

The following websites are suggested as resources for development of social studies lesson plans.

	WEBSITE RESOURCES • Social Studies
Websites	*Wikipedia* *Encyclopedia Smithsonian* *Encarta Online Encyclopedia* *Fact Monster,* An encyclopedia for kids
	All linked websites (designated by the green color) and those listed here are available as clickable links at the book's Premium Website, www.cengage.com/login, for ease of access. These links will be updated periodically to reflect changes and new resources as they become available.

Topic 18

History, Standards, and Internet Resources

History is the Greek word for inquiry. Herodotus (484–425 b.c.e.) is considered the father of written history because he wrote the first prose history (earlier histories were in dialogue or verse) and he was relatively successful in recording factual accounts of events. Students often fail to realize that history is created by historians, often based on inconsistent evidence and secondhand accounts (Fertig, 2005). Respected historians distinguish between facts and interpretations so that readers can decide whether to agree or disagree with the historian's conclusions. Because children trust in the perfection of books and the truthfulness of adults, elementary students will absorb history without understanding that they need to interpret authors' conclusions and draw their own conclusions from the evidence (Barton, 1997a, b; Levstik & Barton, 2001). Teachers can assist students in understanding history by not plowing through history as an endless series of dates and events. They accomplish this rather by creating lessons in which students investigate history as presented in text, primary documents, and realia; by drawing analogies to what they know; and by using questioning and discussion to address children's misconceptions (Barton, 1997c). The ultimate purpose of knowing history is for individuals and their collective societies to learn from past events so that they may further the ascent of humankind.

> *Those who cannot remember the past are condemned to repeat it.*
>
> George Santayana

Have you seen the movie JFK? Have you read the "Warren Report?" They promote very different views of the assassination of John F. Kennedy.

A degree of trust in what we read and hear on the news, as an example, is necessary in a complex society. Reading and listening with **healthy skepticism** is an academic disposition that is necessary for a personal interpretation of history. The ability to distinguish between the author's opinions and the evidence is a form of procedural knowledge. Both must be explicitly taught. The following multiple choice question was given to me by a student and demonstrates the need to interpret and reflect on information:

Which of the following candidates for president would you vote for?
1. Someone who consults astrologers and has a mistress.
2. Someone who took drugs while in college and still drinks heavily during the day.
3. Someone who is a vegetarian, doesn't smoke, and is a war hero.

Folklore (also referred to as *historical fiction*), such as epics like the Iliad from world history, or historical tales like those of Paul Bunyan and Davy Crockett, are fiction or fictionalized versions of the lives of historical people and events. Because folklore is typically presented in the same kind of prose as history, children can misunderstand the difference if teachers are not careful to clarify the distinctions when using the two different forms of historical-based narratives. Both folklore prose and poems like "The Midnight Ride of Paul Revere" are very effective in engaging young students' interest in history and are a great way to support development of reading skills through social studies. Folklore also, but more directly, uses historical tales to promote a more virtuous and democratic view of the world because the stories resonate with students by reflecting the best and common elements of our humanity across time and cultures.

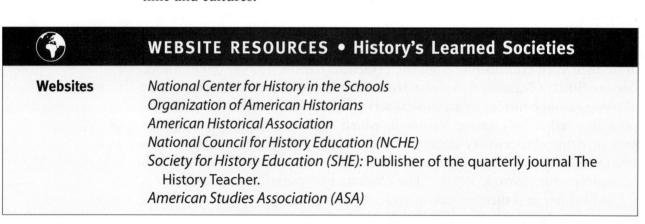

WEBSITE RESOURCES • History's Learned Societies

Websites
National Center for History in the Schools
Organization of American Historians
American Historical Association
National Council for History Education (NCHE)
Society for History Education (SHE): Publisher of the quarterly journal The History Teacher.
American Studies Association (ASA)

Standards for Historical Thinking

Children's study of history rests on knowledge of facts, names, dates, and places. In addition, real historical understanding requires students to engage in historical thinking: to raise questions and to marshal evidence in support of their answers; to read historical narratives and fiction; to consult historical documents, journals, diaries, artifacts, historic sites, and other records from the past; and to do so imaginatively—taking into account the time and places in which these

records were created and comparing the multiple points of view of those on the scene at the time.

National History Standards, (1996)

The National Center for History in the Schools standards were developed in 1996 with funding from the National Endowment for the Humanities and the U.S. Department of Education. Whereas there is little debate about the deficiencies in student knowledge of history (Lapp et al., 2002), there is considerable debate about the ideological perspectives of the recommended content (see ERIC Online ED 477893, *Whose History? The Struggle for National Standards in American Classrooms*, 2002), and there does not appear to be a movement at this time toward their uniform adoption (Stern, 2003). Nevertheless, these standards offer an array of information knowledge and procedural knowledge that can be helpful to teachers of social studies. The following excerpt from Chapter 2, "Historical Thinking," was selected because it is oriented toward procedural knowledge. Even if your state or the federal government never adopts a required set of information of knowledge by grade level, whatever subject matter you select, your goal is to develop procedural knowledge!

Standards for Historical Thinking

STANDARD 1. CHRONOLOGICAL THINKING

    A. Distinguish between past, present, and future.

    B. Identify the temporal structure of a historical narrative or story.

    C. Establish temporal order in constructing student's own historical narratives.

    D. Measure and calculate calendar time.

    E. Interpret data presented in timelines.

    F. Create timelines.

    G. Explain change and continuity over time.

STANDARD 2. HISTORICAL COMPREHENSION

    A. Identify the author and source of the historical document or narrative.

    B. Reconstruct the literal meaning of a historical passage.

    C. Identify the central questions(s) the historical narrative addresses.

    D. Read historical narrative imaginatively.

    E. Appreciate historical perspectives.

F. Draw upon data in historical maps.

G. Draw upon visual and mathematical data presented in graphs.

H. Draw upon the visual data presented in photographs, paintings, cartoons, and architectural drawings.

STANDARD 3. HISTORICAL ANALYSIS AND INTERPRETATIONS

A. Formulate questions to focus their inquiry or analysis.

B. Compare and contrast differing sets of ideas, values, personalities, behaviors, and institutions.

C. Analyze historical fiction.

D. Distinguish between fact and fiction.

E. Compare different stories about a historical figure, era, or event.

F. Analyze illustrations in historical stories.

G. Consider multiple perspectives.

H. Explain causes in analyzing historical actions.

I. Challenge arguments of historic inevitability.

J. Hypothesize influences of the past.

STANDARD 4. HISTORICAL RESEARCH CAPABILITIES

A. Formulate historical questions.

B. Obtain historical data.

C. Interrogate historical data.

D. Marshal needed knowledge of the time and place, and construct a story, explanations, or historic narrative.

STANDARD 5. HISTORICAL ISSUES—ANALYSIS AND DECISION MAKING

A. Identify problems and dilemmas in the past.

B. Analyze the interests and values of the various people involved.

C. Identify causes of the problem or dilemma.

D. Propose alternative choices for addressing the problem.

E. Formulate a position or course of action on an issue.

F. Identify the solution chosen.

G. Evaluate the consequences of a decision.

Using Reading 2, 7, or 12 from the Premium Website as the basis for a lesson plan topic, can you identify one or more of the standards for historical thinking?

What Should Elementary Students Know?

Learning to think about history as a creation of an author is essential. Historians weave stories by making organizational and interpretive choices that they think best explain the historical circumstances, and their organization and interpretation affect our perceptions of events. Some children (and adults, for that matter) tend to think of history as antiseptic and devoid of interpretations. But even when historians do not intend to inject ideology, there are also hazards for consumers of history. Following are the most common themes, interpretations, and hazards found in history.

> *World history is a court of judgment.*
>
> Georg Wilhelm Friedrich Hegel

Organizing Themes for History

The major interpretations of history are made accessible to elementary children by different organizing themes using resources of historians, images, diaries, primary documents, travel logs, secondhand accounts, maps, biographies, anecdotal information, oral reports, and other history accounts. The organizing themes are:

- **Themes:** transportation, growth of democracy, scientific advancements
- **Periods:** American Revolution, Greek civilization, the 1960s
- **Places:** local history, Lexington and Concord, cities, countries, regions
- **Movements:** woman suffrage, civil rights, revolutions
- **Notable figures:** George Washington, Cleopatra, Caesar, Alexander the Great
- **Events:** Gettysburg Address, bombing of Pearl Harbor
- **Technological advancements:** wheel, movable type, combustion engine, computer
- **Topics:** history of baseball, the navy, sailing ships, immigration, Native American history, slavery

Teacher's Tip

Today in History can be used to create a bulletin board and also can be tied into students' birthdays. This item on the History Channel Website allows you to get a list of images and narratives about what happened on a particular day.

For an elementary school teacher, these themes represent a way of organizing a history lesson that may be different from that which appears in your basal textbook. As an example, for lower elementary you might pick 20 notable figures in history or 20 great inventions that changed the world. You could model how to research the figure or invention and then have students make presentations about one of the figures or inventions that you have assigned to each student.

Major Interpretations of History

There are a number of fundamental ways in which history can be interpreted. Using our preceding example, you could focus your introduction or debriefings using the following "great figures" concept for your notable figures lesson and the "great challenges" concept as the precipitating events that lead to new inventions.

- **Great figures** emphasizes the impact of individuals on history. The approach is frequently attributed to Plutarch (45–125 C.E.), who chronicled the lives of well-known Romans and the roles they played in Roman civilization.
- **Great challenges** focuses on the rise and fall of great civilizations based on their responses to new ideas or technology. Western Roman civilization and the Eastern Byzantine response to Christianity are examples of this interpretation. British historian Arnold Toynbee (1889–1975) is credited with developing this perspective.
- **Irresistible forces** propose that ideas can become movements that eventually overcome prevailing institutions. The civil rights movement of the 1960s or the Muslim sweep of the Arab world are examples. Herbert Spencer (1820–1895) applied Darwin's theory of evolution to societies, showing how they evolved through internal and external conflict. He theorized that the groups and societies that adapt the best lead in the development of humankind.
- **Dialectical determinism** proposes that an old idea (*thesis*) will be countered by a new idea (*antithesis*), and that out of the conflict will come new ideas that are a *synthesis*. The German philosopher Georg Wilhelm Friedrich Hegel (1770–1831) developed this interpretation, and Karl Marx (1818–1893) applied it as material dialectic, proposing that history is primarily a struggle between economic classes.
- **Geographical determinism** emphasizes the role of geography in history. The influence of the westward movement in the United States on the adventurous bent of the U.S. psyche, the different development of commerce and industry on the African continent because of lack of harbors and navigable rivers compared to the Americas, and England's development as a sea power are examples of this theory. Frederick Jackson Turner's (1861–1932) frontier thesis serves as the basis for looking at the role of geography in shaping history.

History's Hazards

History requires interpretation and "perspective taking" (Dulberg, 2002). The following are some hazards that you need to help children understand and use.

- **Inference** and **bias determination** is the ability to read (or hear) critically and with skepticism. Children should be presented with multiple versions of the same events and asked to write histories as a way to reveal and examine their own biases.
- **Multiple valid interpretations** require us to accept multiple opinions as legitimate perspectives even though we may disagree and prefer our own or another perspective.

Using the Core Knowledge Elementary Social Studies Textbook Reading 21 or 25 as the basis for a lesson plan topic, can you identify one or more of the organizing themes of history and apply one of the major interpretations of history?

- **Present-mindedness** is the inability to put information in perspective. In the senior year of high school, we think the high school prom and graduation are the most important events in our lives, and we tend to feel the same way at university graduation and marriage. At age 60, we reflect on those events with greater objectivity and often recognize that we were caught up in the times. Children can be asked to write their own histories or chronologies and to rank events and predict what future events might be more important.

- **Historical projection** is the shortcoming of judging historical events by today's standards because we lack the skill of perspective taking—that is, seeing events as the people in their time and place saw them (Barton, 1997b). *Historical empathy* is the opposite of historical projection, and is the ability to view the world as it was seen by the people in the past without imposing today's values on the past (Yilmax, 2007). This problem plagues adults as well as children. As an example, historian Joan Hoff Wilson (1976) states in a U.S. history textbook that "the American Revolution produced no significant benefits for American women" (p. 387). However, there is considerable evidence that the founders' beliefs regarding women's constitutional rights were advanced for their time. A number of changes were introduced in the United States at the end of the revolution that advanced women's rights beyond those of European countries. Women were given the right to inherit, property could be subdivided to provide for inheritance to the spouse instead of being left only to the first-born male (Salmon, 1986), and the divorce laws were liberalized for the benefit of women (Basch, 1995). One can only wonder what historians of the future will write about us if they were to apply their values, norms, and standards to our time.

- **Multiple causation** is the principle that there is almost never a single cause of an event. Edward Gibbon (1734–1798), the author of the famous Decline and *Fall of the Roman Empire*, conceptualized historical changes as having three primary causes: technological improvements; economic, legal, and political development; and cultural achievements. As a bridge to a historical event, children can be asked to identify multiple causes, beyond the amount of time spent studying, of why one student does well on a test and another does not.

> **Teacher's Tip**
>
> Political correctness can be a hazard as seen in this example: "Jefferson Elementary School in Berkeley favored renaming the school Sequoia Elementary because Jefferson owned hundreds of slaves. Under Chief Sequoia, the Cherokee nation owned more than 1,500 black slaves" (Will, 2005).

> **Teacher's Tip**
>
> Oral histories are excellent tools to teach children about history. Children can be asked to collect stories about historical events from grandparents, parents, and relatives and to find differences in interpretations and emphasis.

Teacher's Tip

For an excellent example of teaching students to think like an historian, in Social Studies and the Young Learner you can find tips and a lesson plan in the article, "Teaching the Mystery of History" (Hicks et al., 2004).

History Lesson Plan Ideas and Resources

The following subdivisions of history are suggested as starting points for teachers in developing a topic for a lesson plan. They would probably be found in most states' standards.

To create a lesson plan, you would integrate one or more of the standards for historical thinking, one of the organizing themes of history, and apply one of the major interpretations of history to cover a topic drawn from your content standards for U.S. history.

Calendar and Chronology

Ideas for lesson plans: Present calendar time, including how to tell time, days, weeks, months, seasons, years, and religious and secular holidays; history of the calendar; seasons' relationships to holidays; chronology of periods in world history and U.S. history; family history; and holiday customs of different cultures.

WEBSITE RESOURCES • Calendar and Chronology	
Websites	*Everything You Ever Wanted to Know about Calendars, Time, etc.* *World History Timeline with clickable people events, and maps* *A World Time Zone Map* *Links to Over 200 Timelines*
YouTube	*International Dateline and Time zones*
Sample High-Quality Internet Lessons or Activities	
Lower Elementary	GEM How Old Is Old: Students use decimeter squares to measure their lifespan and create a metric-based timeline going back to ancient Egypt.
Upper Elementary	GEM A Date to Remember: Students create a personal journal with special events and dates.

U.S. History

Ideas for lesson plans: Topics that can be explored include significant lives and contributions (folklore and histories) of U.S. figures (George Washington, Sacagawea, Betsy Ross, Eleanor Roosevelt), time periods (discovery, colonization), events (Boston Tea Party, Appomattox), conflicts (wars, politics, government), and documents (Declaration of Independence, Federalist papers).

WEBSITE RESOURCES • U.S. History	
Websites	*World Wide Virtual Library: U.S. History* *Gateway to Historical Sites* *Gateway to the U.S. Presidents* *Gateway to U.S. Documents* *America's Story:* Interactive information for kids *Songs to Learn History*
YouTube	*Paul Revere's ride, a reenactment*
Sample High-Quality Internet Lessons or Activities	
Lower Elementary	*Edsitement* If You Were a Pioneer on the Oregon Trail: After creating, as a class, oral stories about contemporary cross-country journeys, students learn about the experiences of the emigrants who traveled on the Oregon Trail.
Upper Elementary	*Core Knowledge* Heroes of the Civil War Era: Students learn about heroism and the Civil War.

World History

Ideas for lesson plans: Significant lives and contributions of world figures (Alexander the Great, Mohammed, Joan of Arc, Hitler), time periods (Greek civilization, Renaissance), events (Battle of Hastings, Treaty of Paris), places (Seven Wonders of the World, Waterloo), and documents (Hammurabi's Code, Magna Carta).

WEBSITE RESOURCES • World History	
Websites	*Gateway to World History* *Best of History Websites* *Eyewitness to History* *History Channel* *Antiquity for Kids*
Sample High-Quality Internet Lessons or Activities	
Lower Elementary	*Core Knowledge* Ancient Greece: A Trip Back in Time: Students go back in time to ancient Greece
Upper Elementary	*Core Knowledge* The Mythical, Magical Middle Ages NOT! Students receive a comprehensive lesson on the Middle Ages.

History of Ideas and Technology

Ideas for lesson plans: Origin of ideas (alphabets, democracy); scientific advancements (penicillin, eyeglasses); and technology advancements (steam engine, air conditioning, automobile) by notable individuals including Plato, Galileo, Gutenberg, Alexander Graham Bell, Marie Curie, Florence Nightingale, and Albert Einstein and by civilizations or historical eras (Egyptian, Renaissance, Enlightenment).

	WEBSITE RESOURCES • Ideas and Technology
Video	*Learner.org* Historical Change First grade students in a bilingual class discover in groups using literature and realia the history of farming and its technology.
Websites	*Great Idea Find: For a history of inventions and timeline.* *Gateway to History of Science and Technology.* *Nobel Prize Winners* *National Inventor Hall of Fame by Inventor and Inventions* *History of Inventions* *African-American Inventors* *History of Women in Science*
Sample High-Quality Internet Lessons or Activities	
Lower Elementary	*GEM* Time Line Shuffle: Students are engaged in creating a timeline of significant technology achievements and scientific discoveries.
Upper Elementary	*Edsitement* Thomas Edison's Inventions in the 1900s and Today: From "New" to You! Students are familiarized with life and technology around 1900 in order to better understand how Edison influenced both.

History of the Arts and Literature

Ideas for lesson plans: The significance of art forms; the lives and contributions to the art of notable individuals like Bach, Michelangelo, and Harriet Beecher Stowe; and historically important literature like *William Tell, The Arabian Nights, Brer Rabbit, Aesop's Fables,* "Casey at the Bat," and the *Iliad.*

Websites	*Gateway to All Art*
	Gateway to Literary Classics
	Gateway to Music History
	Children's Classics
	Ancient Mythologies

Sample High-Quality Internet Lessons or Activities

Lower Elementary	*Core Knowledge* Astronomy, Mythology, and Music: Gustav Holst's The Planets Suite is used to teach Roman mythology and astronomy.
Upper Elementary	*Edsitement* Tales of King Arthur: Students learn about the legend of King Arthur as depicted in stories, poems, and artwork.

Assignment 18.1

INTASC Standards 1, 2, 3, 4, 5, 7, and 8

History Lesson Plan Statement of Goals

Download the "Lesson Plan Statement of Goals" (or use another model for lesson planning provided by your professor). Create a lesson plan statement of goals based on one of the elementary social studies textbook history chapters at the Premium Website and your state standard(s). Be prepared to turn in this typed assignment to your professor and to discuss your ideas in class. See Topic 50 for an assignment to create the class notes for this lesson.

Assignment 18.2

INTASC Standards 1, 2, 3, 4, 5, 7, and 8

History: Modify an Internet Lesson Plan

Conduct a site-specific search on the Internet using either the Gateway to Educational Materials (GEM), The National Endowment for the Humanities, or Core Knowledge to identify a lesson plan to teach based on one of the elementary social studies textbook history chapters at the Premium Website and your state standard(s). Print out the Internet lesson plan, complete a lesson plan statement of goals based on the lesson, and submit it with a typed paper that explains how the lesson and any modifications you make to the lesson would achieve your goals.

WEBSITE RESOURCES

Check the Premium Website, www.cengage.com/login, for additional links and links that are periodically updated to reflect new resources as they become available.

Economics, Standards, and Internet Resources

The field of economics appears as an ethical issue in Greek political philosophy. The question was, "What is a just price?" This is related to another key question in philosophy, "What is the purpose of life? Is it wealth? Is it happiness? Will one lead to the other?" These are character and citizenship education questions, and they cannot be divorced from economic considerations because basic needs must be met to develop our full potential as humans (Vanfossen, 2005).

	WEBSITE RESOURCES • Economics Learned Societies
Websites	*National Council on Economic Education*
	National Association of Economic Educators (NAEE)

The following economic standards might best be characterized as *conceptual*, as compared to more *skill-oriented* standards (Miller & Vanfossen, 2008). As examples, the National Council for the Social Studies (NCSS) themes (see Topic 17) use terms such as "explore," "give an example" and "compare," and the history standards' "historical thinking" (see Topic 18) (although there is a separate set of content standards) uses a skill orientation and a separate set of content recommendations. As you will soon recognize, each discipline has shaped its standards differently because the essence of each discipline is, at its core, different.

The National Economic Standards

Listed here are the 20 terms used to identify the national economic standards. Each one of these terms itself represents a number of concepts. A detailed explanation of these standards may be found at Economics America. At the same NCEE Website you can find exemplary lesson plans tied to each concept for each elementary grade level.

1. **Scarcity**: Productive resources are limited. Therefore, because people cannot have all the goods and services they want, they must choose some things and give up others. Students will be able to use this knowledge to identify what they gain and what they give up when they make choices.

2. **Marginal cost-benefit:** Effective decision making requires comparing the additional costs of alternatives with the additional benefits. Most choices involve doing a little more or a little less of something: Few choices are all-or-nothing decisions. Students will be able to use this knowledge to make effective decisions as consumers, producers, savers, investors, and citizens.

3. **Allocation of goods and services:** Different methods can be used to allocate goods and services. People acting individually or collectively through government must choose which methods to use to allocate different kinds of goods and services. Students will be able to use this knowledge to evaluate different methods of allocating goods and services, by comparing the benefits and costs of each method.

4. **Role of incentive:** People respond predictably to positive and negative incentives. Students will be able to use this knowledge to identify incentives that affect people's behavior and explain how incentives affect their own behavior.

5. **Gain from trade:** Voluntary exchange occurs only when all participating parties expect to gain. This is true for trade among individuals or organizations within a nation, and usually among individuals or organizations in different nations. Students will be able to use this knowledge to negotiate exchanges and identify the gains to themselves and others. They will be able to compare the benefits and costs of policies that alter trade barriers between nations, such as tariffs and quotas.

6. **Specialization and trade:** When individuals, regions, and nations specialize in what they can produce at the lowest cost and then trade with others, both production and consumption increase. Students will be able to use this knowledge to explain how they can benefit themselves and others by developing special skills and strengths.

7. **Market prices and quantities:** Markets exist when buyers and sellers interact. This interaction determines market prices and, therefore, allocates scarce goods and services. Students will be able to use this knowledge to identify markets in which they have participated as buyers and sellers and describe how the interaction of all buyers and sellers influences prices. They will also be able to predict how prices change when there is either a shortage or surplus of the product available.

8. **Role of price in market systems:** Prices send signals and provide incentives to buyers and sellers. When supply or demand changes, market prices adjust, affecting incentives. Students will be able to use this knowledge to predict how prices change when the number of buyers or sellers in a market

changes and to explain how the incentives facing individual buyers and sellers are affected.

9. **Role of competition:** Competition among sellers lowers costs and prices and encourages producers to produce more of what consumers are willing and able to buy. Competition among buyers increases prices and allocates goods and services to those people who are willing and able to pay the most for them. Students will be able to use this knowledge to explain how changes in the level of competition in different markets can affect them.

10. **Role of economic institutions:** Institutions evolve in market economies to help individuals and groups accomplish their goals. Banks, labor unions, corporations, legal systems, and not-for-profit organizations are examples of important institutions. A different kind of institution, clearly defined and enforced property rights, is essential to a market economy. Students will be able to use this knowledge to describe the roles of various economic institutions.

11. **Role of money:** Money makes it easier to trade, borrow, save, invest, and compare the value of goods and services. Students will be able to use this knowledge to explain how their lives would be more difficult in a world with no money, or in a world where money sharply lost its value.

12. **Role of interest rates:** Interest rates, adjusted for inflation, rise and fall to balance the amount saved with the amount borrowed, which affects the allocation of scarce resources between present and future uses. Students will be able to use this knowledge to explain situations in which they pay or receive interest and to describe how they would react to changes in interest rates if they were making or receiving interest payments.

13. **Role of resources in determining income:** Income for most people is determined by the market value of the productive resources they sell. What workers earn depends, primarily, on the market value of what they produce and how productive they are. Students will be able to use this knowledge to predict future earnings based on their career plans for education, training, and career options.

Teacher's Tip

For a lesson plan that combines a role-playing strategy and economics content see "Teaching about Saving and Investing in the Elementary and Middle School Grades" cited in Topic 46 at the Premium Website.

14. **Profit and entrepreneurship:** Entrepreneurs are people who take the risks of organizing productive resources to make goods and services. Profit is an important incentive that leads entrepreneurs to accept the risks of business failures. Students will be able to use this knowledge to identify the risks, returns, and other characteristics of entrepreneurship that bear on its attractiveness as a career.

15. **Growth:** Investment in factories, machinery, and new technology and in the health, education, and training of people can raise future standards of living. Students will be able to use this knowledge to predict the consequences of investment decisions made by individuals, businesses, and governments.

16. **Role of government:** There is an economic role for government in a market economy whenever the benefits of a government policy outweigh its costs. Governments often provide for national defense, address environmental

concerns, define and protect property rights, and attempt to make markets more competitive. Most government policies also redistribute income. Students will be able to use this knowledge to identify and evaluate the benefits and costs of alternative public policies, and assess who enjoys the benefits and who bears the costs.

17. **Using cost-benefit analysis to evaluate government programs:** Costs of government sometimes exceed benefits. This may occur because of incentives facing voters, government officials, and government employees; because of actions by special interest groups that can impose costs on the general public; or because social goals other than economic efficiency are being pursued. Students will be able to use this knowledge to identify some public policies that may cost more than the benefits they generate, and explain why the policies exist.

18. **Macroeconomic—income, employment, prices:** A nation's overall levels of income, employment, and prices are determined by the interaction of spending and production decisions made by all households, firms, government agencies, and others in the economy. Students will be able to use this knowledge to interpret media reports about current economic conditions and explain how these conditions can influence decisions made by consumers, producers, and government policymakers.

19. **Unemployment and inflation:** Unemployment imposes costs on individuals and nations. Unexpected inflation imposes costs on many people and benefits some others because it arbitrarily redistributes purchasing power. Inflation can reduce the rate of growth of national living standards because individuals and organizations use resources to protect themselves against the uncertainty of future prices. Students will be able to use this knowledge to make informed decisions by anticipating the consequences of inflation and unemployment.

20. **Monetary and fiscal policy:** Federal government budgetary policy and the Federal Reserve System's monetary policy influence the overall levels of employment, output, and prices. Students will be able to use this knowledge to anticipate the impact of federal government and Federal Reserve System macroeconomic policy decisions on themselves and others.

Used with permission. From *Voluntary National Content Standard in Economics*, Copyright © 1997, National Council on Economic Education, New York. All rights reserved. For more information on the National Council on Economic Education, please visit www.ncee.net or call 1-800-338-1192.

What Should Elementary Students Know?

Because we live communally on a planet with finite resources, the two most fundamental problems of economics are **scarcity** and **distribution of resources**. Or, if put another way, if all things were abundant and available to everyone, there would be little need for economic decisions.

Unit Four Social Studies Disciplines, Standards and Internet Resources

The United States has many types of resources in abundance compared to other nations. Bangladesh has far fewer resources and is one of the poorest countries on the planet. The tension produced by limited resources combined with worldwide population demographics, nations and geographic boundaries and a global economy has led to both conflict and strategies to reconcile differential access to finite natural resources. Our growing understanding of human potential and the effect of wealth on health and education returns civilized people to the original question: "What is fair?"

> Can you envision an economics lesson plan about fairness and personal responsibility for third grade students? What would it be?

It could be argued that crime and poverty would not exist if resources were unlimited and readily available. We use the term *scarcity* to refer to resources that are limited and *distribution of resources* as the process by which cultures decide how to develop and allocate the scarce resources. As a consequence, every nation has an economic system. Some economic systems, such as bartering, are simple; others, like the U.S. system or the global economy, are highly complex.

Economics is the study of money and why it is good.

Woody Allen

Historically, wars, trade, and treaties determined how resources would be allocated. Much of economics since Adam Smith's (1723–1790) landmark book, *An Inquiry into the Nature and Causes of the Wealth of Nations,* (published in 1776) has focused on a debate about the role of government in economic affairs and the best or optimal economic approach to providing adequate opportunity for human potential to be realized and ensuring sufficient redistribution of wealth to minimize class struggles. The movements from 18th-century **mercantilism** to **laissez-faire policies** and from John Stuart Mill's proposals for worker education and taxation to Karl Marx's call for an international workers' revolution are examples of approaches to scarcity, redistribution of wealth, and the role of government.

What is the appropriate role of government in regulation, ownership, and distribution of resources? The competing economic systems of socialism and capitalism are based on differing beliefs about how to increase and promote human initiative, develop natural resources, and allocate products and scarce resources. In both systems, government can play a greater or lesser role in planning and controlling national economies.

In *General Theory of Employment, Interest, and Money* (1936), John Maynard Keynes (1883–1946) was the first economist to explain the complex cycles of recession, inflation, and unemployment. Keynes proposed an important but limited role for government in the world economy. The U.S. free-enterprise system is a relatively unplanned and unregulated capitalist system that promotes private ownership of property and production based on consumer demand. By comparison, the typical socialist system has traditionally had a centrally planned economy with few or no private property rights, and the government determined what, how much, and when products would be produced. The U.S. economy is not a pure free-enterprise system; it promotes redistribution of wealth through direct government policy (taxes, free public education), tax exemption of charitable organizations (churches and nonprofits), and individual altruism (tax deductions for gifts to charity). China and Russia are both moving from unsuccessful highly planned socialist economies to a more capitalist system.

Elementary school students typically begin their introduction to economic concepts through what is commonly referred to as "needs and wants." In its purest sense, *needs and wants* is a character education lesson promoting self-control. Classification of producers and consumers, money, cost, and poverty and wealth are introduced at varying degrees of sophistication during the elementary school experience. Consumer education is a significant part of elementary economics education and often includes simulations of purchasing options and assessment of advertisements, banking, credit cards, and the like.

Economic Lesson Plan Ideas and Resources

The following subdivisions of economics are suggested as starting points for teachers in developing a topic for a lesson plan. They are probably found in most states' standards.

General Economic Concepts

Ideas for lesson plans: Classification of needs and wants (toys, food), goods and services (clothing, hotels), and resources (land, electricity) using local and everyday examples; simulations of barter and payments (trade toys, buy toys); and historical and contemporary presentation of examples of poverty (homeless children, condemned housing) and recession (Great Depression).

	WEBSITE RESOURCES • Economic Concepts
Video	*Learner.Org* Making Bread: Has kindergarten students learning production concepts using an assembly line to make bread.
Website	*National Council on Economic Education* Guide to concepts by grade level.
TeacherTube	*Using Play Dough to Teach Economics Concepts:* An elementary school class simulates supply and demand and opportunity cost.

Lesson plans	*Economic Education Web* Plans based on the national standards. *NCEE* Plans based on the national standards. *James Madison University* Includes plans based on 32 children's books.
Sample High-Quality Internet Lessons and Activities	
Lower Elementary	*EconEdlink* Build Your Community: Students learn about a variety of businesses and their service to a community. They will build a town selecting seven businesses they feel would be the most important to have in order to live in this community.
Upper Elementary	*EcEdWeb* Homer Price (The Doughnuts): Subjects include capital resources, increasing productivity, law of demand, and quantity of demand.

Houghton Mifflin Reading 4, "Needs and Wants," at the Premium Website offers a baseline of information (see Topic 25) for an economics lesson. Can you identify the national standards that this lesson would allow you to achieve with lower elementary students?

American Economic Institutions

Ideas for lesson plans: Simulations and calculations of taxes (tax forms), stock market activity (buy and track a stock), and bank interest earnings (calculate compound interest); historical and contemporary examples of unions (garment workers and Triangle Shirtwaist factory fire, child labor laws) and corporations (history of Ford Motor Company and Andrew Carnegie); work of local charities (United Way); history of money and coin collecting; and current news reports of federal spending on roads and schools.

	WEBSITE RESOURCES • American Economic Institutions
Websites	*U.S. Treasury Department Kids Page* *U.S. Mint* *American Currency Exhibit*
Game	*Stock Market Game*

Sample High-Quality Internet Lessons and Activities	
Lower Elementary	*EconEdlink* Big Banks, Piggy Banks: Students learn that financial institutions protect money from theft and other losses and they also pay interest on money.
Upper Elementary	*EconEdlink* You Can BANK on This! This is one of four lessons offered at this site that cover the scope of banking.

Houghton Mifflin Reading 9, "Using Money," at the Premium Website includes a baseline of information on money, savings, and budgets as well as a story-based lesson. How would you develop these topics and use the story as part of a lesson?

The Economics of Family and Work

Ideas for lesson plans: Classify and describe different types of workers in the community using parents' careers; promote the importance of education to career options; feature guest speakers on careers; promote characteristics of successful workers; focus on local economy with field trip to a manufacturer or a farm; create a family budget including income, loans, and expenses; simulate buying and selling with cash, credit cards, checking accounts, home loans, and auto loans using newspaper and online calculators; demonstrate lost opportunities when buying; introduce magazines like *Consumer Reports* for research; and explain government programs for unemployment, retraining, and food.

🌐 WEBSITE RESOURCES • Family and Work	
Websites	*Bureau of Engraving's Money Factory for Kids* *U.S. Mint Pocket Change* *IRS for Kids*
Sample High-Quality Internet Lessons or Activities	
Lower Elementary	*Core Knowledge* Money for Entrepreneurs: A mini-economy for the classroom in which students join the workforce.
Upper Elementary	*EconEdlink* What Do Other People Want To Be? Students graph people's job choices and identify which jobs would have the most competition.

World Economics

Ideas for lesson plans: Integrate countries' economies into geography for comparisons (United States, Sweden, and Bangladesh), classify countries by political and economic systems (United States, China, and Ethiopia), use current events to explain Third World wages and U.S. imports using production of a tennis shoe as an example, and compare the United States to other nations in terms of trade (imports and exports).

	WEBSITE RESOURCES • World Economics
Websites	*Capitalism* Includes an extensive justification of capitalism as the best system. *The CIA Factbook* Economic Profiles of All Countries *Calculations and Conversions of Money*
Games and Quizzes	*The World Bank*
Sample High-Quality Internet Lessons and Activities	
Lower Elementary	*Education World* And You Thought Gasoline Was Expensive! Students use newspaper ads and charts to compare prices of liquids.
Upper Elementary	*Gateway to Education Materials* Landopoly: A Decision Making Game: A simulation in which students consider both economic and environmental well-being in making land-use decisions.

Assignment 19.1

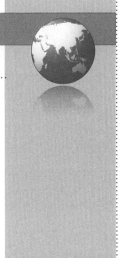

INTASC Standards 1, 2, 3, 4, 5, 7, and 8

Economics Lesson Plan: Teacher Created

Download the "Lesson Plan Statement of Goals" (or use another model for lesson planning provided by your professor). Create a lesson plan statement of goals based on one of the elementary social studies textbook economic chapters at the Premium Website and your state standard(s). Be prepared to turn in this typed assignment to your professor and to discuss your ideas in class. (See Topic 50 for an assignment to create the class notes for this lesson.)

Assignment 19.2

INTASC Standards 1, 2, 3, 4, 5, 7, and 8

Economics: Modify an Internet Lesson Plan

Select one of the 20 national standards and conduct a site-specific search on the Internet using either EconEdlink or EcEdWeb to identify a lesson plan to teach the standard. Print out the Internet lesson plan, complete a lesson plan statement of goals based on the lesson, and submit it with a typed paper that explains how the lesson and any modifications you would make to the lesson would achieve your goals. Be prepared to turn in this typed assignment to your professor and to discuss your ideas in class.

WEBSITE RESOURCES

All linked websites (designated by the green color) and those listed here are available as clickable links at the book's Premium Website, www.cengage.com/login, for ease of access. These links will be updated periodically to reflect changes and new resources as they become available.

Topic 20

Geography, Standards, and Internet Resources

Eratosthenes, a third century B.C. chief librarian at the famous Library of Alexandria, is credited as the first person to use the word "geography." Early humans probably developed mental maps to guide them in their search for life, food, and water. **Geography** is usually pursued or organized as a discipline in one of the following ways:

- **Regional geography** focuses on areas of Earth. Regions may be basically physical or human elements, or some combination of both and may vary in size from continents to small ecosystems.
- **Cultural geography** is similar to that of anthropology and sociology.
- **Physical geography** is closely aligned with geology.
- **Topical geography** focuses on subfields, such as political geography, economic geography, environmental geography, and urban geography.

Cartography is the art and science of making maps (see Topic 30). Regrettably, many people think of maps as the centerpiece of geography. While map interpretation and creation are important tools, the procedural knowledge of geography is extensive and integrates the other social studies fields, such as anthropology, economics, and sociology in unique ways. Understanding history requires an understanding of the locations of people and their resources (Thornton, 2007). At ERIC Online, ED 476500, *The Best of Both Worlds: Blending History and Geography in the K–12 Curriculum* (2003), you can find a number of examples of how to teach both history and geography at the same time. Geographic education helps elementary school children begin to understand their community, region, nation, and planet, and it usually begins with their home, school, and neighborhood in the expanding communities approach (see Topic 6).

> *"Geography is concerned with understanding the spatial dimension of human experience (space and place)."*
>
> *"History is concerned with understanding the temporal dimension of human experience (time and chronology)."*
>
> National Geography Standards

Websites	*National Council for Geographic Education (NCGE)*
	Association of American Geographers
	American Geographical Society

Of the social studies fields, geography may be the most explicit in terms of the procedural knowledge and information knowledge to be taught. Understanding the National Geography Standards and, especially, the themes can greatly facilitate teaching.

The 18 National Geography Standards

According to the NCGE, the geographically informed person should know and understand the following key ideas.

THE WORLD IN SPATIAL TERMS

Standard 1: How to use maps and other geographic representations, tools, and technologies to acquire, process, and report information.

Standard 2: How to use mental maps to organize information about people, places, and environments.

Standard 3: How to analyze the spatial organization of people, places, and environments on Earth's surface.

Teacher's Tip

Should students know the 50 states and capitals? Yes, but it's a question of how you do it! Do not make this a memorization activity. Students should learn about each state in depth. Learn 4 states a week, with an evaluation on Friday for the states of the week. This is a great activity for student research and presentations.

PLACES AND REGIONS

Standard 4: The physical and human characteristics of places.

Standard 5: That people create regions to interpret Earth's complexity.

Standard 6: How culture and experience influence people's perception of places and regions.

PHYSICAL SYSTEMS

Standard 7: The physical processes that shape the patterns of Earth's surface.

Standard 8: The characteristics and spatial distribution of ecosystems on Earth's surface.

HUMAN SYSTEMS

Standard 9: The characteristics, distribution, and migration of human populations on Earth's surface.

Standard 10: The characteristics, distributions, and complexity of Earth's cultural mosaics.

Standard 11: The patterns and networks of economic interdependence on Earth's surface.

Standard 12: The process, patterns, and functions of human settlement.

Standard 13: How forces of cooperation and conflict among people influence the division and control of Earth's surface.

ENVIRONMENT AND SOCIETY

Standard 14: How human actions modify the physical environment.

Standard 15: How physical systems affect human systems.

Standard 16: The changes that occur in the meaning, use, distribution, and importance of resources.

THE USES OF GEOGRAPHY

Standard 17: How to apply geography to interpret the past.

Standard 18: To apply geography to interpret the present and plan for the future.

For more detailed information on the National Geography Standards, go to NGCE.

Download Houghton Mifflin's Reading 8, "Our Country's Geography," from the Premium Website. Can you identify which of the standards are being met by the content covered in the reading?

What Should Elementary Students Know?

Before the national standards were developed, the Geographic Education National Implementation Project (1987) developed Five Geography Themes for teaching geography. The following elaboration on the themes by Richard Boehm and James Peterson (1994) offers an excellent combination of information knowledge and procedural knowledge.

The Five Geography Themes
Location
Position on the Earth's Surface

Location is the most basic of the fundamental themes. Every geographical feature has a unique location—its *global address*. A number of geographic factors give significance to a location. A rich geography lies beyond location, yet the concept of location is crucial to geographical understanding. Location is a basic prerequisite to higher-level geography, just as addition and subtraction are basic prerequisites to advanced mathematical understanding and competency.

Absolute Location

Absolute site has a fixed location on the planet. The most common way of identifying its location is by longitude and latitude coordinates.

Using Grids
Every site has a unique location on planet Earth (or in space). Location can be defined in relation to a reference grid, such as longitude and latitude, or perhaps an alphanumeric grid.

Different Types of Maps and Globes
Maps and globes can be used to find location, but they also show other geographic elements, such as pattern and process. Thematic maps provide the location and distribution of a factor: population, economic systems, climate zones, political divisions, and settlement patterns. Road maps and navigational charts show the routes for travel from one location to another.

Map Projections
Map projections are necessary to transfer information from a spherical Earth to a two-dimensional map sheet. The process of map projection often leads to distortion in distance (size), direction, or shape.

Earth-Sun Relations
The Earth's movement and position relative to the Sun is important in determining climate, seasons, and time zones. Key concepts include solstices, equinoxes, tilt of the axis, daily rotation, and annual revolution.

Relative Location

Relative location is a way of expressing a location in relation to another site. For example, Peoria, Illinois, is 125 miles southwest of Chicago; or Australia is in the Southern Hemisphere; or the Rocky Mountains are between Denver, Colorado, and Salt Lake City, Utah; or Canada is north of the United States.

Locations Have Geographical Explanations

Why are certain features or places located where they are? Relative location can be explained in terms of locational factors of history, economics, or other physical or human factors.

The Importance of a Location Can Change with History

Even though the absolute location has not changed, its relative importance may have increased or decreased because of its changing role in local, national, or world affairs.

Place

Physical and Human Characteristics

Location tells us *where*, and place tells us *what* is there. All places have a set of distinctive characteristics, the features that make them different from or similar to other places. Geographers often divide these characteristics into physical and human phenomena that are spatial and can be mapped. Characteristics of place often can be explained by the human and physical processes that define the geographic patterns of our planet. The geography of a place is a mosaic of factors, including the patterns and processes that define the three remaining fundamental themes: human-environmental relations, movement, and regions.

Physical Characteristics

Landforms

Landforms and the processes that shape the landscape: erosion; deposition by rivers, waves, glaciers, and wind; mountain building; volcanoes; earthquakes; and plate tectonics.

Climate

Patterns of temperature, humidity and rainfall, cells of air pressure, and wind and ocean circulation: the climate of a place affects landform processes, soils, water availability, vegetation, and animal life.

Soils

Natural fertility, suitability to agriculture types and crops, and relations to climate are all important factors of soil.

Natural Vegetation (Flora)

Type of environment: desert, tropical rainforest, tundra, or savanna, and the relationship to factors of soil and climate.

Animal Life (Fauna)
Relationship to environment, climate, soils, and vegetation.

Water
Water bodies, the hydrological cycle, availability of fresh water, areas of water deficit and surplus.

Human Characteristics

Religion
Human belief systems and their imprints on places.

Languages
Human communication and its imprint on places: names of places and features are often geographically descriptive in their original language.

Population Factors
Description, distributions, density, ethnicity, nationality, gender, age, and economic structures, rates of birth, death, and population growth.

Settlement Patterns
Urban, rural, suburban, wilderness areas, and the form of settlements.

Economic Activities
How people make a living, including agriculture, industry, forestry, fishing, and providing services, the imprint of an economic system on the landscape.

Human-Environmental Relations
Relationships Within Places

Spatial patterns and processes develop from the complex interactions and relationships that occur between humans and their physical environments. The geography of our planet is a dynamic system of interacting environmental factors, affected by both natural and human processes.

All environments offer geographical advantages and disadvantages as habitats for humans. How humans behave according to the advantages and limitations that an environment offers can greatly affect a landscape. Key subthemes include:

The Earth as an Environmental System

Interrelationships Between Humans and Environments
Physical and human environments are interconnected, woven together by their interactions and influences. Change in one almost certainly involves change in the other.

The Role of Technology

Humans apply technology to modify their environment. Modification of the environment occurs through agriculture, industry, settlement, lifestyles, and other forms of human activity.

The Problems of Technology

The application of technology can create problems as well as benefits. Air and water pollution, waste disposal, toxic materials.

Environmental Hazards

Humans often cope with hazardous environmental conditions. Environmental hazards can result from either natural or human factors, although both are usually involved to some extent. Examples may be natural, such as:

- Earthquakes, hurricanes, floods, volcanoes, and tsunamis;

or human induced, such as

- Nuclear disasters, oil spills, and heat pollution of water bodies.

Environmental Limits

All environments have limiting factors, such as availability of water, land, and other natural resources and management of environments (coastal zones and lands).

Adaptation

Humans have many ways of adapting to various environments. People in deserts live differently than people in humid tropics or the polar regions. The influence of the environment: ways of making a living, house types, ways of life, and the appearance of the human landscape.

Ethics and Values

Environmental protection or stewardship can conflict with economic development. Do we want bigger and faster cars or expanded industrial capability, or do we want clean air enough to pay the cost?

Different Cultural Attitudes about the Environment and Its Resources

Cultures often have different attitudes toward use and conservation of the environment. One use of the environment may be detrimental to other uses of the same resource.

Movement

Humans Interacting on the Earth

Regions and places are connected by movement or human interactions. Humans are increasing their levels of interaction in communication, travel, and foreign exchange. Technology has allowed us to shrink space and distance. People migrate and travel out of curiosity, of economic or social need, as a response to environmental change, or because they have been forced to move for other reasons. Physical processes are also expressions of movement, such as traveling weather patterns, ocean and wind currents, flowing water, plate tectonics, and volcanism.

Movement: Its Form and Stimulus

Transportation Modes
Private transportation (air, rail, bus, auto, other), public transportation (air, rail, bus, auto, other), and freight transportation (air, rail, truck, barge, ship, pipeline, other).

Movement in Everyday Life
Individual travel behavior, such as journey to work or school and shopping trips. Networks of communication, flows of ideas, and diffusion of culture. Spatial organization of society. Spatial efficiency within market areas in the public and private sectors.

History of Movement
Movement is an important theme in both history and geography. Migration, history of settlements, frontiers. Voyages (and expeditions) of discovery and exploration. Economic stimulus for movements: Economic factors can often stimulate or influence movement. Colonization, mercantilism, current migrations.

Energy and Mass-Induced Movements
Movements associated with the hydrologic cycle (including weather, wind, and ocean currents); tectonic movements (including folding, faulting, and warping); movements associated with volcanism; mass movements, such as landslides and soil creep; and movements within ecosystems.

Global Interdependence

The economies of the world are interrelated, and nations depend on each other for the following.

Movement of Goods, Services, and Ideas
Where do raw materials come from, where are they shipped to? Where do certain products (technologies, services, or ideas) come from? Why?

Foreign Trade
Trade partner countries, tariffs, hinterlands, ports.

Common Markets
Shared labor, markets, production facilities.

Models of Human Interaction

These simplifications help us analyze how humans interact over space and make rational predictions for how similar interactions will occur in the future. Examples include gravity models interactions, based on the size of places and distance, central place theory size and spacing of urban areas, and the relationship of cities to the surrounding region (hinterlands or trade areas).

Regions
How They Form and Change

Regions are geographical tools. They are mental constructs designed to help us understand and organize the spatial characteristics of our planet. Regions may be larger than a continent or smaller than your neighborhood.

Regions can have sharp boundaries that are well defined (such as a state, e.g., California or Illinois), or may have gradational or indistinct boundaries (such as the Pacific Basin, the Great Plains, Silicon Valley, or the Kalahari Desert).

Many regions are familiar to us because of television or the newspapers, or because they are related to other subjects that we study. For the geographer, regions represent a core element of the discipline and are of fundamental importance.

We define our regions by stating criteria and then drawing boundaries. Regions may be based upon crops, types of agriculture, climate, landforms, vegetation, political boundaries, soils, religions, languages, cultures, and economic characteristics. Subthemes include the following.

Uniform Region

Uniform regions are defined by some uniform cultural or physical characteristic. Examples include the Wheat Belt; Latin America; the Gulf-Atlantic Coastal Plain; the Bible Belt; the Sun Belt; New England; the Rocky Mountains; a country, county, parish, or township; and Cajun country in Louisiana.

Functional Region

A **functional region** has a focal point (commonly a city) and is the organized space surrounding that central location. Examples would be a metropolitan area, such as greater New York City, Chicago, Los Angeles, or the San Francisco Bay Area. The Bureau of the Census calls these functional regions

"Metropolitan Statistical Areas." Other functional regions include market areas served by a particular store and districts around schools.

Cultural Diversity

Understanding regions can lead to understanding human **cultural diversity**. Regions are an excellent means for illustrating the cultural differences and similarities between areas of the world and groups of people. Examining and analyzing the cultural characteristics of places and regions lead students to understand the rich diversity of people and the ways they live. Such understanding will lead to more compassionate and nonjudgmental attitudes toward other cultures. Students will also understand ways in which national, racial, or ethnic groups interact with each other in a local, national, or regional context.

Reprinted with permission of NCSS, Boehm, R.C., and Peterson, J.F. (1994).

Download Houghton Mifflin's Reading 3, "Our Earth." How would you develop this lesson using the five themes?

Geography Lesson Plan Ideas and Resources

The following subdivisions of geography are suggested as starting points for teachers when developing a topic for a lesson plan. They would probably be found in most states' standards.

To create a lesson plan, you would integrate one or more of the 18 geography standards and the five themes to cover a topic drawn from your state's content standards for geography.

Geography Skills and Concepts

Ideas for lesson plans: Create a bird's-eye scaled map of room at home and classroom; write directions for fire drill; create a map of the neighborhood; identify local natural resources and effects on economy; compare communities from area and nationally that are very different (Santa Fe and your community); participate in a local ecology project; compare population demographics for class (boys and girls, cultures) and community; calculate relative distance and driving distance; plan field trips to the local downtown, farm, landforms, and water bodies; compare transportation systems; and find directions with a compass.

Website	*National Geographic* Standards-related lessons and activities. *Enchanted Learning for Geography* A collection of geography pages, maps, printouts, flags, quizzes, and activities for students. *U.S. Census Bureau Statistics* *Blank Maps of Countries and States*
YouTube	*Geography Movie: Latitude and Longitude*
Lesson Plan	*National Geographic*
Sample High-Quality Internet Lessons or Activities	
Lower Elementary	*National Geographic* Which Direction Should I Go?: A lesson on directions.
Upper Elementary	*Core Knowledge* Where in the Latitude are You? A Longitude Here: Students learn map and globe terminology.

U.S. Geography

Ideas for lesson plans: Plan a trip across the United States; research and make presentations on selected cities, states, landmarks; find longitude and latitude of locations; create a map of the United States in the schoolyard; create a travel brochure for a destination; compare states by age, birthrate; and create maps of states.

Websites	*National Atlas of the United States* *Gateway to the 50 States* *U.S. Census Data 1790–1960* *Library of Congress* Has a map collection from 1500 to 2000. *Scott Foresman Interactive website for kids.*
YouTube	*US Geography, Regions and States*
Sample High-Quality Internet Lessons and Activities	

Lower Elementary	*National Geographic* Geography Skills and Your Town: Students focus on the five themes of geography by creating books, websites, or multimedia presentations showcasing the unique features of their town.
Upper Elementary	*National Geographic* Mission Geography: USA: Students research and learn about the culture, physical geography, and history of states in each region of the United States.

World Geography

Ideas for lesson plans: Compare climates; create a travel brochure; plan an itinerary to visit an international city and simulate a tour; determine times; have each student research and present a report on a country; compare countries based on education, size; have a virtual tour of the seven wonders of the world; calculate longitude and latitude; and compare historical maps.

WEBSITE RESOURCES • World Geography	
Websites	*University of Texas* Links to the field of geography and extensive collection of maps. *CIA Factbook* *National Geographic* *Google Earth* Download Google Earth for interactive satellite images. *2,500 Live Cameras from around the World* *Children's Geography Books*
YouTube	*Round the World Trip - in under 2 minutes "Tongue Twister"*
Maps	*Atlapedia's Map Collection* *Ancient Maps Gateway*
Sample High-Quality Internet Lessons and Activities	
Lower Elementary	*Core Knowledge* Where in the World is My Slipper?: This unit uses a variety of activities and literature to present the story of Cinderella from five different countries.
Upper Elementary	*Edsitement* On the Road with Marco Polo: Students become Marco Polo adventurers, following his route to and from China.

Assignment 20.1

INTASC Standards 1, 2, 3, 4, 5, 7, and 8

Geography Lesson Plan: Teacher Created

Download the "Lesson Plan Statement of Goals" (or use another model for lesson planning provided by your professor). Create a lesson plan statement of goals based on the content from one of the elementary social studies textbook geography chapters at the Premium Website and your state standard(s). Be prepared to turn in this typed assignment to your professor and to discuss your ideas in class. See Topic 50 for an assignment to create the class notes for this lesson.

Assignment 20.2

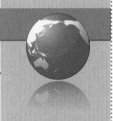

INTASC Standards 1, 2, 3, 4, 5, 7, and 8

Geography: Modify an Internet Lesson Plan

Go to National Geographic's lesson plans and select a standard and grade level. Print out the Internet lesson plan, complete a lesson plan statement of goals based on the lesson, and submit it with a typed paper that explains how the lesson and any modifications you would make to the lesson would achieve your goals.

All linked websites (designated by the green color) and those listed here are available as clickable links at the book's Premium Website, www.cengage.com/login, for ease of access. These links will be updated periodically to reflect changes and new resources as they become available.

Topic 21

Government, Standards, and Internet Resources

Government, at its core, is an attempt by humans to bring order to the societies they create. As humans evolved in culturally and geographically unique locations, different ideas and beliefs emerged about government's role and what form government should take. The study of government falls under the academic discipline of **political science**. Concepts related to citizenship and the formation of nation states should be reviewed in Topic 4 because citizenship and political science are intertwined.

🌐	**WEBSITE RESOURCES • Government and Citizenship** **Learned Societies**
Websites	*Center for Civic Education* *American Political Science Association*

Government Standards

The following standards were developed by the Center for Civic Education, a nonprofit, nonpartisan organization whose mission is to develop competent and responsible citizens committed to the fundamental values and principles essential to the preservation and improvement of U.S. constitutional democracy. Although these appear to be content standards, you should be able to identify the implicit procedural knowledge. Go to the Center for Civic Education for the complete national standards and strategies for teaching to them.

K–4 CONTENT STANDARDS

I.   What Is Government and What Should It Do?
  A.   What is government?
  B.   Where do people in government get the authority to make, apply, and enforce rules and laws and manage disputes about them?
  C.   Why is government necessary?
  D.   What are some of the most important things governments do?
  E.   What are the purposes of rules and laws?
  F.   How can you evaluate rules and laws?
  G.   What are the differences between limited and unlimited governments?
  H.   Why is it important to limit the power of government?

II.   What Are the Basic Values and Principles of American Democracy?
  A.   What are the most important values and principles of American democracy?
  B.   What are some important beliefs Americans have about themselves and their government?
  C.   Why is it important for Americans to share certain values, principles, and beliefs?
  D.   What are the benefits of diversity in the United States?
  E.   How should conflicts about diversity be prevented or managed?
  F.   How can people work together to promote the values and principles of American democracy?

III.   How Does the Government Established by the Constitution Embody the Purposes, Values, and Principles of American Democracy?
  A.   What is the United States Constitution and why is it important?
  B.   What does the national government do and how does it protect individual rights and promote the common good?
  C.   What are the major responsibilities of state governments?
  D.   What are the major responsibilities of local governments?
  E.   Who represents you in the legislative and executive branches of your local, state, and national governments?

IV.   What Is the Relationship of the United States to Other Nations and to World Affairs?
  A.   How is the world divided into nations?
  B.   How do nations interact with one another?

V.   What Are the Roles of the Citizen in American Democracy?
  A.   What does it mean to be a citizen of the United States?
  B.   How does a person become a citizen?
  C.   What are important rights in the United States?
  D.   What are important responsibilities of Americans?
  E.   What dispositions or traits of character are important to the preservation and improvement of American democracy?
  F.   How can Americans participate in their government?
  G.   What is the importance of political leadership and public service?
  H.   How should Americans select leaders?

5–8 CONTENT STANDARDS

I. What Are Civic Life, Politics, and Government?
    A. What is civic life? What is politics? What is government? Why are government and politics necessary? What purposes should government serve?
    B. What are the essential characteristics of limited and unlimited government?
    C. What are the nature and purposes of constitutions?
    D. What are alternative ways of organizing constitutional governments?

II. What Are the Foundations of the American Political System?
    A. What is the American idea of constitutional government?
    B. What are the distinctive characteristics of American society?
    C. What is American political culture?
    D. What values and principles are basic to American constitutional democracy?

III. How Does the Government Established by the Constitution Embody the Purposes, Values, and Principles of American Democracy?
    A. How are power and responsibility distributed, shared, and limited in the government established by the United States Constitution?
    B. What does the national government do?
    C. How are state and local governments organized and what do they do?
    D. Who represents you in local, state, and national governments?
    E. What is the place of law in the American constitutional system?
    F. How does the American political system provide for choice and opportunities for participation?

IV. What Is the Relationship of the United States to Other Nations and to World Affairs?
    A. How is the world organized politically?
    B. How has the United States influenced other nations and how have other nations influenced American politics and society?

V. What Are the Roles of the Citizen in American Democracy?
    A. What is citizenship?
    B. What are the rights of citizens?
    C. What are the responsibilities of citizens?
    D. What dispositions or traits of character are important to the preservation and improvement of American constitutional democracy?

From "How can citizens take part in civic life?" Reprinted with permission. National Standards for Civics and Government, Copyright © 1994, Center for Civic Education, Calabasas, California.

Houghton Mifflin's Reading 16, "Citizenship and Democracy," offers a baseline of information on citizenship and democracy. Which of these standards could we achieve by developing this content into a lesson?

What Should Elementary Students Know?

People were first bound together in **societies** based on shared geography. As the regional culture developed, bonds expanded to include customs, language, dress, and the like. The method by which a society is ruled is **government**. The term "state" can be used to refer to one of the United States, but on the world stage it refers to a **sovereign** (meaning "autonomous") **state** with borders recognized by other nations. There are almost 200 sovereign states in the world, each with a recognized border and an autonomous government.

> It is an axiom in political science that unless a people are educated and enlightened it is idle to expect the continuance of civil liberty or the capacity for self-government.
>
> *Texas Declaration of Independence*

Plato and, most people are surprised to learn, the Founders of the United States were opposed to unqualified democracy. In the purest sense, **democracy** requires everyone to vote on every issue or proposal and, strictly speaking, the majority always rules. In a **direct democracy**, citizens vote directly for leaders and laws. Plato and the authors of the U.S. Constitution believed in **representative democracy**, in which representatives are expected to be well informed, protect the **rights of the minority** and not be easily swayed by passions or self-interest. Setting aside the practical problems of direct democracy in highly populated communities, this is why the U.S. president is elected by an electoral college and why the general population does not vote on referenda and propositions at the national level.

Countries may call themselves "democracies," but some do not meet the critical attributes of free elections and a system that ensures free speech and assembly, which are prerequisites to free elections. The purpose of **constitutional government** is to limit the powers of elected officials during their terms of office and to guarantee certain fundamental rights by subjecting everyone to a basic set of rules and procedures.

Students must learn about governments and their histories if they are to intelligently define their beliefs and turn those beliefs into a coherent ideology that they find fulfilling on a personal level. That comprehensive worldview is known as an **ideology**.

Ideology

The word *ideology* has its origins in the Greek language and refers to the study of ideas. There are two forms of ideology: personal and communal. Personal **ideology** refers to a single person's worldview. It is shaped by experiences, knowledge, ideas, beliefs, and one's psyche. **Communal ideology** refers to a society's way of thinking in its specific time and place.

Historical Perspective

The communal ideology of contemporary U.S. culture has its roots in the ideology of the 18th and 19th centuries. The founders of the U.S. used the ideology of "respect for the rule of law," "inalienable rights," "all men are created equal," and "government by consent of the people," derived from the philosophers of ancient Greece; the "Atlantic Tradition" philosophers, such as Locke and Rousseau; and Judeo-Christian beliefs to replace the feudal system ideological view of humanity. They originated a republic based on free enterprise, constitutional law, and democracy.

The citizens of Asian, African, Eastern European, and Middle Eastern nations have different ideological traditions, although there is little disagreement that a worldwide adoption of democratic ideology is the driving force in the ascent of humankind on the current world stage. As the peoples of the world have had increasing contact with one another, conflicts have arisen over ideologies as well as over resources. It is worth noting that almost all ideologies claim a belief in freedom and rule by the people. This was the case with the 20th-century ideologies of communism and fascism, which were adopted by some European nations, though neither their citizens nor the citizens of nations they conquered experienced what was the equivalent of democratic freedom or self-rule in the United States at that time. Today, nations that many U.S. citizens see as undemocratic, such as Iran, Syria, Cuba, and North Korea, can point to constitutions that claim freedom and rule by the people.

All cultures and societies are not equal at the same time in terms of fostering and protecting rights as part of their communal ideology. As an example, in 1860, U.S. culture was sharply divided on political and ideological grounds as it related to the issue of slavery. The U.S. Civil War finally ended slavery in the United States but only after other nations had outlawed it in their countries. Is it possible, however, to appreciate attributes of Southern culture in 1860 United States while opposing the ideological forces that promoted slavery. Making such distinctions is very important, particularly as U.S. citizens think of their relationship with Middle Eastern countries.

Slavery still exists in some countries today, but that does not mean that we cannot learn from other qualities of those countries. During the early medieval period in Europe many Arab cultures flourished, and they are credited with significant advancements in mathematics and science. Since the end of the Middle Ages, the intellectual and human rights advancements of Western civilization have been unparalleled, in spite of such atrocities as the treatment of the First Americans, the Inquisition in Spain, and the Holocaust in Europe. Differences in ideology among civilizations that come in contact with each other have been sources of conflict throughout human history and continue today.

Conflicts among ideologies and nations often result from the role of the state and from the environment that the government creates for the individual. Citizens of the United States generally believe that the U.S. concept of the relationship between the people and the state is superior to the rights and obligations found in the ideologies of communism, fascism, or religious fundamentalism. Governments with totalitarian regimes are thought by U.S. citizens to be undemocratic because they suppress what U.S. citizens consider to be basic rights. Government leaders like those in North Korea and Iran would argue that their form of democracy works for their people at this time in their place.

Ideology and Politics

Ideology (one's view of life) often reflects itself in one's political views, hence a *political ideology*. We most often associate the term "ideology" with political orientations like liberal and conservative, and in the United States they are ascribed to the Democratic and Republican parties, respectively.

You may consider yourself liberal on some issues and conservative on others, which is typical of many U.S. citizens.

The U.S. political system is based on democratic ideological principles and guarantees the right to personal ideological beliefs and the freedom to espouse those beliefs, but it limits the practice of certain cultural customs and actions that might conflict with the U.S. democratic ideology. For example, Mormons are not permitted to practice polygamy, and it is illegal to discriminate in housing and the workplace based on "race" or ethnicity. However, members of the Jewish or Muslim faith who are in prison are entitled to special meals because of their religion's dietary laws. Often, the limits of ideologies are determined by the United States' **independent judiciary**, which must balance the rights of individuals against the good of that state. The impartial U.S. judicial system (although not perfectly impartial) that is relatively devoid of corruption and cronyism is more uncommon in the world than most U.S. citizens realize and has brought a degree of stability to the society that is unprecedented in world history. Many believe U.S. citizens' respect for the rule of law and an independent judiciary will be recorded as two of the most notable accomplishments of U.S. civilization. The many cultural variations that we experience in people who are different from ourselves are accommodated by the daily goodwill exhibited by individuals whose idea of citizenship has been fostered by a universal public school system that leads them to tolerate, if not appreciate, what is different from their family and community experience. From the nation's inception, the founders promoted education as a way of ensuring a thriving democracy. Many of us believe that the lack of worldwide, broad-based public education that allows a free exchange of ideas and promotes civility remains the primary stumbling block to a more democratic world.

> *Any man who is under 30 and is not a liberal has no heart; any man who is over 30 and is not a conservative has no brains.*
>
> Winston Churchill

Do you think your students should know your political affiliation or ideology?

In what we perceive to be less democratic nations, religious traditions and ethnic or gender discrimination are allowed to supersede what U.S. citizens consider basic human rights. For example, Saudi Arabia requires females to be veiled in public, and a caste system still exists in India although it is a democratic state. Conversely, many people from other societies view the United States' "open" culture as decadent, wonder why we allow pornography and vulgarity in the name of free speech, or associate the disintegration of the traditional family with the women's liberation movement. Many derogatory observations about U.S. culture are legitimate; others are not. However, there is significant evidence that few people in the West would give up the intellectual, cultural, and economic advantages of Western civilization, and many in less culturally diverse and accepting regions of the world wish their own countries were more open and democratic. U.S. children should come to appreciate that today's unparalleled opportunities for personal, economic, and civic growth are uniquely available in the United States and other ideologically Western countries.

The goal for educators is to help students decide their own democratic, ideological perspective in a reflective and thoughtful way. Character traits important to a teacher's success are linked to his or her ideology. You can be optimistic or pessimistic, a Democrat or a Republican. **Skepticism** is a healthy, if not essential, quality trait that leads citizens to press for explanations and information so that they can make informed judgments. **Cynicism** can easily lead to apathy. It is a pessimistic view of the future. A teacher who is excessively cynical can destroy the optimism, energy, and enthusiasm needed by the next generation of citizens. Understanding the concepts and terms in this topic is crucial to modeling the civic dispositions we seek in children and adults.

A great many people think they are thinking when they are merely rearranging their prejudices.

William James

Government Lesson Plan Ideas and Resources

The following government topics can serve as the basis for lessons created by teachers.

Democracy is the recurrent suspicion that more than half of the people are right more than half of the time.

E. B. White

U.S. State and Local Government

Lesson plan ideas: Role-play significant speeches and events, learn and perform patriotic songs, create timeline of Amendments to the Constitution, hold mock elections, hold mock trials, consider school and classroom rules, study primary documents, review current events by using pictures without captions from the newspaper survey opinions on social issues (homelessness, crime), and use children's literature from National Council for the Social Studies booklists.

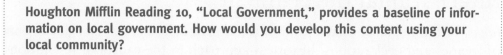

Houghton Mifflin Reading 10, "Local Government," provides a baseline of information on local government. How would you develop this content using your local community?

WEBSITE RESOURCES • U.S. and Local Government	
Video	*Learner.org* State Government: Fourth grade students learn about state government's three branches and how a bill becomes law.
YouTube	*Schoolhouse Rock* Three-Ring Government
Lesson plans	*American Heritage Education Foundation*
The National Archives	*Teaching with Primary Documents—Constitution Day*
Primary Documents	*Avalon* For primary documents like the Magna Carta.
Websites	*Political Science Resources on the Web* *Gateway to Current Political Goings Ons* *Public Agenda* For current issues. *Civics Online for Kids* *Bensguide to U.S. Government for Kids*
Puzzles	*Constitution Facts*
Music	*American Patriotic Songs* *Justice for Kids*
Sample High-Quality Internet Lessons or Activities	
Lower Elementary	*American Heritage Foundation* The Declaration of Independence: Students use a radio script strategy to discover the reasons for the Declaration of Independence.
Upper Elementary	*Edsitement* Declare the Causes: The Declaration of Independence: Students use primary documents and analysis to figure out why the colonists wrote the Declaration of Independence.

International Government

Ideas for lesson plans: Virtual tour of the United Nations, primary documents of treaties and declarations, historical approach to the causes of revolutions, rights around the world, classification and comparison of types of governments around the world, creation of profiles of countries and leaders, and review of cartoons about current events.

WEBSITE RESOURCES • International Government

Websites
World Fact Book
Gateway to International Political Science Resources
Amnesty International
Free Speech around the World
United Nations

Sample High-Quality Internet Lessons or Activities

Lower Elementary
GEM Raise the Flag for the European Union: Students create flag as an activity to understand the European Union.

Upper Elementary
National Geographic World Hunger: Students learn about world hunger.

Assignment 21.1

INTASC Standards 1, 2, 3, 4, 5, 7, and 8

Government Lesson Plan: Teacher Created
Download the "Lesson Plan Statement of Goals" (or use another model for lesson planning provided by your professor). Create a lesson plan statement of goals based on one of the elementary social studies textbook government or citizenship chapters at the books' Premium Website and your state standard(s). Be prepared to turn in this typed assignment to your professor and to discuss your ideas in class. See Topic 50 for an assignment to create the class notes for this lesson.

Assignment 21.2

INTASC Standards 1, 2, 3, 4, 5, 7, and 8

Government: Modify an Internet Lesson Plan

Conduct a site specific search on the Internet at either the Gateway to Educational Materials (GEM), the National Endowment for the Humanities, or Core Knowledge to identify a government or citizenship lesson plan, print out the Internet lesson plan, complete a lesson plan statement of goals based on the lesson, and submit it with a typed paper that explains how the lesson and any modifications you would make to the lesson would achieve your goals.

WEBSITE RESOURCES

All linked websites (designated by the green color) and those listed here are available as clickable links at the book's Premium Website, www.cengage.com/login, for ease of access. These links will be updated periodically to reflect changes and new resources as they become available.

Topic 22

Social Sciences, Topical Approaches, and Internet Resources

While history, economics, geography, and government have traditionally represented the core of social studies, the **social sciences** (anthropology, sociology, and psychology) are also part of social studies and play an essential role in students' character and citizenship education. In addition, there are topical approaches, such as environmental education and current events, which typically require use of more than one of the social studies for a more complete understanding.

 WEBSITE RESOURCES • Social Science Learned Societies

Websites	*American Anthropological Association*
	American Psychological Association
	American Sociological Association

The Social Sciences

The social sciences share modes of reasoning that are empirical in their orientation. They are based on facts, artifacts, statistics, and observations that are used to prove or develop hypotheses. Two historical periods, the **Renaissance** (1260–1700) and the **Enlightenment** (1700–1800), were the precursors of the social sciences' revolution. The reliance on observation and deductive reasoning as the basis of knowledge proposed in these eras stood in sharp contrast to the beliefs espoused by religious leaders during Europe's **Middle Ages**. As an example, nobles were believed to have been selected by God for their special status, and the poor and peasantry were in their proper place because they were not worthy of higher status. The development of nations, the rebirth of democratic notions of equality (some as old as Greek civilization), and the emergence of secular universities, capitalism, and industrialization made it possible for the social sciences to produce a broader understanding of the human condition and human potential. Being out of work, as an example, was seen not necessarily as caused by laziness but possibly by economic conditions; being uneducated was no longer synonymous with being unintelligent; and behaving abnormally was not blamed on possession by evil spirits.

The social sciences rely on **observation** of behaviors, sometimes through **data** and **surveys** to gather facts that are typically analyzed statistically to determine **norms**. **Normative information** is at the center of most social sciences and is commonly used to shape public opinion and public policy. Trends and statistical projections form the basis of expectations of **normative behavior**. When information demonstrates that some behaviors are outside the norm, social scientists want to know whether it occurred by chance and, if not, what influenced the behavior; whether those influences form a discernible and statistically valid pattern; and whether changes in the social system reduce the likelihood of occurrences. For example, we know that high school dropouts are likely to end up on welfare and that children from homes with only one parent are even more likely to do so. Organizations like Big Brothers and Big Sisters are a direct response to information about students who are at risk for dropping out of school and/or live in single-parent families.

Psychology focuses on the behavior and experiences of people as individuals. Wilhelm Wundt (1832–1920) established the first psychology laboratory in Germany, and William James (1842–1910) in the United States is credited with writing the first general psychology textbook, *Principles of Psychology*. An example of a lesson plan idea would be to lead a discussion on bullying, examining why some kids do and why it is wrong.

Sociological thinking can be found as far back in history in the writings of Confucius (circa 580 b.c.e.). The term "sociology" (coined by Auguste Comte, 1798–1857) focuses on the interactions of people with other humans and with their environments. Surveys, interviews, field studies, and observations are the tools sociologists typically use to gather the data from which they draw conclusions. Sociologists, for the most part, limit their investigations to current topics and issues. A lesson for an elementary classroom where students learn about sociology practices would be to have students conduct surveys of family members or their classmates regarding their TV viewing habits and then teach students how to create a graph of the results.

Cultural anthropology commonly overlaps with sociology because both disciplines focus on the interactions of human beings and their environments. Both have a scholarly interest in poverty, crime, gender, enculturation, values, belief systems, rituals, traditions, race, cultural stratification, population, and other topics. However, anthropologists investigate historical as well as contemporary populations—preliterate peoples, ancient civilizations (Greece), and contemporary cultures (aborigines, Western teenagers). At Gateway to Educational Materials (GEM), you can find the Native American Board Game, an activity in which students first examine the game Monopoly to learn about their own culture, and then create a game based on American Indian culture.

History is, strictly speaking, the study of questions; the study of answers belongs to anthropology and sociology.

W. H. Auden

Physical anthropology has its origins in **archeology**, which uses artifacts and fossils to trace and understand the history and culture of human beings. When anthropology is mentioned, Indiana Jones, the fictional archeologist from the movies, commonly comes to mind. Charles Darwin's 1859 treatise, *The Origin of Species*, served as a major impetus to the scientific investigation of the evolution of humankind by anthropologists. At the PBS Website, you can find "Be An Archeologist," an activity in which children simulate an archeologist's activity and reassemble an ancient clay pot.

What Should Elementary Students Know?

At the elementary school level, these social sciences are at the center of the expanding communities approach to scope and sequence (see Topic 6) whereby students start by learning about self, then about family, school, neighborhood, and community, all of which offer content for lessons focused on modes of reasoning in the social sciences. Often the social sciences are used to model for students how to collect and present facts and analyze the information to draw concepts and, finally, form beliefs. Current events and issues (see later in this topic) are often a great starting point for a lesson using the social sciences' modes of reasoning because the way anthropologists, sociologists, and psychologists study such matters results in the kind of objective, detached analysis that is a prerequisite to defining public policy choices.

Transpection is looking at one's own culture and, therefore, oneself through the eyes of those outside the culture. Creating opportunities for students to look at U.S. culture and their assumptions and behaviors as part of that culture through the eyes of someone from a Third World country, as an example, brings about the kind of information and concepts essential for objectivity and introspection. These dispositions are also essential for examining other cultures.

> *Anthropology is the science which tells us that people are the same the whole world over, except when they are different.*
>
> Nancy Banks-Smith

The following is a social science mode of reasoning strategy that can be used to compare peoples or communities. These key social science questions could be taught to children as questions that should be asked when examining contemporary or historical cultures and societies (Fraenkel, 1980).

The Key Social Science Questions
1. Who were the people being studied?
2. When did they live?
3. Where did they live?
4. What do artifacts tell us about them?
5. What kinds of work did they do and where did they do it?
6. What did they produce or create?
7. What did they do for recreation?
8. What are their family patterns?
9. How did they enculturate?
10. How did they govern and control their society?

11. What customs and beliefs did they hold?
12. What events, individuals, or ideas are they especially known for and how did these affect their lives?
13. What unique problems did they have?
14. How did they attempt to deal with these problems?

Assignment 22.1

INTASC Standard 1

The Nacirema

Visit the Nacirema, at the University of Missouri, or search the Internet for "Nacirema," and read and print out the brief history of the Nacirema people. Use the key social science questions to analyze the Nacirema people and be prepared to share your answers with the class and turn in the assignment to your professor.

WEBSITE RESOURCES • Social Sciences

Video	*Learner.org* Understanding Stereotypes: Fifth grade students use the history of the Negro Baseball League to understand stereotypes.
YouTube	*Go to YouTube and type in "sociology," "anthropology," or "psychology" for background knowledge podcasts on various topics.* *Sociology Virtual Library* *The World's Indigenous Peoples*
Lesson Plans	*Scholastic's Expanding Communities* *Do I Have Culture?*
Sample High-Quality Internet Lessons or Activities	
Lower Elementary	*National Geographic* Funny Business: Students learn about the nature of laughter across cultures and species. *(Arts Edge)* Native American Chants and Movement: Students use First Americans' culture to appreciate dance as part of culture.
Upper Elementary	*Edsitement* Australian Aboriginal Art and Storytelling: Students learn about Australia's indigenous people and the role of art and storytelling in cultures. *Edsitement GEM* Mapping Your Neighborhood: Students investigate the sociology of their neighborhood.

Topical Approaches

Topical approaches to social studies have been developed by individuals and groups who believe that knowledge of these fields should be part of the social studies curriculum. Most, if not all, of the topical approaches appeared in social studies education literature prior to the adoption of the ten National Council for the Social Studies (NCSS) themes, and they are now accommodated, to some degree, by the themes. Topical approaches provide a wealth of well-developed ideas, strategies, and resources that can aid a teacher in meeting state standards and the needs of students. In the following sections, we explore some of the most common topical approaches to teaching social studies.

Current Events

Current events lessons resonate with students because the topics are in the news and are an important part of their lives. Because current events are contemporaneous, ongoing, and often subject to opinion—if not controversy—teachers need to carefully consider their own beliefs as they craft lessons. Most current issues are best understood in a historical and/or cultural context, and the teacher may not know or have access to the kind of background information necessary for thoughtful development of the content. As an example, do you think violent crime is up or down in the last 10 years? Public Agenda is a nonprofit organization that makes an admirable effort to present objective information and multiple perspectives on public policy issues such as health care, poverty, crime, etc. From Public Agenda, you can learn that violent crime in the United States is down almost 40 percent! Public Agenda has charts, statistics, and opinion papers that you can use in class and as background information. In addition, the NCSS site is updated almost daily with tips and background information on teaching current events.

Similarly, how many of us knew Afghanistan's history, or even where it was located, before we became aware of its involvement in the terrorist attacks of September 11, 2001? In the absence of books to draw on for background information about current affairs, the Internet can be a particularly valuable resource. The World Factbook at the Central Intelligence Agency Website can answer many questions about Afghanistan, for example.

Traditional children's periodicals in the school library like *Junior Scholastic*, *Weekly Reader*, and *Young Citizen* are excellent resources for use in the elementary school classroom. The local newspaper and recorded broadcasts of local television news can be used in class as sources of information and as materials for various kinds of learning experiences.

Teachers have the unique opportunity to examine current events in a more thoughtful, informed, and deliberate way than commonly occurs in the media, community, or home. Classroom examination of statistics, opinions, causes and effects, timelines, and pros and cons through interviews, newscast simulations, analysis and discussion, debates, videotaped news broadcasts, trial simulations, and case studies can influence the way children begin to think about problems both in and out of school.

Current Issues Lesson Plan: Teacher Created

Download the "Lesson Plan Statement of Goals" (or use another model for lesson planning provided by your professor). Create a lesson plan statement of goals based on one of the topics at Public Agenda. Be prepared to turn in this typed assignment to your professor and to discuss your ideas in class. See Topic 50 for an additional assignment to create the class notes for this lesson.

Career Education

Career education is intended both to inform students about careers and about the skills and education needed to prepare for them and to inspire students to pursue careers that they may perceive as being beyond their reach. Many of the goals, ideas, and strategies of career education are woven into other topics in this book. Ideally, all children should have all career choices available to them by the end of high school, when they will typically be mature enough to begin to narrow down their own career choices. Not all children will choose careers that require postsecondary education, but at the elementary level we should provide the skills that will give them the choice. One reason career education is important at the elementary level is that by middle school students may be tracked or unknowingly opt out of the sequential math courses that are crucial to keeping all their career options open.

The tougher the job, the greater the reward.

George Allen

Employers have consistently cited poor attitudes; lack of self-confidence; lack of goals; poor motivation; lack of enthusiasm; lack of drive; little evidence of leadership potential; and inadequate reading, writing, and math skills as reasons they do not hire young people (Charner, 1988). The social studies curriculum is important to career education not only because it should explicitly provide opportunities for children to develop academic skills that will allow them to keep their career options open, but also because it can nurture habits that are needed to achieve career goals.

Career Education Best Practices

The following ideas should be helpful as you plan career education lessons.

It has become appallingly obvious that our technology has exceeded our humanity.

Albert Einstein

1. Expose students to different career paths and the academic and personal attributes needed to enter into those careers because it can be motivating.

2. Provide guest speakers and literature about different professions so that students can learn about unfamiliar professions.
3. Require challenging tasks that lead to the personal habits of dedication, persistence, and hard work so that students have more career options.
4. Focus on the essential social studies skills and procedural knowledge to place students in a position to attain careers and professions that they are introduced to by their teacher during social studies lessons.

Assignment 22.3

INTASC Standards 1, 2, 3, 4, 5, 7, and 8

Career Education: Modify an Internet Lesson Plan

Download the "Lesson Plan Statement of Goals" (or use another model for lesson planning provided by your professor). Using GEM, type "career" into the search box to locate a lesson plan on careers appropriate to elementary education and create a lesson plan statement of goals. Be prepared to turn in this typed assignment to your professor and to discuss your ideas in class. See Topic 50 for an assignment to create the class notes for this lesson.

Environmental Education

Environmental education is often considered a subset of global and geography education and can easily be combined with instruction in science. Environmental education is concerned with the health of the land, air, and water in the United States and around the globe. Debate among scientists and political leaders has left many citizens bewildered about air quality, global warming, water quality, and other issues. Statistical information may seem inconsistent, and predictions by authorities are often in conflict. Some advocacy groups may be providing data that are not objective.

Download Houghton Mifflin Reading 8, "Our Country's Geography," from the Premium Website and read Lesson 2, "Protecting the Land." How could you use this in a lesson?

The goal of environmental policy is to achieve a better environment. Resources are scarce, and society must be willing and able to pay the cost. For this reason, teachers are advised to pursue environmental education in an economic context; otherwise it is based on an unrealistic premise. **Tradeoffs** as well as **markets, incentives**, and **disincentives** are crucial concepts in environmental education. As an example, when students are organized to pick up trash left around the school, the *tradeoff* is staying in class to learn more mathematics. A second example involves electric cars. While electric cars have no emissions, the electrical plants needed to supply them with kilowatts do have emissions. The adverse impact from increased production and disposal of acid for batteries also needs to be part of the calculation. Saving the Amazon rain forest is, unfortunately, often an ideologically based lesson that does not consider competing market forces and tradeoffs. Many desperately poor people in developing nations perceive U.S. advocates of saving the rain forest as having already depleted many of their resources in pursuit of a higher living standard, a standard that they now propose to deny to inhabitants of other areas.

> *We must all hang together, or assuredly we shall all hang separately.*
>
> Benjamin Franklin

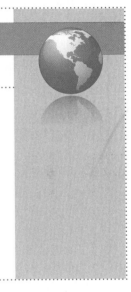

Assignment 22.4

INTASC Standards 1, 2, 3, 4, 5, 7, and 8

Environmental Education: Modify an Internet Lesson Plan

Download the "Lesson Plan Statement of Goals" (or use another model for lesson planning provided by your professor). Using the North American Association for Environmental Education, locate a lesson plan on environmental education appropriate to elementary education and create a lesson plan statement of goals. Be prepared to turn in this typed assignment to your professor and to discuss your ideas in class. See Topic 50 for an assignment to create the class notes for this lesson.

Law-Related Education

Law-related education often focuses on the U.S. legal system, the Constitution, and court cases. At the elementary level, teaching the reasons for laws is paramount, and law should be examined through grade-appropriate aspects of civic life like littering, street signage, lost and found objects, and dog leash laws as well as through analogies with school and classroom rules. Law-related education is part of citizenship education. The emphasis should be on concepts like duty, responsibility, and sacrifice of some individual rights for the good of the many. An introduction to the Constitution and Bill of Rights is commonly included. Role playing and simulations can be used to introduce students to court proceedings, legal terms, and players in the legal system.

A framework for law-related education was developed at the Institute for Law and Citizenship Education at Virginia Commonwealth University (McBee, 1994). The institute's framework presents four big ideas that should be part of law-related education in elementary school settings:

> *It may be true that the law cannot make a man love me. But it can keep him from lynching me, and I think that's pretty important.*
>
> Martin Luther King, Jr.

1. Power
2. Justice
3. Liberty
4. Equality

In addition, the following concepts can serve as a basis for lesson planning.

Sources and Concepts	Dispositions
1. Authority	1. Effective group participation
2. Origins of democracy	2. Apperception of others' perspectives
3. Constitution, Bill of Rights	3. Democratic problem solving
4. Laws	4. Fairness process
5. Contracts	5. Consideration of needs and circumstances
6. Civil rights	6. Compromise
7. Civil disobedience	7. Need to obey rules and laws
8. Community vs. individual needs and rights	8. Tolerance of disagreements
9. Rights of U.S. citizens	
10. Historical legal documents and cases	
11. Reasons and needs for laws	
12. Consequences	
13. Rights	
14. Rights of a child	
15. Majority vs. minority	
16. Rule making	
17. Rule breaking	
18. Comparative rules for home, school, community, and states	

Assignment 22.5

INTASC Standards 1, 2, 3, 4, 5, 7, and 8

Law Related Education: Modify an Internet Lesson Plan

Download the "Lesson Plan Statement of Goals" (or use another model for lesson planning provided by your professor). Conduct a general search for a lesson plan on the Constitution, Bill of Rights, law education, mock trials, and so on appropriate to elementary education and create a lesson plan statement of goals. Be prepared to turn in this typed assignment to your professor and to discuss your ideas in class. See Topic 50 for an assignment to create the class notes for this lesson.

Essay	**ERIC Online** *ED367848,* Smart Consumer Lesson Plans (1997): Has lessons related to consumer education *ED440044,* Infusing Functional Law into the Classroom (2000) *ED381482,* Living the Law by Learning the Law (1994) *ED409188,* Resources, People and the Planet: Lessons for a Sustainable Future (1996)
Websites	*EPA Environmental Education* *Center Earth Guide* *Global Schoolhouse*
Documents	*Landmark Supreme Court Decisions*
Lesson Plan	*American Bar Association's Law Day Planning Guide*
Games	*Law Focused Education, State of Texas*
	All linked websites (designated by the green color) and those listed here are available as clickable links at the book's Premium Website, www .cengage.com/login, for ease of access. These links will be updated periodically to reflect changes and new resources as they become available.

Unit Five

21st Century Literacy and Basic Skills in Social Studies

Topic 23

Reading Strategies for Social Studies

"Before you can walk, you have to crawl," is a common expression and the mantra that defines the essence of education at the elementary school level. This unit focuses on the basic skills necessary to build more sophisticated social studies concepts that are essential to the ideas inherent in citizenship and character education. Few would disagree that reading is at the center of basic skills.

There are numerous ways to approach teaching students how to comprehend social studies content and using social studies to improve students' reading skills. But the best practice in both cases is to incorporate reading into a comprehensive social studies lesson plan so that the reading material allows you to develop big ideas and procedural knowledge with your students.

Text Genres

Your students' ability to read is influenced by two broad **genres of text**:

- **Narrative text**, which is a significant portion of the elementary school language arts program, is used primarily to teach basic reading skills, and allows students to form general knowledge from fiction and non-fiction stories (Duke, Bennett-Armistead, & Roberts, 2003). Such narratives are "story driven" and usually chronologically organized. Stories, such as the "Three Little Pigs" fairy tale entice children into the joy of reading and can also be used in social studies for character education. This story genre with its plot, unknowns, character development, and intrigues provides a motivational element for young readers that cannot be easily achieved with the kind informational text found in typical social studies textbooks. However, for lower elementary social studies textbooks, one can find story-based approaches for social studies content as well. For an example of a social studies story-based reading passage on economics in a social studies textbook that could be *infused* (see Topic 7) into your language arts bloc or used to build a social studies lesson, download Houghton Mifflin Reading 9, "Using Money: Max Malone Makes a Million," from the Premium Website. Such stories in textbooks and children's books are an effective strategy for introducing children to social studies content.

- **Informational** (or expository) **text**, which is the traditional text structure used in books such as history or geography textbooks, is used to inform the reader about social studies content (Flood & Lapp, 1986; Hoyt, 2002; Yopp & Yopp, 2000; Hirsh, 2006). Science, mathematics, social studies, etc., each have different approaches to "laying out" their information in a textbook, and within social studies fields there are differences. As examples, history presents information, typically, chronologically, and geography textbooks often take regional approaches. The Core Knowledge series, Readings 21, 23, and 25 at the Premium Website offers excellent examples of comprehensive informational text at three grade levels.

A significant transition from narrative text to informational text takes place around fourth grade (Hart & Risley, 2003) due to textbooks shifting to a more traditional, informational text format. The new format requires a different reading approach that teachers at the lower elementary level must prepare their students for. Success in reading informational text relies more heavily on a rich vocabulary, fluency, and automaticity (see next topic). Motivation to read must shift from the intrinsic engagement with plot and character of narrative text, to one in which gaining knowledge for its own sake becomes a priority. Teachers can begin to use the social studies content found in textbooks to create a **baseline of information** as a prelude to an engaging lesson plan. The concept of a *baseline of information* is to require and hold students accountable for reading social studies textbook sections through in-class or homework activities prior to teaching about the subject and then **scaffolding** on top of the reading material though an engaging social studies lesson.

It can be argued that the kinds of social studies informational text found in too many elementary basal textbooks are isolated vignettes that inhibit the sustained development of social studies concepts by teachers (Palincsar & Duke, 2004; Duplass, 2007). As a result, both within and between grades students are not required to move through increasingly more complex procedural knowledge and information knowledge vocabulary and concepts in their social studies textbooks like the kind of building-block approach one sees in mathematics textbooks, as an example. The lack of such tiered reading materials is partly attributable to a nonexistent scope and sequence by grade level and believed to be one of the main reasons social studies is not perceived as having the same rigor as disciplines like mathematics and science (Duplass, 2008). It is also believed to contribute to reading comprehension scores stalling at fourth grade

Teacher's Tip

In addition to traditional textbooks, **primary documents** like diaries (see Houghton Mifflin Reading 12, "Conflicts Grow: Emma's Journal"), the Gettysburg Address (see Core Knowledge Reading 24), and an **artifact** like a **broadside** of a slave auction are also information text of another kind and enrich your lessons and engage students beyond traditional textbooks.

because students must have a command of social studies vocabulary that is tiered from week to week and year to year (Hirsch, 2006). Text should serve as a baseline of information for the teacher to wrap a lesson plan around in order to develop social studies knowledge (see Topic 25 for an example of how to scaffold instruction with a baseline of information).

Teaching Social Studies Reading Skills

The ability to independently analyze written information and form ideas and beliefs is a goal of reading instruction in social studies. Students need to be taught how to systematically question and interpret social studies text (Massey & Heafner, 2004). During the postreading activity (see Topic 26) the teacher should explore text material by using the following approach as a guide to develop students' social studies reading skills.

Close Reading refers to the ability to extract and construct meaning from text (Paul and Elder, 2006). Close reading consists of five levels that the teacher should focus on when teaching students how to read social studies content:

1. **Level 1: Paraphrasing** consists of paraphrasing the text sentence by sentence, paragraph by paragraph, passage by passage.
2. **Level 2: Explication** includes stating the main point, elaborating, drawing analogies, and citing additional examples.
3. **Level 3: Analyzing the logic** includes
   What is the author's purpose?
   What is the key question the author is trying to answer?
   What is the author's point of view?
   What are the author's assumptions?
   What are the implications?
   What information is the author using and is it accurate?
   What are the inferences?
   What are the concepts and generalizations?
4. **Level 4: Assessing the logic** requires a judgment about the text clarity, logic, significance, fairness, and relevance.
5. **Level 5: Speaking in the author's voice** involves having the students be able to dialogue as if she or he were the author. Could you explain it to others with the clarity of the author?

It is a wise man who only believes half of what he reads and hears. It is a genius who knows which half.

British comic Benny Hill

It is important to specifically select narrative passages to teach how to read social studies content just as you would select information knowledge on the American Revolution or local history for a lesson plan topic. A lesson with an announced purpose, such as, "Today we are going to learn how to figure out what an author is really telling us," is *explicit teaching* (described in Topic 8) of reading skills in social studies at its best.

The Four Key Criteria for Selecting Reading Material

The selection of passages for students to read should be based on at least two realities. First, in a year, it is highly unlikely that you will cover, much less have students read, the entire social studies book. Second, students will not retain facts over the long term, but they will retain concepts based on facts if they are allowed to construct them. And by tying the facts to concepts, they will more likely remember the fact examples you used.

With that in mind, there are four key questions to ask in deciding what social studies passage from your textbook the children should be expected to read.

1. Can a big idea or cultural literacy be developed with the content?
2. Can their reading and interpretations skills be enhanced?
3. Can other materials (Internet, CD-based encyclopedia, etc.) be used to enrich the textbook's content during the following lesson plan?
4. Can the content be made relevant to students' lives as part of a lesson plan?

Reading assignments should always be part of a lesson plan that includes instruction related to the passage.

Reading at Home and School

Students should be expected to read both at home and in school.

Homework Assignments

The practice of assigning social studies passages as homework fulfills two primary goals: (1) it develops students' independent reading skills, and (2) it makes instruction efficient, because rather than using classroom time, you make good use of their time out of class for an activity that students can complete on their own, at their own pace.

It is good practice to expect students to read grade-appropriate material before you develop the ideas associated with it. It is a commonsense approach to have students demonstrate that they have completed the assignment by answering basic factual questions either as *bell work* at the beginning of the school day or as part of a lesson, usually at the beginning (see Topic 40 for one approach to questioning that can support reading). The pre-reading options explained in the following section should precede a reading homework assignment.

Reading in Class

Reading during class provides an opportunity to develop students' ability to read social studies information using a strategy such as the aforementioned *close reading* approach and for the teacher to assess students' reading ability. In social studies, it is important for students to read during class as part of a planned lesson plan to teach social studies reading skills when you are first instructing them how to read narratives, maps, graphs, diagrams, charts, primary documents, statistics, and so on. Developing lesson plans focused on different types of social studies reading materials (text, a chart, primary document, etc.) is just as important as developing lesson plans around traditional topics such as the U.S. Civil War or the geography of the Southern Hemisphere. After students have been taught how to read text and such specialized materials as maps in a prereading activity, as an example, they can then be expected to read new material at home in anticipation of classroom instruction.

The Three Phases of Reading

Teacher's Tip

A **picture walk** is a prereading strategy in which the teacher promotes reading strategies by leading students through the pictures, text boxes, and charts that illustrate the reading passage.

The three phases of reading are **prereading**, **reading**, and **postreading** (adapted from Avery & Graves, 1997). Because the reading passage you plan to use should be choreographed into your lesson plan, these three phases would be part of the instructional sequence model (see Topic 8).

Prereading Options

One of the main goals of prereading is to prepare students for the reading. The "Okay, kids, open your books to page 73 and start reading" approach is not acceptable. You should motivate your students with an attention-getter, preview the reading to entice students, and then use one of the four strategies listed in Table 23.1 or the many others that can be found at websites like Read/Write/Think.

Reading Options

The reading strategies listed in Table 23.2 have relative advantages and disadvantages. A teacher should vary his or her approaches by using different options, although this author does not recommend *rotational* or "round-robin" reading due to its inefficiency and negative impact on weaker readers.

Of these reading strategies, how many have you experienced and what were your least desirable and desirable? Be able to explain why you feel the way you do.

Table 23.1   Prereading Options

Strategy	Considerations
Preteach Vocabulary	Assures knowledge of new terms. Terms and definitions can be placed on the chalkboard during in-class reading.
Preteach Concepts	Points student toward the key ideas. Can be particularly effective with a graphic organizer.
Promote Objectives	Focuses on what you want students to get out of the reading. Verbal questions or an Anticipation Guide are often used to focus on the expected outcomes.
Promote Reading Strategies	Can be used to highlight upcoming images or tables that are part of the reading. Gives students a heads-up to look for figurative, biased, covert, subtle, and emotional appeals.

Table 23.2   Reading Strategies

Strategy	Consideration
Reading as Homework *(Students read at home.)*	Develops independent reading skills. Requires students to focus on information knowledge. Is effective only if the teacher has an evaluation following the reading, either as bell work or as an assessment prior to instruction. The reading material must be at the appropriate reading level. Adapting strategies like the SQ3R method can improve comprehension prior to development of the content in the classroom.
Reading Aloud by the Teacher *(Teacher reads the content.)*	Models the joy and practice of reading. Should include teacher sharing of metacognition. The most straightforward approach to modeling metacognition is for the teacher to articulate his or her own thinking while reading a passage of text. This "talking-out-loud" approach explicitly teaches the underlying thinking process that one should use when reading. Failure to model metacognitive processes can result in students' failing to understand and acquire the full set of skills they need to become lifelong learners. Provides a model of correct pronunciation and how "good" reading sounds. Students do not practice reading; they just listen. Can be boring, so use short, interesting pieces.
Independent Silent Reading *(Students read a passage in silence.)*	Reading takes place in class, and the teacher can circulate to provide individual assistance to students with weaker reading skills. This strategy can be greatly enhanced by use of an Interactive Notebook, the SQ3R method or the marking up strategy (see postreading). Without an evaluation, the teacher does not know who is actually reading the material or what students' level of comprehension is, so this strategy should be paired with an activity to monitor comprehension.
Rotational or Round-Robin *(Each student reads a paragraph or passage aloud.)*	This strategy is the least efficient approach. Weaker readers often feel embarrassed; when weaker readers' turns come up, other students may appear irritated. Stronger readers are bored. Better to have reading in supervised small groups.

(Continued)

Table 23.2 (Continued)

Reading in Groups *(Each student reads a paragraph or passage aloud in a small group.)*	Heterogeneous groups of four allow everyone to read multiple paragraphs. Teacher can assign stronger readers to help weaker readers, or assign roles like reader, questioner, note taker, etc. Weaker readers are not as inhibited in smaller groups. Students can reflect and share ideas for reinforcement and uniformity of understanding. Teacher must circulate among groups.
Student-Teacher Shared Reading *(Teacher begins to read and then asks students to read; teacher reads and asks questions to ensure comprehension; or teacher assigns short sections to be read independently and guides the discussion.)*	Has similar shortcomings to rotational or round-robin reading, if not carefully choreographed. Questions can be interspersed to keep everyone attentive and to ensure a baseline of content knowledge.
Choral Reading *(All students read in unison.)*	Allows weaker readers to follow along in a large group with anonymity and little apprehension, but the teacher cannot assess individual reading ability and participation. Often students do not participate, and their minds wander.
Dramatic Reading	This is a powerful approach often used with passages and children's books in which there is tension in the story. Children learn the joy of reading and the powerful images that words create.
Reading Questions *(Created during group reading or individual silent reading; students are required to create and write questions they have as they are reading. These questions become part of a postreading activity.)*	Encourages students to think about their thinking while they are reading. Is time consuming, but effective.
Mental Images *(Have students, during group or independent reading, create mental images in their minds' eyes, and then draw them and possibly storyboard the images.)*	Encourages young learners with marginal writing skills to think about their thinking while they are reading. Gives the student an accommodation to express their understanding of the passage other than through writing. Is time consuming, but effective.

Postreading Options

Every reading should be followed by a postreading activity (see Table 23.3) in which the teacher develops some of the ideas to reinforce the concepts or ideas found in reading—that is why you're the teacher. Or put another way, it is not appropriate to have students read a social studies passage and not have it followed by a comprehensive lesson, debriefing, discussion, lecture, tasks, etc. The postreading can be the end of the lesson or it flows into a content presentation in which the teacher develops new but related big ideas or procedural knowledge and introduces new information knowledge.

Table 23.3 Postreading Options

Strategy	Considerations
Lesson Plan	The text passage is developed with a comprehensive lesson that uses the facts and concepts in the passage as a baseline to develop procedural knowledge and big ideas.
Debriefing	Debriefing (in which the teacher asks questions about the reading in a whole class setting) should not be limited only to the facts, but should also be elevated to the concept level. Teacher-centered probing of students allows them to summarize, synthesize, and report their construction of the information. The teacher can engage students with additional concepts.
Summarizing	Summarizing is not as effective as debriefing, and students will learn not to read because they anticipate that the teacher is going to summarize. Reciprocal teaching allows students to summarize with other students.
Discussion	Students in heterogeneous groups of four or five should focus on discussion questions provided by the teacher that require predicting or analyzing, and the teacher should circulate among the groups.
Simulation	Students create a simulation (role playing) to demonstrate their understanding of the reading. Requires a debriefing by the teacher after each skit.
Project	Students are given an art project, writing assignment, or other project to demonstrate or apply their knowledge. The RAFT strategy helps students to analyze and reflect upon their reading through personal writing.
Basal Worksheets and Graphic Organizers	Many textbook companies provide worksheets to accompany social studies textbooks. These tend to be fact-based and evaluate only lower-level learning. It is better to use graphic organizers.
Marking-Up Strategy	In this approach students return to the reading and are led through a process of "marking up a document" (see Assignment 23.2 to learn about this strategy) so as to clarify for all the students the important parts of the reading.

Assignment 23.1

INTASC Standards 1, 2, 3, 4, 5, 7, and 8

Reading Plan

Based on one of the Houghton Mifflin K–6 Social Studies Series readings at the Premium Website, prepare a prereading–preteach vocabulary, a reading in groups, and postreading plan–debriefing that details how you will approach having your students read the content prior to your instruction. Be prepared to discuss your results in class and submit the assignment to your professor.

TEACHSOURCE VIDEO CASE ASSIGNMENT 23.2

INTASC Standards 1, 2, 3, 4, 5, 7, and 8

Metacognition and Reading

View the TeachSource video, *Metacognition: Helping Students Become Strategic Learners*, at the Premium Website and answer the viewing questions in the case. Although the case is about a middle school class, the explanation of metacognition and the use of the "marking-up strategy" is important to learn about so you can adapt it to your elementary classroom. Be prepared to discuss your answers and submit the assignment to your professor.

WEBSITE RESOURCES • Reading

Video	*TeachSource* Teaching Struggling Readers: Key Strategies for the Inclusive, Elementary Classroom *Learner.org* Using Resources: Focuses on how to make the most of the resources that can be used in teaching social studies, from artifacts and primary sources to children's literature and the Internet. You will find an adaptable mini-lesson that uses children's literature to examine what constitutes a good citizen.
Website	*Read/Write/Think* For reading strategies. *School District's* List of reading strategies with examples. *TeAchnonogy* Has printables, rubrics, etc. that can be used as part of reading strategies.

Sample High-Quality Internet Lessons or Activities

Lower Elementary	*Read/Write/Think* Book Buddy Biographies: Intermediate and Primary Students Working Together: The success of a year-long Book Buddy program hinges on those first few days at the beginning of the year. Students come to know each other on a more personal level by creating personalized biographies by interviewing each other.
Upper Elementary	*Read/Write/Think* A Daily DEAR Program: Drop Everything, and Read: A structured independent reading activity.
	All linked websites (designated by the green color) and those listed here are available as clickable links at the book's Premium Website, www.cengage.com/login, for ease of access. These links will be updated periodically to reflect changes and new resources as they become available.

Topic 24

The Crucial Role of Social Studies Vocabulary

The importance of **vocabulary** to reading cannot be overstated. Both Information and procedural knowledge vocabulary are essential to sustained understanding of social studies because they are building blocks to the development of more sophisticated concepts, ideas, and beliefs as students progress through school (Hirsch, 2006; Willingham, 2006).

Reading and vocabulary go hand in hand. Both are at the center of the elementary education curriculum and should also be a focal point of social studies instruction for elementary students. With reading and instruction comes the ability to develop a richer vocabulary by which children can communicate their ideas verbally and in writing, the capability to be a lifelong learner, and exposure to more sophisticated logic and modes of reasoning. Reading in social studies, particularly through trade books (see Topic 39 for strategies and the National Council for the Social Studies list of notable children's trade books) engages and excites students with connections to everyday life.

> **Teacher's Tip**
>
> Low socioeconomic status (SES) students entering kindergarten are three times more likely to score in the bottom quartile on assessments of reading (Cortese, 2007).

Vocabulary and Reading

Children learn about 1,000 to 5,000 new words a year (White, Graves, & Slater, 1990). Children initially learn their first words through the home, and these words become resources for reading (Walsh, 2008). Research (see Hart & Risley, 2003) has uncovered what is known as the "30,000-word gap." There is a 30,000-word gap that develops between elementary school–aged children from professional families and low SES (see Aikens & Barbarin, 2008) children, with working-class families' children falling roughly in the middle. This gap becomes most evident in fourth grade, where the demands of the curriculum begin to require **comprehension** of the more sophisticated *informational text*

> *There are worse crimes than burning books. One of them is not reading them.*
>
> Joseph Brodsky

rather than just the basic skill of **decoding** used in lower elementary grades with mostly *narrative text* (Chall, Jacobs, & Baldwin, 1990). Structured pre-reading and postreading (see Topic 25) activities are crucial to the development of children's decoding and comprehension skills with social studies informational text.

A vocabulary word is a trigger to access a concept. However, vocabulary that is found in text is static and devoid of a conversational context. As a result, words found in text require greater development by the teacher than new words provided during verbal instruction (Nagy & Scott, 2000). Learning by reading requires: (1) **fluency**: the momentum and speed with which one reads, and (2) **automaticity**: quick and accurate recognition of words and phrases (Nagy & Scott, 2000). Without these two acquired capabilities, students become so bogged down in deciphering words and phrases that by the end of the sentence, paragraph, or page they have lost sight of the facts, concepts, and generalizations presented in the text. Without the information contained in the vocabulary words, students are unable to perform feats of analysis and synthesis (Willingham, 2003a, 2003b).

Types of Social Studies Vocabulary

Parker (2001) has identified various types of vocabulary that students encounter in social studies and for which teachers must flush out a *commonsense meaning.*

1. Technical terms: *plateau, century, longitude, polls, legislature*
2. Figurative terms: *political platform, Cold War, Sun Belt, pork barrel*
3. Words with multiple meanings: *cabinet, mouth, bank, revolution*
4. Locality-specific terms: *grits* (southern breakfast dish), *bayou* (predominately used in Louisiana to refer to a body of water), *coulee* (Chinese immigrant working on the transcontinental railroad), and *Oklahoma Sooner*
5. Alike words: *peasant* for *pheasant, principle* for *principal, alien* for *allies*
6. Acronyms: *NATO, NASA, OPEC, NAFTA, NCAA, MADD*
7. Quantitative terms: *century, decade, GNP, acre*
8. Names: *Lewis and Clark, the American Revolution, 1776, Gettysburg*

Bias in Vocabulary—A Unique Problem to Social Studies

Unlike math and science, social studies vocabulary can be biased. The "Ramadan War" and the "Yom Kippur War" were the same war and are typically used in either pro-Arab or pro-Israeli text. One book's "freedom fighters" might be another book's "terrorists."

> Is Osama Bin Laden a freedom fighter or terrorist? Was Richard the Lion Hearted a freedom fighter or terrorist? In whose textbooks would either be depicted as one or the other?

More subtle biases are reflected in phrases like "Women were given the right to vote" rather than "Women won the right to vote." Such bias can stem from ethnocentrism as well as ideology. Griswold (1986) points out that describing Lebanon as located in the "Near East" and India and Japan the "Far East" reflects a Eurocentric view dating from the time England was the dominant world power, or at least controlled mapmaking. England is nearer to Lebanon and farther away from Japan. Rather than passing over this kind of terminology, the teacher should use the language to expose the bias so that students can become more intuitive and discerning as consumers of social studies information.

> Should you say "Christmas break" in your classroom or "winter break?"

Historical Expressions

Etymology is the study of the origin of words and expressions. Social studies expressions and words are a rich resource for introducing students to vocabulary and giving the words a context. Words and expressions can start a lesson or become the focus of a lesson. Following are some examples.

- *Pork barrel:* The term goes back to the early 1800s, when pork was packed in barrels, and hungry farm workers reached in to help themselves to slabs of salt pork. By 1900 *pork barrel* had become political slang meaning federal government projects or funding that provide benefits or jobs to particular areas or people.
- *Kangaroo court:* This was a court for commoners set up by the British in Australia. Australia was originally a British penal colony, and the court was indifferent to what happened to the people who were sent there. The court was known for trumped-up charges and swift justice, and that is how the term is used today.
- *Dirt poor:* Only the wealthy could afford floors of wood or tile; the poor had dirt floors.
- *The whole ball of wax:* This means that everything is included. In old English law, when an estate was being divided, each parcel of land was identified on a small piece of paper that was wrapped in a ball of wax. The balls of wax were placed in a hat, and each heir took a ball of wax to select the parcel of land he would receive. If there was only one heir, the estate would not be divided and he received a single ball of wax.

- *Loophole:* During the Middle Ages, architects built narrow windows called loopholes at the tops of castle walls. A loophole was big enough to fire a longbow or crossbow out of while running little danger of being wounded in return by attackers. When cannons and firearms made loopholes obsolete, the name was transferred to any figurative "opening" that made it possible to evade an agreement or a law.
- ***Don't throw the baby out with the bath water:*** This admonition stems from medieval times, when hot bath water was scarce. Men, then women, and finally the children and babies of the household all bathed, one after another, in the same bath water.
- *Upper crust:* In the Middle Ages, bread was divided according to status. Workers got the burnt bottom of the loaf, family members got the middle, and guests got the top, the "upper crust."

For more expressions and their origins, you can go to the Phrases & Expressions Website.

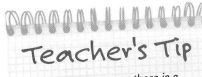
Techniques Used to Enhance Vocabulary Acquisition

Whether through reading or instruction, students are exposed to what Christie (1998) calls "uncommonsense vocabulary." These new words and expressions must be "unpacked" from their unfamiliar wording to a *commonsense* meaning (Beck et al., 1998). For example, the Emancipation Proclamation would be unpacked to mean "a law that freed slaves" for lower elementary students. As students move through the grades, the term's meaning becomes more multifaceted and is further explored with more sophisticated modes of reasoning (it only freed slaves in the southern states still in rebellion). A primary goal of instruction is for the teacher to unpack technical terms into commonsense meanings during **teacher talk**. When new words are introduced in text materials, unpacking them as part of prereading, reading, and postreading activities can increase motivation and allow students to read with greater fluency and automaticity.

McCullough (1958) suggests a number of techniques that the teacher should plan to use when teaching the various types of vocabulary to children. These techniques are listed in Table 24.1.

Best Practices for Teaching Vocabulary

There does not appear to be a single best way to learn vocabulary. Following are some basic principles that can serve as a guide. They are based on the findings

Table 24.1 Vocabulary Techniques

Strategy	Example
Picture Clues	*The sloppy banks* . . . [teacher provides a picture]
Verbal Clues: The president's *cabinet* meets weekly.	*The members are official advisers to the president.*
Experience Clues	*When we came to a fork in the road* . . .
Comparison and Contrast Clues	*The president* vetoed *the first bill, but he* allowed *the second to become law.*
Synonym Clues	*The Democratic party adopted its* platform; *this* plan *must be voted on by the delegates to the convention.*
Summary Clues	*What people know and believe to be true, how they act, are part of their culture.*
Definition Clues	*To* lobby *is to accost, address, or solicit a legislator in order to influence legislation to one's own advantage.*
Mood Clues	*His* disrespect *for his captors was evident in the way he scowled at them.*
Familiar Expression Clues	*The card said "Happy Holidays."*

of Brett, Rothlein, and Hurley (1996); Beck, McKeown, and Omanson (1987); Teal (2003); and others.

1. Teach the concept before presenting the unknown word.
2. During reading, students learn significantly more vocabulary when teachers explain new words when they are first encountered rather than waiting until the end of the reading activity.
3. Encourage students to determine the meaning of new words by inferring the meaning from the context, using a dictionary, or some other means.
4. Students should manipulate words by comparing them to experiences and describing how they relate to other words.
5. Use repetition so that students encounter a new word many times, make sure that discussions of words are extensive, and require that students explain their use of words.
6. Create and display a word web, matrix, or list or use a crossword puzzle assignment to preview new vocabulary as an alternative to listing words and definitions.
7. When students are reading silently in class or during a homework reading assignment, have them record on the left column of a piece of paper the words they understand and on the right column the words they don't understand. Review both by calling on students to provide explanations prior to instruction.
8. Debrief homework reading assignments and in-class readings by referring to and using the new vocabulary.
9. Require a vocabulary notebook.

INTASC Standards 1, 2, 3, 4, 5, 7, and 8

Vocabulary Development

Visit the Learner.org Website and view the Video Lesson, *State Government and the Role of the Citizen* for an upper elementary lesson that uses vocabulary cards and concept organizers. Using the Houghton Mifflin Readings 12 and/or 13 at the Premium Website, prepare a short paper explaining how you would apply this approach to the history topic presented in the readings.

	WEBSITE RESOURCES • Reading and Vocabulary
Essay	***ERIC Online*** *ED413576,* Building a Strong Vocabulary (1997) presents 12 strategies for building vocabulary; This is a 196-page book.
Vocabulary Games, etc.	*Awesome Library*
Website	*TampaBay Reads* A comprehensive list of generic vocabulary for grades 1 through 5 of words students should know. *Literacy Matters* Offers strategies to improve vocabulary acquisition.
Sample High-Quality Internet Lessons or Activities	
Upper Elementary	*Read/Write/Think* Acquiring New Vocabulary Through Book Discussion Group: Using Pink and Say, students acquire vocabulary about the Civil War using group approaches. *Read/Write/Think* Using Word Storms to Explore Vocabulary and Encourage Critical Thinking: A vocabulary strategy called "word storms" is used to explore social issues related to the role of working dogs' contribution to society.
	All linked websites (designated by the green color) and those listed here are available as clickable links at the book's Premium Website, www.cengage.com/login, for ease of access. These links will be updated periodically to reflect changes and new resources as they become available.

Topic 25

Textbooks and Social Studies Instruction

Using Textbooks in Social Studies Instruction

Textbooks continue to be the mainstay of school-based education and play a central role in social studies education (Thomas B. Fordham Institute, 2005; Zhao and Hoge, 2005). Textbook publishers are subject to market forces and the ideological orientations of the times, but they aspire to a high degree of credibility. Elementary social studies textbooks have been criticized as shallow, excessively inaccurate, and biased (McGowan, Erickson, & Neufeld, 1996; Cruz, 1994; Hirsch, 2006; Duplass 2007). The field of social studies has been criticized for too much reliance on book-based instruction in which students absorb and reproduce trivial information (Scheurman & Newman, 1998). For example, having students read and complete standardized worksheets is not a best reading practice, nor is it good social studies education. Creating lessons in which students are challenged to create summaries or graphic organizers like timelines, storyline organizers, and problem solution organizers (see the Premium Website for graphic organizers), requires thinking skills rather than just recall and reporting.

Teacher's Tip

Introduce the textbook to students by teaching what they are, why certain words are in bold type, what purpose tables and callouts have, and how to examine pictures, headings, and so on. Explain the table of contents and index. This is best done at the beginning of the year, before you start using the textbook.

A Typical Historical Reading Passage

The following brief passage is typical of material in fourth and fifth grade textbooks. It will be used to model the choreography of social studies reading material and instruction into a coherent lesson.

Caribbean Settlement

Columbus made four voyages. On his first voyage on October 12, 1492, Columbus landed on San Salvador (Spanish for "Holy Savior") Island in the Bahamas. Later, Columbus discovered other Caribbean islands. He set up a fort on the island called Hispaniola. The first peoples Columbus met were the Tainos and the Caribs. He thought he was near the East Indies, so he called them "Indians."

Spain wanted to colonize the Caribbean Islands. In 1502, Nicolas de Ovando was named governor of Hispaniola. Colonists from Spain followed the governor to Hispaniola, which is now Haiti and the Dominican Republic. He brought colonists who wanted to make money by farming and mining. One of their problems was not having enough people to do the hard work.

To get enough workers, the colonists tried to make slaves of the Indians. This did not work. Many Indians died when they were forced into slavery. The Spanish tried to solve the problem by capturing Indians from other islands. But many of these Indians died, too. Later, slaves were brought from Africa.

Even after all of these things were tried, there were still not enough people to do the work. Many of the colonists quit and returned to Spain. Some moved to other islands in the Caribbean. Some of the colonists moved to Puerto Rico in 1508. The Spanish leader who brought them there was Ponce de Leon. Another leader, Juan de Esquivel, took colonists to Jamaica in 1509. The largest Caribbean island, Cuba, was settled in 1514.

Before you read the following section, do you think you would use this reading passage on the Caribbean Settlement based on your learning about the four key criteria for selecting reading material that were introduced in Topic 23?

Choreography of Reading and Instruction

The following example of choreographing textbook reading material into your instruction is based on the preceding passage and the *instructional sequence model* explained in Topic 19.

Lesson Plan Topic: The Settlement of the Caribbean

TEACHER BACKGROUND INFORMATION

The discovery of the "New World" should be analyzed in the context of multiple causation. The discovery was driven largely by curiosity, economics, nationalism, Roman Catholic evangelism, and the desire for wealth and glory. Western Europe's civilization was more technologically advanced than the civilizations of the Americas and Africa in the 15th century which facilitated the ease with which other peoples were conquered and implied to Europeans that they were also superior. Combined with the belief that the unknown world had unlimited resources, these forces shaped the mindsets and behaviors of the explorers and colonists toward the inhabitants, economic systems, governance, and environment of the New World.

Resources

(A few examples from the social studies–rich Internet):
- **Mariner.org** has timelines, maps, and other information on the Age of Discovery.
- **About.com** has Images, maps, and background information on the Atlantic slave trade.
- **Library of Congress, The Born in Slavery collection**: "A broadside advertisement for the sale of slaves in America."
- **Dictionary of Tiano people's language.**
- **Athena Review** includes 15th-century maps of the Caribbean and a drawing of the Tiano people.
- I Abolish.

Big Ideas
- The comparison of the concept of *economies of scale* to enterprises during the discovery period of the Americas and today.
- People's motivations in supporting slavery. Is it wrong to treat people badly? How do you know when you are treating people badly?
- Did the colonists think they were treating the Caribes and Tiano people badly? Can you judge the colonists by today's standards?
- What makes some people think they are better than other people?

Standards
National Council for the Social Studies themes and strands:

Time, Continuity, and Change: Demonstrate an understanding that people in different times and places view the world differently.

Power, Authority, and Governance: Recognize and give examples of the tensions between the wants and needs of individuals and groups, and concepts such as fairness, equity, and justice.

Production, Distribution, and Consumption: Describe how we depend upon workers with specialized jobs and the ways in which they contribute to the production and exchange of goods and services.

Method/Instructional Sequence

Attention-Getter

Questions: What is slavery? "Slavery" is defined as bondage: the state of being under the control of another person or a condition of control over a person against his or her will, enforced by violence or other forms of coercion. Is slavery fair? Why do you think people enslave other people?

Teacher's analogy: Compare slavery to bullying by a stronger person, and relate it to technologically more advanced societies' encountering less technologically advanced societies. Sometimes the clash of cultures leads to prejudice.

Do you think there is slavery today? Use current examples from Asia and Africa; refer to Joseph in the Old Testament and slavery in the 18th and 19th centuries in the United States.

Review

Call on students to recall what they know about the story of Columbus.

Prereading

Use the preteach vocabulary approach by pronouncing each proper name and place name in the reading. If students whose first language is Spanish are in the class, you can ask them to pronounce the words.

Reading

Provide each student with a data retrieval chart (Table 25.1) prior to reading. Use the *group reading approach*: Place the students in heterogeneous groups of four and require each student to read one of the four paragraphs aloud. Then require the students to complete the cells in the table that were left blank. When all groups are finished, show a transparency of the completed chart.

Table 25.1   Data Retrieval Chart

Dates	Discoverers	Discoveries	Reasons
	Columbus		Make Money
		Hispaniola	
1508			
		Jamaica	
1514			

Postreading Debriefing/First Content Presentation

Start by asking, "Why do you think explorers came to the new world?" Write students' answers on the chalkboard. Redevelop and provide examples for their answers by explaining the four primary reasons: adventure, nationalism, Roman Catholic evangelism, and the search for wealth and glory. Next, with the headings in Table 25.2 ask questions and record on the transparency until the organizer is complete.

Why do people want to make money?
Is it wrong to want to make money?
How do people make money today?
How does McDonald's make money?

Explain concepts of location, raw materials, efficiency (economies of scale), shift work, too many workers, too-high pay, not enough customers, not enough profit, and so on, by using the Socratic method to analogize the elements of the Caribbean story to a popular fast-food chain like McDonald's or Burger King until Table 25.2 is complete.

Table 25.2 Parallel Construction Organizer

McDonald's	Caribbean Exploration
Similarities	
Needs workers to be efficient.	Needs workers to be efficient.
Must sell hamburgers for more than it costs to make them in order to stay profitable.	Needs to mine ore (silver, gold) and harvest farm products that are worth more than they cost to produce in order to make a profit.
Good location needed for profit.	Good location needed for profit.
Differences	
Service company: buys raw materials (buns, hamburger) and people (unions) make the products.	Production company: people use tools to harvest raw materials for other people to consume.
Has employees.	Has slaves.

Guided Practice

Place students in heterogeneous groups that are different from the reading groups. Display a transparency of Table 25.3 with only the headings (A, B, C, & D) filled in. Using the Socratic method, complete section "A" by referring to the answers on the chalkboard.

Table 25.3   Story Analysis Organizer

A. Why Were Workers Needed?		
To make money.	Mining and farming.	Efficiency.
B. What Was Tried First?	**What Was Tried Second?**	**What Was Tried Third?**
Colonists did the work.	Made slaves of the Indians.	Slaves were brought from Africa.
C. Results	**Results**	**Results**
Not enough workers.	Indians died; not enough workers; brought Indians from other islands.	Still not enough workers.
D. Final Outcomes		
Discovered and colonized new islands; Africans were enslaved and brought to the New World.		

Teacher's Tip

It is a best practice to have each student complete a product like a graphic organizer even when students work in a group, so that each student's performance can be evaluated.

Explain the difference between inferred and explicit language, using this example: If you say, "This is my homework," a listener infers that you did your own homework. Explicit language would be, "This is my homework, and I did it all by myself." Ask students for other examples and explain that they should look for inferences in the reading. This is an important reading skill, and it is social studies procedural knowledge. The answer to "What was tried first?" is "The colonists did the work," which is an inferred answer that students often miss unless they are taught the strategy of inferences.

Inform the students that they are to complete sections "B," "C," and "D" in groups. Circulate around the room, assisting with questions as necessary, but require students to devise the answers.

Second Content Presentation by the Socratic Method

Have groups report their answers from Table 25.3, clarifying, correcting, and elaborating as needed.

- Do you think the Spanish explorers were wrong to enslave the Caribbean Indians and Africans?
- Do you think they thought it was wrong?
- Can we blame them today for what they did 400 years ago?
- Do we do anything today that people 400 years from now will say is wrong?
- The Caribbean story explicitly mentions that the Indians died, but it doesn't mention that the Africans died. Why? Answer: Author oversight? Did Indians actually die at a greater rate than the African slaves? Why would Indians die at a faster rate? Answer: Because the whole population of Indians was enslaved; many unhealthy African slaves died crossing the Atlantic; Indians lacked immunity to European diseases.

The headings and chronology of any lesson should vary, depending on the goals and topic. Evaluation is important, but it is not always formalized in a test or activity at the end of a lesson. In addition, there is not time to evaluate all learning at every stage, so teachers must also rely on observation of student attentiveness and participation.

Assignment 25.1

INTASC Standards 1–8

Choreography of Reading and Instruction

Select any passage from Houghton Mifflin readings at the Premium Website and choreograph your instruction based on the model and principles developed with the Caribbean example in this topic. Be prepared to discuss your results in class and submit the paper to your professor.

WEBSITE RESOURCES

Check the Premium Website, www.cengage.com/login, for additional links and links that are periodically updated to reflect new resources as they become available.

Topic 26

Children's Literature and Social Studies Instruction

Children's literature adds significant value to an elementary social studies program because it often provides the kind of rich social studies knowledge essential to the development of reading skills, can tap into students imaginations, and often focuses on the kinds of values questions important to character and citizenship education (Chick, 2006 & Carr, 2005). Books rich with graphics (often referred to as **graphic novels** for young children) make learning to read easier (Lyga, 2006).

Trade books, like those recognized for excellence by the National Council for the Social Studies (NCSS) and the National Council for Teachers of English (NCTE) are an essential part of literature-based social studies either as teacher-centered read-a-louds (often referred to in the literature as **big book readings**) or as books for students to independently read. As an example, the core knowledge curriculum approach to character and citizenship education tends to use classics such as "William Tell" and "The Boy at the Dike" (see the Premium Website, The University of Virginia Electronic Text Center) to explore values. The expanding communities approach, in contrast, tends to use more contemporary stories like "Citizenship and Democracy" or "Using Money" which can also at be found at the Premium Website. Both trade books and passages such as these support literacy goals, motivate at-risk students and English language learners, and allow differentiated instruction for gifted students (Edmunds, & Bauserman, 2006; Walker-Dalhouse, 1993). In addition, you can find children's stories in anthologies such as *The Book of Virtues: A Treasury of Great Moral Stories* (Bennett, 1996) that can become the basis for compelling character and citizenship education lessons when reinforced with discussions and debriefings.

The standards set for the Orbis Pictus Award for outstanding children's nonfiction books sponsored by NCTE should serve as a guide for teachers when selecting books to use in their classroom. The standards include:

1. **Accuracy**—facts current and complete, balance of fact and theory, varying point of view, stereotypes avoided, author's qualifications adequate, appropriate scope, authenticity of detail
2. **Organization**—logical development, clear sequence, interrelationships indicated, patterns provided (general-to-specific, simple-to-complex, etc.)
3. **Design**—attractive, readable, illustrations complement text, placement of illustrative material appropriate and complementary, appropriate media, format, type
4. **Style**—writing is interesting, stimulating, reveals author's enthusiasm for subject; curiosity and wonder encouraged; appropriate terminology; rich language

For trade books, both fiction and nonfiction, a lesson plan should "wrap around" the trade book. The teacher needs to contextualize the book's content by providing background information and then focusing the debriefing on the big idea(s).

> At the Premium Website, download the Core Knowledge Reading 20, "Boy at the Dike." Take a moment to read it and think about what concepts it is promoting and how you would use it in class.

The prereading, reading, and postreading strategies discussed in Topic 23 apply when teachers use social studies–themed children's literature as a whole-class dramatic reading, as an example. But there are other strategies for using reading materials, such as a book club in the classroom or checking out books from the school's learning resource center. Regardless of approach, teachers need to structure the reading experience with instructional activities that give opportunities to reinforce character and citizenship values and for students to master social studies content and modes of reasoning. As an example, if you were fortunate enough to have five copies each of five different children's books, you could have students read them in groups and the students could **role-play** (see Topic 46) scenes for the other groups or create a Decision Prediction Organizer (see "Graphic Organizers" at the Premium Website). After they complete these tasks, the teacher debriefs students to ensure understanding.

Independent Reading of Children's Tradebooks

Teacher's Tip

Communicating the need for independent reading to parents and actively soliciting their involvement in their children's reading assignments are essential. This message should be part of your introductory letter to parents and included in your "School Welcome Back" event.

When literacy and learning social studies are your goals, it is not enough to simply assign books for students to read. A book of 50 or 100 pages seems intimidating to some children. Students need a structured approach to reading books as an independent activity. A strategy for having students read tradebooks requires a number of steps from selecting and getting the books to integrating the books into a structured lesson plan.

Following is an example of a lesson that requires each student to read a book over a two- or three-week period. In this plan, the students are independently reading different books—and, to a degree, at their own pace. The lesson is based on the big idea of success.

A Focused Children's Book Lesson

Topic: Success
Grade Level: Third through sixth.
Big Idea: What does it take to be successful?
Goals:
    Each student will read a biography.
    Each student will create a web of the book.
    Each student will write a paper about the successful person in the book he or
        she is reading.
    Each student will make a presentation to the class about the successful person.

NCSS Theme: Time, Continuity, and Change
    Strand B: Demonstrate an ability to use correct vocabulary associated with time
        such as past, present, future, and long ago; read and construct simple timelines;
        identify examples of change; and recognize examples of cause-and-effect
        relationships.
    Strand C: Compare and contrast different stories or accounts about past
        events, people, places, or situations, identifying how they contribute to our
        understanding of the past.

PREPARATION

Meet with the school librarian two months in advance of the lesson and provide a list of 100 successful individuals. If you need help identifying contemporary and historical successful men and women from different cultures, consult *100 Women Who Shaped World History*, by Gail Meyer Rolka (1994), and *100 Men Who Shaped World History*, by Bill Yenne (1994). Amazon.com and Barnes & Noble have excellent search engines for identifying children's books on notable figures.

Ask the school librarian to collect enough grade-appropriate children's biographies from the list so that each student can have one book for three weeks. The librarian will probably make use of interlibrary loan to obtain the books. An alternative is to collect money from parents or the Parent Teacher Association (PTA) to set up a permanent collection of biographies in your classroom.

Write the book titles on individual slips of paper that the students will draw from a hat or a box. Select one book for yourself (I selected *Joan of Arc*) and prepare a web and a grade-appropriate paper as models for students.

ATTENTION-GETTER AND CONTENT PRESENTATION 1

Day 1

Write on the board: "Name five people you think are successful. Do not name your teacher or a relative, but name someone we all know." Divide the students into groups to develop the list, and have the groups report out names. Probe and have students justify the names. If necessary, suggest names that students might not think of, such as Mother Teresa, Laura Bush, and Oprah, to ensure diversity. Write the names on poster paper, and tape the poster on the wall.

> **Teacher's Tip**
>
> Your PTA or school may allow you to apply for a grant. A good use of grant money is to buy a set of grade-level biographies to be used all year each year.

Day 2

Write on the board: "List five attributes or qualities that a person must have to become successful." Divide the students into groups to develop the list, and have the groups report the attributes they decided upon. Probe and emphasize such qualities as working hard, practicing their skills, not necessarily being the smartest or most attractive, developing the talent they had, being well rounded. Write the attributes on poster paper, and tape it to the wall.

Day 3

Write on the board: "List five advantages or benefits of a person who has become successful." Divide the students into groups. Probe and emphasize that not all have money or fame, that they like what they do. Have the groups report out benefits, write them on poster paper, and tape the poster to the wall. Point out that the successful people they listed are well known, and ask whether someone has to be well known to be successful. Since the class listed only well-known people, most of the people on the list are wealthy and famous. Tell students that some successful people are not wealthy or famous. Give examples of professions like carpenters and teachers.

Day 4

Write on the board: "List three careers that you think you could be successful in, and be prepared to tell everyone what qualities you have that will help you be successful." Have each student answer. Probe and point out that each career requires them to get a good education. For instance, carpenters need to know math, professional basketball players need to know economics in order to spend their money wisely; and doctors need to learn a lot of science.

CONTENT PRESENTATION 2: MODELING

Step 1

Show students the 48-page book *Joan of Arc* by Angela Bull. The book is designed for children from 5 to 8 years of age. Explain that you have read the book, and that they will all read a book about a successful person during the next three weeks.

Show a web such as the one in Figure 26.1 on the overhead, and explain that you drew the web after reading the book. Explain that based on facts you found in the book, you concluded that Joan of Arc was brave, religious, loyal, and smart. Then for each adjective, starting with brave, show the students that you placed an index card in the book at page 24 with the note "Battle of Orleans—Brave." Explain that after you read the book and created the web, you had to find proof to support your

Figure 26.1   Web of Joan of Arc

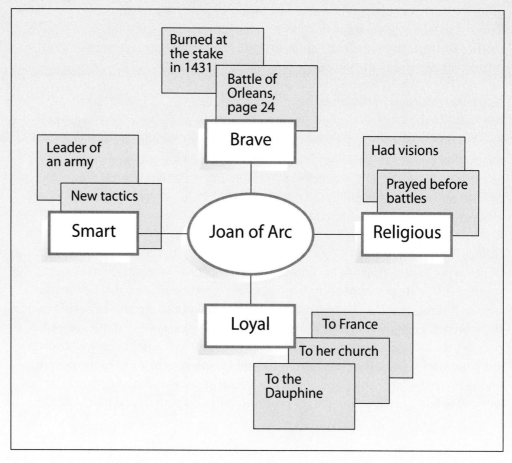

claim, and that what Joan did in the Battle of Orleans is proof of her bravery. Explain that this is what historians call "documentation and footnoting," and tell students that they will do the same thing for the successful person they read about.

Step 2
Divide students into small groups, and give each group a copy of your grade-appropriate paper. Tell them that the paper is a model that they can use to write their papers after they create the web. Have the students discuss the headings and citations, and encourage questions about how to choose the headings as well as the attributes. Hand out index cards for students to use to mark pages in their books.

Step 3
Show students the page of notes (outline, headings, etc.) that you will use for your presentation, then make a presentation explaining why Joan of Arc was successful. Tell students that this is how you want them to present their successful people.

Teacher's Tip

I selected this Joan of Arc example because when I was in third grade I had an appendectomy, and my mother brought me biographies to read (in the old days you were required to stay in bed for 10 days). The first one I read was about Joan of Arc. Books on George Washington, Abraham Lincoln, Dwight D. Eisenhower, and others soon followed. I still attribute my interest in reading biographies of virtuous and courageous people to this first experience.

Step 4
Take out the hat or box with the folded pieces of paper listing the book titles, and have students each draw one and tell the class whose names they drew.

Step 5
Take the students to the library or distribute the books. Have each student write the number of pages the book has on a piece of paper and divide the number by 12. Then tell the students that the number is how many pages they must read each night. Each day, randomly call on students to tell what they learned about their people so far.

Step 6
On day 13, put students in groups to develop their webs.

Step 7
In the same groups, have them write their papers, create notes for their presentations, and practice their presentations with their group. Make a transparency of each web.

Step 8
Schedule five students a day to present their successful people, and invite parents to attend their children's presentations.

You can expand upon this reading assignment in a number of ways:

- Students could use the Internet to learn more about the people and find pictures of them or of the places or events in the book. Perhaps students can even take a virtual field trip (see Topic 48).
- Students could create reenactments (see Topic 46).

Variations on This Approach

This strategy should not be limited to biographies. It can be modified to accommodate a range of social studies topics and can be used with books or Internet sources for research projects. For each topic, students could be required to create chronologies, maps, outlines, summaries, simulations, presentations, drawings, or fictional accounts from participants' perspectives. The following books are resources that can be used to identify potential topics, trade books, and Internet sites that would help you develop focused lesson plans in which independent reading is a primary goal.

- *100 Great Cities of World History,* by Chrisanne Beckne
- *100 Explorers Who Shaped World History,* by Jerome Prescott and Tony Chikes
- *100 African Americans Who Shaped American History,* by Chrisanne Beckner
- *100 Inventions That Shaped World History,* by Bill Yenne and M. Grosser

A Book in One Hour

A second approach is known as the **book-in-one-hour method** (Childrey 1980). As an example, a teacher would use a trade book at the fourth-grade level, such as *Number the Stars,* by Lois Lowery (1998), which is a story of Jews escaping Nazi-controlled Holland during World War II. The paperback version is 137 pages long. The teacher would tear the book into roughly 20 sections and number each section in order. Each student would read one section in about 15 minutes, take notes, and prepare to verbally summarize it. The teacher would write the main characters' names on the chalkboard as a reference. The students, in the order of the numbered sections, then proceed to tell the story to the rest of the class.

The students will want to know what came before and after their passages. The suspense and peer pressure ensure that each student thinks carefully about how he or she will articulate a summary.

Trade Book Resources

Children's fiction and nonfiction books are an excellent starting point for developing lesson plans. Each year, *Social Studies and the Young Learner,* published by the NCSS, includes a special edition on children's books with advice on how they can be integrated with the 10 NCSS themes. As mentioned previously, the NCSS Website provides an annual list and summary of children's books published since 1997 that are excellent for social studies education.

Trade books can be used in read-alouds. The teacher can appear in period dress or in character in order to do a dramatic reading. A book like *America: A Patriotic Primer* (Cheney, 2002) can be used to inspire students to consider how to make the world a better place and become better persons themselves. Each letter of the alphabet is dedicated to a theme, like "T" for tolerance, or a significant historical figure, like "J" for Thomas Jefferson. The book is limited to U.S. culture, but can a version based on world history be far behind?

Assignment 26.1

INTASC Standards 1, 2, 3, 4, 5, 7, and 8

Trade Book Lesson Plan

Go to the NCSS Notable Trade Books Website and identify a trade book to use in the creation of a social studies lesson. Purchase or check one of the books out of the library and provide a synopsis of the book, identify the big idea(s) and state standard that it fulfills, and explain how you would use it to teach a social studies lesson. Be prepared to turn in the assignment to your professor and to discuss your ideas in class.

	WEBSITE RESOURCES • Reading

Essay	***ERIC Online***
	ED380793, Twenty-Five Habits to Encourage Reading (1995):
	  A list of suggestions to encourage reading.
	ED451483, Read-A-Louds with Young Children (2001):
	  A how-to book with examples and concepts.

Website	*Read/Write/Think* This site has comprehensive, high-quality reading and writing lesson plans using children's trade books.
List of Tradebooks	*Carol Hurst Reading* The website is a collection of reviews of great books for kids. *Barahona Center for the Study of Books in Spanish* Has a listing of children's books in Spanish. *University of Virginia Electronic Text Center* Downloadable children's classics for use in the classroom.

Sample High-Quality Internet Lessons or Activities	
Lower Elementary	*Read/Write/Think* Little Red Riding Hood: Used to compare fiction and nonfiction with text sets. *Read/Write/Think* What if Everybody Did That? A story is used to create a citizenship lesson about classroom rules. *Edsitement* Aesop and Ananse: Animal Fables and Trickster Tales: Introduces students to the virtues found in Aesop's fables.
Upper Elementary	*Read/Write/Think* A Bad Case of Bullying: Uses literature response groups with students for a Character and Citizenship Education lesson. *Core Knowledge* Tales from Arabia: Lessons in Literature and Character: The teacher integrates a bulletin board display with Arabian Nights stories as part of a lesson about the Middle Ages and the age of exploration. *Read/Write/Think* Martin Luther King, Jr., and Me: Identifying with a Hero: A biography is used for students to consider their role as citizens.
	All linked websites (designated by the green color) and those listed here are available as clickable links at the book's Premium Website, www.cengage.com/login, for ease of access. These links will be updated periodically to reflect changes and new resources as they become available.

Topic 27

Writing and Presentations

John Dewey (1915) said there is "all the difference in the world between having something to say and having to say something" (p. 35). Unlike disciplines like mathematics and science, social studies is more directly relevant to students' lives because it is about "real world" people, places, and events. Because students come to school with some social studies information knowledge, ideas, and beliefs which they have learned vicariously, no matter how naïve, social studies lessons can tap into their experiences giving children a chance to voice and refine their perspectives.

Writing, at its core, forces students to reconstruct and make sense of ideas and their beliefs. The writing process requires young learners to conceptualize, organize, reflect, and structure their thoughts, skills that are essential to the development of their character and role as citizens. Including writing assignments in social studies lesson plans enables teachers to assess students' knowledge and provides students a skill to become productive members of society and participate in the democratic process.

While authoring documents may be an end in itself, most oral presentations should be preceded by some form of writing in preparation for a presentation, as a best practice.

Teacher's Tip

The Northwest Regional Educational Laboratory (NWREL) developed the Six + 1 Trait Analytical Writing Rubric, which is an excellent example of the kind of rubric that can be used to promote writing in social studies

Writing in Social Studies

Preparing reports, keeping journals, taking notes, and outlining are essential parts of the learning process. The teacher should provide students with a model of such strategies so they can more easily conceptualize what the final product should look like and contain. This can often be achieved by saving an exemplary document from a student from the prior year. In addition, the teacher should structure the learning and writing experiences in a step-by-step process and should check on progress to ensure higher rates of success. Rubrics, are yet a third strategy to improve success rates.

Even though writing results in an end product, writing should be thought of as a process because that is the way it works in the real world. Students should be expected to write some papers on their own and collaboratively. Coauthoring can be particularly effective with heterogeneous groupings when the better writer understands that part of his or her role is to help the other student learn to write better. Self-assessment is yet another strategy that has proven effective (Andrade & Valtcheva, 2009). The following process should be used with writing assignments in social studies.

The Five-Step Writing Process

The complexity of writing tasks varies by grade level, but whether writing a paragraph or a longer paper, teachers should provide students a consistent pattern to improve their writing. The **process writing approach** that follows is considered a best practice and is adapted from Leu and Kinzer (1999).

I am returning this otherwise good typing paper to you because someone has printed gibberish all over it and put your name at the top.

English professor,
Ohio University

1. **Prewriting**: First and foremost, prewriting is an opportunity for students to gather their thoughts about the information and the organization of the topic. In social studies, writing may follow a lesson, a reading, a discussion of a reading, or the presentation of a graphic. The prewriting activity may involve creating a web of ideas, outlining, listing vocabulary, identifying headings, creating a chronology, or comparing ideas in groups. It may also include teacher modelling or presentation of an example of the kind of report expected.

2. **Drafting**: The purpose of drafting is to put an initial set of ideas down on paper and then receive feedback from the teacher or peers. Since this activity requires brainstorming and a degree of creativity, it is advisable to set a time limit so that the students will start writing.

3. **Revising**: Elementary-level children have traditionally been trained to focus on the quality of their penmanship, punctuation, and spelling while revising, but this is the primary focus of the fourth step, editing. During the revising stage, they should reexamine the logical progression of ideas, headings, sentence structure, content, and word selection. Peer review is an excellent strategy for both revising and editing.

4. **Editing**: It is difficult to edit one's own work, and authentic assessment requires asking a peer to edit the revised draft. Students can be taught the following editing process by teacher modelling.

a. First, the author reads the draft aloud to the peer.

b. Second, the peer reads the draft aloud to the author, but pauses at each problem, explains the problem, marks the problem, and recommends a change.

c. Third, the author accepts or rejects the recommended changes and rewrites the document.

   Elementary students should also learn the traditional editing signs for capitalizing letters, checking spelling, inserting commas, making deletions, adding insertions, starting new paragraphs, transposing letters or words, and inserting periods.

5. **Publishing and sharing**: The final step is publishing the paper in its final form. The work should be shared with the class or prepared for an event like an open house, depending on the kind of report produced.

Four Types of Writing

Risinger (1987) identified four types of writing. All four can be used to give social studies more meaning and to allow students to be creative.

1. **Reporting**: Students are directed to compile information with a minimum of critical or original thinking. ("Write a paper about four major events of the American Revolution.")

2. **Exposition**: Students are asked to explain an idea, conduct a critical investigation, synthesize issues, or bring a fresh point of view to a problem. ("Make a list comparing British and U.S. reasons for the American Revolution.")

3. **Narration**: Students are asked to write a story, an anecdote, a tall tale, a legend, a short story, a drama, or a vignette. ("Pretend you are a reporter, and write a fictitious story that includes some facts about the Boston Tea Party.")

4. **Argumentation**: Students are asked to evaluate, defend, or oppose an idea or belief. ("Write a letter to your fellow colonists detailing the reasons why they should not declare independence.")

> **Teacher's Tip**
>
> The **writers workshop** is a model that has been adopted by a large number of schools and is a great strategy to have students write about social studies topics (Lewison, & Heffernan, 2008).

Social Studies Writing Products

The following sampling of products can be effective with elementary social studies students.

- **ABC report:** The ABC report is 27 pages long, with a cover page followed by one page for each letter of the alphabet. The author of the report identifies content that can be associated with a letter. For example, if the topic is the American Revolution, "A" could be arms used in the revolution, "B" could be the Boston Massacre, and so on. The author writes a sentence or paragraph, depending on what grade he or she is in, about the topic on each page. Students could also be given the option of creating or including images. Students can be divided into three-person groups, with two group members responsible for nine letters each and one for eight letters and the cover.

- **Biography:** One of the best ways to understand history is to write a biography. Children can be asked to interview relatives, create a family tree and chronology, and then write a biography of family members or an autobiography.

- **Classroom newspaper:** Students can write articles and gather pictures to create a children's newspaper of current events or a newspaper of school and family events.

- **Magazine report:** A magazine report involves the creation of a magazine-like article with photographs, drawings, and other images either created by students or taken from published magazines. Students can be asked to make up a story based on a contemporary event, such as the last presidential election, or a historical event, such as Lexington and Concord. Social issues like poverty and crime are also excellent content for magazine reports.

- **Newscaster report:** A newscaster report is intended to emphasize public-speaking and writing skills. Students can script information from newspapers or magazines to create a simulation of the evening news. Other students can videotape the newscast, and students can take a copy home to show their families. A variation is to conduct news reports of events from history. Each student could select an event (the Lincoln assassination, the surrender at Appomattox, the Boston Tea Party), research it, write a script, and be videotaped reporting the event and interviewing the participants.

- **Note taking:** Learning to take notes can improve students' success. The Cornell note-taking system is useful, even though it was designed for college students. Elementary students can be taught to divide a piece of paper into two columns, one about one-third of a page wide and the other about two-thirds of a page wide. The student writes key words in the left column and notes from the lecture, video, or written material in the right column. During the early stages of learning to take notes, students can be guided to identify key concepts, indent brief explanations, and draw diagrams.

- **Outlining:** Outlining should emphasize sequencing and hierarchies of ideas. The classic outline form is *I, A, 1, a.* When it is applied to text narrative or a lecture, this format emphasizes the sequence, the hierarchy of ideas, and the importance of organization.

- **Picture-story sequencing:** This is used with lower elementary children. The teacher creates cartoon-like frames or has the children create them. The students organize the frames into a chronologically correct story. A picture-story sequence of great North American wars might use pictures of flags and First Americans for the French and Indian War, of George Washington for the American Revolution, and of a burning White House for the War of 1812.

- **Medium report:** A medium report is particularly appropriate for lower elementary students. After instruction, children are required to draw pictures and print vocabulary words in a medium that creatively reflects the lesson. For a lesson on Columbus, the students draw a foot locker on construction paper. Students create construction paper cutouts of items that Columbus would need for a voyage, such as a compass, a map, vegetables, and a barrel of fish by drawing pictures of these items on a separate sheet of paper and labeling each item. Other media that the teacher could use instead of a foot locker include a First American tepee, a colonial farmhouse, a turkey, a military tank, and a covered wagon.

- **Response journals:** Students can react to a lesson or a book in response journals. They can be expected to record their thoughts after a simulation, discussion, big-book reading, video, or guest speaker. Students can be asked to react to "what if" scenarios or to respond from the perspective of a character from history. Other approaches could be based on such stimuli as
  - This reminds me of a situation I found myself in . . ."
  - The person is like me because . . ."
  - I did not like this person because . . ."

- **Reading-writing center:** The teacher equips part of the room with all the reading and writing materials required for assignments in which students can work independently. For example, a teacher might make copies of two- or three-page biographies of the first 10 presidents and create a rubric based on the who-what-when-where-why-how method (refer to Topic 17) that requires each student to read the biographies and answer the questions. The teacher should provide clear directions on using the reading-writing center before students begin working there.

- **Essay:** An essay should emphasize organization and proper citation of sources. The teacher should provide an example of an end product and guide students in authoring their papers. Simple, uniform citation methods should be provided for elementary children.

- **Take-turns paper:** This kind of paper requires students to work in pairs or foursomes and to take turns adding the next sentence.

Teacher's Tip

If the teacher breaks down writing assignments into manageable steps, students feel less intimidated and have a greater likelihood of success.

These writing assignments often take many hours. The teacher should scaffold the steps for each assignment and provide frequent detailed feedback as each step is completed.

Student Presentations

The primary goals of student presentations are to improve students' writing and presentation skills and to validate their comprehension of social studies knowledge. But a more subtle goal that is important to becoming an engaged and effective citizen is the ability of students to see themselves as advocates and develop the confidence to make arguments, even in the less structured settings such as the discussion in class and while working in groups. The kind of modelling, direct instruction, and role-playing (also see Topic 26 strategy for presentation skills development) that should be part of instruction to prepare students for presentations can have a positive effect on students personal advocacy (Boyd, et al., 2007). The same principles and best practices a teacher learns for presenting lessons to a class hold true for elementary students who make presentation and should, therefore, serve as the basis for teaching children how to make verbally communicate to an audience.

Some children are natural performers; they are uninhibited and love being the center of attention. Others get anxious when they have to stand in front of an audience and make a presentation (Boyce, et al., 2007). It is for the development of the anxious child that children should be introduced at an early age to the preparation and performance of presentations. Both uninhibited and more timid students need a structure for preparing and making presentations. They will all be helped when a thoughtful teacher coaches them through the process and works more closely with students who are more timid.

Why do you think some people are apprehensive about making presentations?

Strategies for Improving Comfort Level for All Students

The following strategies can ease students' anxiety.

1. Tie the presentation into a project, such as an ABC report, timeline development, creation of a map, or a book report. Having the subject matter well in hand will build confidence (see Topic 26).
2. Implement a step-by-step protocol to convert a written project into a presentation. Begin by teaching outlining, the use of index cards to take notes, and the creation of props (transparencies, pictures). Then provide feedback on student materials.

3. Let the more timid students rehearse their presentations in front of you with no one else around.
4. Require students to rehearse their presentations at home in front of their parents or siblings, if possible.
5. Place students in groups to prepare and rehearse their presentations.
6. Encourage students to visualize the entire presentation in their minds' eyes.
7. Have students write out a few questions that they expect or want the audience to ask, and be prepared to answer them.

Keys to a Great Presentation

Discuss the following ideas with students as they prepare for their presentations.

1. Don't try to memorize your entire presentation, just know the key ideas and tell us about the subject.
2. Be enthusiastic.
3. Make eye contact.
4. Begin with an attention-getter.
5. Avoid fill-ins like "ah," "so," "you know," "well," "uh," and "um."
6. Use good posture.
7. Use hand motions.
8. Close with something interesting, such as a famous quote or a provocative question.
9. Use humor (this is not the same as being funny).
10. Stay within the time limit.

Teacher's Tip

Debating, using formalized, grade-appropriate rules and forums, can be implemented at the elementary level, but be cautious. While debaters hone their skills in preparation, argument, counterargument, logical thinking, and questioning, they also become competitive and lose sight of the search for truth by using reason and collaboration. *Debate Central* at the University of Vermont offer articles, streaming video, topics, and techniques for presentations and debates.

Assignment 27.1

INTASC Standards 1, 2, 3, 4, 5, 7, and 8

ABC Report

Using the NWREL Six + 1 Trait Analytical Writing Rubric develop a rubric for an ABC report. Create a model of an ABC report using one of the Core Knowledge Readings 21, 23, or 25. Be prepared to discuss your results in class and submit the assignment to your professor.

Assignment 27.2

INTASC Standards 1, 2, 3, 4, 5, 7, and 8

Strategy for Reluctant Writers

View the TeacherTube video "Tech Tip for Reluctant Writers (Elementary Level)" by searching TeacherTube or clicking on the link at the Premium Website. For a 2nd grade class, find a social studies image in Google Images or another source that you can apply this strategy to. In a one page document (attach the image), list the social studies topic, the big idea, and the most important information knowledge and procedural knowledge you would cover with your students prior to the writing assignment. Be prepared to discuss your results in class and submit the assignment to your professor.

WEBSITE RESOURCES • Writing and Presentations	
Video	*TeachSource* Elementary Writing Instruction: Process Writing: This workshop shows how teachers use historical fiction about the Middle Ages to develop students' writing skills
Booklet	**ERIC Online** *ED502942*, Helping Your Child Become a Reader is a booklet you can distribute to parents by the U.S. Department of Education that explains how parents can help their children become better writers and readers.
Sample High-Quality Internet Lessons or Activities	
Lower Elementary	*Read/Write/Think* Acrostic Poems: All About Me and My Favorite Things: Students write free-verse acrostic poems about themselves using the letters of their names to begin each line. *Read/Write/Think* A Daily DEAR Program: Drop Everything and Read: This is a structured independent reading activity.

Upper Elementary	*Edsitement* A family "travel log": Students create a travel log as they travel through cyberspace to find out what's happening in their ancestral homelands.
	Thirteen.org This Just In! Nile Network News Update: Students conduct research on engineering, scientific, architectural, and artistic contributions of the ancient Egyptians and share their findings by producing a TV news broadcast presentation.
	All linked websites (designated by the green color) and those listed here are available as clickable links at the book's Premium Website www.cengage.com/login, for ease of access. These links will be updated periodically to reflect changes and new resources as they become available.

Topic 28

Artifacts, Primary Documents, and Realia

The use of **artifacts,** such as an image of the original page from the diary of Lewis and Clark's expedition, an ancient map of the "New World,"or a political campaign poster; **primary documents,** such as the Declaration of Independence or a transcription of the diary entry of the Lewis and Clark expedition; or **realia,** such as a more contemporary artifact like a sombrero, stimulate students' interest in social studies. But they require instruction on how to read or interpret them (Kobrin, 1996). Primary documents such as London and Boston newspaper accounts of the burning of Washington, D.C. in 1814 can be used to expose students to multiple perspectives on events of the past and apply the subjective and contradictory renditions to present day events, thus requiring students to use critical thinking skills. The Internet has placed many of these kinds of resources at your fingertips. You should select these kinds of resources because they can be used to:

- **Create a question:** why did people invent sombreros?
- **Challenge a belief:** an "upside down" image in which the southern hemisphere is on top of the globe
- **Encourage empathy:** a picture of homeless children from a newspaper
- **Introduce a contradiction:** comparing Lincoln's two famous but apparently contradictory statements for the Lincoln-Douglas debates
- **Produce a new insight:** a comparison of the Israeli and Iranian constitutions, both of which establish religious states

Teacher's Tip

Selecting grade-appropriate artifacts, realia, and primary documents requires the same kinds of thoughtfulness as you use in selecting topics and reading materials. If in doubt about the appropriateness of an image or reading passage, seek out a colleague's opinion. Would it be appropriate to use photographs of German concentration camp victims with third-grade students?

Primary Documents

Primary documents are original records created at the time historical events occurred or after events in the form of memoirs and oral histories. These primary documents or sources fall into two categories: (1) **text-based,** such as diaries, newspapers, letters, manuscripts, speeches, journals, interviews, memoirs, and government documents (which can be artifacts if in pictured in their original state; and (2) **images** and **recordings**, such as photographs, audio recordings, moving pictures, or video recordings. Both kinds of primary sources are the raw material to interpret the past.

The Core Knowledge series at the Premium Website has two primary documents: Reading 22 has excerpts of Patrick Henry's "Give Me Liberty" speech and Reading 24 has the Gettysburg Address by President Abraham Lincoln. How would you use these in a lesson?

Text-Based Primary Documents

Because vocabulary and sentence structure in historical primary documents will likely be archaic and not likely be grade-level reading material, your students reading skills may not have prepared them for the more and challenging reading assignment. As a result, teachers need to preview new vocabulary and give context to the document as part of a prereading activity. At the end of this topic you will find a list of website resources where you can find suitable primary documents and images. In addition, at the National Archives, you can view lessons and rubrics that can be modified for the elementary school level for use with primary sources. At learner.org, you can view the video lesson, *Using Primary Sources*. This exceptional video details a strategy to be used with upper elementary students that includes primary documents, group activity, and a graphic organizer for a lesson on colonial America.

Images

Using images (such as a child arriving at Ellis Island, an etching of the Boston Massacres, or the front page of the *New York Times* announcing the end of World War II in Europe) in social studies is effective because it allows children to use a medium they are familiar with and, in the case of lower elementary students, reading skills are not always necessary (Barton, 2001). The very nature of images as compared to linear text incorrectly suggests they are less complex because we tend to subsume the image as a whole, but in fact images are very complex because of their nonlinear format and, often, emotional appeal (Ortony, 1993). As a result, images have created new challenges for social studies instruction (Werner, 2004). When reading text, people control the mental pictures they create in their minds' eyes based on the author's words. When we encounter an image, it is thrust upon our psyche by appealing directly to our **affective domain**.

Images can be classified as **static** (a picture or a cartoon) or **moving** (film or video). Moving images have the greatest visceral impact. The media of delivery for static images include books, magazines, the Internet, video projectors, and computer monitors. Moving images are found in theaters and on television, the Internet, videotape, film, and multimedia CDs. Static images can be compiled into a sequence to create quasi-moving images, and parts of moving images can be placed in a fixed medium.

In a book or text-based primary source, such as the "Give Me Liberty . . ." document at the Premium Website, the reader must integrate the time and place into an evaluation of the intent of the author in order to develop an objective idea from the information. A scene from a movie such as *Schindler's List* is powerful because it provides rich images and sounds, places the viewer in the event, and creates a desired affective impact with no required reading. Films, television, and even static images don't rely on our imaginations to create the pictures; all they require is for us to *suspend disbelief* that he or she is not really there in person. For example, if your professor showed you a picture of a Holocaust victim, you would have a certain kind of response. If your professor were to say, "A victim of the Holocaust," you would create the picture in your mind's eye. Essentially, images make viewers part of an event, whereas words place them outside it.

Creating mind's-eye images based on words requires more work than viewing images that have been provided. To oversimplify, images do not require the viewer to cognitively shape what they see. The goal of all media—from storytelling to books to I-Max theaters—is to communicate viscerally and cognitively.

> **Can you think of an image from history that particularly impacted your affective domain?**

Topic 29 provides a sequence for teaching students how to analyze charts, a kind of image, and you should refer to Topic 23's "Close Reading" for ideas on how to interpret images. These two approaches should be used as a guide in teaching students how to decipher primary sources, artifacts, and realia. Teaching students to evaluate a source using a systematic approach and set of questions is as valuable as what the students will learn from the actual source itself.

Realia

Realia are physical objects, and are also referred to as "artifacts." An item like an ancient coin from the Roman Empire, for example, is typically considered an artifact, whereas a current-day wedding gown from Ethiopia would be considered realia. Realia can include such items as clothing, adornments, utensils, toys, magazines, military items, coins and bills, postcards, games, photographs, flags, tools, and household items. They tend to be things you can touch, but not paper. For elementary students, items from five years ago can be enlightening. Although realia websites have images of coins, arrowheads, and other artifacts, the effectiveness of realia is tied to the tactile quality more than to the visual quality. Simply put, realia is most effective when students can touch and manipulate the items.

Questions to Ask with Primary Documents, Realia, and Artifacts

Some questions about realia and artifacts that can spark a discussion follow.

1. What is it?
2. What is it made of?
3. What is its use?
4. How old is it?
5. How was it made?
6. Where was it made?
7. What does it tell us about the people?
8. Was it valuable or scarce?
9. What is its history, its predecessor, and its contemporary equivalent?

At learner.org, there is an exceptional online video lesson titled, *Explorations in Archeology and History*, in which a teacher explores the students' family history through their personal artifacts.

Can you think of artifacts or realia from your family or home that could be used in a social studies class?

Assignment 28.1

INTASC Standards 1, 2, 3, 4, 5, 7, and 8

Cartoon or Picture Interpretation

Go to the Political Cartoonist Index Website (or Google "political cartoons.") Find a cartoon or a picture to print, create a transparency of the image, and bring the transparency to class. Develop a series of questions that you could use with elementary students to analyze the cartoon. The "Eight Questions for Analyzing Information" should be helpful in this

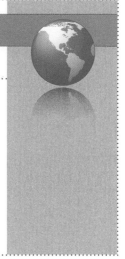

(Continued)

Assignment 28.1 (*Continued*)

INTASC Standards 1, 2, 3, 4, 5, 7, and 8

regard (see Topic 23). You may want to use the following outline, inserting questions and key ideas after each step.

Step 1: Display the image.
Step 2: Interpret the image.
Step 3: Draw conclusions about the message of the image.

Be prepared to share your outline and image with the class and to turn in the assignment and transparency to the professor.

Assignment 28.2

INTASC Standards 1, 2, 3, 4, 5, 7, and 8

Collect Primary Documents or Realia

Go to the Premium Website and select one of the following Houghton Mifflin Readings.

- Reading 2, "The First Americans"
- Reading 7, "Coming to America"
- Reading 12, "Conflict Grows"

Search the Internet to collect five related primary documents, images, or images of realia that could be used to enrich the lesson and be prepared to submit this assignment to your professor and explain your ideas in class.

Over 10,000 images are available by using Google images. Another great resource is the History and Images Index at the Library of Congress. This is a gateway to historical pictures, caricatures, postcards, prints, and posters.

Lesson Plans	***ERIC Online*** *ED442126,* Jamestown Changes (2000): This lesson plan examines the original census statistics of the colony. ED364449, Brother against Brother: The Civil War (1993): This lesson plan uses the Emancipation Proclamation as a primary document. *U.S. National Archives* The National Archives has over 60 lesson plans using primary documents and "worksheets" that can be used to analyze the documents.
Primary Documents	*American Memory of the Library of Congress* A gateway to primary documents. *European Primary Documents* A gateway to European primary documents.
Images	*Google* Has over 10,000 images.

Sample High-Quality Internet Lessons and Activities

	Edsitement What Was Columbus Thinking? Students use excerpts from Columbus' diary and letters in a lesson on the discovery of the Americas. *Edsitement* Colonial Broadsides: A Student-Created Play: Students collaborate in interpreting broadsides and creating a timeline.
	Check the Premium Website, www.cengage.com/login, for additional links and links that are periodically updated to reflect new resources as they become available.

Topic 29
Charts and Statistics

Charts are powerful learning devices; yet our ability to understand them is sometimes questionable. **Charts** (including tables, graphs, and diagrams) are typically compiled as an alternative or supplement to narrative. Typically, that information is statistical or numerically based, such the figures in this topic. **Statistics** can be presented in both narrative and graphic formats. This kind of normative data is often the product of empirical studies. The presentation of this kind of information requires reading skills and interpretation skills that are different from those used to understand typical narrative.

Charts

Students are typically not taught how to create or interpret charts, teachers often ignore them when instructing, and students often ignore them when reading (Duplass, 1996a). Because the interpretation of charts often requires a different kind of reading—if not a higher level of analysis—than narrative, readers often skip them, thinking that the same information will be presented in narrative form. However, charts can be particularly informative precisely because they condense complex information into a simplified form. They can also be deceptive because readers may misperceive the apparent straightforward approach as less likely to be misleading.

Chart images have particular relevance to the social studies teacher's quest to cultivate problem-solving skills and build an informed citizenry. One of the most effective ways to teach children about charts is to have students create them for the teacher to use during lessons as transparencies or as boardwork; another is to teach about charts when they are encountered in reading materials.

Teaching Students to Create Charts

The teacher should identify a number of essential components of charts when teaching students how to create a chart. A chart has both *literal information* and *figurative information*. **Literal information** is usually raw data or summations of raw data. **Figurative information** is deduced from the presentation of the data; it is the implied idea that the author is conveying, and it is effectively communicated by the type of chart and the headings selected to present the literal information.

> Page forward to Figure 29.1. There are **nine pieces** of *literal information*. But, what is the author trying to convey with the *figurative information*, **particularly by item 1 being an "exploded" slice of the pie chart?**

One of the most important contributions a teacher can make is to ensure that students understand that charts are constructed out of data that are collected by surveys or other research or found in reports, books, and other sources. For this reason, the teacher should start teaching about charts with data that clearly lend themselves to a chart presentation. The instructional process should proceed through the following sequence.

Instructional Process

1. Frame a topic relevant to students' experiences or to the social studies content. The following example uses data about how students spend their day.
2. Define categories of information to be collected.
3. Collect data or provide raw data based on the categories.
4. Calculate literal information that can be used in meaningful comparisons.
5. Create a chart that includes:
   a. Selection of chart type (figure, bar graph, diagram) that best conveys the figurative information;
   b. Determination of the title, date, source, categories, and labels; and
   c. Determination of the literal information, linear connections, axis titles, data labels, and scale.
6. Compare and contrast the literal and figurative information, proceeding from left to right, top to bottom, line by line.
7. Extend learning by relating the information to the students' experiences or the social studies content.
8. Assess the effectiveness of the chart as a form of communication and expose possible bias in the choice of categories and chart format.

Example of an Instructional Sequence to Teach About Charts

This strategy involves the creation of two charts (Figures 29.1 and 29.2) as a class project. The lesson is designed for upper elementary students using an active learning approach and starting with their daily activity. A pie chart and a stacked bar chart are used to show how the same literal information is conveyed in two different types of charts.

Figure 29.1   Student Average Daily Activity

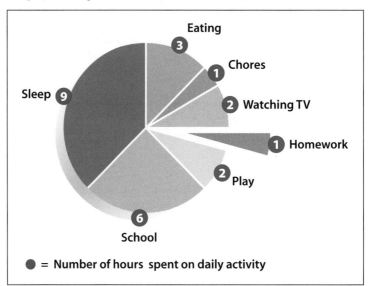

Source: Fourth-grade class at George Washington Elementary School, 2002.

Segment 1: Pie Chart

1. **Attention-getter:** Introduce the topic, "Let's see how we spend our time."

2. **Content presentation 1:** Whole-group discussion using the list, group, and label method results in students' reporting their daily activities to identify the categories for the charts. The teacher explains that the class will be surveyed to collect data. Using the right-side columns of Figure 29.2 as a model, have each student record how he or she typically spends time during a day. The teacher explains that this is a survey.

3. **Math integration:** Surveys are collected, and teams calculate averages for each of the categories. The results are placed on the chalkboard by category. The number of hours should add up to 24.

4. **Content presentation 2:** The teacher creates a class pie chart, Figure 29.1, and explains that pie charts are one of the best forms to show the ratio of categories (allocation of time) to the total (24 hours). Reading a chart is modeled and explained. The teacher reviews the chart proceeding from left to right, top to bottom, line by line. Emphasis is placed on the components of the chart (not the content) that appear in Figure 29.1: titles, type of chart, labels, slice sizes as reflective of a proportionate share of a whole, and source.

5. **Independent practice:** Each student is asked to create a personal pie chart based on his or her original response to the survey.

6. **Content presentation 3:** In a whole-class activity, the teacher reviews Figure 29.1 and the student's personal charts for content by proceeding from left to right, top to bottom, line by line. The teacher conducts a whole-group discussion focused on comparison and contrast of the

literal and figurative information in and between the two charts and inferences that can be drawn within and between the charts. This involves questions like "Who watches the most TV?"

7. **Extension:** The teacher ends the lesson by focusing a whole-group discussion on homework and its relationship to success. The teacher's decision to have the homework slice of the pie chart "exploded" would serve as the basis for an examination of bias in the construction of a chart image.

Segment 2: Stacked Bar Chart

1. **Content presentation 4:** The teacher introduces the concept of a stacked bar chart (left-side columns of Figure 29.2). The teacher reviews the chart proceeding from left to right, top to bottom, line by line. Emphasis is placed on the components of a stacked bar chart.
2. **Guided practice:** In groups of four, students convert the data from the pie charts to the stacked bar charts using the second chart as a fill-in-the-blank handout.
3. **Writing integration:** The teacher has students employ their writing skills to explain the data in narrative form.
4. **Extension:** The learning episode is extended in a whole-class activity.

The teacher asks students if a being from outer space could read this chart and reasonably conclude that people do not take baths or attend religious services. The teacher leads a whole-class discussion clarifying individual preferences for pie charts, stacked bar charts, tables, or narratives in order to assess the effectiveness of the chart as a form of communication.

Teaching Students to Interpret Charts

Teachers must emphasize the importance of the literal and figurative information contained in charts that students find in books, magazines, and other sources so that the author's intent, and perhaps biases, are made obvious.

Instructional Process

The following steps should be used when presenting a chart for interpretation.

1. Present the chart.
   a. Explain the type of chart (line chart, figure, pie chart).
   b. Identify the title and make connections to the facts, concepts, and generalizations of the social studies topic.
   c. Evaluate the reliability of the source and date.
2. Examine the categories of the literal information from left to right, top to bottom, line by line to ensure a baseline of understanding of the axis titles, headings, scale, and data labels.
   a. Define the categories to reveal the reader's assumptions.
   b. Explore other possible categories based on the topic.

Figure 29.2 Student's Average Daily Activity Stacked Bar Chart

	Class Averages				Individual Student		
Class Average Categories	Hours in a Day (24 hours)	Cumulative Percent	Percent in a 24 Hour Day		Individual Student Categories	Hours in a Day (24 hours)	Cumulative Percent	Percent in a 24 Hour Day
Sleep	9	100%	38%				
Sleep							
Sleep							
Sleep							
Sleep							
Sleep							
Sleep							
Sleep							
Sleep							
School	6	62%	25%				
School							
School							
School							
School							
School							
Eating	3	37%	13%				
Eating							
Eating							
TV	2	24%	8%				
TV							
Play	2	16%	8%				
Play							
Chores	1	8%	4%				
Homework	1	4%	4%				

Source: Fourth-grade class at George Washington Elementary School, 2002.

3. Examine the literal information from left to right, top to bottom, line by line to ensure a baseline of understanding.

4. Generate and record figurative information to discover the possible inferences by hypothesis testing:

   a. Based on the literal information;

   b. Based on the literal information compared to the title; and

   c. Based on the literal information compared to the social studies topic.

5. Extend learning by predicting future outcomes based on the literal and figurative information.
6. Assess the effectiveness of the chart as a form of communication, and expose possible bias by the choice of categories and chart format.

Statistics

Descriptive statistics explain or summarize facts about a population, as in the example of how students spend their time. **Inferential statistics** are used to infer or predict from a sample—for example, using the data from one fourth-grade class to predict the use of time by all fourth graders. Statistical information can be presented in charts like those in the preceding section, or it can be presented in narrative form. Children need to learn to interpret and present data in both forms as part of social studies instruction. Whether in narrative or chart form, reading statistical data should follow the close reading approach (refer to Topic 23), particularly Level 2:

What is the author's purpose?
What is the key question the author is trying to answer?
What is the author's point of view?
What are the author's assumptions?
What are the implications?
What information is the author using and is it accurate?
What are the inferences?
What are the concepts and generalizations?

In addition, there are key concepts about statistics that elementary children can learn. *Food for Thought,* by the Population Reference Bureau, is an excellent upper elementary lesson plan that includes geography, statistics, and active learning.

Interpretation and Bias in Statistics

Statistics are used to persuade as well as to enlighten. For this reason, examining their presentation is necessary to reveal the author's intent.

Charts

Statistics in a chart form can be misleading simply because of the structure selected by the person who creates the chart. Figures 29.3 and 29.4 present the same data in two different ways. The only differences are that Figure 29.3 starts at $0, uses increments of $10 million, and shows each year, while Figure 29.4 starts at $20 million, uses increments of $1 million, and shows two years.

> *There are three kinds of lies: lies, damned lies, and statistics.*
>
> Benjamin Disraeli

Figure 29.3   State Payroll

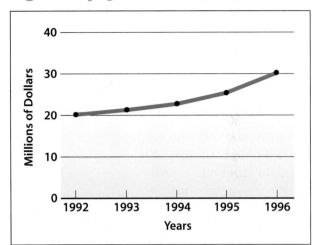

Figure 29.4   State Payroll

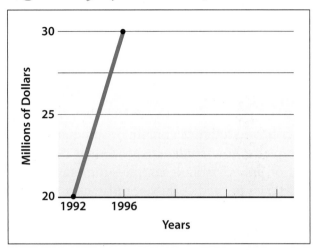

 If you read only Figure 29.3, what conclusion would you reach? If you read only Figure 29.4, would you draw a different conclusion?

Narrative

Having students convert charts into narrative and narrative into charts is a best practice for learning about statistics. The teacher should first model an examination of different samples of narrative and charts that include statistics. The following could be used to begin to teach inference and bias. Based on the information in Figures 29.1 and 29.2, the following two statements could be made:

Statement 1. "The typical student in the fourth-grade class at George Washington Elementary School spends two hours a day watching TV, *but only* one hour a day on homework."

Statement 2. "The typical student in the fourth-grade class at George Washington Elementary spends two hours watching TV a day and one hour on homework per day."

Statement 1 has an unequivocal inference due to the use of the words "but" and "only." Statement 2 is more neutral because a decision was made to replace "but" with "and" and to leave out "only." The decision to select one set of words and sentence structure over another usually depends on whether the goal is to persuade or to inform. Children should be taught how to detect both forms of communication and to write both ways as a procedural knowledge skill.

Key Concepts for Teachers

Statistics in social studies narrative require special attention. Take the statement "80 percent of all U.S. children can talk by the time they are two and a half years of age." Most readers take this to imply "normal" behavior, and parents might conclude that something is wrong if their child is not talking by that age. However, the age at which a child first talks can be affected by siblings, by parents' educational level, by the amount of reading material in the home, by the amount of TV that is watched, and by parental verbal interaction, among other factors. A "normal" child might be part of the 20 percent who don't speak until they are older. On the other hand, such "norms" are guidelines by which we can identify behaviors that might be worthy of further investigation—by a speech pathologist, for example.

Key Concepts for Elementary Students

Most of the following concepts are mathematically oriented and can be extended into math lessons depending on the age of the students.

- **Averages** like the average height of the class can be used to demonstrate a range of numbers and how an average can be misleading.
- **Proportion** is a relative measure of differences. "There are 15 girls in the class and 5 boys, for a ratio of 3 to 1" is a *ratio*, whereas "75 percent of the class is girls and 25 percent boys" is a *percentage*.
- **Probability** depicts the likelihood that something will happen. It is frequently used to make predictions: "Based on poll data, it is likely that John will win the election," or "90 percent of the people on welfare did not graduate from high school."
- **Relative** and **absolute descriptions**: "I lost half of all my money in the stock market" is a *relative description* of an undesirable event and elicits sympathy. However, if the same person says, "I lost $100 in the stock market today," this *absolute description* might cause you to be less sympathetic. Similarly, an automobile dealership might advertise that its customer satisfaction rating went up by 50 points. But the dealer might be using a 1,000-point scale, and the increase may have been only from 100 to 150.
- **Correlation** and **causality**: It is easy to confuse correlations and causes. In a *correlation*, when one event occurs another event is also likely to occur, but one is not necessarily the cause of the other. The positive *correlation* between years of education and income and the negative correlation between wearing seatbelts and automobile deaths probably involve cause-and-effect relationships. But despite the positive correlation between sales of umbrellas and suicide rates, no one would think that one causes the other. (Communities with higher amounts of rainfall and fewer hours of sunshine have higher rates of depression and suicide than sunnier communities with higher rates of sunshine.)

Assignment 29.1

INTASC Standards 1, 2, 3, 4, 5, 7, and 8

Teaching a Graph

Use the example of an "Instructional Sequence to Teach Charts" in this topic to develop a grade-appropriate instructional sequence using one of the charts from the Premium Website's readings.

Reading 4, "Needs and Wants," page 129

Reading 7, " Coming to America," page 172

Reading 14, "The Great Depression, " page 598

Be prepared to share your ideas with the class and to submit the assignment with the content presentation and the chart to your professor.

Check the Premium Website, www.cengage.com/login, for additional links and links that are periodically updated to reflect new resources as they become available.

Topic 30

Creating and Interpreting Maps

When someone says the word "geography," typically the first thing that comes to mind is a map. Even though geography educators consider maps essential to children's understanding of the world, maps are only one tool and one aspect of geography education, as explained in Topic 20. In fact, cartographers do not use the term "maps" but instead refer to these documents as **projections**. From early civilization to the mid-20th century, mapmakers could only "project" what, for example, the continents looked like because photographic images of large land masses did not exist until satellites and space exploration in the 1960s made them possible. Now we can produce actual pictures instead of drawing projections. The free Google Earth is, by any standard, an exceptional interactive program for examining the Earth's surface that you can use with students in your classroom.

The purposes of the following four-question pretest are to help you learn important information knowledge and procedural knowledge about maps that you will also want to teach your elementary students and to demonstrate how a pretest can be used as an attention-getter and organizing scheme for a lesson.

Map Quiz Pretest

1. Which is bigger, Greenland or South America?

   A. Greenland   **B.** South America

2. Reno, Nevada, is _____ of Los Angeles, California.

   A. Northeast   **B.** Northwest   **C.** Southeast   **D.** Southwest

3. The west coast of South America is in the _____ time zone.

   A. Eastern   **B.** Central   **C.** Mountain   **D.** Pacific

4. It will get colder as you travel north.

   A. True   **B.** False

Why Map Reading Is Often Difficult for Children

For a number of reasons, teachers need to be very thoughtful and thorough when teaching children to draw, complete, and interpret maps.

1. **Maps are visual abstractions.** A bird's-eye view, which adults take for granted, is a novel idea to lower elementary children. One of the best ways to overcome this problem is to start with the familiar such as having students create bird's-eye view drawings of their classroom or homes.

2. **Maps distort the globe in converting a sphere to a plane.** This is evident when looking at Mercator and Robison projections at the same time. Examples of each can be found at the Alabama Maps Website. In teaching world geography, you will find it better to use a globe or an image of a globe than a map.

3. **Maps need to be carefully presented to ensure that students will understand them.** You shouldn't rush through maps; take the time to examine them in a systematic way (see "Toads on Logs" later in this topic).

4. **Children are egocentric.** When someone asks a child a question, the child is inclined to answer from his or her own perspective. So if you ask a child in Miami if it will get colder if he or she travels north, the child will almost always answer that it will. A child in Argentina would answer no, because Argentina is below the equator.

The Essence of Maps

There are two of key elements to all maps that teachers should be particularly attentive to.

The term **orientation** refers to the relationship between directions on a map and compass directions. Most maps today have the north at the top of a map.

Map scale refers to the consistent ratio (10,000 miles equals one-fourth inch, as an example) used to draw the map. This allows the reader to estimate relative sizes of the entities (such as land masses) and distances between entities with a degree of accuracy.

Common Types of Maps

Maps are graphic representations of all or part of Earth's surface drawn to scale on a two-dimensional plane with cultural and natural features depicted by symbols. Learning about the different types of maps and their names is part of the necessary procedural knowledge and vocabulary essential to elementary social studies education. The Enchanted Learning Website has a large collection of map and geography materials that can be used to create lessons.

A **base map** is a general-purpose map that shows the locations of land and water. The Mercator and Robison projections are world wall maps commonly used in schools that have the typical attributes of base maps. Base maps often show and label rivers and lakes; state and local boundaries; and roads, towns, and cities.

> What variables determine temperature at locations on Earth? Topic 36 offers a problem-solving active learning experience for geography that answers this question.

Physical maps include topographic maps that use *contour lines*, joining points of equal height or depth, to indicate elevation. Other physical maps, called "relief maps," use different colors or shadings to indicate elevation. (For an example of a relief map, see Houghton Mifflin Reading 8, page 37, at the Premium Website.)

Teacher's Tip

It is a best practice to use a globe rather than a world map in teaching world geography. Twelve-inch beach-ball, inflatable globes are relatively inexpensive in school supply stores. Purchase five so that students can use them in groups.

Thematic maps primarily portray information on a single topic or a set of topics. A thematic map may feature cultural information, such as population, or physical information, such as annual rainfall. (For an example of a population map, see Houghton Mifflin Reading 14, page 598.)

Many types of maps are combinations of base and thematic approaches. **Political maps** have features such as the outlines of countries, states, and cities. (For an example of a map of the United States that also indicates the number of electoral votes, see Houghton Mifflin Reading 15, page 673.) **Road maps** show major and minor highways, cities, and towns, often also marking campgrounds, parks, and other tourist features. **Weather maps** show weather conditions such as fronts, temperatures, rain, snow, and fog at a particular time or temperature or precipitation ranges during a particular period.

These examples of maps are by no means exhaustive. Students at the elementary level should learn about different kinds of maps—both contemporary and historical versions.

Creating and Interpreting Maps

The instructional sequence for teaching about charts and diagrams outlined in Topic 31 should be used to teach about maps as well. The teacher should begin analyzing a map by proceeding from left to right, top to bottom, item by item, making sure to cover each component before proceeding to the unique information knowledge of the map.

The best way to help children understand maps is to have them create maps. With lower elementary students, the teacher can begin by having them draw maps of their bedrooms or houses, the classroom, the schoolyard, and the neighborhood, which is referred to in the literature as the **small-world approach** (Gertig & Silverman, 2007). After the teacher has modelled ways to create and interpret maps, the **Toads on Logs** mnemonic device (Lapham, 2001) can help children remember to include the key map components.

1. Title at the top
2. Orientation for the compass rose (see Houghton Mifflin Reading 3 page 75 for an example of a compass rose)
3. Author for your name
4. Date for the date you created the map
5. Scale to explain the size of the map
6. Legend to explain the symbols used in the map (See Houghton Mifflin Reading 17, page 358, for an example of a legend.)
7. Outline of the perimeter of the map
8. Grid to mark off the distances on the perimeter
9. Source to identify the source(s) you used to create the map

The teacher should use this mnemonic to examine maps for literal understanding and then discuss the figurative meaning in the lesson.

A number of geography websites provide maps. Following are sites that are most appropriate for elementary education.

Assignment 30.1

INTASC Standards 1, 2, 3, 4, 5, 7, and 8

Integrating History and Geography

One way to combine geography and history in a lesson is to use historical maps. The Perry-Castañeda Library Map Collection at the University of Texas is an outstanding source. Using one of the Core Knowledge readings from the Premium Website, download at least three historical maps that are relevant to the reading you selected and explain in your paper how each one would be used in a lesson. Be prepared to share your maps with the class and submit this assignment to your professor.

Assignment 30.2

INTASC Standards 1, 2, 3, 4, 5, 7, and 8

Map Skills: Modify an Internet Lesson Plan

Conduct a site-specific search on the Internet using either the Gateway to Educational Materials (GEM), National Geographic, or Core Knowledge Websites to identify a lesson plan for teaching map skills related to local, state, U.S., or world geography. Print out the Internet lesson plan, complete a lesson plan statement of goals based on the lesson, and submit it with a typed paper that explains how the lesson and any modifications you would make to the lesson would achieve your goals.

WEBSITE RESOURCES • Maps

Video	*Learner.org* China Through Mapping is an exemplary lesson on teaching map skills through active learning strategies.
TeacherTube	How to Read a Map, video with techno music and cartoon robots
Website	*About.Com* Blank maps of countries and the U.S. states. *National Atlas* Historical and contemporary maps of the United States. *Library of Congress* Historical maps from 1500 to 2000.
Lessons Plans	*National Geographic* Search "Expeditions" for maps.

Sample High-Quality Internet Lessons and Activities

Lower Elementary	*Teachervision:* This lesson plan in map making is based on the children's book, Make Way for Ducklings.
Upper Elementary	*Core Knowledge:* Students create 3-D maps of their state.
	All linked websites (designated by the green color) and those listed here are available as clickable links at the book's Premium website, www.cengage.com, for ease of access. These links will be updated periodically to reflect changes and new resources as they become available.

Topic 31

Chronological Thinking and Timelines

Teacher's Tip

Teaching the time, days, months, and calendar is a part of social studies instruction. One of the best ways to teach time is to have each child create a clock out of a paper plate and clock hands out of construction paper. The child should manipulate the clock as you teach time.

Chronological thinking is essential to understanding history. Timelines are important tools in teaching children about time periods and chronology. Historians use timelines so that they can more clearly make observations, draw conclusions, and support propositions about events or trends in history.

Chronological Thinking

Children in lower elementary grades may have difficulty understanding concepts of duration and sequence, which is a prerequisite to understanding time. Analogies like "It will take as long as *Sesame Street*," give children some idea of how long an event will take. Finding similar analogies to time, such as "This would have been about the time your great-great-grandmother was your age" can give some sense of distance from the current day. One early goal in elementary education is to make sure that all the students know how to tell time. The lesson should also include learning the seasons, days, months, and years. Children should be able to perform the tasks shown in Table 31.1.

Table 31.1   **Children's Ability to Think Chronologically**

Age	Children Can
3–5	Sequence events like their birth order with that of siblings and days of the week.
6–8	Add ages to birth order, like brothers' and sisters' ages, and match events to dates, like 1492 and Columbus.
9–11	Place persons and events in time periods, like George Washington and the Revolutionary Period, and make relative time placements, like "The Civil War was about 150 years ago."
12–14	Understand most confusing terms (see Table 31.2) and generalize dates to periods, like "The year 1860 is in the 19th century."

Table 31.2 Indefinite Time Expressions and Confusing Terms

Indefinite Time Expressions	Confusing Terms
See you later!	*century*
until recently	A.M. and P.M.
in the Middle Ages	*decade*
in the days before radio	*time zones*
in pioneer days	B.C./B.C.E or A.D./C.E.
at the beginning of modern times	*quarter to*
prehistoric times	*half past*

Adapted from Saxe, 1992.

A method for helping children understand basic time periods is to segment a student's day into "wake-up" to "go to bed" and relate events to morning, afternoon, and evening. This can also serve as an analogy to historical periods or sequence.

Another goal of lower elementary education is to move students from indefinite to definite time expressions and to clarify confusing time-related terms and concepts. The teacher can model increasing precision in time expressions and can teach key terms as vocabulary. Table 31.2 lists some indefinite time expressions and potentially confusing terms.

Timelines

Timelines require students to apply definite time frames to information knowledge. The term "timeline" is not always consistently used to describe the same thing. An Internet search for "timeline" will produce a *chronological listing* of events from a time period like the American Revolution rather than the more traditional form of a timeline. Sequencing events is not the same as creating a timeline both because the sequence may or may not include dates, and, more important, it is not a graphic image that depicts the distance in time between events.

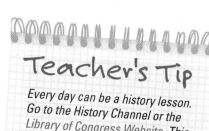

Teacher's Tip

Every day can be a history lesson. Go to the History Channel or the Library of Congress Website, This Day in History, for a listing of events that you can put on the chalkboard so students can find out more about what happened on the day they were born.

Teachers should use timelines to place historical events in the appropriate time periods, sequence, and relative distance from each other. Of equal importance is having students create timelines. Timelines can be either vertical or horizontal. Students should be taught the following rules for creating timelines, and teachers should model the rules as part of instruction. For examples of different kinds of timelines, see Houghton Mifflin's Readings 12 and 13, which have a running timeline, and Houghton Mifflin's Reading 1, which has a timeline that introduces first grade students to the concept of time at the Premium Website.

Rules for Timelines

Effective timelines are:

1. **Properly titled.** For example, "Timeline: Important Events of the 1900s" is the title of Figure 31.1.

2. **Drawn proportionately.** In Figure 31.1, the 1900s are divided into 10-year increments, and the space between the decades is equal.

   a. Any period and any increments are appropriate as long as the increments are of equal duration. This is a graphic image, so it is essential for the spaces between the years to be of equal distance.

   b. When drawing a timeline on the chalkboard, the teacher should mark a middle and two end points, then subdivide the two sections proportionately. In the case of Figure 31.1, the two sections are 1900 to 1950 and 1950 to 2000. Mark off the years proportionately and begin writing with a date and narrative "1929 Stock Market Crash" and then draw a line to the appropriate spot on the timeline between 1920 and 1930.

   c. If the timeline is created in advance as a transparency, the teacher should use a ruler to ensure equal distances between dates. When a timeline is created using word-processing software, tabs or tables will help keep the spaces equal.

3. **Clearly labeled.** If the timeline is on a transparency, the labels can be completed in advance and revealed as the event is presented. If the timeline is on a chalkboard, the teacher first creates it on paper and then adds the labels sequentially as they are presented. A more active approach is to have individual students come to the chalkboard or overhead projector to label the events on the timeline.

4. **Graphically rich.** Timelines should be visually appealing. Although Figure 31.1 is a traditional timeline, pictures and images can be used instead of text to define events in a timeline for young children. For example, a musket could be used to stand for Lexington and Concord.

Figure 31.1   Timeline:Important Events of the 1900s

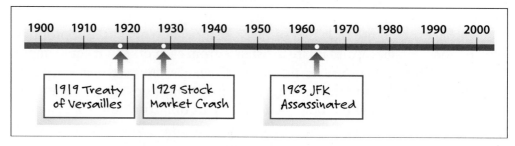

Look at the "Timeline Graphic Organizer" at the Premium Website. You will note that there are two timelines. The lower one is a **focused timeline**. A focused timeline allows you to enlarge a segment of the upper timeline by drawing lines from a period of time in the upper time to the lower timeline. This is an effective strategy when you have events that you want to focus on, or the span of time and events you are teaching about lends itself to a focused timeline.

There are a number of websites on time and historical chronology that can be used as background information or in class with students; see listings at the Premium Website.

The Escalator Model

The **escalator model** (like the escalator in your local mall) combines time and cause and effect to depict an escalation of a set of events in history. The model makes explicit what is often implicit in the selection of events to be included in a timeline.

Figure 31.2 is an example from the American Revolution. The information could just as easily have been portrayed in a timeline. But the visual relationship shows an *escalation* of events, not just a sequence. In a lecture, the teacher could have students volunteer dates to be added. Do you know any of the dates?

Figure 31.2   Escalator Model of the American Revolution

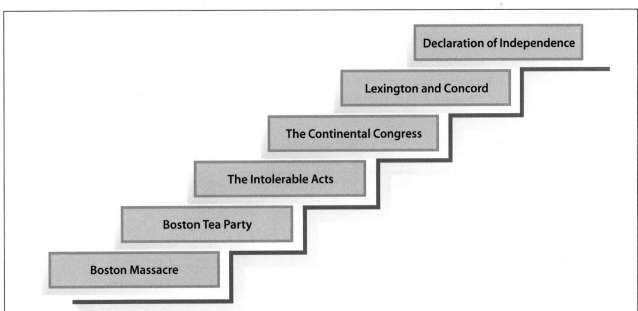

Assignment 31.1

INTASC Standards 1, 2, 3, 4, 5, 7, and 8

Time Periods and Data Organizers

Create a table using the format of the data organizer at the Premium Website. In the first column, include the following headings: Time Periods, Decade, Games You Played, Transportation, Location, and New Inventions. In the first rows, include the following: Third Graders, You, Parents, Grandparents, and Great-Grandparents. Conduct oral interviews with relatives to collect the information to put in the cells. Be prepared to share your ideas with the class and to turn in your organizer to the professor.

Assignment 31.2

INTASC Standards 1, 2, 3, 4, 5, 7, and 8

Lower Elementary Timeline

Go to the History Place (or search for "Lincoln time line.") The History Place has a timeline of Abraham Lincoln's life. Select five or six important events, and construct a timeline using the rules presented earlier and the timeline organizer at the Premium Website. Assume that the timeline is for lower elementary students, so use images (original or clip art) instead of text to depict the events. For example, to depict the Molasses Act in a chronology of events leading up to the American Revolution, you might show a jug labeled "Molasses." Bring your timeline to class, and be prepared to share your ideas with the class and turn your timeline in to the professor.

WEBSITE RESOURCES • Timelines and Chronology

Websites
Smithsonian Institution American history timeline.
National Internet Library History of time.
History World Timeline of world history.
Hyper History An interactive timeline.
TeAchnology Online Create timelines online.

Unit Five **21st Century Literacy and Basic Skills in Social Studies**

Teacher Tube	*Lesson in Time* A video that teaches time
Sample High-Quality Internet Lessons and Activities	
Lower Elementary	*Beacon* Post Office Stamps: Has students create stamps based on people from history and then place them on a timeline. *U.S. Mint* Charting History with Pennies is a lesson plan where students use pennies to create a timeline.
Upper Elementary	*Beacon* Timeline Shuffle: Has students create a timeline as part of a unit lesson on significant discoveries.
	All linked websites (designated by the green color) and those listed here are available as clickable links at the book's Premium Website, www. cengage.com, for ease of access. These links will be updated periodically to reflect changes and new resources as they become available.

Unit Six

Social Studies Instructional Approaches

"We teach them that the world can be an unpredictable, dangerous, and sometimes frightening place, while being careful not to spoil their lovely innocence. It's tricky."

Topic 32

Strategies and Direct and Indirect Instruction

The terms **strategies**, **instructional approaches**, and **methods** are frequently used interchangeably in education literature. For the purposes of this text, instructional approaches and methods are both types of strategies used to instruct students. *Instructional approaches* are, for the most part, fundamental or underlying strategies used to instruct students, such as concept formation, critical thinking, and so on. *Methods,* which are presented in Unit 5, are typically procedures, like lectures and cooperative learning; tactics, like the use of analogies; and tools, like the Internet.

Social studies shares many of the same strategies with the other disciplines you will teach. The application of these strategies to social studies will be the primary focus of this unit and topic. But as stated previously in this text, when applied to social studies instruction, these strategies require a nuanced application because social studies has both *definite* and *indefinite information* (see Topic 2) with the later being subject to personal opinion and ideology.

Teaching is more than the sum of its parts (Hansen, 1994) and as the expression goes, "Great teaching is hard to define, but I know it when I see it." The success of a teacher requires a considerable grasp of **pedagogical content knowledge (PCK)**. PCK requires the integration of **subject matter knowledge** (which may come from college courses in history, etc. that you have taken or by going to an encyclopedia, such as Wikipedia, or other sources to bring yourself up to speed on a topic you are not familiar with); **curriculum knowledge** (such as standards, etc., which were presented in the earlier units of this textbook); and strategies (or **pedagogy**) so that you can present the knowledge in a way that makes sense to your students (Shulman, 1986, 1987). This and the next unit are dedicated to strategies to build your PCK so that you can transfer the social studies procedural knowledge and information knowledge about a subject to your students.

The Purpose of Strategies

Social studies instructional approaches and methods are intended to:

1. Deliver information knowledge.
2. Provide opportunities for students to develop their procedural knowledge.
3. Have students consider big ideas (BIs) and adopt new beliefs.
4. Have students learn to apply their developing academic disposition.

Many people have an extraordinary command of facts (information knowledge) and are adept at winning spelling, geography, and history bees. Such students should be commended for the self-discipline and memorization skills that helped them achieve these goals. Many other people fail dismally in such competitions but are adept at analyzing information, organizing data to make it meaningful, and interpreting facts (procedural knowledge).

> **Which type of student do you think will be better prepared for a productive life and citizenship: one who can master information knowledge or one who excels at procedural knowledge? Which would you want your child to be? Is it really an either-or proposition?**

If a teacher's only goal is for students to acquire information knowledge, methods like lecturing and having students read the textbook and fill out worksheets are the most efficient approaches to instruction. But a teacher who wants students to think, to learn how to think analytically, and to acquire procedural knowledge needs to use other kinds of instructional approaches. Even, lecturing (which is frequently criticized as a method) based on completed reading assignments using high-level questions and activities that require analysis and application can teach children that their responsibility is to think and can help them learn how to think in increasingly sophisticated ways. The following topics on approaches and methods provide key concepts that will allow you to select and effectively use strategies to teach both definitive and indefinite social studies knowledge.

Best Practices for Selecting Strategies

The pivotal question is: What strategies work best with social studies? Because teaching is both an art and a science, however, the variables are too amorphous and the outcomes not sufficiently precise for anyone to reach a definitive conclusion. Teaching would be easy, and like a factory, if we could use one strategy and *all* students would learn!

We know that students remember more if they are required to generate or reconstruct the information rather than just receiving it from the teacher as if they were little containers to be filled up with water (Slamecka & Graf, 1978).

This kind of **active learning**, in which students reconstruct the knowledge requires them to be mentally (sometimes emotionally) engaged in what they are learning and generating connections, that is, engaged in their own learning to avoid what is referred to as **shallow knowledge** (Willingham, 2003a, 2003b).

While we may be certain about some principles of learning, issues such as the impact of homework and class size on learning, are still debated. In these areas, research and practical experience often conflict, and research results may be less than objective. If you look long enough, you can find research that claims to demonstrate that the amount of homework does not have a significant effect on students' success. Such research typically asserts that the average improvement of an experimental group was not significantly different from that of the control group. Similar studies can be found suggesting that differences in class size do not matter, either. But studies claiming that smaller classes and more homework have no significant impact on learning defy our personal experience; we expect that more of the students in a class of 10 taught by a highly qualified professional will learn more than will students in a class of 25, and we expect that students who do homework will learn more than students who do not. In fact, both have a positive effect for most students (see Cooper, 2001; National Research Center on Education in the Inner Cities, 2000). In the studies that indicate no difference, it may well be that the teacher with a class of 10 students may not have changed his or her methods to suit the unique opportunities of a class of 10, and the homework assignments were so poorly conceived that they didn't make a difference (see Topic 46).

Teachers should select their strategies on the basis of research findings and on common sense if empirical data are lacking or questionable. The topics in this unit and the next provide strategies based on theory, research, and common sense. When selecting your strategies, consider the following.

1. Use multiple strategies so that each student has the opportunity to develop the skills to learn in different ways.
2. Use strategies that work for you and that you are comfortable with, but develop a repertoire of strategies that appeal to all of your students.
3. Use strategies that research and/or common sense indicate are most likely to succeed.
4. Do not reject a method if common sense and experience indicate that it works.
5. Design all lessons (instruction, reading assignments, practice, and tests) so that students are unable to avoid thinking about the BI and the procedural knowledge.

Direct and Indirect Instruction

Direct teaching of the whole class together does not mean a return to the formal chalk-and-talk approach, with the teacher talking and pupils mainly just listening. Good direct teaching is lively and stimulating.

It means that teachers provide clear instruction, use effective questioning techniques, and make good use of pupils' responses.

Numeracy Task Force, 2004

Direct instruction (also referred to as "direct teaching," "explicit instruction," "clinical teaching," "target teaching," "whole-class instruction," "teacher-led instruction," "lecture," and "teacher-centered instruction"), puts the teacher at center stage for that part of the lesson plan. Detractors label it as less effective than indirect teaching methods (Lamber & McCombs, 1995; Shuell, 1996). In **indirect instruction** (also referred to as "indirect teaching," "group learning," "discovery learning," and "student-centered instruction"), the teacher creates an instructional sequence in which students work more independently—as individuals, in pairs, or in groups—to construct knowledge rather than primarily hear about it. The multiple terms used to describe these two approaches to instruction can be confusing. For example, when is teaching not "student centered"? And even indirect instruction planned in an instructional sequence typically is preceded by some form of direct teacher talk, if not direct instruction. Table 32.1 classifies a number of direct and indirect strategies, all of which should be used during your instructional sequences.

Direct Instruction

A teacher using *direct instruction* should explicitly plan to also include a high degree of student engagement as part of the direct instruction. At learner.org, you can watch the video, *State Government and the Role of the Citizen*, that combines many of the best elements of a lecture with questions that insure student engagement. The Topic 25's "Settlement of the Caribbean" is also a good example of this student-engagement approach, and the multiple lecture types recommended in Topic 39 would serve the same purpose. Organized with this goal in mind, direct instruction is one of the most effective and efficient forms of teaching. In a comprehensive review spanning 30 years of research on direct instruction's effectiveness, Adams and Engelmann (1996)

Table 32.1   Direct and Indirect Instruction Strategies

Direct Instruction	Both Direct and Indirect Instruction	Indirect Instruction
Lecture	Concept formation	Hands-on activities
Modeling	Inductive reasoning	Individual projects
Display of graphic organizers	Deductive reasoning	Cooperative learning (discussions, projects, etc.)
Teacher-led discussion	Problem-based instruction	Group learning (discussions, projects, etc.)
Debriefings	Discovery learning	Peer tutoring

found that it produced far superior gains to other forms of instruction in almost all subject fields and for students with different abilities. Drawing partly from the research of Shuell (1996) and Eggen and Kauchak (2001), we can say that direct instruction is most effective when:

1. The content is definitive, straightforward, and well defined.
2. The content needs to be mastered by all the students, such as facts or how to draw a map to scale.
3. The content would be difficult for students to master in indirect instruction without direct instruction first, such as concepts like *supply and demand* or *longitude and latitude*.
4. The goal is to model for the students how to integrate the facts, concepts, generalizations, and ideas of an organized body of knowledge like a topic such as the American Revolution.
5. The goal is to introduce a **baseline of knowledge** or **prerequisite knowledge** to set up an indirect instruction approach to follow (for example, about landforms) and then having students in groups create a graphic organizer of landforms.

Best Practices for Direct Instruction

Many of the following best practices are a restatement of the instructional sequence recommended for planning lessons in Topic 20. The inclusion of both guided and independent practice in that sequence, however, is a specific attempt to integrate indirect instruction with direct instruction. Additional best practices such as lecturing, modeling, and questioning can be found in direct instruction methods in the next unit. Following are some best practices for direct instruction.

- Limit the time of direct instruction to the student's attention spans.
- Open lessons by reviewing prior knowledge.
- Use an overview or analogy to create a context.
- Provide a short statement of goals.
- Present new material in small steps, with student practice or application after each step.
- Give clear and detailed instructions and explanations.
- Ask a large number of questions.
- Periodically check for understanding.
- Guide students during practice segments of the instructional sequence.
- Provide systematic, immediate feedback and corrections.
- Monitor students during tasks.
- Involve all students.
- Maintain a brisk pace.
- Teach skills to the point of *overlearning*.
- Introduce materials.
- Praise and repeat student answers.

Indirect Instruction

Indirect instruction has been promoted as an alternative to the direct instruction method, which dominated education until the early 1960s, because (a) it appeals to students' different learning styles; (b) students should learn to learn in many different ways; (c) it capitalizes on social interactions in ways that whole-class, direct instruction cannot; (d) if the teacher plans astutely, students are required to not only learn the knowledge but also to initiate and manage their own learning; and (e) the burden of managing one's own learning is strategically shifted to the student, whereas in direct instruction it can become a process of passively receiving information. The research on indirect instruction indicates that it, too, is successful when it is employed effectively (Jacques, 1992; Michaelsen, Fink, & Knight, 1997; Slavin, 1990). Unlike direct instruction, which can fail when done poorly because of student passivity and boredom, indirect instruction may fail because the teacher does not clearly define the tasks, provide adequate structure and monitoring, or hold students accountable.

Best Practices for Indirect Instruction

In addition to the following general best practices, you can find more detailed practices explained in the next unit in the topics on group learning, practice, and homework.

- Carefully plan the transition from direct to indirect instruction.
- Carefully define the tasks, such as creating a Venn diagram or reading in a group.
- Monitor the students' progress, by observing individual or group progress and joining in when necessary.
- Establish clear time limits for the activity and its outcomes.
- Ensure equitable participation by all students in groups though monitoring or using a strategy like mandated taking turns.
- Establish student-to-student communication rules for group activities.

Direct Versus Indirect Instruction: Three Examples

As a comparison of the two approaches, consider the following examples. Assume your goal in the lesson was to teach students the differences between humans and animals. This may sound like a science topic, but it is anthropology as well and is really focused on critical thinking.

Direct Instruction 1: The teacher lectures using a transparency with a table of columns for humans and animals, sequentially identifying a critical attribute of each that the teacher has conceptualized. The teacher asks students to take notes. *Boring*!

Direct Instruction/Indirect Instruction 2: The teacher leads a discussion using a table on the chalkboard with columns for humans and animals, asking students to hypothesize the unique attributes of each and asking follow-up questions to probe individual students' thinking as they offer ideas. The teacher then adds correct conceptions, offers modifications or solicits them from students, and tactfully rejects misconceptions while completing the columns and rows on the chalkboard. *Students are engaged*!

Indirect Instruction: In this indirect approach, the teacher gives students a blank Venn diagram, puts them in groups, and asks them to hypothesize which attributes animals and humans have in common and which they do not have in common. Students are then asked as a group to offer their ideas and rationale, while the teacher serves as an interlocutor, probing and suggesting alternatives. *Students are engaged and manage their own learning*!

Which of the above is your favorite way of learning? Why?

🌐 WEBSITE RESOURCES • Strategies

Video	*Learner.org* Groups, Projects, and Presentations provides ideas on active learning and alternative assessment.
	Learner.org Explorations in Archeology and History is an exceptional example of lecture with a visual aids.
	Learner.org China through Mapping, Making Bread Together, and Explorer's in North America provide excellent examples of the choreographed use of both direct and indirect instruction.
	Houghton Mifflin Multiple Intelligences: Elementary School Instruction demonstrates a multiple intelligences approach to active learning.
Essay	**ERIC Online**
	ED459110, Social Studies for the Elementary and Middle Grades: A Constructivist Approach (2002): A 480-page book of strategies employing the constructivist approach.
	ED448424, Classroom Strategies for Interactive Learning (2001)
	ED425112, The Classroom Mini-Economy (1996): Provides lessons, resources, and simulations for economics education.
	All linked websites (designated by the green color) and those listed here are available as clickable links at the book's Premium Website, www.cengage.com, for ease of access. These links will be updated periodically to reflect changes and new resources as they become available.

Topic 33

Concept Formation

We often forget what learning looks like through the eyes of children, and we make poor assumptions about what children do and do not know. Teachers' ideas about how children form concepts should shape their teaching strategies.

The word "concept," as used in *concept formation* (also referred to as "concept attainment" in the literature) means the process of turning what we hear and see in a classroom into our personal **conceptualizations** or **conceptions**. That is what Piaget described as *schemas* (Piaget, 1929). So **concept formation** means that students create an understanding of individual facts, concepts, and generalizations as well as the overall relationships among them. The teacher's job is to provide conceptual models that are the most accepted or correct according to the discipline's **community of practice**. All of these forms of knowledge become *conceptualizations,* the "airy" thoughts lodged in our psyches. Teachers use various strategies to transfer their more sophisticated and well-formed conceptualizations to students.

Teachers' conceptualizations about social studies topics are far more complex than the conceptions of elementary school–aged students' and, therefore, must be presented to students in increments of complexity. Teachers first introduce less information to their students and then help students make sense of it. As you are presenting your conceptualizations of knowledge, students will either:

1. Acquire the knowledge by
   a. Taking it into existing **schemas**.
   b. Taking it into newly formed schemas.
   c. Using **rote memorization** (putting it into temporary storage).

Or the student will:

2. Fail to successfully acquire the knowledge because
   a. The existing personal schemas are inadequate.
   b. The teacher has given insufficient clues to place the information into the right context.

> *I can't understand why people are frightened of new ideas. I'm frightened of the old ones.*
>
> John Cage

Figure 33.1   Concept Objects

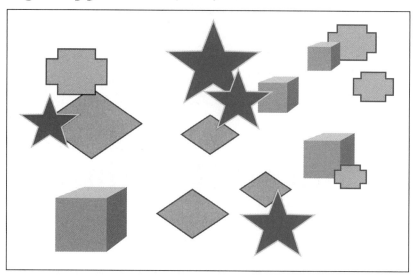

c. The student used inadequate or incorrect schemas and thus distorted the message.

d. The student was not actively engaged mentally (Piaget, 1929; Piaget & Inhelder, 1958).

Teacher's Tip

Graphic organizers are effective in teaching concepts because they present a simple visual image of a complex idea. See the Premium Website for examples.

For students, revising their conceptions of concepts, generalizations, ideas, and beliefs is not just a matter of adopting the teacher's more sophisticated conceptualizations but rather of evaluating, reorganizing, and integrating existing and new conceptions into their own personal schema and belief system (Duit, 1999; Schnotz, Vosniado, & Carretero, 1999).

Figure 33.1 is an abstract example related to the concept formation process presented in a training session on how to teach critical thinking by Bernoff (1992).

Is the organization of the objects in Figure 33.1 satisfactory to you? Why? Why not? What do the objects represent? Do you feel compelled to reorganize the objects?

Assignment 33.1

INTASC Standards 1, 2, 3, 4, 5, 7, and 8

Concept Formation

Write a step-by-step description of how you would rearrange the objects in Figure 33.1. In addition, create a drawing of your reorganization. You should be prepared to share your ideas with the class and submit the assignment to your professor.

Social Studies Concept Formation

When using the concept formation strategy with the lecture, discussions, or group method, the teacher must initially decide on the appropriate schema students should adopt. This can be rather straightforward for *definite social studies knowledge* (what are the three branches of government?), but for *indefinite social studies knowledge* (why do people rob banks?) the schema will end up being different for each student based on values and ideology. Often, a graphic image can be used to show students what the concepts are and how they should be organized. In the long term, after having seen such a structure developed and modelled by the teacher, students should take responsibility for deciding on the schema or conceptualization for the future knowledge they will be exposed to, which is a form of procedural knowledge and becomes an academic disposition.

Graphic Organizers and Concept Formation

The purpose of Assignment 33.1 was to have you begin to think about how more than one correct conceptualization of an idea can exist in social studies. Now let's take a look at the relationship of concept formation to indefinite and definite knowledge using three graphic organizers.

- Figure 33.3 reflects *definite information*, and there is only one appropriate conceptualization, regardless of maturation.
- Figure 32.2, however, is an elementary grade–appropriate conceptualization. But at the high school or college level, students would be expected to understand that this **parallel construction** of President of the United States and Prime Minister of Great Britan is imperfect because the two positions have very different degrees of power, etc. Rather than think of this as *indefinite knowledge*, it is best to recognize that the spectrum of knowledge starts with a **naive conceptualization** and ends with **expert conceptualizations** of the same concept. My understanding of physics, as an example, is more sophisticated than my granddaughter's but is far more naive than a science professor's understanding of physics.
- Figure 33.4, "Criteria for President" represents the unique *indefinite knowledge* aspect of social studies, in which a teacher may help frame some of the criteria for someone to decide who should be president (but even this would be open to opinion) as a prerequisite to each student deciding who should be president based on his or her own ideology.

A teacher can present concepts to students so that they get the most sophisticated, grade-appropriate conceptualization. Figures 33.2, 33.3, and 33.4 can be used to convey concepts to students learning about the U.S. presidency by providing context compared to another nation's head of state and within the U.S. government, and then a way of making a personal decision about who should be president. In figure 33.2 the **comparable entities strategy** is used to create a schema with a new conceptualization with the use of **parallel construction**.

Figure 33.2   Heads of Government

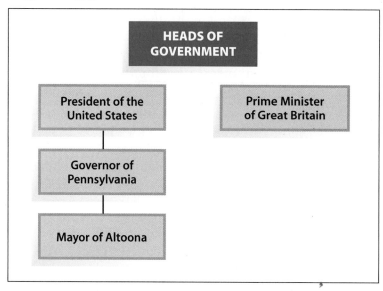

Figure 33.3   U.S. The Branches of Government

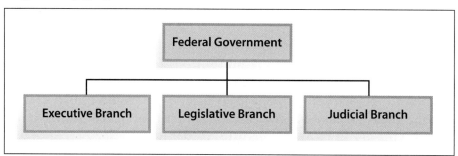

In a hierarchy organizer, the relationship of a cell to other cells is defined as superordinate, subordinate, or coordinate. **Superordinate** ideas are higher than related **subordinate** ideas; the subordinate idea can be a subset of the former or an attribute can make it lesser (for example, a governor has less authority than a president). **Coordinate** cells represent equalities of two entities; mayors of two cities are an example. In Figure 33.2, the concept is *heads of state*. The U.S. president is superordinate to the governor of Pennsylvania, and the mayor of Altoona is subordinate to the governor of Pennsylvania. Prime minister is coordinate to the president.

Values, Concept Formation, and Indefinite Knowledge

When teaching with indefinite knowledge, the goal is very different from teaching with definitive knowledge. The following is an example of how to integrate the demands of value formation, concept formation, and knowledge into a lesson.

Figure 33.4   Criteria for President

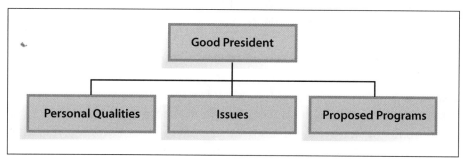

Lesson Plan Example: Presidential Election

This example is assumed to be taking place during a presidential election year, but it could be modified for a mayoral or gubernatorial election.

You should download Houghton Mifflin's Reading 10, "Local Government," for an example of a textbook treatment of the topic of voting. How would you develop this content into a lesson? What is the definitive and indefinite knowledge?

Using the Socratic method, the teacher would use Figures 33.2 and 33.3 (possibly blank) in an overhead projection or as a chalkboard display to ask students to supply definitive information about each while filling in the blanks and illuminating the concepts in a whole-class setting. Next, using an analogy appropriate to elementary students, the teacher would ask, "If you were going to pick a new friend, what criteria would you use?" The teacher would use this **analogical bridge** to the question, "How would you decide to select one person for president over another?"

The discussion would lead to the creation of a diagram like that shown in Figure 33.4 on the chalkboard. Note that the goal of Figure 33.4 is to focus on a structure and process for making such a decision because it deals with indefinite knowledge, as opposed to a method in which the teacher tells the students what criteria should be used or which candidate to select. The students could be divided into groups to develop; debate; and discuss a list of qualities, issues and proposed programs; rank them; and weight them under each of the headings.

Students could be asked to interview a parent about the three categories of personal qualities, issues, and programs that are being discussed in the presidential election. Students could be asked to apply their criteria to candidates in the upcoming election by writing a paper on whether they think each candidate has the personal qualities and how each stands on the issues. A simulated election could be held. Later in the year, the students could be asked to apply the same procedural knowledge to a local or state election.

In this example, deciding who the "best" candidate is or what the "most important" issues are is not the teacher's job, and it is not even the primary goal of the lesson. The teacher's goals are to:

1. have the students acquire the citizenship disposition that they have an obligation to go through a deliberate analysis in selecting their president, and
2. convey the idea that each student should make up his or her own mind based on his or her personal assessment. Having them develop this kind of conceptualization prepares them to think about candidates in a structured, purposeful way, so that in the future they can make thoughtful decisions as adults in a democratic society.

This is an example of explicitly teaching an academic disposition and procedural knowledge. Focusing on the process of thinking when teaching subjects that both require individual choices and may be controversial ensures that students are not indoctrinated.

It is possible to store the mind with a million facts and still be entirely uneducated.

Alec Bourne, A Doctor's Creed

Concept Formation Best Practices

The concept formation approach has a number of best practices. The teacher should:

1. Assess information by having students dialogue to reveal their conceptions, misconceptions, and naive social theories.
2. Expect students to generate opinions, explain key ideas, formulate questions, and reflect on opinions.
3. Expect students to listen to others' opinions, consider new ideas, and formulate responses.
4. Expect students to reflect on their thinking (metacognition) by having them report on key decision points, the process they used, and how they recognized that their new idea was better than the old one.
5. Systematically use one concept to bridge existing schema to the more appropriate or correct schema.
6. Debrief students on their new schema.
7. Relate the new schema to other topics so as to broaden the schema.
8. Use graphic organizers to help students capture the framework for the concepts.

Assignment 33.2

INTASC Standards 1, 2, 3, 4, 5, 7, and 8

Concept Formation Lesson

Download Houghton Mifflin's Reading 15, "The Twenty-First Century Begins," from the Premium Website and review page 675 on the Iraq War. Assume you are preparing a lesson based on the Iraq war. Based on the "Lesson Plan Example: Presidential Election" in this topic and the concepts *bias* and *indoctrination* (review Topic 4), prepare a description of how you would teach about the Iraq war. Be prepared to discuss your results in class and submit the assignment to your professor.

	WEBSITE RESOURCES • Concept Formation
Video	*Learner.org* Celebrations of Light: Lower elementary students focus on concepts in a lesson on different cultures' holiday celebrations. *Learner.org* Understanding Stereotypes: Fourth grade students discover the concept of stereotypes through indirect instruction.
Lesson Plan	**ERIC Online** *ED 429896* Teaching about War to Help Create a More Humane World (1998): A lesson plan that uses a concept formation approach. *Critical Thinking Community* The Concept of Family: An upper elementary lesson on teaching the concept of family.
Essay	*ED 406303,* Fractured History and Geography: An Examination of Why Students Choose "Wrong" Words to Write and Talk about Social Studies Topics (1998): Provides an analysis of and solutions to misconceptions in elementary social studies.
Concept Maps	*Education Oasis* Concept maps for downloading.
	All linked websites (designated by the green color) and those listed here are available as clickable links at the book's Premium Website, www.cengage.com/login, for ease of access. These links will be updated periodically to reflect changes and new resources as they become available.

Topic 34

Active Versus Passive Learning

If you are under 30 years of age, you most probably have been exposed to **activities-based instruction** in elementary school and may think of activities as being social studies. This conceptualization of social studies instruction continues to be played out in classrooms with great frequency. Activities-based social studies is exemplified by a newspaper photo that recently appeared in a local newspaper titled "A Lesson in China" showing three U.S. third-graders, one wearing a kimono and all three enjoying a meal of rice, ginger ale, and fortune cookies at a classroom table. The caption indicates that this meal followed the study of a Chinese girl and her culture. Dressing up in traditional Asian clothing and the meal as a **culminating activity** to a lesson should not be confused with active learning.

Activities

Activities are not necessarily **active learning** (Pica, 2008). Activities can include participating in a medieval festival, preparing a Thanksgiving dinner prior to the Thanksgiving holiday, simulating a factory assembly line, and reenacting a battle. Such activities are great culminating events and are thought to "lock-in" students' memories of what they have learned. However, social studies content seems to be particularly prone to teachers substituting such activities for challenging active learning experiences (Frasee & Ayers, 2003).

In this case from the newspaper, the lesson may have lost its way because some of the content is suspect, at least in the culminating activity. Remember, the students should—due to the lesson—understand why some food is eaten and garments are worn in some cultures and not others.

1. The girl in the picture was wearing a kimono; a kimono is Japanese, not Chinese.
2. The Chinese consume a significant amount of rice, and thus using it as a **cultural archetype** for China is appropriate.
3. Ginger is neither indigenous to China nor a primary crop of China; it is a tropical plant. Ireland is credited with the invention of ginger ale in 1851.
4. San Francisco and Los Angeles both claim to be the place where the first fortune cookies were invented around 1900. The Chinese people are unfamiliar with them, except from what they have learned from Americans.

No doubt the children had fun with this Chinese meal activity, but they were not necessarily active learners because active learning must take place during the instruction, not just as an add-on activity. Regrettably, some teachers mistakenly create such activities and leave out the lesson, and this has contributed to a perceived lack of rigor and importance in elementary social studies. For an example of a lower elementary lesson with substantial geography content and active learning, to which a Chinese meal might be added as a culminating activity, go to learner.org for the video lesson, *China through Mapping*.

Active Learning

Active learning requires teachers to create strategies in which students are active agents on a mental, emotional, and/or physical level in the construction of knowledge through meaningful tasks (Pica, 2008). The Chinese meal could be an activity within an active learning strategy if it were preceded or followed by meaningful learning. First, the geography of China, with some history would be taught. The indigenous foods of a culture can serve as a motivating device to create interest where students could be required to analyze their own types of food, compare their food with China's, and relate the local climate to regional food choices. These tasks require critical thinking and would represent an active learning approach. Through the Socratic method, a number of big ideas could be related to this information knowledge:

Teacher's Tip

In the National Assessment of Educational Progress (2002), the top three most reported activities by students were worksheets (87 percent), reading the textbook (77 percent), and memorizing (61 percent). This is not active learning!

How does food reflect a region climate and culture? How have a global economy and communication brought all cultures into closer contact; made different food products available to more people; and exposed all peoples to new, creative ways to make food? To achieve a multicultural goal, children could be asked to identify and teach the other students about a food based on their national origin. A children's tradebook could be added to enrich the information.

The Houghton Mifflin readings at the Premium Website have a number of appropriate and meaningful sample culminating activities that could be part of an active lesson: For example, Reading 5 includes the creation of a post-card, Reading 6 has a "hands tree" created by students, and Reading 10 includes a poster to promote voting. To see how a teacher combines active learning, visual aids, and a culminating activity that is exceptionally well done, go to learner.org, and view *Explorations in Archeology and History*.

Can you think of the components of an active learning lesson that would precede these three culminating activities?

Time Constraints

Activities like the Chinese meal consume valuable teacher preparation and classroom time. Time becomes more precious each year because of the demands for basic skills instruction created by high-stakes testing and frequent school-based activities (assemblies, announcements, etc.) that interrupt the daily routine of teaching. Teachers must ask, "Is this the best use of two hours during the school week?

If parents were given the chance to vote, do you think they would rather see improvement in students' math or reading skills rather a culminating activity?

The Role of Passive Learning in Student Development

Passive learning is almost always teacher-centered instruction (lecture or direct instruction), with students seated at their desks working on tasks, and is often characterized by memorization, note taking, recitation, drill, and practice as the primary instructional methodology. Learning the virtues of patience, diligence, and persistence; embracing multiple learning strategies; employing memorization skills; and practicing note taking are vital to students' long-term success. From the start of their education, students should come to understand that it is their responsibility to learn, regardless of the degree of boredom, the teacher's skill (or lack thereof), or support at home, and that not all learning will be entertaining.

Not all learning can be fun, but it should all be meaningful. Creative teachers can make most learning engaging. We engage students when we require that they reconstruct the knowledge that they acquire. Efficiency often dictates less pleasurable learning strategies

Teacher's Tip

Passive learning can be minimized and active learning emphasized by allocating many passive activities (reading, drill, and practice) to assigned homework and making the most effective use of the classroom for communal and active learning experiences that are best delivered at school.

with less personal attention and more self-responsibility. As students progress through the school system, the burden for motivation and learning shifts more to them; this transfer of duty is an essential part of the maturation process required by the organized school system as well as the workplace, and it should be a goal of every teacher.

Converting Passive Learning to Active Learning: An Example

Most of the strategies in this text are intended to help you to convert many passive learning opportunities into active learning experiences. The "Lewis and Clark" lesson in Topic 20, the lesson on the "Settlement of the Caribbean" in Topic 27, the focused children's book lesson in Topic 28, and creating a chart in Topic 31 all meet the criteria for active learning. The learner.org videos, *Explorations in Archeology and History* and *China Through Mapping*, are exceptional examples showing how teachers orchestrate active learning with both direct and indirect instruction.

The whole art of teaching is only the art of awakening the natural curiosity of young minds for the purpose of satisfying it afterwards.

Anatole France

Learning vocabulary, for example, is often taught as a passive activity in which students copy vocabulary words and their definitions from the text and teachers hold the students accountable with a test or application. At first glance, it might seem impossible to turn learning vocabulary into an active learning experience. However, Spencer Kagan has developed a variety of active learning approaches, and the Kagan Website is an excellent starting point for ideas on active learning using cooperative learning (see Topic 46).

As an example, one vocabulary strategy drawn from Kagan's ideas is easy to prepare and choreograph. For a class of 20, place 10 vocabulary words on yellow cards and 10 definitions on red cards. Give each student one card, and place the definitions on an overhead. Play music while students find a partner (like musical chairs) to discuss each definition and word and try to determine if the word and the definition match. When the students have paired up, they return to their seats, and the pairs report the word and definition. This is an active learning experience because the students are participating agents on a mental, emotional, and/or physical level in the construction of the meaning of the words and concepts.

The lesson on China discussed at the start of this topic could be organized as an inquiry-based lesson plan, a form of active learning. To learn more about the active learning model called "inquiry-based learning," you can go to Thirteen.Org's Concepts to Classrooms series for the video workshop *Inquiry Based Learning*.

Did you participate in an active learning experience in elementary school, or did you observe one during your field experiences that you can share with the class?

Assignment 34.1

INTASC Standards 1, 2, 3, 4, 5, 7, and 8

Active Learning Internet History Lesson Plan

Conduct a search on the Internet using the Gateway to Educational Materials, the National Endowment for the Humanities, or Core Knowledge to identify a lesson plan related to history that you believe is an active learning lesson as opposed to an activity. Print out the lesson plan and be prepared to share your plan with the class and submit the printout to your professor.

WEBSITE RESOURCES • Active Learning

Video

Learner.org, Engaging Students in Active Learning: Demonstrates classroom strategies to stimulate thinking and bring social studies concepts to life for their students.

Learner.org, Groups, Projects, and Presentations: Provides ideas on active learning and alternative assessment.

Essay

ERIC *Online*

ED459110, Social Studies for the Elementary and Middle Grades: A Constructivist Approach (2002): A 480-page book of strategies employing the constructivist approach.

ED448424 Classroom Strategies for Interactive Learning (2001).

ED425112 The Classroom Mini-Economy (1996): Provides lessons, resources, and simulations for economics education.

All linked websites (designated by the green color) and those listed here are available as clickable links at the book's Premium Website, www.cengage.com/login, for ease of access. These links will be updated periodically to reflect changes and new resources as they become available.

Topic 35

Critical Thinking Skills

When I discovered critical thinking, my teaching changed. Instead of focusing on questions that had "right" answers, I wanted children to think through situations where the answer was in doubt. I expected them to decide which of two or more conflicting theories, procedures, beliefs, observations, actions or expert claims made the most sense.

Wright, 2002

We all, to some degree, bring to the classroom an ability to think critically. In social studies, critical thinking is crucial to citizenship and character education because it gives us the tools to examine issues important to our personal growth and the advancement of humankind (Van Hover & Van Horne, 2005). Teachers of social studies are expected to move students to increasingly more sophisticated ways of thinking critically about the knowledge they are acquiring, public policies, and personal actions. To do this, teachers need to construct lessons that integrate information knowledge and procedural knowledge in a way that allows students to internalize the ways of thinking critically and then apply their newly acquired critical thinking skills. This is crucial because "students remember what they think" (Willingham, 2003b). There are two main ways by which students are exposed to the disposition of critical thinking:

Teacher's Tip

Critical thinking must be taught in the context of content, not just for advanced students, and must be explicitly taught and practiced

(Willingham, 2007).

1. They observe teachers' modeling the use of more sophisticated ways of thinking critically than they currently possess; and
2. Teachers (or fellow students) ask questions that stimulate the critical thinking essential to the construction of knowledge.

Examples such as the procedural knowlege and big idea in the "Lewis and Clark" lesson in Topic 11, the questions asked in the "Settlement of the Caribbean" lesson in Topic 27, and a teacher modeling the use of the

"Key Social Studies Questions" (see Topic 22) demonstrate how teachers should orchestrate all lessons that create opportunities for students to acquire a critical thinking disposition.

Inductive and Deductive Reasoning

Critical thinking begins with your understanding the two fundamental ways in which we reason, **inductive** and **deductive reasoning** processes.

Inductive reasoning is the process of drawing conclusions from observations (see Figure 35.1). It is an open-ended process in which observations, hypothesis, or assertions are explored and scaffolded up to an idea or belief. If a child's only exposure to a homeless person was to see (pardon this biased example, but it seems necessary to make the point) a disheveled, White male adult on a street corner holding a sign asking for money, that child could reach a mistaken and biased conclusion that a White male adult is the typical homeless person. Until, perhaps a social studies lesson on homelessness in which students were exposed to the full spectrum of homeless people (children, women, people of color, etc.), would a less naïve idea or belief emerge.

Deductive reasoning is the process of applying a generalization to an illustration (see Figure 35.2). It is focused on proving or applying a theory rather than discovering a theory out of information. Using the homeless person example again, assume a student has the generalization that homelessness affects all kinds of people, then such a student could see disheveled children and conclude that they might be homeless.

> ## Teacher's Tip
>
> Rather than think of history as something you tell students about, think of it as something they will discover as a critical thinking skills strategy. One approach is the **detective strategy** that sets up a history lesson in which students become detectives (Fuchs, 2006).

Figure 35.1

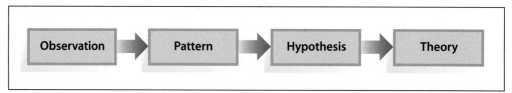

Figure 35.2

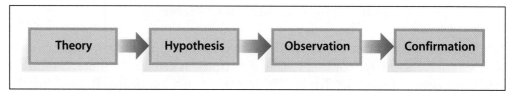

Active Learning Approaches to Deductive and Deductive Reasoning

Reasoning as a focal point of critical thinking, can be organized as an active or passive experience as well as a deductive or inductive experience. The following examples use the definitions of "island" and "peninsula" to demonstrate the possible combinations.

Inductive Active Learning

1. The inductive approach starts with pictures of islands and peninsulas. Students might be divided into groups and asked to analyze the pictures to see if they can place them into two categories based on similarities that form a pattern.
2. When they have grouped the islands in one stack and the peninsulas in another stack, students would be asked to develop a hypothesis that would include a definition or the *critical attributes* of stack X and stack Y.
3. Each group might present a definition, and the teacher would probe for their thinking by asking questions or showing more pictures.
4. A debriefing would include confirming the definition, reinforcing that X is an *island*—a body of land surrounded by water—and Y is a *peninsula*—a body of land surrounded by water on three sides.
5. Students would record the definition.

Deductive Active Learning

1. The teacher writes the definitions of "island" and "peninsula" on the board.
2. Students are given pictures and asked to apply the definition to the illustrations.
3. After they have placed the islands in one stack and the peninsulas in another stack, students would be expected to justify their decisions.
4. A debriefing would include reinforcing the concept.
5. Students would record the definition.

> **Which way do you prefer to learn—by inductive or deductive reasoning? Why?**

In both cases, the teacher is promoting a correct formulation of the concept and a **mental map** of the concepts and their relationships to each other by having students identify the island's and the peninsula's **critical attributes**. Both inductive and deductive strategies require students to do the critical thinking by use of their observation, analysis, prediction, and justification skills. Almost anything we teach can be structured into one of these two approaches. In various forms, this process is referred to as "critical thinking," "thinking skills," or the "discovery method." It is active learning because students construct knowledge.

Teacher's Tip

Another passive deductive approach is the extensive use of **worksheets**, which typically use the find-and-record strategy. This approach is often used by teachers who think that their job is to teach a textbook or facts. Unlike graphic organizers, few worksheets require students to construct or reconstruct knowledge; therefore, little thinking is required.

Passive Learning

The very nature of inductive reasoning makes it difficult to imagine a passive inductive learning approach. However, passive deductive reasoning approaches are very popular. They do not require thinking or discovery and are frequently used by teachers, even though they are not best suited to the goals of elementary social studies.

1. The teacher gives the definitions of "island" and "peninsula."
2. Students record the definitions.
3. The teacher may or may not show examples.
4. Students memorize the definitions.
5. Students are tested.

Hypotheses in Social Studies

Critical thinking learning experiences in social studies often begin with a question or presentation of a problem that forces students to form a hypothesis. In science we think in terms of testing a hypothesis in an experiment that has unequivocal results. In social studies, we are typically unable to conduct experiments with controlled conditions. In social studies, we focus on gathering data on phenomena that have already occurred in the real world and on making logical assertions that can be used to accept or reject a hypothesis.

A **hypothesis** is an untested idea or an educated guess that is followed by inductive or deductive reasoning to explain a phenomenon. The following hypotheses provide an example, "most homeless people are addicted to drugs," or "most homeless people are lazy." These are **stereotypical generalizations** that would benefit from a systematic examination of the underlying hypothesis. With the first question, one finds published information or can gather data through drug testing to determine if the hypothesis is true. The second question is a values question and, thus, subject to personal opinion that may be supported or not supported by data about homeless people and their job histories. As a strategy, one of the benefits of hypothesis testing is that students come to appreciate the role of data in reaching the most objective conclusions. Teachers often place students in groups (see Topic 43) and use the case study method (see Topic 47) to gather information, analyze their findings, and reflect on their beliefs prior to and after the analysis steps as part of character and citizenship education lessons. If hypothesis instruction is teacher centered, the focus is on questioning in a whole-class environment and presenting data. Some typical social studies questions that can be used to form hypotheses and learn a big idea through critical thinking are:

1. In history, why do people rebel against a government?
2. In geography, why are sombreros worn in Mexico and fur hats in Russia?
3. In economics, why are some people poor and other people rich?
4. In government, why do the House of Representatives and the Senate have different numbers of members?
5. In social sciences, what are the causes of poverty?

Asking "Why do people rebel against a government?" as an attention-getter for a lesson on the American Revolution should stimulate students and immediately focus their attention on a big idea. When students develop a list of reasons or **subordinate hypotheses** about why people might rebel against a government, they are developing and forming **generalizations** or **concepts**. Students can then use those generalizations as hypotheses that are in need of facts from the American Revolution to support or reject their hypothesis or to add new subordinate hypotheses. In science and in social studies, we accept the idea that hypotheses and conclusions can change based on new evidence or new analysis.

Speculation and **prediction** are important components of hypothesis testing and, for that matter, critical thinking. Both require questioning the facts and concepts that are advanced by others, and both are crucial to teaching and learning social studies. For example, what would the United States be like if the colonists and England had resolved their differences? What would happen if citizens did not have to go to school? Such questions give meaning that cannot be found in passive instruction in which the teacher tells students the answers. Social studies instruction should allow students to make informed and rational decisions based on speculation and prediction. Students need to be exposed to the process of developing plausible hypotheses and testing them.

Critical Thinking: The 10 Academic Virtues

Tishman, Jay, and Perkins (1992) identify seven **thinking dispositions** that should be acquired by students. Their dispositions have been expanded into the following 10 academic virtues that teachers can foster by constructing active learning experiences for their students.

1. **To be broad and adventurous:** The tendency to be open minded; to explore alternative views; to be alert to narrow thinking; the ability to generate multiple options
2. **To have sustained intellectual curiosity:** The tendency to wonder, probe, find problems, to have a zest for inquiry; to be alert for anomalies; the ability to observe closely and formulate questions
3. **To clarify and seek understanding:** A desire to understand clearly; to seek connections and explanations; to be alert to lack of clarity and the need for focus; an ability to build conceptualizations
4. **To plan and be strategic:** The drive to set goals, to make and execute plans, to envision outcomes; to be alert to lack of direction; the ability to formulate goals and plans
5. **To be intellectually careful:** The urge for precision, organization, thoroughness; to be alert to possible error or inaccuracy; the ability to process information precisely
6. **To be respectful of evidence:** The aspiration to accept new evidence and formulations of data and concepts
7. **To seek and evaluate reasons:** The tendency to question the given, to demand justification; the ability to weigh and assess reasons
8. **To be metacognitive:** The tendency to be aware of and monitor the flow of one's own thinking; to be alert to complex thinking situations; the ability to exercise control of mental processes and to be reflective
9. **To be tolerant of ambiguity:** To resist the drive to bring closure to problem solving and decision making for the sake of inquiry and thoughtfulness
10. **To be skeptical:** The inclination to require proof and logical analysis as demonstrative of ideas and generalizations and to look for flaws

Assignment 35.1

INTASC Standards 1, 2, 3, 4, 5, 7, and 8

Remodeled Lesson Plans

Download one of the remodeled lesson plans from criticalthinking.org. Print out the lesson plan and be prepared to share how your plan changes from a "regular" lesson plan to one that focuses on critical thinking. Then, be prepared to share how you would apply the principle to one of the Houghton Mifflin Readings at this book's website.

Critical Thinking Strategies	***ERIC Online*** *ED438208,* Turning Points in History: People, Ideas, Events (1999): Has lesson plans that require students to think critically. *ED408570,* Cooperative Learning in the Thinking Classroom: Research and Theoretical Perspectives (1997): Provides illustrations of cooperative learning to support a thinking skills emphasis. *ED414209,* Enhancing Social Studies through Literacy Strategies (1995): Bulletin 91 includes literacy-based strategies to enhance critical thinking
Websites	***Critical Thinking on the Web*** A comprehensive resource on critical thinking approaches and strategies. ***The Center for Critical Thinking*** Includes articles on critical thinking and strategies/examples on how to convert lessons to critical thinking lessons.
	All linked websites (designated by the green color) and those listed here are available as clickable links at the book's Premium Website, www.cengage.com/login, for ease of access. These links will be updated periodically to reflect changes and new resources as they become available.

Topic 36

Problem Solving and Decision Making

The examples of deductive and inductive reasoning in the previous topic are part of the critical thinking processes used in **problem solving** and **decision making**. Problem-solving and decision-making approaches share many of the same qualities. Scientists and mathematicians solve problems that typically are focused on definitive content and thus do not engage people's emotions, or what we call the **affective domain**. Solving the division problem 24 divided by 7 is unencumbered with controversy or in need of a value decision, because there is only one answer. Social studies also has opportunities to solve problems, such as calculating the distance between Chicago and Los Angeles and determining why a vacation to Disney World is less expensive in March than in July. But when problems have social or personal implications, particularly when they deal with indefinite information, like drunk-driver laws, crime, or abortion, decision making becomes the primary vehicle for understanding because ideology, values, and virtues come into play.

Problem Solving

Problem solving is a process of seeking an explanation of observed phenomena, it should be used at all levels of elementary education, and is almost always an active learning experience (West, 2007). Problem solving is both a process and an acquired academic disposition. Whimbey and Lockhead (1980) identified traits that are associated with successful and less successful problem solvers, which have been adapted to create Table 36.1.

Table 36.1 Characteristics of Problem Solvers

Successful Problem Solvers	Unsuccessful Problem Solvers
Are concerned about accuracy.	Fail to observe and use all the facts.
Break problems into parts.	Are not systematic in their work or thinking.
Avoid guessing.	Do not identify relationships fully.
Have a positive attitude.	Are sloppy in collecting information.
Are energetic in the process.	Show inadequate reflection.

The Five Steps in Problem Solving

There are many variations of the steps in problem solving, depending on how specific one wants to be. The following version is based on Beyer (1988) and Kalsounis (1987).

1. **Become aware of the problem:** The teacher introduces a topic like poverty and leads an introductory discussion.
2. **Gather data:** Students are given packets of information or are directed to resources for individualized collection of data, or the teacher can present information.
3. **Form hypotheses:** Students are placed in groups to form a hypothesis about the causes of poverty and who the "poor" are.
4. **Test the hypotheses by analyzing, evaluating, and interpreting data:** Students examine data to determine if their hypotheses are accurate. Students could use the "Hypothesis/Proof," "Problem/ Solution," and "Cause/Effect Organizers" from the Premium Website to construct their ideas.
5. **Reach a conclusion:** Students report their findings and conclusions, perhaps using graphic organizers.

I cannot teach anybody anything; I can only make them think.

Socrates

   You should teach the problem-solving process so that students can name the steps and apply them in sequence to a problem you present (Watson & Linder, 2004). Your success in creating problem-solving lessons is dependent on your ability to give students just enough information to place them in proximity to the answers, but not so much that figuring out the solutions on their own is impossible or too easy. The following example requires students to create the categories of phenomena (causes) that might affect temperature as well as determine their effects. With this two-step structured approach, the teacher is emphasizing problem solving by the systematic **brainstorming** of the possible set of causes and the effects to be rejected or accepted as the causes of the differences in temperature.

A Problem-Solving Example: Juneau and Chicago

In a typical passive approach to teaching about the variables that affect temperature and climate, the teacher might list the variables on the board, give definitions of each variable, and explain how each affects climate. To demonstrate how to restructure what you may think of as mundane social studies content into a critical-thinking, active-learning, problem-solving lesson, the following is an example of how to teach the same thing in which children must figure out what makes the temperatures in Juneau, Alaska and Chicago, Illinois different.

1. Show a map of North America on which Juneau and Chicago and their longitudes and latitudes are clearly labeled.
2. Explain longitude and latitude.
3. Ask students which place they think is colder. They will probably say Juneau because it is farther north than Chicago.
4. State the problem: In the month of December, the average temperature of Juneau, Alaska is warmer than the average temperature of Chicago, Illinois. Explain *average* by having the tallest and shortest students come to the front of the class and measuring them.
5. Place students in groups and ask them to figure out (hypothesize) why Juneau is warmer by completing a cause/effect organizer like the one at the Premium Website.
6. With a cause/effect organizer on the board (see Table 36.2), ask what things affect the growth of a tree. By questioning, fill in columns 1 and 2 in Table 36.2, elaborating on each. From this analogy and with a globe and world map to consult, the students should begin brainstorming about Juneau and Chicago.
7. Once students have finished, have different groups report one item for the first column and probe their thinking. Then have groups report the effect for each item listed in the first column and probe their thinking. As the students report, introduce topographical maps and other additional data to demonstrate and support the correct hypothesis.
8. Probe, confirm, and elaborate for each item and effect.

Table 36.2   Trees

Things That Affect Their Growth	Possible Effects
Water	Too little: They could die.
	Too much: They could die.
Sunlight	Too little: They could die.
Food	Too little: They could die.
Wind	Too much: They could die.
Bugs	Too many: They could die.

Assignment 36.1

INTASC Standards 1, 2, 3, 4, 5, 7, and 8

Why Is Juneau, Alaska, Warmer?

With another colleague, complete a "Cause/Effect Graphic Organizer" found at the Premium Website. In the first column, list the possible causes for Juneau's being warmer than Chicago; in the second column, list the effects.

Decision Making

There are basically two kinds of decision making learning experiences in social studies education.

1. **Non-values–based decision making** that involves choosing between alternative solutions because there is seldom one absolutely right solution or answer (i.e. it involves indefinite information). Is a bicameral legislature better than a unicameral legislature? There are pros and cons to each approach or solution as to how to provide the best representation of the people and people can reasonably disagree on which is best.

2. **Values-based decision making** inevitably calls forward someone's personal values and ideology into the decision-making process and can be influenced by emotions. "Are the driving under the influence laws too harsh or too lenient?" could arouse an emotional override of detached logic by someone whose family has been harmed by an intoxicated driver, but even if that's not the case, in the end someone's values and ideology related to punishment for crimes will influence his or her position on the topic.

Decision making starts with the introduction of a problem. Sometimes getting involved parties to reach an agreement about the problem is the problem. For example, what do you think the problem in the 2000 presidential election, Busch vs. Gore, was? **Framing** the problem (see Topic 37) may be based on ideology, different knowledge bases, and/or bias. So even two people of goodwill may find two very different solutions to a problem that they frame differently. Furthermore, implicit in social studies decision making is the notion that an individual would act on his or her decision and would promote the belief or make some kind of a change to the existing belief. In the 2000 presidential election, the Democratic and Republican parties agreed to disagree about who should be president, but both agreed that the voting process needed change, at least in Florida.

Eight Steps in Decision Making

Naylor and Diem (1987) have identified eight steps in decision making. Note that step 2 includes the five steps in problem solving. A lesson on homelessness illustrates the process.

1. **Recognize the situation as one in which a decision needs to be made:** People are homeless, and we need to solve the problem.
2. **Clarify the problem:** Follow the problem-solving steps.
3. **Identify relevant values:** Put children in groups to discuss their feelings and attitudes about people who are homeless.
4. **Indicate the desired outcome (goal):** Have the groups indicate what they think should happen to homeless people.
5. **Propose and consider a range of potential alternatives:** Expect the groups to come up with solutions such as more low-income housing, jobs, and orphanages.
6. **Project the likely consequences for each alternative (both positive and negative):** Expect the groups to identify higher taxes and other consequences.
7. **Choose the best alternative, or rank the alternatives based on analysis of projected consequences and consistency with the stated goal and one's values:** Have the students forge a consensus.
8. **Apply the decision and assess the consequences:** Have the groups report their decisions.

The teacher should emphasize the importance of the deliberate steps in the process as a crucial form of procedural knowledge.

Children's Literature-Based Decision Making

In Topic 47 you will find a list of types of case studies that teachers can use to create case studies or scenarios on which students can exercise their decision-making skills. Children's literature can serve as an excellent source for decision-making lessons (Kay, 2006). Riecken and Miller (1990) provide key questions for children's books and a list of 25 children's books suitable for teaching decision making. Following are some of the questions they recommend using in a decision-making lesson based on a tradebook and should be used as a follow up to the close reading strategy in Topic 23. The teacher should concentrate on reinforcing the process of reflection, thinking, and decision making as equally important to the story itself.

1. What is the problem?
2. Why is it a problem?
3. What has to be decided?

4. What are the options?
5. Given the situation, what are three different things you think the character can do?
6. What would you do if you were in this situation?
7. Did the character's solution work?
8. What can the character do now?
9. Are some options better than others?
10. What are the benefits and consequences of each option?
11. Have you ever had to make a similar decision?
12. What would you do?

Decision Making and the Teacher's Role

Decision-making lessons are part of citizenship and character education because students must learn to balance their objectivity with their personal value set or self-interest. The teacher is not to be a provider of answers, but rather a provocateur or "devil's advocate" who forces students to consider alternative positions by posing alternative perspectives. The teacher needs to focus on building a sense of community and trust to create the context for thoughtful decision making. In the lesson itself, the teacher serves as guide through the analysis using the decision-making and problem-solving steps. This kind of systematic approach creates a framework for students to think critically about issues and to reflect on their biases and thinking in the process. Teachers should teach the steps using content rather than teaching the content using the steps. Just as students should be able to recite the seven continents, they should be able to recite the eight decision-making steps.

Simulations and case studies let students use information knowledge from history or contemporary life to progress through the decision-making process under a teacher's guidance. Children's stories like "Jack and the Beanstalk," vignettes from the *Book of Virtues*, the story of George Washington and the cherry tree, a newspaper story on homeless families, or (for upper elementary students) the bombing of Hiroshima provide the opportunity to take students through a lesson using the eight steps of the decision-making model and reach decisions based on their values and ideology.

At the Premium Website, you can download Houghton Mifflin Reading 20, "The Boy at the Dike." How would you turn this story into a decision-making lesson?

Assignment 36.2

INTASC Standards 1, 2, 3, 4, 5, 7, and 8

Create a Decision-Making Lesson

The Gateway to Educational Materials Website displays over 600 lessons in social studies when you do a search for "Decision Making and Social Studies." Search for a high-quality lesson, print out the lesson plan, and be prepared to share your plan with the class and submit the printout and your reasons for considering it a good plan to your professor.

WEBSITE RESOURCES • Problem Solving and Decision Making

Lesson Plan Strategies	**ERIC Online** *ED368568,* The No Waste Anthology: A Teacher's Guide to Environmental Activities K–12 (1993): Has a number of decision-making lesson ideas. *ED457118,* Teaching Character Education Using Children's Literature (2001): Has a list of children's literature, lesson plan ideas, and examples. *ED377046,* Counting on People: Elementary Population and Environmental Activities (1994): Has a number of decision-making lessons on population.
	All linked websites (designated by the green color) and those listed here are available as clickable links at the book's Premium Website, www.cengage.com/login, for ease of access. These links will be updated periodically to reflect changes and new resources as they become available.

Topic 37

Values Formation

The *first question* one faces when thinking about values education is: Whose values will be taught? Your values, society's unclear and ambiguous values, the parents' values? And, if we just promoted agreed-upon current values, there would never have been an end to slavery in the United States or legislation giving women the right to vote.

> If you were going to teach about families to a second grade class, how would you define them? Would you include gay parents as one model? Perhaps you have personally strong views about population, would you not include single parents with six or more children? What might be thought of a just a simple lesson on the family can quickly become a thorny issue for the teacher!

There are some civic values that many people can agree upon that are necessary as part of citizenship and character education development and that are essential to the operation of a school. Promoting the values that underlie rules, such as cooperating with classmates, being attentive, coming prepared for class, and being respectful can generally be agreed upon as necessary for the orderly conduct of the school. And there is an assumption that this socialization will be habit forming and transferrable to students' actions in society at large.

Courage is the ladder on which all other virtues mount.

Clare Booth Luce

The *second question* is: How do students learn appropriate behaviors and adopt beliefs of what is generally accepted as right and wrong? You will have some children in your class who come well prepared by their parents for the collaborative requirements necessary to be successful in school. Some of these children come to this awareness due to their own disposition; others require skilled parenting. Children come to understand which ideas and actions are undesirable or desirable by interaction with their parents and others who give them feedback and through observation of the behaviors of others. Children adopt acceptable and unacceptable behaviors based on a complex set of decisions requiring a high degree of reflection. Beliefs can change as a result of changes in behaviors, and behaviors can change as a result of changes in beliefs. Rewards and punishments and acceptance and rejection by others play a key role in reshaping undesirable behaviors in children. The focus of instruction in values education is to introduce ideas that encourage children to adopt productive behaviors and beliefs. Doing the "wrong thing" might result from not thinking things through as opposed to having a wrong idea. Inculcating civic and personal values by teachers and parents is more difficult, by most accounts, because of the abundance of media children are exposed to today. Such media has a unique and substantial influence on children's behaviors and ideas (Sanchez, 2005).

The *third question* is: How should children be taught right and wrong thinking and behavior in a classroom and school setting? Topics 3, 4, and 5 set the stage for your consideration of how to think about this question, and at the Premium Website is a Bonus Topic on classroom management, which is intertwined with values formation. The field of values education as an instructional strategy is divided into two instructional approaches:

1. **Values analysis** (also referred to as "values clarification") is commonly used to describe an instructional approach in which students are asked to consider their existing beliefs, with the teacher emphasizing the process of analysis and reflection as the way to more sophisticated thinking about right and wrong.

2. **Values inculcation** (which also includes **moral development** and **service learning;** see Topic 48) is considered a more direct approach. With this method, the teacher is both emphasizing analysis and promoting a specific virtue necessary for personal development and for fulfilling one's obligations as a citizen in a democracy. Arguably, one of the hallmarks of a democratic society is that even during values inculcation teachers should emphasize analysis and reflection, in contrast to teachers in countries or schools that promote a single ideological perspective. Concept formation, critical thinking, problem solving, and decision making are tools to assist students in addressing problems that require choices that require the integrating of their personal beliefs, new ideas, and objective information.

The *fourth question* is: How is our success at values education to be measured? Are teachers successful if children can articulate the right thing to do, or can we only evaluate our success if we observe them doing the right thing? Does the answer come from looking back at how a person has lived his or her life or the ethics of our culture?

Regardless of your personal answers to these questions, teachers have a special duty because society commissions them, like parents, to guide the moral development of children: This concept is known as in **loco parentis**—you stand in the place of the parent as a moral compass. Values education strategies can

Unit Six Social Studies Instructional Approaches

be controversial with parents because the teacher may be promoting a more or less democratic ideology than is found in the home, and because children are being asked to think for themselves rather than to blindly maintain the perspectives of their parents, teachers, family, or culture—all in the hope that they will make the right decision and act on it.

> What is your duty in the case of a student who expresses a bigoted view? If it is also the parents' view, do they have the right to keep you from interfering with the values they want to impart to their offspring? Do you have a greater obligation to help the student consider a more democratic ideology? Do you have a greater duty to the other students to affirm a more democratic ideology?

Kohlberg's Principles

No discussion of values education would be complete without consideration of the fundamental work of Lawrence Kohlberg (1969, 1987). Kohlberg's analysis rests on Jean Piaget's concepts of cognitive development. The focus of Kohlberg's work is on how individuals think about ethical issues, not on how they feel. Through interviews with children, Kohlberg identified how individuals pass through stages of conceptualizing issues of right and wrong at various points in their lives. Two main criticisms of the Kohlberg model are that it may be culturally biased and gender biased. Shweder (1982) has argued that the model is based on a Western ideological view of ethics, and Gilligan (1982) has maintained that females' orientation toward compassion and caring is different from males' orientation to rights and rules. Critics notwithstanding, Kohlberg has had a profound influence on how we think about values formation.

More recent research (Hauser, 2006), suggest two principles at work when making moral judgements that appear to bridge all cultures and genders and that seem to be encoded in human biology. Because of this encoding we seek out a "moral system" to reconcile the tension between our emotions and intellect. One, emotions do not appear to have much effect on our judgments about right or wrong, and two, emotions have a significant impact on what we decide to do. To elaborate, we generally do not commit wrongful acts because we know they are wrong, intellectually, and we also don't want to pay the emotional price for doing the wrong thing (refer to "the corollary problem" in Topic 3, "Character Education"). Two examples may help. Humans have some morally impermissible thoughts that "pop" into their heads ("I want to kill him/her"): It appears that it is our emotions that restrain us from acting on those kinds of thoughts. Conversely, humans may have morally permissible thoughts ("I need to save that person who is drowning") but do not intervene due to emotions.

Men are equal: it is not birth but virtue that makes the difference.

Voltaire

Kohlberg focused on the intellectual aspect of morality and identified how humans from childhood through adulthood think differently about right and wrong. In addition, the **defining issues test (DIT)** is an instrument developed as an objective measure of people's moral reasoning levels using Kohlberg's stages of moral development.

Kohlberg's Stages of Moral Reasoning

Kohlberg identified three levels and six stages of chronological moral development (see Table 37.1).

Table 37.1 Kohlberg's Stages of Moral Reasoning

Level	Stage	Characteristics of the Orientation
Preconvention Behavior is governed by external forces like parents and teachers rather than by an intrinsic notion of right or wrong.	1	**Punishment and Obedience** Typical of children under 10 years of age.
	2	**Instrumental Relativist** Reciprocity orientation; typical of children around 10 years of age.
Conventional Conformity to social norms is a major Consideration.	3	**Interpersonal Concordance** Acceptance orientation; typical of preteens and teenagers.
	4	**Authority and Social Order Maintaining** Typical of young and mature adults.
Postconventional Individuals try to define morality in terms of abstract principles; they see rules as practical manifestations of ideas or values.	5	**Social-Contract Legalistic Interpretation** Interpretation of principles typical of young and mature adults.
	6	**Universal Ethical Principle** Few people are believed to reach this status.

To help you understand the above distinctions, the following two examples should help. Children are not "little adults"; they think in a fundamentally different way from adults. Children in the *punishment and obedience stage* will behave the way parents and teachers want them to behave, not because like adults they have reasoned their way to the right choice, but because they fear rejection or not being loved, or overt punishment. Middle school children in the *interpersonal concordance stage* will behave primarily in a way that wins them the acceptance of their peers which is a stronger influence than fear of rejection or punishment from their parents, so parents think of them as rebellious.

Values Analysis

Acknowledging what one believes is the first step to analyzing what one values and developing the flexibility to change when confronted with new ideas or unpredictable circumstances (Blatt & Kohlberg, 1975). Values analysis is a character and citizenship education strategy that provides the vehicle to integrate what we know, what we feel, and what we do based on a balancing of our internal thoughts about right and wrong. Table 37.2 provides the framework for the way a teacher should organize a discussion of topics that we want students to consider as part of their character and citizenship development. These topics or dilemmas tend to come in two forms: (a) **current issues** that are subject to opinion and values, such as poverty or immigration, as opposed to definitive social studies content that is devoid of subjectivity (such as what came first, the Spanish-American War or World War I), or (b) **moral dilemmas** that set up cases or scenarios for students to consider that require a judgement about right or wrong and what is the best thing to do. These moral dilemma cases may be based on real-world cases such as the bombing of Hiroshima, classroom or school situations—a teacher-created story about cheating, and literature such as "Jack and the Beanstalk" or "The Hundred Dresses" (a lesson about courage and teasing), which can be retrieved at the Boston University School of Education Website. These kinds of cases can be found on the Internet by searching for "Kohlberg" or "moral dilemmas." For the classic case of the Heinz Dilemma, go to Wikipedia and enter "Heinz Dilemma."

Table 37.2 Steps in Value Analyses

Teacher	Student
Set Focus	
Provides a stimulus.	Internalizes and becomes motivated.
Briefing	
Provides content.	Internalizes content.
Uses questioning to clarify facts and concepts.	Reflects on facts and concepts.
Dialogue	
(Teacher does not give personal opinions but asks questions.)	
Solicits students' observations and opinions.	Articulates initial opinions, ideas, and beliefs.
Evaluates students' levels of valuing.	Reflects on others' opinions, ideas, and beliefs.
Introduces higher-level thinking if not proffered by students.	Reflects on clarifications and recasts opinions.
Clarifies and recasts opinions, ideas, and beliefs as needed.	Identifies alternatives for adoption.
Encourages personal choice.	Chooses an alternative for adoption.
Listens.	Explains reasons for choice.
Debriefing	
Uses questioning to help students summarize reasoning.	Reflects on personal decision.
Expands on dilemma.	Evaluates reasoning, decision, choice.
Summarizes.	Moves to higher moral reasoning.

Teacher's Tip

When students ask a teacher, "What do you think?" your response should be, "It is not important what I think. What do you think?" This is a clear message that their ideas are important and that you are there to help them think, not to pontificate.

A classroom, like no other environment, provides opportunities for students to hear other children thinking about moral dilemmas at both a lower stage and a higher stage in their moral development. Using Kohlberg's model, students in an elementary classroom may be thinking at stages 1, 2, and 3. When students at stage 2 are exposed to the thinking of students at stage 1 and stage 3, they come to affirm their rejection of the lower-level thinking and aspire to or adopt the higher-level thinking because it makes more sense. And, the teacher is there to pose questions and challenge students to further students along in their conceptualizing, if not adopting, higher-stage thinking (Blatt & Kohlberg, 1975).

The value analysis process works best when the teacher asks questions that lead to more virtuous considerations. The process is used in the content presentation section of a lesson plan to outline how to lead a discussion. The steps in Table 37.2 were adapted from Maxim (1991).

The kind of planned discussion depicted in Table 37.2 would be part of the *instructional sequence* of a lesson plan. It has a number of positive outcomes.

1. Moral considerations and thinking are not developed in a haphazard and inconsistent process, as they would be on the playground.
2. The teacher can ensure a deliberate process and nurturing environment during the discussion, which promotes thoughtfulness and civility.
3. The teacher provides insights at a higher moral level than do peers, strangers, or acquaintances who might have personal agendas.
4. Considerations of such problems preempt unfavorable outcomes of the potentially painful and disastrous trial-and-error method.

Coming to know the right thing to do is the beginning of a moral life, a disposition that is crucial to becoming a whole person and a good citizen. Acting on those beliefs is a function of the virtue of courage. The more examples people acquire of right actions, the easier it is to find the courage to do the right thing.

Based on your understanding of virtues and character education, is there anything you would change about the "Decision and Prediction Organizer" at the Premium Website? Do you think it is an effective tool to use with moral dilemmas?

Kinds of Dilemmas

In preparing to lead students in exploring moral dilemmas, teachers must be aware of the variety of dilemmas and quantity of sources. All moral dilemmas, however, have one common element—tension. A conflict is created that causes tension and forces students to choose one course of action over another. Moral dilemmas can be categorized into four types; each has strengths and weaknesses.

1. **Contemporary dilemmas** are typically drawn from current events. They can be controversial, and may be too sensitive for discussion. California's Proposition 187, which limits funding for certain services for illegal immigrants, or public pressure for a new gun control law following a school shooting are examples of current issues that can be crafted into moral dilemmas. Sometimes it is best to convert an issue into a figurative dilemma because this allows children to consider it with greater objectivity.

2. **Figurative dilemmas** are available in films, cartoons, literature, and teacher-crafted stories. Figurative dilemmas allow children to vicariously consider complex ideas of right and wrong. After the value analysis, the teacher debriefs students about their personal attitudes, which gives the issues personal meaning.

3. **Personal dilemmas** address issues of immediate concern to children. They typically come out of classroom experience, or they are crafted by teachers based on students' experiences. What should a child who breaks a toy do? What should the consequences of not doing homework be? These childhood concerns can be written as stories to be read by the students or presented as read-alouds. Discussions of the right and wrong actions can be used to preempt undesirable behaviors.

4. **Historical dilemmas** are based on historical events or heroic acts. Truman's decision to use the atomic bomb is an event, and John F. Kennedy's *Profiles in Courage* provides examples of historical figures who faced moral dilemmas.

Sources of Dilemmas

The following ideas, adapted from Raths, Harmin, and Simon (1978), can be used to craft a values education lesson.

1. Acted-out scene from a play or movie
2. Advertisement
3. Cartoon
4. Classroom management problems that present teachable moments
5. Clip of a news broadcast
6. Editorial
7. Excerpt from a speech
8. Famous quotes
9. Conflicting aphorisms
10. Historical event
11. Incident at school
12. Letter to the editor
13. Literature—fiction
14. Literature—nonfiction
15. Newspaper or magazine story
16. Open-ended question
17. Oral interview
18. Picture without a caption
19. Primary document
20. Popular song lyrics
21. Picture with a caption
22. Scene from a movie or TV show
23. Tape recording of local people with strong viewpoints

Values Inculcation Approach

Values inculcation is a more direct approach to having students adopt specific values than the value analysis approach and is used to promote specific democratic values and virtues. Literature, big ideas, expressions of the day (like many of the quotes in this textbook), anecdotes, and aphorisms can serve as starting points for lessons that promote specific virtues or democratic principles.

Using Literature to Promote Virtues

Literature is a valuable source of moral dilemmas for children. The endings of most stories can be left out, forcing students to consider what they would do, in which case literature becomes a *values analysis approach*. In most cases, however, literature is used to promote a virtue because the author wrote the story to promote a way of thinking. For example the short story, "The Gift of the Magi," by O' Henry, is a poignant story of sacrifice (a virtue a democratic society promotes) that can be read to children. Because there is a moral dilemma in the story (as in most good fiction), instead of provoking debate about the right thing to do, it simply tells what was done so that the reader will aspire to similar acts of sacrifice. If you are unfamiliar with the very brief story, read it at the Gutenberg Project. Two other sources of stories that promote virtuous actions are *Myths and Hero Tales: A Cross Cultural Guide to Literature for Children and Young Adults*, by Alethea Helbig and Agnes Regan Perkins (1997), and *The Book of Virtues: A Treasury of Great Moral Stories*, by William J. Bennett (1996). There are also websites that offer free downloadable versions of many stories from these sources.

> **What is the moral lesson one is supposed to get from "Goldilocks and the Three Bears" or "The Three Little Pigs and the Big Bad Wolf?"**

Using Big Ideas to Develop Values Lessons

Another simple but effective approach to values inculcation for lower elementary students is to develop a lesson around big ideas that are particularly relevant to their lives. The following socialization topics from Jordon and Metais (1997), as an example, can be used to promote personal identity and socialization.

Teacher's Tip

When using literature as a read-aloud and when students may not be familiar with the characters or language, it is a good practice to create a chalkboard display to preview the character, places, and events.

Good ways to make friends
- Talk to other students about their interests.
- Share your things with them.
- Include them in what you and your other friends are doing.

Good ways to keep friends
- If you say you will do something for a friend, make sure you do it.
- Wait for them, so that they don't get left behind.
- Keep the secrets that they share with you.

Guaranteed ways to have no friends
- Boast about yourself, and tell everyone how great you are.
- Talk about yourself without listening to what others have to say.

Guaranteed ways to lose friends
- Badmouth them when they are not around, and tell their secrets.
- Be jealous of their successes, and be jealous if they like other people.

Using Aphorisms to Develop Values Lessons

An **aphorism** is a statement of a truth or principle. Because aphorisms tend to be short, to the point, and metaphorical, they are easily remembered and can be very powerful. An effective strategy is to write an aphorism on the chalkboard every day or every week and to lead a discussion of what the message is and how it should affect students' behaviors, beliefs, and ideas. The aphorisms in Table 37.3 create intellectual disequilibrium by forcing students to think about and reconcile competing ideas.

Table 37.3 Competing Ideas

He who hesitates is lost.	Look before you leap.
Birds of a feather flock together.	Opposites attract.
You are never too old to learn.	You can't teach an old dog new tricks.
Variety is the spice of life.	Don't change horses midstream.

You can find resources for aphorisms and quotes at Timeless Aphorisms and On Matters of Grave Concern.

Best Practices for Values Education

With an instrument like the DIT (described earlier), empirical studies and anecdotal information can be collected about individuals and groups with different kinds of scores. This information has been used to identify teaching practices and child-rearing techniques that can influence the development of higher levels of moral reasoning at earlier stages in life. Teachers should consider the following strategies for values formation.

1. Plan and lead discussions of topics that present moral dilemmas.
2. Encourage students to participate in service activities.

3. Encourage students to take on leadership roles at school and in organizations.
4. Encourage culturally diverse discussion groups.
5. Use role-playing techniques to create discussions of moral dilemmas.
6. Encourage parents to involve their children in meaningful discussions of issues that require moral reasoning.
7. Encourage a college education (of all variables, education has the highest positive correlation with DIT scores).
8. Help students discover and examine alternative formulations of possible decisions.
9. Give students opportunities to make public affirmations: Focus on reasons for decisions.

In a addition to the assignments listed here and in Topic 3, see two more assignments related to values and character education in Topics 38 and 41, both make use of YouTube videos.

Assignment 37.1

INTASC Standards 1, 2, 3, 4, 5, 7, and 8

The Heinz Dilemma

Go to the Center for the Study of Ethical Development or search the Internet for "Heinz Dilemma." Print out a copy of the Heinz Dilemma and bring it to class. The dilemma requires you to consider whether Heinz should or should not steal a drug and to identify the ideas that most influenced your decision. The dilemma will be used to illustrate Kohlberg's theory of moral development, explained in this topic. Use the dilemma to complete the "Decision and Prediction Organizer" from the Premium Website. Be prepared to turn the organizer in and to discuss your decision in class.

Assignment 37.2

INTASC Standards 1, 2, 3, 4, 5, 7, and 8

Planning a Moral Dilemma Lesson

Create a dramatic personal dilemma that will engage students, and prepare a typed explanation using the steps of leading value analysis. Be prepared to share your ideas with the class and turn in the assignment to your professor.

Unit Six Social Studies Instructional Approaches

Assignment 37.3

INTASC Standards 1, 2, 3, 4, 5, 7, and 8

Planning a Moral Dilemma Internet Lesson

The Random Acts of Kindness Foundation promotes the virtue of kindness. The extensive website has true stories, quotes, lesson plans, and activities that you can use to promote kindness among your students. Select and print out a lesson plan and be prepared to share the idea and your thoughts on the plan with the class and turn in the assignment to your professor.

	WEBSITE RESOURCES • Values Education
Video	*Learner.Org,* Unity and Diversity: A discussion about the teacher's role in promoting values of diversity.
Essay	**ERIC Online** *ED 370075,* Teaching Values Through Children's Literature (1995). **NCSS Statement,** Fostering Civic Virtue: Character Education in the Social Studies.
Lesson Plan Strategies	*ED 440911,* Building Good Citizens for Texas: Character Education Resource Guide. Elementary School (2000): Provides a yearlong plan for character education. *ED 484717,* Kids in Action: A Guide for Involving Elementary Students in Civic Participation. K–5 Social Studies (2004).
Children's Book List	*Character Counts* List of children's books, each tied to a virtue. *Aesop's Fables* The online collection of 655+ fables.
Websites	*Teaching Values.com,* Free e-books and list of classic and contemporary children's books, video and music for the classroom.
	All linked websites (designated by the green color) and those listed here are available as clickable links at the book's Premium Website, www.cengage.com/login, for ease of access. These links will be updated periodically to reflect changes and new resources as they become available.

Unit Seven

Social Studies Methods

Topic 38

Modeling and Metacognition

My daughter-in-law found herself having to correct Lizzie, her two-and-a-half-year-old: "You're not listening, and I have had enough!" A little later, when Lizzie was playing "family" with her stuffed bears, Lizzie modeled her mother by fussing and wagging her finger at the baby bear and said, "I have enough!" Children model adults', and other children's behaviors, sometimes for the good, sometimes for the bad (Horner, et al., 2008).

Modeling is one of the most powerful ways to transmit values, behaviors, and reasoning skills to students because students learn by observing and emulating the teacher and the other students (Bandura, 1979; Nauta & Kokaly, 2001). The complexities of the serendipitous human interactions in everyday life and the classroom are not entirely controllable, but teachers are expected to use modeling (and be "role models") as a purposeful strategy to teach children how to do things, how to behave, and how to think (Wilford, 2007). The role of the teacher as a modeler is particularly important in elementary education because the children are typically exposed to the one teacher all day long. As a result, the teacher plays a crucial role in shaping students' academic disposition, ideology, and temperament.

Types of Modeling

There are three kinds of modeling in the classroom setting: personal, tasks, and metacognitive.

Personal Modeling

In **personal modeling** the teacher serves as a role model by the way he or she conducts discussions, shares ideas, organizes the classroom, and orders the learning experience. Because students are constantly making judgments about a teacher's character, teachers should carefully choose the words and ideas they articulate and the actions they take. In addition, a teacher can identify students who model appropriate behaviors and strategies so that other students might choose to adopt similar approaches and ideas. This personal role modeling is, arguably, more important to social studies educators because it is part of the socialization process that is used to prepare students for the personal growth as human beings and participation in the civic life necessary for democracy.

Teacher's Tip

Teachers should never shout or become angry in front of their students because that teaches students that they should shout and do not have to control their anger.

Tasks Modeling

Tasks modeling takes place when the teacher demonstrates a task that students will be expected to replicate. The teacher can perform an identical or similar activity so the students can observe the process, or the teacher can provide a sample of an end product and describe the process that led to its creation. If students are expected to create a map, an ABC report, a timeline, or a Venn diagram, the teacher should present and explain such a model so that students have a clear understanding of the task. Often, students who have easily conceptualized a task like creating a timeline can be called upon to show and explain their work as a way of modeling the task for other students. A teacher may be aware of a student's particular interest or ability and will ask the student to model a task. For example, a student who is particularly poised and articulate could model making a presentation after the teacher worked with him or her.

How to read social studies textbooks and information knowledge, such as that explained in Topic 25, and how to apply basic skills knowledge are skills well suited for tasks modeling. An example of teacher modeling on how to pronounce words is available at the Premium Website, see TeacherTube, Teaching Reading with Modeling - Word Decoding. There is also the kind of tasks modeling that fits more in the vein of character education where teachers explicitly teach civility or social skills necessary for success as a productive member of society. In the TeacherTube video, Responsive Classroom Morning Meeting - Greeting we see this kind of modeling and perhaps even more important, we see an example of instruction in a topic that many teachers would take for granted.

Metacognitive Modeling

Metacognition is the intellectual function of the mind that is used to control and direct thinking; it involves "thinking about your thinking" (Flavel, 1979; Beeth, Ozdemir, & Yuruk, 2003). It is particularly necessary in social studies when the lesson focuses on a process of deciphering information, interpreting assertions, or drawing conclusions when the lesson involves indefinite information.

The following example is intended to make clear the need for metacognitive modeling. Take the example (since this is an example of what *not* to do, it is what is referred to as a "nonexample") of a high school student watching a mathematics teacher solve a problem at a chalkboard and then expecting students to solve a similar problem. The teacher would deliberately proceed through a series of steps to derive the results, such as the steps needed to apply the distributive property to a set of numbers, remember $a(b + c) = ab + ac$? *But*, assume the teacher did not share his or her thinking while listing the steps to the solution on the board. While the teacher had a destination and a road map in his or her mind' eye, the students had no sense of where they were going because the teacher did not share (model) the most important part, the metacognition that was taking place in her or his mind. So the students would typically memorize the steps, but they wouldn't understand how or why the teacher made the decisions to move from one step to the next or the goal. Metacognitive modeling can make up for two shortcomings found in teaching:

1. **Zone of proximal development.** In its simplest form, teachers must plan new learning to begin where students' knowledge has plateaued (the beginning of the "zone") and move students through the new knowledge with decreasing degrees of support to the new knowledge at the end of the zone (Berk & Winsler, 1995). The process of teachers (or other students) verbally sharing their thinking is the **scaffolding** process that moves students toward the end of the zone (Luria, 1979; Smagorinsky, 2007).

2. **The curse of knowledge.** This principle states that some teachers know their subject matter so well that it is difficult to put themselves in the shoes of novice learners and, thus, fail to find a starting point (the end beginning of the zone) and further fail to model their metacognition because it seems to obvious to himself or herself (Heath & Heath, 2007).

With planned metacognitive modeling, the teacher can potentially overcome these two barriers to students acquiring the desirable social studies knowledge.

Modeling Approaches

Both teachers and other students consciously or unconsciously model behaviors that can be either desirable or undesirable. In the classroom, the teacher needs to correct undesirable behaviors or thinking by redirecting the students through explanation or their own modeling of the desirable behavior or thinking.

Student Modeling

Students exhibit both productive and unproductive thinking and behaving that serve as models for other students. Because classrooms are spontaneous and interactive environments, unproductive modeling cannot be eliminated. A student who reaches a faulty conclusion and proclaims that "all poor people are lazy," as an example, has articulated a conclusion that is based on an inadequate analysis. When something like this happens, the teacher's first consideration should be to focus on the thought process rather than the conclusion. By redirecting the student who made the statement to reconsider his or her thought process, the teacher can guide him or her to eventually reach a different belief about poor people.

A situation like this can also be an opportunity for the teacher to make use of the student as a productive model by capitalizing on his or her naive thinking process. A common approach to exposing and reflecting on faulty generalizations and to develop the thinking of all students is the **Socratic method**. By leading the student though a reexamination of the possible characteristics of poor people with a series of structured questions that lead to a more logical conclusion, all students observe a better line of reasoning. A second possibility is to conduct an examination of how one might examine the attributes of poor people using metacognitive modeling approaches (described later). Students who provide productive modeling in their first answer can be used as examples by merely confirming their thinking and having them explain not only their conclusions but also how they arrived at those conclusions.

Teacher Modeling

Teachers should be productive models of thinking and behaving. Teacher modeling forms part of the **hidden curriculum** in which students pick up on the teacher's unstated thinking process as well as part of the **planned curriculum** in which the teacher is more purposeful in explaining his or her thinking to students. Teacher modeling of how someone sophisticated in the use of procedural knowledge examines an issue, such as crime or a topic such as the Civil War, lets students witness higher-order thinking firsthand and as it is occurring.

Arguably, metacognition is the most neglected form of modeling, even though it is the most important to the formation of procedural knowledge. The most straightforward approach to modeling metacognition is for the teacher to articulate his or her own thinking while examining an issue, reading a passage of text, or performing a task. This **thinking-out-loud strategy** (Woods, 1998) explicitly demonstrates the underlying thinking process of the teacher. The teacher's failure to model metacognitive processes can result in students' failure to understand and acquire the full set of skills that will empower them to be lifelong learners.

A teacher can implement metacognitive modeling as part of the planned curriculum in a number of ways.

- **Decision making and problem solving:** Just providing students with the decision-making or problem-solving steps (refer to Topic 36) is not enough. Unless the teacher also models how to think during the sequence, students will not learn the metacognitive process of applying the steps. With lower elementary students, for example, a teacher could conduct a case study on whether to talk to a stranger who stops the car in front of a child's home. At pivotal points in the analysis the teacher would share his or her thinking, if a student doesn't share his or hers, in the form of statements such as "I am wondering how close I should get to the car of a stranger," "should I talk to a stranger," and "should I call my mom?"

- **Reading:** The process of metacognitive modeling is particularly effective during reading instruction (Clay, 2005). During *shared reading* (refer to Topic 23) with students, the teacher asks rhetorical questions or makes comments to demonstrate the kinds of questions and thoughts that students should process while reading. For example, while reading about the Lincoln assassination, the teacher might say, "I am wondering what impact this will have on how the North and South reconcile." The teacher could ask a student to share what he or she is thinking. By sharing his or her metacognition, the teacher is encouraging deep reading (Birkerts, 1995), that is, reading for meaning. This metacognitive process can be used not only with content, but also with procedures: "I need to look up that word" or "What word do I want to use to label this row [of a data retrieval chart]?"

- **Questioning:** The teacher asks a question and then explains how she or he would think about answering it. The teacher shares not the answer but the thinking process. A teacher who asks, "Why did the explorers come to the New World?" might continue, "I wonder why I would volunteer to go somewhere that I didn't know much about?"

Elementary school teachers should not assume that their students have been exposed to thinking about thinking. Consistent use of metacognitive modeling techniques will help students understand the important role they play in reasoning and understanding.

In your observations of elementary school teachers, how frequently have you seen teachers using metacognitive modeling? Can you think of a specific example from your current experience as a student?

Assignment 38.1

INTASC Standards 2 and 9

Modeling

Please log on to Teacher Tube and search for "Children See and Children Do" or access the video at the Premium Website. Write a one or two paragraph reflection paper of what you see happening in the video.

Video	*TeachSource*, Metacognition: Helping Students Become Strategic Learners: Although this case depicts middle school students, the same metacognitive strategy could also be used at the elementary school level.
Essays	***ERIC Online*** *ED457222*, Students Reflecting on What They Know (2001). *ED438583*, How to Monitor Listening More Efficiently: Meta-Cognitive Strategies in Listening (2000). *ED446872*, Motivating Students to Be Self-Reflective Learners Through Goal-Setting and Self-Evaluation (2000). *ED446269*, Sound Thinking with Thinkback (2000). *ED453521*, Metacognition: Effects on Reading Comprehension and Reflective Response (2001).
	All linked websites (designated by the green color) and those listed here are available as clickable links at the book's Premium Website, www.cengage.com/login, for ease of access. These links will be updated periodically to reflect changes and new resources as they become available.

Topic 39
Lecture

Lecture-type instruction at the elementary level is often referred to as **direct instruction** or **teacher-centered instruction**. Naturally, lectures at the college level should be very different from those at the elementary school level because they would not be appropriate for elementary school children based on their maturation and attention spans. For the purpose of this text, we will use the term **lecture** in the broader sense of instruction in which the teacher is at the center and is verbally delivering information to students. The goal of the topic is to introduce you to multiple ways of lecturing that is appropriate for the elementary school classroom.

Lectures are the most efficient way to convey information. At the end of a lecture a teacher may be able to say, "I taught them," but the students have not necessarily learned what was taught; hearing information, even when enhanced with visuals or models, does not guarantee that students have reconstructed the new knowledge or big ideas. This is one of many reasons why extensive use of questioning (see Topic 40) and guided and individual practice (see Topic 44) are crucial parts of the instructional sequence at the elementary level.

Because of time constraints, you will find it necessary to lecture. In fact, even elementary students need to learn how to persist through lectures because they exist in the real world. However, you will be most effective when you conduct lectures:

- more as discussions,
- limit the duration to the attention spans of the children,
- and purposefully integrate different types of lectures and organizing patterns into the content presentations of your instructional sequence (see Cusik, 2002).

Types of Lectures

The types of lectures presented in Table 39.1 are based on Bonwell and Eison's (1991) ways to vary lectures so that they are effective in the classroom. One attribute common to these lectures is that they are purposefully interrupted with **breakout groups** (see Topic 43) and/or individual tasks. At the elementary level, this is crucial because students have limited attention spans. In general, lectures for lower elementary are shorter than the time suggested and for upper elementary they can be longer.

Table 39.1 Types of Lectures

Lecture Type	Process
Feedback Lecture	*Lecture:* 10 to 15 minutes. Students are given an outline of the lecture beforehand. The teacher lectures based on the outline, with students filling in the outline with information.
	Breakout group: 15 to 20 minutes. Students are given questions to answer based on the lecture and their notes.
	Debriefing: 10 to 15 minutes. The Socratic method is used and is structured around the questions given to the students. The teacher uses a list of big ideas, key concepts, and facts to ensure understanding.
Guided Lecture	*Lecture:* 10 to 15 minutes. Students are given a list of objectives to achieve during the lecture, but students cannot write or take notes—they can only listen and ask questions. The teacher lectures from an outline of big ideas, key concepts, and facts.
	Individual assignment: 5 to 10 minutes. Students are to write down all the information they can recall.
	Breakout group: 10 to 15 minutes. Students work in groups to reconstruct the big ideas, concepts, and facts.
	Debriefing: 5 to 10 minutes. Students ask questions to fill in and expand on missing information. The teacher calls on other students to respond and uses a list of big ideas, key concepts, and facts to ensure understanding.
Responsive Lecture	*Breakout groups:* 15 to 20 minutes. The teacher, perhaps once a week, sets aside time for questions on material covered during the week. Students develop and rank open-ended questions from a recent topic for the teacher to answer, with at least one question from each student.
	Lecture: 15 to 20 minutes. The teacher asks why each question is important in addition to answering it. Student volunteers should also be called on to answer the questions.
Demonstration Lecture	*Lecture: 15 to 30 minutes.* The teacher lectures from an outline of big ideas, key concepts, and facts.
	At points during the lecture, the teacher stops to demonstrate a procedure or process, such as how to find the longitude and latitude of St. Louis.
	Demonstration: 15 to 20 minutes. The demonstration can occur anytime during the lecture. The demonstration is laced with questions to draw out of the students the next steps in the demonstration
	Debriefing: 5 to 10 minutes. Teacher calls on students to explain or demonstrate the process or procedure.
Pause Procedure Lecture	*Lecture:* 20 to 40 minutes. The teacher lectures from an outline of big ideas, key concepts, and facts, with students taking notes but stops every five minutes or so.

(continued)

Table 39.1 (Continued)

Lecture Type	Process
	Breakout pairs: Every 5 minutes. The teacher pauses to allow pairs of students to share notes to correct and collect missing information.
	Debriefing: 5 to 10 minutes. The teacher calls on students to respond to teacher prepared questions to summarize the big ideas, key concepts, and facts.
Think/Write/Discuss Lecture	*Lecture:* 20 to 30 minutes. The teacher lectures from an outline of big ideas, key concepts, and facts.
	At least four key questions are planned by the teacher at pivotal points in the lecture.
	Student response: 2 to 3 minutes. The teacher pauses after each question for students to write answers to the question.
	Debriefing: 5 to 10 minutes. The teacher calls on students to share their written answers to the questions. The teacher repeats and summarizes big ideas and concepts and all students record answers.
Lecture with Graphic Organizer	*Lecture:* 15 to 30 minutes. Rather than taking notes, students are provided a handout of a graphic organizer (web, Venn diagram, etc.), map, or other visual to complete while the teacher lectures.
	The teacher completes the same organizer on the chalkboard or a transparency on the overhead projection.
	Debriefing: 15 to 20 minutes. The teacher circulates during the lecture, making sure students are completing the organizer, etc. and probing for concepts by asking questions of the class as she observes what students are recording.
Socratic Method Lecture	*Lecture:* 15 to 30 minutes. The lecture is structured on a series of carefully sequenced questions. Literally, all the information is developed out of students responses to questions prepared by the teacher.
	This kind of lecture usually follows a reading assignment so that students have a *baseline of knowledge*, although many questions require students to use logic and inference skills. This lecture can be longer because the number of questions increases students' engagement in the lesson by breaking up listening activity with answering activity.
Traditional Lecture	*Lecture:* 15 to 20 minutes. The teacher has a set of class notes that the students are expected to record and primarily reports information.
	Review: Check to make sure students have the key concepts and facts.
	Such lectures today should be infrequent in an elementary school and are presented here more as a *nonexample*. They should be converted into one of the other types of lectures.

Organization of Lectures

The way a lecture is organized will determine its effectiveness. The lecture organizing schemes in Table 39.2 are adapted from the University of Pittsburgh Website (2007) and the University of Illinois Website (2007). The organization of a lecture is based primarily on the nature of the content.

Table 39.2 Organization of Lectures

Organization Format	Definition	Example
Cause and Effect	Focus on cause-and-effect relationships.	"The British persecution of Pilgrims led them to leave their homes and come to the New World. Why do people come to America today?"
Chronological	Demonstrate the order of events.	"Let's take each of the events leading up to the Civil War . . ."
Compare and Contrast	Identify significant differences and similarities.	"Let's compare the advantages and disadvantages of electric cars and gas-powered cars."
Conflicting Generalities	Pose one principle, then force the examination of a counter principle.	"Now that we understand what freedom of speech is, can you always say anything you want?"
Part to Whole	Emphasize how a big idea is composed of several concepts.	"Before we can understand crime, we need to look at how economics, education, and culture contribute to criminal behavior."
What-Why	Emphasize application of a concept.	"Now that we understand the differences between the Senate and the House, let's look at the reasons the founders organized things this way."
Parallel Elements	Compares two events or ideas based on a set of common elements.	"Let's see if we can classify the reasons for the American Revolution and the American Civil War into culture, economy, issues, and beliefs."
Problem-Solution	Identifies a problem and then identifies solutions.	"What causes a recession?"
Ascending-Descending Order	Arranges topics according to their importance or complexity.	"Let's arrange the following states in order by population and by square miles."
Rule-Example	Either begins with a rule, followed by examples and then restatement of the rule; or begins with examples, followed by analysis of the rule.	"In the United States we have a right to privacy. Can you give me some examples?"

Best Practices for a Good Lecture

At the elementary level, there are a number of practices that teachers should use when lecturing. Lectures can be successful when the teacher:

1. Presents the content in small steps.
2. Focuses on a single big idea.
3. Plans and asks many questions.
4. Plans and gives many examples and analogies.
5. Interrupts the lecture with individual or group activities.
6. Constantly checks for student understanding.
7. Doesn't talk too fast.
8. Changes inflection, volume, and pitch.

Teacher's Tip

Images, and even sounds, are so readily available on the Internet that no teacher should consider lecturing without the use of transparencies and other resources from the Internet to enrich the experience.

9. Uses eye contact to keep everyone involved.
10. Holds students responsible for the content.
11. Employs concept-related humor.
12. Shows enthusiasm about the subject.
13. Promotes note taking by speaking slowly and repeating important information.
14. Gives motivational cues ("On Friday you will need to create a legend for a map of Florida").

Assignment 39.1

INTASC Standards 1, 2, 3, 4, 5, 7, and 8

Create a Lecture Based on Lecture Types

Download the Core Knowledge Reading 23, "First Americans, Colonies and the Slave Trade," from the Premium Website and review the topics. Create a step-by-step lecture based on the content of the reading and one of the lecture types. You should expect to share your idea with the class and submit this assignment to your professor.

Assignment 39.2

INTASC Standards 1, 2, 3, 4, 5, 7, and 8

Content for Organization of Lectures

Download the Core Knowledge Reading 21, "The Ice Age, Egypt and World Religions" from the Premium Website and review the topics. Using a table similar to Table 39.2, write an example from the content in Reading 21 for each of the organization formats. You should expect to share your idea with the class and submit this assignment to your professor.

Assignment 39.3

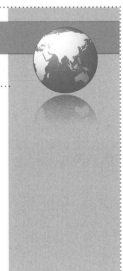

INTASC Standards 1–8

Internet Resources

Download Core Knowledge Reading 25, "The Enlightenment, French Revolution, and Napoleon: History," from the Premium Website and review the topics. Based on the content in Reading 25, find five high-quality resources on the Internet that could be used as background knowledge, lesson plan, activities, or in-class with students. Print out a copy of each and explain how each would be used. You should expect to share your idea with the class and submit this assignment to your professor.

Check the Premium Website, www.cengage.com/login, for additional links and links that are periodically updated to reflect new resources as they become available.

Topic 40
Questioning

Questioning students ensures that all students participate in class and are active learners. In citizenship and character education, it is particularly important because the right question from teachers compels students to reflect on what they know and what they value. Questioning has its origin in the **Socratic method,** a specific kind of instruction used by Socrates that depends entirely on asking students questions. Socratic method requires teachers to methodically plan a series of questions that leads students to the critical attributes of a subject. For what most philosophers would agree is an excellent example of the Socratic method, read the *Meno* at the MIT Classics Website to see how Socrates asks a student to define what it is to be virtuous.

Well-formed questions are essential to teachers who believe that their primary focus should be students developing their critical thinking skills and learning the executive processes of the domain (Brogan & Brogan, 1995). Unlike when students provide written answers to written questions, with verbal questioning students have an opportunity to elaborate and adjust their responses based on their interaction with the teacher, and other students as well, to put forth unique insights. Questioning is one of the easiest ways to convert instruction from a passive to active learning experience, but it must be planned and purposeful (Schurr et al., 1995). A popular indirect teaching strategy that attempts to increase both discussion and thoughtfulness is the *Socratic Seminar* (Mee, 2007). In this method, students engage each other with questions under the guidance of the teacher, rather than led by the teacher.

> *The problem today isn't that we don't have the answers, but that we don't have the questions.*
>
> Marshall McLuhan

A former student told me that one of her students complained to her parent that the teacher was asking her too many questions, and the parent complained to the teacher that it was "cruel to put students on the spot." How would you respond to the parent?

If you have recently observed an elementary class, you will have possibly noticed some teachers call on the same relatively small group of students almost all the time and "shop" questions around the classroom until someone, anyone has any answer. This is an unproductive practice, because it communicates to the students that you do not care about all your students enough to call on them, you just want an answer from someone, anyone. Conversely, making sure all students participate during questioning, communicates that you care about each and every one of them. In a given week, students should have to answer questions an almost equal number of times, and raising one's hand should not be a stimulus for the teacher to avoid calling on students who less frequently volunteer. Students should be questioned because we care about them as individuals—even if at times the student hasn't prepared well enough to answer the question and her or his ego suffers in the short run as a result.

Questions can be used to:

1. Evaluate students' preparation and comprehension. For example, when students read a passage about community workers, the teacher should question them about it to ensure a baseline of information before developing the big ideas.

2. Diagnose students' strengths and weaknesses. In this case a teacher might ask a student to list and categorize community workers in order to determine the student's ability to categorize. The teacher would then ask additional questions of students who were having difficulty with the task.

3. Develop, review, and/or summarize content. It is better to organize the questions you will ask students than to organize what you will tell the students. In other words, rather than telling students who all the community workers are, ask them to volunteer answers.

4. Develop higher-order thinking. With modeling from students or the teacher, mundane facts can be turned into big ideas and procedural knowledge. This is particularly important in character and citizenship education (Elkind & Sweet, 1997).

A Protocol for Questioning

The following protocol can positively influence how your students feel about questions and reduce the anxiety that some students experience even when they know the answers. The first task in this process is to create a thoughtful atmosphere.

Creating an Environment Conducive to Questioning

Creating an environment conducive to questioning or discourse is essential to social studies education. Newmann (1988) identified a number of indicators of a "thoughtful classroom."

1. Classroom interaction focuses on sustained examination of a few topics rather than superficial coverage of many. That is, big ideas and procedural knowledge are emphasized.
2. Students are given sufficient time to think before being required to answer questions.
3. The teacher presses students to clarify or justify their assertions (rather than merely accepting and reinforcing them indiscriminately).
4. The teacher models the characteristics of a thoughtful person. The teacher shows interest in students' ideas and their suggestions for solving problems, models problem-solving processes rather than just giving answers, and acknowledges the difficulties involved in gaining a clear understanding of problematic topics.
5. Students are encouraged to generate original and unconventional ideas in the course of the interaction.

To view a video of an upper elementary lesson in which the teacher effectively uses questioning to engage students, go to learner.org's *Explorers in North America*.

To organize your questions, you need a strategy that takes into account different types of questions.

Choosing Grounded and Ungrounded Questions

There are a number of ways to think about the questions you will pose during lectures and discussions. The first way is to divide your questions into those that are grounded and those that are ungrounded.

Grounded questions are those that students should know the answers to because they have been taught the information in class or were expected to acquire it, perhaps in a homework reading assignment. For example, if you just taught that Columbus' three ships were the *Nina, Pinta,* and *Santa Maria* or if you required students to read a paragraph with that information as homework, they should know the answers to questions about the names of the ships because the information is *grounded* in content that has been assigned. During verbal questioning with grounded information, students need to be held accountable. If not, they will soon learn they don't have to read or pay attention and you will not likely move up to the kind of questions that require reflection and analysis.

To transform your classroom into one where all students are active participants in questioning, their answers need to be part of your evaluation scheme. Students (and parents) should be told of the importance of questions as being equivalent to verbal testing and that not being prepared to answer grounded questions will affect their grade. When a student fails to answer a grounded question, indicate—verbally, by facial expression, or by body language—that you expect an answer because he or she has a duty to study and assist the other students by answering a fair share of questions. If you don't want to keep your gradebook open during questioning, you need to make mental notes and record scores at a later time. In either case, your grade reports should include a category for "answering questions," just as you have a category for "tests." Problems of inattention and incomplete assignments will dissipate when questioning is elevated to the level of a performance evaluation.

Grounded questions should not be limited to simple recall of facts. Students should also be held accountable when they are unwilling or fail to infer, predict, or deduce an answer that you have framed in a question. For example, if after reading "Goldilocks and the Three Bears," a teacher were to ask, "What do you think the three bears thought when they returned home from their walk?" the student should be expected to respond with a thoughtful answer even though the teacher did not explicitly teach the answer and it does not explicitly appear in the story. However, these kinds of questions should not be treated in the same way, in terms of a grade, as fact-based questions for which there is really little excuse for not having the answer.

✎ **Ungrounded questions** are asked as part of an attention-getter or content presentation because they rely on serendipitous knowledge. Students may not know the answer through no fault of their own. The question "Does anyone know what the president said yesterday about . . . ?" is an example of an ungrounded question. Students cannot be held accountable if they do not volunteer an answer or if they give a wrong answer.

Types of Questions

Bloom's *Taxonomy of Educational Objectives* (1956) offers a format for structuring effective and efficient questions. Many teachers may not recognize that preparing questions is an essential component of lesson planning and that successful teachers take care to craft questions that force students to think at higher levels. The following examples of different levels of questions should help you prepare lesson plans.

- **Knowledge questions** check memory only. A knowledge question should have a followup question or should be framed to access both knowledge and a higher-order thinking skill.
    - *Base question:* Who is the president?
    - *Follow-up question:* Can you tell us some of the things you would want to do if you were president?
    - *Combined question:* Who is the president, and can you tell us some of the things you would want to do if you were president?
- **Comprehension questions** check memory and comprehension. A comprehension question should have a followup question or should be framed to access both comprehension and a higher-order thinking skill. Comprehension

Teacher's Tip

Questions are so important to thinking skills development that you should place a sign in the back of the classroom: "Ask Questions. Wait for Answers."

questions usually require the student to explain the answer in his or her own words.

- *Base question:* Can you explain needs and wants?
- *Follow-up question:* Would you give the class an example?
- *Combined question:* Can you give the class an example of a need and an example of a want, and tell us the difference?

- **Application questions** require students to use their knowledge and comprehension by applying it to a situation.
  - *Base question:* Can you go to the map and find the longitude and latitude of Tampa, Florida?

- **Analysis questions** require the student to scrutinize information knowledge and explain its significance.
  - *Base question:* What are some of the reasons a family may be unable to meet its needs?

- **Synthesis questions** require the student to combine information knowledge to form a new idea based on relationships.
  - *Base question:* Based on knowing the longitude and latitude of a place, what other things can you hypothesize?

- **Evaluation questions** require a student to use a set of criteria to make a reasoned judgment.
  - *Base question:* Based on what the president said he would do, do you think he is doing a good job?

The process of questioning is as important as the questions themselves, as we will see in the next sections.

Wait-Time Approach

The wait-time approach is based in part on the research and principles of **wait time** (Rowe, 1972) and **think time** (Stahl, 1980), among others. The most basic principle is that a question is followed by a minimum of three seconds of silence so that every student has time to collect his or her thoughts and devise an answer. Then a student is selected, and a second wait time is used for the student to collect his or her thoughts prior to answering. By waiting for as long as it takes the student to answer, the teacher conveys an unequivocal message that he or she cares about the individual and that the student must take responsibility for learning. After only a week of consistent use, you should see a change in students' responses and their preparation for class. Some of the positive aspects of this strategy are:

1. All students are motivated to develop answers.
2. The length and correctness of students' responses increase.
3. Silence and the number of "I don't know" responses diminish.
4. The number of volunteered answers to ungrounded questions increases.
5. Scores on academic achievement tests increase.
6. Teachers tend to increase the number of higher-level questions.

7. The classroom becomes a quieter and more civil community of learners.
8. Students become more active agents in their own learning.

A Comprehensive Classroom Questioning Approach

Because each teacher has a different approach to questioning, students should be briefed about your approach at the beginning of the term. On the first day of class, explain that questioning is important and how questions will be handled in class. This explanation can have a dramatic effect on the quality of the learning environment. Explain the difference between grounded and ungrounded questions, and tell them the following.

1. During grounded questions, they need not raise their hands because you care about each one of them, so you will call on all students an equal number of times during the course of a week.
2. You will always ask the question before calling on a student, so that students will have plenty of time to think about the answer.
3. You will keep track of students called on and their answers because questions are evaluated like a test.
4. Each student is important and is in school to learn. You will give them time to remember what they learned and time to share it with the class. They have to be thinking and paying attention during their reading, while you are teaching, and during questioning.
5. You will wait in silence for as long as it takes the student to answer. The student always has to answer. Correct, thoughtful answers result in better grades. Partial answers are acceptable. You will not call on another student before the student has given you an answer or has said that he or she does not know the answer.
6. If the first question required only the reporting of knowledge or comprehension, you will usually ask the same student to apply, analyze, synthesize, predict, or evaluate the reported information.
7. Students who wish to comment or expand upon another student's answer may raise their hands only after there is a period of silence in which all students consider whether they want to comment.

You should be consistent with the application of this framework by using it in all subject fields and on an everyday basis if you want your students to enjoy the benefits of the questioning-centered classroom.

Best Practices for Questioning

The following additional questioning practices should guide teachers in a classroom of active learners.

1. Create and announce your questioning framework at the first class.
2. Use wait time.
3. Ask all students an equal number of questions.
4. Prepare questions that focus on higher-order thinking.
5. Since answers to verbal questions are part of assessment, make sure they are reflected in students' grades.
6. Praise correct answers.
7. Call on other students to repeat a particularly good answer.
8. Encourage students to answer to the class, not just to you.
9. Form questions that are precise and definite, not ambiguous.
10. Encourage students to ask qualifying questions.
11. Keep questions short and to the point.
12. Avoid fill-in-the-blank questions.
13. Don't ask for trivial information.

Assignment 40.1

INTASC Standards 1, 2, 3, 4, 5, 7, and 8

Grounded Questions Lecture

Download Houghton Mifflin Reading 8, "Our Country's Geography," from the Premium Website and review the chapter. Assume your students read the material the night before as homework. Create a list of grounded questions to teach this material by listing a series of questions (followed by the expected answers in parentheses). Be prepared to turn in the assignment to your professor and to discuss your ideas in class.

Assignment 40.2

INTASC Standards 1, 2, 3, 4, 5, 7, and 8

Bloom's Taxonomy Questions

Download Houghton Mifflin Reading 11, "Community Resources," from the Premium Website and review the chapter. Create an example question for each of Bloom's six categories (followed by the expected answers in parentheses). Be prepared to turn the assignment in to your professor and to discuss your ideas in class.

Essays	**ERIC Online** *ED370885,* Using "Think-Time" and "Wait-Time" Skillfully in the Classroom (1994). *ED461411,* Reformulating Useless Questions for Classroom Instructions (1988). *ED366530,* Integrating Thinking Skills into the Third Grade Social Studies Curriculum (1993). *ED383706,* Wait-Time: Effective and Trainable (1995).
Teacher Tube	*Socratic Seminar*
Websites	*The Socratic Method*
	All linked websites (designated by the green color) and those listed here are available as clickable links at the book's Premium Website, www.cengage.com/login, for ease of access. These links will be updated periodically to reflect changes and new resources as they become available.

Topic 41

Analogies

Analogies are essential and powerful tools of instruction because they connect the known to what we don't know (National Research Council, 2000). Analogies serve as the bridge from an existing idea students may have to a new idea (Duplass, 1996). Hoffman (1983) estimates that the average English-speaker uses over 3,000 analogies or metaphors per week as an expeditious means of conveying ideas.

> **How many times a week do you think you say, "it is just like . . ."?**

The word "analogy" is frequently used to describe metaphors and similes. But if we use the word loosely to mean a general comparison, then we could say that an analogy happens when we compare two examples: "This is like that." As an example, "*Boy* is to *girl* as *rooster* is to *hen*" is an effective analogy with children, because they have an idea what a boy and girl are, but not a rooster and hen. Analogies work in part because they create metacognitive tension (the "What?" immediate response when we hear or read an analogy) between what we know and do not know (Manhood, 1987). In this boy-rooster analogy, the tension is created because we generally think of boys/girls and roosters/hens as two very different things (humans and lower-level animals), but they are alike in two very important ways, they are both male/female and animals. A new idea (gender) is formed from the one-to-one relationship by analogizing two existing distinct categories (people and chickens) but with a common attribute (male/female [Marzano, Gaddy, & Dean, 2000; Ortony, 1979]). Analogies are among the most powerful ways of creating a bridge to a new idea or concept, but to be effective, they must start with something the student knows (Baldwin et al., 1982; Block, 2001).

Types of Analogies

Analogies can take a number of forms and have a consistent pattern in social studies.

Similes

Similes are explicit comparisons of two unlike things, usually starting with the words "like" or "as." "Reason is to faith as the eye to the telescope," by the philosopher David Hume, is an example. This kind of analogy draws direct connections from one idea to another, usually by saying, "It is just like . . ." For example, a teacher using the term "prime minister" for the first time can quickly and efficiently create a bridge to this new concept by saying, "It is like the president of the United States." Teachers can draw analogies between U.S. civilization and Roman civilization (they both have senates, economies, rights for citizens, etc.), for example, so that students can compare and contrast the two.

Metaphors

Metaphors are implied comparisons of two unlike things in which the words "like" and "as" are not typically used. Referring to Cleopatra, Shakespeare wrote, "She was a morsel for a monarch." Metaphors are more complex and subtler than similes; because they use figurative language, they can be more powerful than similes. They may also require more analysis, which presents opportunities for teachers of social studies to model analytical thinking and close reading. President Theodore Roosevelt's statement, "Walk softly but carry a big stick," expresses a complex set of ideas about the United States' position on the world stage. If a teacher says, "I came to a fork in the road," elementary students will want to know if the teacher leaned down to pick up the fork unless the teacher clarifies the meaning.

Allegories

Allegories are figurative comparisons using children's literature such as fairy tales and fables with fictional characters to *analogize* events to one's own life. "Goldilocks and the Three Bears" and "Jack and the Beanstalk" are allegorical tales intended to teach a big idea. From the perspective of social studies education, these two stories are vehicles to draw children into consideration of circumstances that require rethinking what it means to be virtuous: One is about breaking and entering and the other is about stealing. Allegories provide powerful citizenship and character education lessons and they can be drawn from many cultures and allow students to consider the kind of person they want to be or fear becoming.

Few of today's children's books of fairy tales and fables would sell many copies if they were not heavily laced with pictures. While **picture books** are more enticing than books printed with relatively few images, they do not require students to create the variety and volume of mental images that were needed in the past. Having to create a mental image of Jack and the giant provided a different kind of experience than looking at a picture book provided by the publisher. Dramatic readings by teachers of allegorical tales also have the advantage of expecting students to be active learners, if teachers promote strategies which encourage the children to close their eyes and imagine the scenes and characters. With extensive and powerful media, one can suspect this is becoming a lost art.

Media

Media (sound recording, movies, videos, still pictures, television, and theater productions) are figurative illuminations, like allegories, but in another form. The movie *Saving Private Ryan* (while not appropriate for children, you can see a seven minute clip of the landing on D-Day in World War II at YouTube, if you are unfamiliar with the film) offers viewers the experience of war without actually being in physical danger themselves. Media can provide more intense and direct connections to the senses than the written word can. A reenactment in which children reenact Rosa Parks's dilemma when the bus driver tries to force her to give up her seat on the bus is an example of a role-playing activity that creates a bridge to a big idea.

Analogical Construction

Constructing social studies analogies includes **framing** the analogy and selecting its components. Analogies have a **topic, topic characters,** a **story,** a **vehicle,** and **vehicle characters** (see Table 41.1). Teachers should plan analogies to ensure that the vehicles and characters have appropriate and as accurate **parallel construction** as possible. This is known as *framing* the analogy. Table 41.1 shows an analogy for the Civil War.

Table 41.1 **Parallel Construction: Civil War**

Topic	Vehicle
United States in 1860	Family
Topic Characters	**Vehicle Characters**
Civil War	Argument
North	One brother
South	Another brother
Story	
"The Civil War is like two brothers fighting"	

Pitfalls of Analogies

Because analogies are so powerful, they can be used to overtly or covertly mislead or misinform people. For example, Nazis overtly compared Jews to rats during World War II. But compare this subtler analogy from a Toronto newspaper to the overt Nazi propaganda: "Starbucks coffee shops are spreading through Toronto faster than head lice through a kindergarten class." This may seem on the surface to be neutral because it does not state an overt objection or support for Starbucks. But upon reflection, the choice of the vehicle *lice* can be judged to reflect the author's opinion of the undesirability about the multiple locations of Starbucks in Toronto.

Analogies are efficient and potent, but culture and age differences can also limit their effectiveness (Readence, Baldwin, & Rickelman, 1983; Tierney, 1991). As an example, a teacher in a recent social studies class who was preparing to draw an analogy asked if anyone knew who Lewis and Clark were. A student whose first language was not English said that he was Superman and she was his lover in the popular 1990s *Lois and Clark* TV series. Obviously, any analogy built around these names might have a rough going with this student. And as a second personal example from my own teaching: I recently drew on my childhood experiences and referred to my students as the "peanut gallery" when they were too talkative for me to get their attention. Because all of them were born well after the *Howdy Doody* show had left the air, they didn't know what to make of it, and some of you, as readers of this textbook, may not either!

In addition, analogies are by nature imperfect because the vehicle characters used to draw the comparison cannot be perfectly identical. The office of the president of the United States is not exactly the same as the office of the prime minister of England. Analogies, therefore, must be understood to be imperfect but still vital to instruction. Once the bridge is crossed, we can refine the meaning of the other vehicle character.

> Using "Goldilocks and the Three Bears," can you frame the story to create two different perspectives? One perspective might be sympathetic to Goldilocks, and the other might be sympathetic to the bears.

Using Analogies with Controversial Issues

In teaching, analogies are most commonly used in lectures, in giving follow-up explanations to students, and discussions. They can also be used in the case study method (see Topic 47). Typically, the teacher will create a metaphorical story for the case study. This can be especially helpful in discussing current events and controversial issues. When emotions are running high in the community or school, discussions about some topics may be counterproductive when the topics are approached head on. The teacher can use a metaphorical story to develop basic concepts without the children's knowing, at first, that they are discussing the controversial issue. Because it is "just a story," more objectivity can be brought to the issues. Students use inductive reasoning as they draw conclusions from the facts of the metaphorical case. Later, they use deductive reasoning to apply the generalizations to the real-world controversial issue. If nothing else, students must confront the reasons their decision about the real-world case is different than their decision about the metaphorical case (see Assignment 41.1 as an example of this approach to controversial issues).

The following is an example of using an analogy to have students consider a controversial topic. Consider this example as occurring immediately following the 9/11 attacks.

In a first grade classroom, a student has invited his uncle as his "VIP guest" to talk to the other kids. The child introduces his uncle and says; "I asked him to come because he is a Muslim."

The first question from a well-intentioned first-grader is: "My dad says Muslims killed people with a plane and that they are bad," referring to the World Trade Center attack.

VIP Guest: "Does everyone have cousins?" Children, "Yes."

VIP Guest: "Have any of your cousins done something bad?" One child: "Yes, he took some cake when he wasn't supposed to and blamed it on me."

VIP Guest: "Because that one cousin did something bad, is everyone in your family bad?" (paraphrased from the Showtime series, *Terror Cell*, 2006)

> **Handling controversial issues is not easy. What is your assessment of this dialogue?**

Assignment 41.1

INTASC Standards 1, 2, 3, 4, 5, 7, and 8

Creating an Analogy for a Controversial Issue

How does a person living in Mexico or another country become a legal immigrant to the United States? To answer this question, you can go to the U.S. Department of Justice Website to learn more about U.S. immigration policy. California residents passed Proposition 187, which denies public schooling and most taxpayer-funded nonemergency health services to illegal immigrants (the proposition is currently being contested in the courts). Conduct a search for "Proposition 187" on the Internet to learn more about different perspectives about the initiative.

(Continued)

Assignment 41.1

INTASC Standards 1, 2, 3, 4, 5, 7, and 8

For this assignment, write a story/analogy that you could use with children as a case study (Topic 47) for decision making about Proposition 187. Assume that you have a classroom of multicultural children, some of whom may be illegal immigrants. Your challenge is to create a bias-free analogy that deals with the ideas and beliefs associated with immigration and Proposition 187. Complete the equivalent of Table 41.1, and be prepared to share your answers in class and turn in the assignment to your professor.

Assignment 41.2

INTASC Standards 1, 2, 3, 4, 5, 7, and 8

Character Education and Perils of Analogies

What is the moral of "Jack and the Beanstalk?" This is a more complex tale than you may think. View this YouTube video, identify the moral issues, and create a list of questions you would use in debriefing the story with 3rd grade students.

	WEBSITE RESOURCES • Analogies and Controversial Issues
Video	*Learner.org,* Dealing with Controversial Issues.
	All linked websites (designated by the green color) and those listed here are available as clickable links at the book's Premium Website, www. cengage.com/login, for ease of access. These links will be updated periodically to reflect changes and new resources as they become available.

Topic 42

Concept Organizers

Concept organizers, graphic organizers, and **concept maps** describe various, typically paper-based, visual images that assist teachers in having students develop concepts (see Topic 14 for their use as assessment tools). The use of concept organizers in lectures, discussions, group activities, case studies, and homework assignments is a better approach than the typical fill-in-the-blank worksheets that one too often sees in use in schools. And, importantly, it is their visual simplicity that makes the images so successful (Stone, 2002).

? When you have observed elementary classrooms, what was your experience with worksheets, in contrast to concept organizers?

Teacher's Tip
The "Inspiration" Website offers a software tool that can facilitate visual learning.

Teachers can use most of the organizers found at the Premium Website to organize processes, concepts, or facts, and a large number of websites have downloadable concept organizers (see end of this topic). Frequently, teachers create unique concept organizers that they conceptualize based on the specific information knowledge and procedural knowledge they are teaching.

Concept maps and organizers are important tools for a number of reasons.

1. They are appropriate to almost all grade levels.
2. They visually enhance learning.
3. They accommodate different learning styles.
4. They are easy to teach from and use.
5. They can include both information knowledge and procedural knowledge.

354

6. When teachers use them, they model how to construct knowledge.
7. When students make or complete them, students must reconstruct knowledge.

Examples of concept organizers can be found at the Premium Website, and in Houghton Mifflin's Reading 15, "The Twenty-First Century Begins," page 678 and in Reading 12, "The Conflict Grows."

Selection of Concept Organizers

You may want to keep three considerations in mind in deciding on one of the many types of concept organizers.

1. Which type of organizer should be used? Would a Venn diagram, a data retrieval chart, a timeline, or a cause-and-effect diagram most effectively convey the ideas? The selection of the graphic organizer is important because it typically defines the kind of procedural knowledge that will be used to connect the information knowledge.
2. What type of information knowledge is to be recorded? For example, data retrieval charts lend themselves to categories, whereas events are best shown in timelines and escalator diagrams.
3. How should the information knowledge be organized? In the case of a data retrieval chart, decide what vertical and horizontal headings will create meaningful relationships among the data in the cells. For timelines, determine how long the time period should be and what the important benchmarks are.

Lecturing with Concept Organizers

Teachers often use concept organizers as organizing schemes for lectures and display them as overhead transparencies and/or hand them out to students. Not only is a concept organizer a valuable visual cue about the organization of the lecture, it is also a valuable model of how to organize concepts into schema and, during lecture, the teacher is modelling their use. For example, see Figure 42.1, a "Hierarchy Organizer" used to explain Roman civilization. The items in boxes are **concepts** (*empire*) or **facts** (*Augustus, 7 kings*), and the terms between the boxes are **connectors** ("had," "started as"). This pattern and terminology should be used consistently and shared with students. Note that the engineering and architecture sections are not complete; could you complete them?

Also note that a different teacher might choose to emphasize other concepts and facts. There are multiple right configurations, but there are also inaccurate conceptual depictions—so teachers need to thoroughly plan the

Figure 42.1

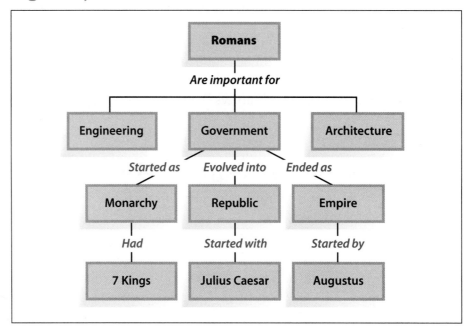

organizers they use and have prototypes of the "ideal" organizer ready to use for feedback when students are expected to create them.

One teaching approach is to exhibit the completed Figure 42.1 as a transparency and to deliver a lecture with questioning that includes more detailed information on each component. A second approach is to require students to draw an identical hierarchy organizer, filling in the missing concepts, facts, and connectors and recording notes as instruction progresses. A third option is to distribute copies of a blank hierarchy organizer, rather than having the student draw it, and have them fill it in as in the second approach. In all three cases, as the teacher progresses through each of the topics framed in the organizer, he or she should introduce images taken from the Internet that illuminate the concepts. The wealth of images about the Roman Empire on the Internet makes it possible for a teacher to provide an image for almost every example concept or fact included in the concept map.

Group Activity Approach with Concept Organizers

The active learning in the lecture approach is limited to looking at images, replicating or filling in the concept organizer, calling on students for answers, asking follow-up questions to develop concepts, and perhaps taking notes. However, one of the goals of any concept organizer is for students to capture the entire image in their mind's eye. Requiring students to create a concept organizer after a lecture and note taking, discussion, or other activity often involves a higher level of engagement and critical thinking by students because they reconstruct the information; accommodates individual differences by allowing students to use different kinds of concept images; and forces them to conceptualize their understanding of the concepts rather than the teacher's view.

For example, assume that you modeled the use of the hierarchy concept organizer in a lecture on the Roman Empire. Now you want students to read a passage in their textbook on the medieval period. You could use a timeline organizer for the medieval period so students learn how to use timelines. Or, you could—now that they have experience with a hierarchy concept organizer— put them in groups, and have them create one for the medieval period to explain its civilization as was done for the Roman Empire. You could then cover the big ideas related to the components of the society, like serfs, lords, and the economics of a castle and fief system, in a lecture. As a practice activity (see Topic 44), students might create a compare-and-contrast organizer to contrast the Roman and medieval civilizations.

The following is an example that demonstrates one approach to the use of organizers.

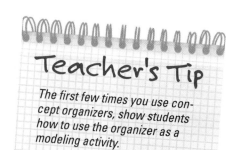

Teacher's Tip

The first few times you use concept organizers, show students how to use the organizer as a modeling activity.

A Geography Example

Table 42.1 contains a number of concepts and connectors that would be taught to elementary students as part of a lesson on the basic components of the Earth using a **guided lecture** organized as a **part-to-whole** lecture (refer to Topic 39). Assume that you would teach about these concepts as discrete entities with a globe, examples, and images from the Internet. Following the lecture, students would be divided into groups, and Table 42.1 would be displayed as a transparency. Students would be reminded of the Roman civilization organizer they completed earlier in the year and told that their

Table 42.1   Concepts

Concepts	Connectors
Continents	Are at
Earth	Divided into
Gulfs	Includes
Islands	Is made up of
Lakes	
Land areas	
Oceans	
Rivers	
Water bodies	

organizer should be similar (a hierarchy of concepts linked by connectors) using the concepts and organizers in Table 42.1. Note that the concepts are presented in alphabetical order, as are the connectors. Tell students that the rules for this kind of active learning experience are that each concept must be used, but only once, and that the connectors may be used more than once or not at all. Before having students create concept maps, the teacher should present a model of the concept map with different content.

Assignment 42.1

INTASC Standards 1, 2, 3, 4, 5, 7, and 8

Create a Concept Organizer
Use the contents of Table 42.1 to create a concept map based on the model in Figure 42.1 and be prepared to share your answers in class and turn in the assignment to your professor.

Reading with a Concept Organizer: The Guided Reading Escalation Model

Students can be expected to create a concept organizer from a reading assignment as a *baseline of information* (see Topic 44) prior to a debriefing or lesson or as a postreading activity. The purpose of having students use concept organizers based on a reading passage is for them to develop:

1. The skill of identifying and recording relevant information correctly;
2. The skill to reconstruct the knowledge from narrative to conceptual form;
3. The procedural knowledge of organizing the information based on the relationships of the facts and concepts; and
4. The intuition that is part of an academic disposition to select the best concept organizer to project the information knowledge.

A Whole Year Approach to Using Graphic Organizers

The **guided graphic organizer approach** is intended to introduce students to the use of graphic organizers through a structured, scaffolded approach with increasing degrees of difficulty during the course of a year. Table 42.2 illustrates the sequence with a sequential listing of 10 typical U.S. history passages starting with the Vikings and ending with the "Acts" (the Tea Act, etc.). The sequence starts before the first reading, which is when the teacher gives students

Table 42.2 Guided Reading Escalation Model Example

Steps	Readings Sequence	Distributed When	Individual or Group	Concept Organizer Type Data Organizer
1	1st Reading *Vikings*	Prior	Group	Headings and Some Data
2	2nd Reading *Early Explorers*	Prior	Individual	Headings and Some Data
3	3rd Reading *Jamestown*	Prior	Group	Headings Only
4	4th Reading *Plymouth*	Prior	Individual	Headings Only
5	5th Reading *French and Indian War*	After	Group	Headings Only
6	6th Reading *Northern Colonies*	After	Individual	Headings Only
7	7th Reading *Middle Colonies*	Prior	Group	No Headings
8	8th Reading *Southern Colonies*	Prior	Individual	No Headings
9	9th Reading *Mercantilism*	After	Group	No Heading
10	10th Reading *The Acts*	After	Individual	No Heading

After using a number of concept organizers (not just the *data organizer* used here for illustration purposes), students should be expected not only to reconstruct information into concept organizers but also to select or create the concept organizer that best depicts their conception of the passage.

a data retrieval chart with the headings indicated and some data filled in. Students work in groups, and each student completes his or her chart. By the 10th step, the student receives a blank concept organizer after the reading and is required to create his or her own conception of it without the support of peers. By the 11th step, students select the concept organizers rather than the teacher, thus taking charge of their own learning and exhibiting the capacity to interpret and project the parts of a reading that they find most compelling. It is not necessary to proceed through all 11 steps. Steps can be skipped if the teacher perceives that students are ready for a more advanced step.

To simplify the illustration, the only concept organizer listed in Table 42.2 is a *data organizer*. This does not mean that the teacher has to use only passages that lend themselves to a data organizer in the first 10 reading assignments. The content of the reading should determine the concept organizer that is used. In the real world, four or five different organizers might be used in the first 10 readings. Each time a new organizer is used, the teacher should begin with the first step. For example, if the first reading uses a data organizer and the second reading lends itself to a timeline organizer, students would be given a timeline organizer with some information filled in before the second reading. If the third reading also uses a data organizer, the teacher would move on to the second step.

Students are permitted to work in groups when a new degree of difficulty is reached. This collaborative approach increases success rates, but the goal is for each student to be capable of individually selecting and completing a concept organizer to convey his or her ideas by the end of the year. In all cases, each student completes his or her own organizer. The teacher models his or her thinking when introducing a new concept organizer and moves students to the point where each student selects an organizer as well as completes it.

This strategy does not have to be used only in social studies; its use in the other subjects would benefit students' entire education. By taking students through this kind of systematic approach, the teacher is making sure they have the needed skills to determine the best way to interpret and explain reading passages.

The goal of the guided graphic organizer model is to reach the 11th step as early as possible in the school year. A box of concept organizers would be kept at a resource table, and after reading a passage a student would be expected to select one that he or she believes will best reconstruct the passage and most clearly communicate the ideas to someone else. Having students not only read but also select the best method to explain the passage empowers them to be lifelong learners, fosters autonomy, and ensures the highest level of reconstruction of knowledge.

Assignment 42.2

INTASC Standards 1, 2, 3, 4, 5, 7, and 8

Create Graphic Organizers

Download the Core Knowledge Readings 21, 23, and 25 from the Premium Website and review the topics in the chapters. Prepare three unique graphic organizers that could be used with each chapter. Prepare a one-page summary to explain how each would be used in lecture, group activity, or reading approaches. Attach the graphic organizers to your summary and be prepared to discuss your results in class and submit the assignment to your professor.

Essay	***ERIC Online*** *ED424882,* Using Mind Maps to Teach Social Problems Analysis (1998). *ED473056,* Improving Organizational Skills Through the Use of Graphic Organizers (2003).
Websites	*TeacherVisions Graphic Organizers* *Education Oasis Graphic Organizers* *Scholastic*

Sample High-Quality Internet Lessons that Use Graphic Organizers

Lower Elementary	*EconoEd* How Much Is That Doggie? Uses a Venn diagram and work sheet for students to consider the purchase of a pet.
Upper Elementary	*Core Knowledge* Getting to the Core of World and State Geography uses a number of graphic organizers.
	All linked websites (designated by the green color) and those listed here are available as clickable links at the book's Premium Website, www.cengage.com/login, for ease of access. These links will be updated periodically to reflect changes and new resources as they become available.

Topic 43

Group Learning

Grouping students for learning activities is a powerful and essential tool for the elementary school teacher. **Group learning** fosters the kind of collaboration needed for effective citizenship, allows the teacher to change the class tempo, reduces teacher-centered instruction, and increases student participation (Hendrix, 1999). Unless the teacher guards against it, a few students in the group may take over and do the majority of the work or monopolize the discussion, while other students become non-participants—both of these possibilities should not be permitted by the teacher.

Groups can be categorized as informal **breakout groups** and more structured **cooperative learning groups**. Jacobs et al. (2002), Johnson, Johnson, and Holubec (1994), Kagan (1993), and Slavin (1990) offer a number of principles and practices that are applicable to both breakout groups and cooperative learning groups. They provide some of the foundation and many of the strategies proposed in this topic. The Cooperative Learning Website is sponsored by Kagan. Both sites are worth visiting.

Grouping Methods

The following are some frequently used grouping methods used in social studies. It is a good idea to use several methods over time so as to vary the group processes.

1. **Paired sequences:** Students write notes on small pieces of paper. Each pair of students compares notes and puts the notes in an order that reflects the organization of the new information.
2. **Pairs compare:** Members of pairs work independently but are allowed to check each other's work.

3. **Match mine:** One of the pair must draw an image, and the other must write a description.
4. **Paraphrase pairs:** The teacher requires one student to paraphrase the other student's statement, verbally or in writing.
5. **Interview pairs:** After a content presentation or reading assignment, two students interview each other about the information.
6. **Group graphic organizer:** A group designs a graphic organizer based on a content presentation or reading assignment.
7. **Line opinion:** Students stand and form a line from strongly agree at one end to strongly disagree at the other, reflecting their opinions about a topic.
8. **Agreement circle:** Students stand in a circle and step in when they agree with the teacher's statement.
9. **Student timeline:** Students write the date and event on a piece of paper and form a line based on the date.

Breakout Groups

The breakout group strategy is frequently used while lecturing (refer to examples in Topic 39). Typically, the teacher pauses, announces a task, and assigns students to groups of two, three, or four. Students either turn to each other in their desks or move around to form the groups. The type of tasks students complete in breakout groups often include:

- Discussing a topic;
- Devising an answer to a question or hypothesis;
- Completing a graphic organizer as a group or as individuals; or
- Preparing a simulation, presentation, or demonstration.

While the possibilities are infinite, students should report their conclusions to the class or submit their projects, and the teacher should **debrief** the group activity.

Typically, students are given a challenge that can be completed in 5 to 30 minutes. Breakout groups can be organized around existing seating, but it is best to vary the members of the groups so that each student learns to work with all other students. In groups, students can exercise their critical thinking and collaboration skills and participate in a task at a level of quality and degree that would not be possible if the same assignment were given as individual work or to the whole class. Breakout groups are planned as part of a lesson plan and should be formed quickly. They have short-term goals and typically lack the formality and structure of cooperative learning.

While the breakout groups are meeting, the teacher circulates among them to ensure that everyone is on task. For evaluation purposes, if a product like a

graphic organizer is to be created, typically each student should create his or her own while working with the other students so that each students is assessed individually on his or her work. Participation in the discussion or activity should be observed and graded as well. Students must be held accountable for their work in groups, so if questioning is used during a debriefing, the teacher must remember to call on different students on different days and to record their participation and questioning grades.

Cooperative Learning

Cooperative learning is an effective group learning method that is very structured compared to breakout groups. To be successful in cooperative learning, students must master interpersonal skills, a crucial goal that is shared by social studies education and cooperative learning. Cooperative learning promotes thinking skills and positive interdependence among students, while holding each student accountable. The cooperative learning structure helps students develop these skills by providing specific rules and roles during the group activity.

The Key Elements of Cooperative Learning

Following are some of the requirements for effective cooperative learning.

1. **Teacher supervision** is needed to establish the rules. The teacher should observe groups to ensure that all students are gaining from the experience. If a student is off task or misbehaving, the teacher should join the group to reinforce the rules or answer questions about the assignment.
2. **Heterogeneous groups** ensure that students of different abilities and backgrounds learn to work together to achieve a goal.
3. **Positive interdependence** is achieved through group goals, joint rewards, divided resources, and role assignments. Students are responsible for their own behavior in the group.
   a. Students are accountable for contributing to the assigned task.
   b. Students are expected to help any group member who wants, needs, or asks for help.
   c. Students will ask the teacher for help only when everyone in the group has the same need.

4. **Face-to-face interaction** encourages eye contact and verbal and nonverbal responses. Students explain, discuss, solve problems, and complete assignments as a team.

5. **Individual accountability** requires students to be held accountable for individual tasks that will help the group meet its overall goal. Some possible roles include:
   a. Leader
   b. Recorder
   c. Timer
   d. Encourager
   e. Reader
   f. "Go-fer"
   g. Artist
   h. Proofreader
   i. Checker
   j. Observer

6. **Social skills** are behaviors that enhance positive interaction and communication among group members. Children learn to compete at a young age, but we must teach them to collaborate and use social skills in a cooperative group as well. The teacher needs to review behaviors and establish rules. Students must:
   a. Take turns.
   b. Share information.
   c. Use quiet voices.
   d. Listen to the person speaking.
   e. Use time wisely.
   f. Politely criticize ideas, but never people.

7. **Group processing** is a discussion of how well the group has functioned. Key words for this element are "participation," "feedback," "reinforcement," "clarification," and "refinement." Group processing allows for closure when a cooperative assignment is completed.

8. **Evaluation** should include both an individual performance assessment and a team assessment.

Cooperative learning focuses on the socialization and civility goals of social studies education, while the teacher can effectively convey information and procedural knowledge. In addition, the interactive process supports multicultural education goals, and many of the projects can be designed to appeal to multiple intelligences.

Primary Cooperative Learning Models

There are numerous models and types of cooperative learning depending on your lesson goals. Table 43.1 provides brief descriptions of the most common models.

Table 43.1 Primary Cooperative Learning Models

Name	Brief Description
Co-op	Students work in teams, and each contributes to an assigned product by accepting responsibility for a part of the project, like an ABC report.
Corners	Students form a team in each (in this example, 3 corners) corner of the room, representing a teacher-determined idea, such as rural communities vs. suburban communities vs. urban communities. Each team discusses its ideas of the critical attributes of each. Each corner shares its idea, and then the teams listen to and paraphrase ideas from the other two corners.
Inside-Outside Circle	Students stand in pairs in two concentric circles. The inside circle faces out, the outside circle faces in. Students rotate as they answer questions on a topic that was taught or assigned as a reading and respond to each partner in the circle.
Jigsaw	The number of members in a team is determined by the number of separate subtopics. The American Revolution would be divided into geography, before the war, the war, after the war, and so on. All teams have the same topics and subtopics. Each student on the team becomes an expert on one of the subtopics by working with the experts from the other teams. Upon returning to the primary team, the student teaches the other members about the subtopic.
Learning Together	In addition to completing the assigned task, the group dynamics that lead to the success or failure of the teams and its members are explicitly analyzed as part of the process following completion of the task.
Numbered Heads Together	Every team member is numbered. (In a team of four, students would take numbers 1 through 4.) The teacher poses questions; team members consult to make sure that everyone knows the answer; the teacher calls a number; and the student responds.
Pairs Check	Students work in pairs in teams of four. One coaches while the other solves a problem. Then they alternate. After every two problems, the pairs check their answers.
Round-Robin	Each team member takes a turn to share with classmates.
Roundtable	Each team member writes one answer as a paper and pencil are passed around the group.
Student Teams, Achievement Divisions	STAD teams are organized following a lesson, and members help each other master the knowledge. Students take individual quizzes, and team evaluation is based on the success of individuals.
Team Word Webbing	Teams create webs, with all students contributing simultaneously on a piece of chart paper or at the chalkboard.
Teams, Games, Tournament	TGT is the same as STAD, but quizzes are replaced with a tournament in which teams compete with each other. Low achievers from one team compete with low achievers of other teams, and each member earns points.
Team-Assisted Individualization	TAI combines group and individualized learning. Students on a team work individually on a self-paced assignment, and members check on each other and help solve problems.
Think, Pair, Share	Students think about a topic, pair with another student to discuss ideas, then share their revised thoughts.
Three-Step Interview	Students take turns interviewing each other in pairs, then share information they learned.

Adapted from Kagan (1989).

TEACHSOURCE VIDEO CASE ASSIGNMENT 43.1

INTASC Standards 1, 2, 3, 4, 5, 7, and 8

Cooperative Learning Lesson

For this assignment, view the TeachSource Video, *Cooperative Learning in the Elementary Grades Classroom—Jigsaw Model*, in which students study the Greek Olympics. After watching the video, list and explain three concepts or strategies that you found particularly useful. Be prepared to submit your assignment to your professor and to discuss your ideas in class.

WEBSITE RESOURCES • Group Learning

Video	*Concepts to Classroom* Cooperative and Collaborative Learning: An online video demonstration of cooperative learning techniques. *TeachSource* Inclusion: Grouping Strategies for Inclusive Classrooms. *TeachSource* Inclusion: Classroom Implications for the General and Special Educator.
Essay	*ERIC Online* ED264162, Cooperative Learning in Social Studies Education: What Does the Research Say? (1985).
NCSS Statement	Ability Grouping in Social Studies
Website	*Jigsaw Helper* This site offers lesson plans that use the Jigsaw method.
	All linked websites (designated by the green color) and those listed here are available as clickable links at the book's Premium Website, www.cengage.com/login, for ease of access. These links will be updated periodically to reflect changes and new resources as they become available.

Topic 44

Practice and Homework

The idea of **practice** is something teachers often associate with practicing mathematics problems, but it is as an essential component of social studies instruction because it is where students practice applying procedural knowledge. In this textbook, practice is conducted in class under the teacher's supervision. This is typically either **guided practice** or **independent practice** as described in Topic 9. **Homework** can be a kind of independent practice that takes place at home, but it can also be a strategy to create a *baseline of information* through reading or other kind of assignment upon which a teacher will draw for instruction.

Automaticity and Overlearning

As an adult, you can add 2 + 2 without noticeably thinking about it. **Automaticity** refers to the skill of being able in social studies for students to use procedural knowledge rapidly and with little conscious effort. With automaticity, you don't have to commit substantial memory to the process and thus free up memory for reconstructing and making meaning of knowledge that is more complex (Willingham, 2003a, 2003b). **Overlearning** is the way thinking processes become automatic. It means learning something to a point of mastery so that it can be replicated repeatedly, automatically, and over extended years. Automaticity results from overlearning, which requires *practice*—not just explanation or exposure to the concepts by the teacher. Sustained practice over the time period of a course, a semester, a year, or several years is the overlearning strategy that allows students to develop automaticity.

Practice in Social Studies

Most teachers associate practice with reading, writing, and arithmetic rather than with social studies. Teaching a math procedure like adding two-digit numbers and carrying over the remainder is followed by student practice with new problems. Social studies also has to be practiced. For example, when procedural knowledge about gathering facts using a graphic organizer like the "Who, What, When, Where, Why, and How Organizer" is used (refer to Topic 17), students could be given individual information packets or a reading about historical figures or events, and they would be expected to apply the method to the new "problem," once the teacher had modeled the procedural knowledge methodology. This would be practice!

> **Can you think of other examples of basic skills or procedural knowledge and content that can be practiced in social studies?**

Guided Practice

Guided practice always takes place in the classroom. The teacher actively interacts with students, providing over-the-shoulder instruction. Students can be expected to apply the procedure as individuals, or they can be allowed to complete their individual assignments in groups. They are permitted to consult with other students while working, but not to copy results. Each student is responsible for his or her assigned project or task or, in the case of cooperative learning, his or her contribution to the group project. The task is usually graded to ensure that students take it seriously, but it is typically given a lower value than a test since it is the students' first practice. In group guided practice, the teacher can give both group and individual grades, but never just group grades.

Independent Practice

Independent practice can take place in the classroom or as homework. The student is expected to complete the task without assistance from the teacher, other students, or anyone else. It is best to have an independent practice follow a guided practice as an in-class activity or a homework assignment. Both types of practice should involve applying the procedural knowledge skill to new information knowledge. For example, in a lesson on longitude and latitude, the teacher might model how to locate the city of New Orleans by longitude and latitude. The guided practice would require groups to apply the knowledge to New York City, and the independent practice would require each student to find a different city's longitude and latitude.

Sometimes limitations on classroom time will allow using only guided practice or independent practice rather than both. The result is that students get less practice than they might need to completely understand the task.

Independent practice is graded to ensure that students take the assignment seriously. It is typically given a lower value than a test and a higher value than guided practice.

Teacher Supervision of Practice

As a general rule, once the teacher has taught the knowledge and explained the directions for the practice, he or she should minimize responses to questions from students so as to encourage students to pay attention during the instruction and explanation of direction, and encourage students' taking responsibility for their own learning during practice. Instead, the teacher could use the Socratic method to draw the analysis and conclusion (answer) out of the student (s) who is asking question(s). Questions could be redirected to another student in the class, group or pair.

If a student persists in asking questions over weeks of practice, the teacher might ask the student if he or she understands before the group activity begins. The teacher could counsel the student privately. This encourages listening skills, metacognition, and responsibility and demonstrates that the student knew or should have known the answer. A teacher who does not handle questions this way will have taught students that they don't have to pay attention and will have begun an unending process of answering questions.

Homework

Homework is a form of independent practice. Teachers have traditionally depended on it to further the education of students given the limited amount to time in the classroom. One of the first considerations a teacher must make while planning lessons is what can and should he or she relegate to homework and what should he or she cover in class. Time outside of school is used to ensure that all the learning that needs to take place during a school year is completed. Parents often see homework as an indicator of a productive classroom and their child's development.

The Value of Homework

There are advocates and opponents of homework. Disagreements about the value of homework stem in large measure from what individuals identify as its purpose as well as from the complexity of measuring its academic effects (Cooper, 2001).

Advocates see homework not only as improving academic performance but also as improving study habits, developing autonomy and self-discipline, promoting efficiency by effectively using both the classroom and the home for learning, and facilitating parental involvement in children's education. Such goals lead them to conclude that homework is too valuable not to be used as strategy. Research demonstrates that homework has a positive long-term, if not short-term, effect on children's academic success (Cooper, 1989; Lamare, 1997). Objections to homework often stem from poorly thought-out homework assignments and policies and cultural changes that have resulted in parents not seeing homework as a priority.

When homework is well conceived and required in moderation, it can be an effective strategy in the development of the child's potential. O'Rourke-Ferra's 1998 article "Did You Complete All Your Homework Tonight, Dear?" is an excellent summary of opinions about and research on homework. The report can be obtained by going to ERIC Online and entering "ED425862."

Because homework is completed outside of the classroom and requires integration into family life, parental support is essential. In single-parent and dual-income families, long workdays and commutes make it difficult for some parents to commit the time needed to supervise children's homework. Some parents feel that homework is less important than social or athletic events and that it therefore intrudes on their lifestyle. Teachers, as a result, have the additional challenge of persuading parents that homework is crucial to their children's future and that the parent, teacher, and child make up a team that needs to use homework to maximize learning. Teachers need to weed out unnecessary and mundane assignments that may legitimately lead parents to conclude that the homework is "busy work."

The Goals of Homework

Well-conceived homework has four goals and a number of advantages as shown in Table 44.1.

Table 44.1 Homework Goals and Advantages

Goals	Advantages
• To practice skills learned in class	• Makes efficient use of home and class time
• To learn a baseline information in advance of a lesson	• Improves academic performance
• To apply concepts learned in the classroom by completing projects	• Promotes valuable study habits
	• Improves students' attitudes
• To learn self-discipline	• Promotes productive relationships between parents and children

Teacher's Tip

Except for an assignment needed to form baseline knowledge for the next day's lesson, it is a best practice to assign all homework for the week on a Friday even though the individual assignments are due on different days of the upcoming week. This allows students and parents to work the homework into their weekend and weekday schedules. It also gives students an opportunity to acquire self-discipline and organizational skills.

Parents' Duties

Successful homework starts with parents' cooperation (see Bonus Topic F, "Parent-Teacher Relations," at the Premium Website). Parents should not be viewed as a substitute for the teacher when expertise is needed to complete an assignment at home because not all parents have the training. While teachers can and should provide a consistent learning environment in their classrooms with well-thought-out routines, each home is unique and ranges from stable to unstable family units. Parents can be called upon and should be expected to monitor their children so that homework is completed on time and according to the directions provided by the teacher.

Whereas teachers express frustration with students who do not do homework, parents express frustration when children have too many seemingly trivial assignments and when assignments are not clearly explained. Teachers should consider holding a homework seminar for parents during the first week of class and/or explaining homework at the open house and parent-teacher meetings. Teachers need to send a letter to parents at the beginning of the school year encouraging them to adopt the following practices.

1. Provide a specific and consistent time each day for homework so that it becomes a valuable part of the daily routine.
2. Designate a specific place where homework is to be done, preferably in your presence (at the kitchen table).
3. Limit distractions by eliminating TV during homework.
4. Check the child's understanding of the assignment prior to starting.
5. If there is a problem in understanding the assignment, the child should contact a study club member or homework buddy. The child should not give answers to or receive answers from other children.
6. Children should not do homework with their friends; homework is independent practice.
7. If the child encounters a problem, use the Socratic method to have the child arrive at a conclusion.
8. Never do your child's homework by telling him or her the answers.
9. Expect the work to be neat and orderly.
10. Check the work for accuracy if you have the expertise.
11. Sign each homework assignment whenever possible.

Teachers' Duties

Teachers must also give greater attention to the planning, amount, and value of homework. They must assure parents that:

1. Only homework that students should know how to do if they were paying attention in class will be assigned.

2. Reading assignments will follow a prereading activity and/or be followed by bellwork or a postreading activity. Students will be held accountable for reasonable factual information.

3. Homework assignments will always be doable without the need for a particular expertise, if children were paying attention in school.

4. The assignment will be clear and definite, and children will be able to do it at home, even if they do not have computers or other specialized materials.

5. A parent workshop on homework will be held during the first week of school, and the same information will be sent home with the students.

6. Students will be assigned to a study club or homework buddy.

7. The amount of time students will be expected to spend on homework will be limited. For lower elementary students this means about a half-hour a day and for upper elementary students an hour a day, on Monday through Thursday.

8. Children will have homework every day.

9. Homework will be collected, read, and graded and feedback will be provided within two days of receipt. Marking will include positive comments as well as notes about mistakes. Homework that reflects improvement will be praised.

10. Students will be required to use a homework planner.

11. Daily check-in and checkout of homework will be required. They will be self-regulated activities performed by students.

12. Some homework will be mandatory and some will be optional.

13. Students will have options—for example, they will be able to choose among creating a sentence with vocabulary words, defining the words, or creating a cartoon with the words.

14. Assignments will be written on the chalkboard at beginning of class, not at the end as an afterthought.

15. As students leave, they will be reminded about the homework due the next day.

> **Teacher's Tip**
>
> During the first day of class, create **homework buddies**. In twos or threes, students exchange phone numbers and are expected to call a buddy if they need assistance.

How much homework do you think is reasonable for lower elementary and upper elementary students? How should you decide what is the right amount in your school?

Assignment 44.1

INTASC Standards 1-8 and 10

Homework Handout

Prepare a letter to be sent home to parents describing your policies and expectations for homework. Be prepared to turn in your assignment to the professor and to discuss your ideas in class.

WEBSITE RESOURCES • Homework

Essay

ERIC Online

ED394690, Study Skills Begin at Home (1990): Offers tips to pass on to parents for lower elementary students.

ED436295, Helping Your Child with Homework (1999): Provides tips for parents on helping their children with homework.

ED452628, Five Homework Strategies for Teaching Students with Disabilities (1999): Offers a number of strategies for accommodating special students.

ED428325, Needed: Homework Clinics for Struggling Learners (1999): Suggests how to organize a well-planned clinic on homework for students and parents.

Websites

Homework Central A useful site that supports students and parents with practices and content for homework assignments.

Check the Premium Website, www.cengage.com/login, for additional links and links that are periodically updated to reflect new resources as they become available.

Topic 45

Discovery Learning, Self-Directed Learning, and Learning Centers

Discovery learning (or **inquiry-based learning**) has its origins in the work of Jerome Bruner (1967) and is based on the principle that students should discover facts, concepts and generalizations for themselves, rather than having teachers explain the ideas to them. Teachers can learn the art of creating lesson plans that require the kind of fact gathering, critical thinking, and active learning (described in Unit 6) that allows students to reach conclusions with social studies content. Self-directed learning and learning centers are specifically based on discovery learning principles, but also serve to meet the individual needs of today's learners expected by differentiated instruction.

The need to customize learning experiences has taken on greater importance as a result of the diversification of U.S. classrooms (Allan & Tomlinson, 2000). This customization, is often referred to as **differentiated instruction** ([Smutny, 2003; Tomlinson, 1999, 2001] see Topic 8, "Lesson Planning" and Bonus Topic A, "Teaching Diverse Populations" at the Premium Website). Teachers accommodate individual differences through a variety of means by their choice of content, methods, projects, and the legally mandated **individualized education programs** for exceptional children. This topic focuses on **self-directed learning** (independent study, individualized instruction, etc.), which often includes the use of **learning centers, learning packets,** and **learning contracts** and, while effective strategies in and of themselves, accommodates individual differences as well.

Self-directed learning and individualized instruction is sometimes misunderstood to mean that students work only by themselves. The focus of individualized instruction is on individual students' responsibility for work and products, but many tasks are completed while students work together and, at the elementary level, in frequent consultation with the

Teacher's Tip

With individualized instruction, students are allowed to work at their own pace, but this does not mean that there are no deadlines. Instead, the teacher should provide checkpoints and observe students to monitor progress.

teacher. Typically the teacher defines the parameters of tasks that are used to assess the student's knowledge.

Keys to Discovery and Self-Directed Learning

Self-directed learning, whether organized as learning centers, contracts, or packets, has a number of crucial attributes. In the following list, these attributes are applied to a social studies lesson on countries around the world.

1. **Students take charge of their own learning.** The teacher organizes resources and expects students to independently collect information from them and to complete prescribed tasks, which might include making a map, creating a timeline, putting together an organizational chart of the government, or creating a statistics chart of population demographics for an assigned country.

2. **Direct teacher supervision is minimized.** After an overview or modeling, the teacher responds to students' questions or reviews drafts of their products. Teachers are able to allocate more time to students who need help.

3. **Learning has specific and measurable objectives,** which can be communicated by a list of objectives, a template of a population demographics chart, a specific graphic organizer, a model of a map, and an oral examination.

4. **A minimum standard** is set for page length, specific products, and required knowledge.

5. **Optional objectives allow for additional effort by students.** A student can choose to create a fictional firsthand account of an event, a biography of a notable figure, or a skit about a historical event. The teacher may provide the options, orz students can propose creative alternatives for the teacher's approval.

6. **Students can also choose how to demonstrate mastery of optional objectives.** They may have a menu of ways to demonstrate chronological understanding—a timeline, a listing of events in order, or an escalator model.

7. **Students set their own paces, and deadlines vary based on individual differences and student preferences.** Students are given a time frame for completion of the entire project, and other activities are available to those who choose to finish faster. Often, the teacher provides time in which students can choose to work on their projects, do homework in school, or work on other assignments.

In addition to acquiring social studies knowledge, learners practice and exhibit life skills such as self-direction, responsibility, decision making, resourcefulness, accountability, time management, and creativity. These kinds of dispositions are as much the focus of individualized instruction as is traditional content. Talking with students individually and as a group about these attitudes is crucial to their development.

Learning Centers

Learning centers or stations are powerful tools for individualizing learning and are frequently used in elementary schools (Stuber, 2007). However, they require a high degree of planning and numerous resources. Such planning pays off with highly active and motivated students. In addition to the general attributes just listed, learning centers:

1. Are rich in resource materials like those listed in Table 45.1.
2. Provide for collaborative and individual performance, so students who prefer to work in different ways have options.
3. Include performance-based assessment by requiring products as well as traditional testing.

Learning Center Approaches

Each of the following approaches might be used at different times during the school year.

1. A **permanent learning center** is an ongoing learning center in a fixed location in the classroom. All students can be required to visit the center during a period of time. It can also be used as an incentive by allowing students who complete work correctly and either early or on time to visit while others are still working. The materials and focus of permanent centers change over time to support current learning. A reading station with reading materials or maps from social studies would qualify as a permanent center. Some teachers use a computer as the focus of the learning center, with a listing of websites for students to visit or software to support basic skills.

2. A **temporary learning center** might be created for a week or two to support individualized instruction on a topic being developed in class, like the American Revolution or communities. Maps, brochures, and stories about the topic would be available for students to use in projects or for general learning.

3. A **whole-class learning center** requires the most preparation and completely alters the nature of instruction for a fixed period of time. Although it is not required, it is best to think about a whole-class learning center as part of interdisciplinary or thematic lessons (Topic 17). Very little whole class direct instruction takes place, and

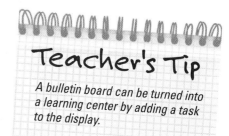

Teacher's Tip

A bulletin board can be turned into a learning center by adding a task to the display.

Table 45.1 Learning Center Organization

Skills: *What Students Practice or Demonstrate*		
Classifying	Communicating	Comparing/Contrasting
Computing	Creating	Critiquing
Demonstrating	Drawing Conclusions	Evaluating
Investigating	Listening	Measuring
Preparing	Problem Solving	Reading
Record keeping	Researching	Summarizing
Thinking	Vocabulary Development	Writing
Products: *What Students Create*		
Advertisements	Collages	Diagrams
Diary entries	Dioramas	Displays
Editorials	Essays	Experiments
Games	Graphic images	Graphs
Interviews	Journal entries	Letters
Models	News stories	Pictures
Poems	Puzzles	Reports
Scrapbooks	Timelines	
Resources: *What Students Use to Gather Information*		
Art supplies	Audiotapes	CDs
Computers	Filmstrip	Flash cards
Games	Globes	Graphic images
Internet hook-up	Laser disks	Library books
Magazines	Maps	Newspapers
Pamphlets	Pictures	Posters
Puzzles	Tapes	Textbooks
Timelines	Videotapes	

Adapted from Schurr, et al. (1995).

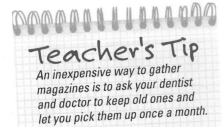

Teacher's Tip
An inexpensive way to gather magazines is to ask your dentist and doctor to keep old ones and let you pick them up once a month.

usually there are five centers—one in each corner plus the teacher's desk. Collaboration with other same-grade teachers is almost a necessity because of the work involved in creating a whole-class learning center.

The whole-class learning center approach provides an opportunity to work in small groups with students who need remediation or enrichment while others are actively engaged in self-directed learning.

Whole-Class Learning Center Example: Australia

Assume that four third-grade teachers decided to create a whole-class thematic unit on Australia to be used by each for a week in his or her classroom. Each teacher would agree to take responsibility for developing one of the four stations and filling it with materials, assessment tools, and objectives related to a unit about Australia.

- *Station 1:* The social studies station would include anthropology, geography, history, and government information.
- *Station 2:* The literature and arts station would have children's books, magazines, stories, pictures, and songs.
- *Station 3:* The science station would include information on animals and geology.
- *Station 4:* The math station would have math problems using Australian themes (add kangaroos, calculate miles using the relative location of cities).

In addition to gathering resources, each teacher needs to create written objectives or tasks for each station, defining what the students must do to master the information or skills and how they can demonstrate their mastery to the teacher.

On the first day of the whole-class learning center, the students would enter a reorganized room. Assuming a class has 25 students, five desks would be located in front of each station, with five at the teacher's desk. The teacher would introduce students to each center and give them their objectives for the week.

Each station should have packets and materials sufficient for about seven students to be working there at one time. The teacher's station is used for calling students together in homogeneous academic groupings for about 45 minutes at a time for focused work on basic skills or advanced skills in reading, writing, and math. Although the experience starts out with students staggered at stations, they are allowed to select the order in which to complete their required tasks and how many elective tasks to complete. Some teachers use signup sheets to schedule time at a station; others prefer to keep it less formal. By the end of the week, all students are required to complete a minimum number of tasks at each station. There are sufficient tasks to keep all students actively engaged for the full week.

At the end of the week, the teachers move the centers to the next classroom and replace the consumables (graphic organizers, maps). The first classroom returns to a more typical instructional motif.

Have you observed or participated in a whole-class learning center strategy? Can you think of some social studies topics that might lend themselves to this strategy? Describe the types of materials and resources you might include in a social studies center based on heroes or community.

Types of Learning Centers

Several types of learning center arrangements are intended to meet the needs of individualized instruction.

1. **Content centers** include materials on the current lesson. For world geography, for example, the teacher might put websites of different countries in the Favorites folder of the computer's browser software and have tradebooks on cultures of different countries and different kinds of maps available. Content stations are usually integrated into the lesson plan topics that are currently being studied. If visiting the stations is optional, the center would be classified as one of the following.

2. **Enrichment centers** include materials on topics that expand on a lesson. These stations are sometimes used to reward students who complete work correctly and either early or on time. They may be prescribed for students who are academically advanced. For example, when the War of Independence is being studied, students who have completed their tasks could go to a computer in an enrichment center to visit websites with battle sites like Bunker Hill, primary documents like the etching of the Boston Massacre, or George Washington's Mount Vernon. If the enrichment center is not computer based, the teacher could have fiction or nonfiction reading materials on the War of Independence for students' use.

3. **Reinforcement/remediation centers** provide additional focused activities for students to practice or relearn previously taught or new skills and knowledge.

4. **Exploratory centers** offer experiences on topics that might not be covered in class. They allow students to investigate topics with grade-appropriate materials collected by the teacher. An example is a computer-based collection of websites on the history of technology that the teacher doesn't plan to cover during the year. A virtual tour could be taken of Greenfield Village in Michigan or the National Maritime Museum.

The last three types of learning centers can also be organized by content. A center on the American Revolution might include enrichment, reinforcement, and exploratory information. Conversely, enrichment, reinforcement, and exploratory stations could include content from any and all of the content areas.

Organization of Learning Centers

So that students are familiar with the organization and processes of learning centers, it is wise to use a consistent approach to organizing all the centers for all the subjects you teach. Table 45.1 provides a listing of skills to be used, products to be created, and resources that are necessary for students to work independently in learning centers.

Assessment of Learning Center Performance

Learning centers are performance based, and directions should be written in terms of behaviors or outcomes. The independent and self-paced nature of learning centers also requires unique reporting requirements. The best practice is to give students responsibility not only for learning but also for keeping records and reporting their accomplishments. The following are the two most common practices.

1. **Station-based record keeping:** Each student has an individual chart in a station folder at each station. Students are expected to fill in the charts each time they visit, noting the length of the visit and checking off completed tasks. Products are placed in a file box that is kept at the station. The teacher periodically checks the stations and engages students who are not proceeding to expectations or whose products do not meet specified standards.

2. **Student-based record keeping:** Each student is given a folder with a packet of check sheets for each station, and the student creates a portfolio of work for submission by a certain date. As with station-based record keeping, the students are expected to complete the chart each time they visit, noting the length of the visit and checking off completed tasks. In this case students keep their own folders, which travel with them.

Learning Packets

Learning packets can be thought of as a learning center's materials placed in individual packets for each student. Packets are used to organize projects. Unlike the learning centers approach, learning packet tasks can be based solely on the textbook, but the better practice is to have a variety of materials (readings, maps, charts, pictures) in each packet and to place some materials that the students can use as references in a center. The kinds of resources, products, and skills listed in Table 45.1 are also used to define the learning packet's tasks and evaluation scheme.

Students can work in groups or individually. As in learning centers, there should be a minimum set of tasks and optional tasks. Time is scheduled for students to work on their packets, and completed packets are turned in for evaluation. Although acquiring social studies knowledge is the primary objective, the dispositional skills of collaborating, time management, diligence, and self-control are equally important from a citizenship education perspective.

Webquests

Webquests combine computer technology, group learning and self-paced instruction into an effective lesson. Webquests require students to gather information from the Internet rather than having the information provided to them

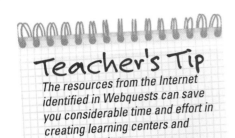
by the teacher. You can create your own Webquest, although many comprehensive Webquests are online, providing both information about how the lesson should proceed and the links needed to be accessed by students to complete the quest. At the University of South Florida, for example, you can access a design center should you want to create a Webquest or modify one of 75 social studies Webquests like *Plan a Trip to Japan* and *The Influence of Women on History* at the USF Social Studies Education Webquest Teachers' Resource Center. To learn more about Webquests, go to Thirteen.org's Concept to Classroom's video workshop on Webquests.

Learning Contracts

The **learning contract** method has the following attributes.

1. It is a prearranged, written agreement between the teacher and the student (and sometimes the parent).
2. The student commits to doing specific learning tasks within a given time frame to earn a specified grade.
3. The learning is self-directed once the contract is signed.
4. The contract is unique to each child.

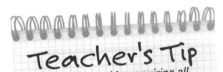
Learning contracts can be powerful tools for building self-control and a sense of self-satisfaction. Many contracts are structured around independent projects that students are assigned. Others are created for students who initiate ideas for projects based on special interests.

Learning contracts can be very effective with students who are highly self-motivated and who need enrichment. In addition, they can be effectively used with students who fall behind in their schoolwork. While completing current work, such students can be given a chance to make up work. In these cases, it is often wise to bring the parent into the arrangement because the additional work may require the parent's cooperation.

A learning contract should include:

1. Student's name
2. Date
3. Reason for the contract

4. Objectives, which should be written in unambiguous language, like "The student will . . ."
   a. Neatly outline Chapter 12 in no less than two pages free of misspellings and grammatical errors.

b. Create and color-code a map of England showing 6 water bodies, 10 of the largest metropolitan areas, and 5 landforms in their correct locations.

c. Make a 5-minute presentation to the class on England's . . ."

5. Due date

6. Outcome: "If completed on time and as specified, the student will receive an A and the assignment will be worth 20 points."

6. Signature of teacher, student, and parents.

Assignment 45.1

INTASC Standards 1, 2, 3, 4, 5, 7, and 8

Webquest

For this assignment, select one of the social studies Webquests at USF Social Studies Education Webquest Teachers' Resource Center. After reviewing the teacher's and student's section, prepare a paper explaining how you could modify the lesson to meet the needs of your elementary school students. Be prepared to submit your assignment to your professor and to discuss your ideas in class.

WEBSITE RESOURCES • Self-Directed Learning and Learning Centers

Essay	***ERIC Online*** *ED497353*, Determining Fair Grades for Students with Special Needs: A Standards-Based Model (2007). *ED44323*, Alternate Performance Indicators (APIs): The Development and Examples of APIs for Students with Disabilities (2000). *ED411274*, Empowering Students Through Negotiable Contracting (1997).
Website	*Discovery.com* Learning center resources.
Lesson Plan	*Core Knowledge's* The One Out of Many lesson plan uses learning packets.
	All linked websites (designated by the green color) and those listed here are available as clickable links at the book's Premium Website, www.cengage.com/login, for ease of access. These links will be updated periodically to reflect changes and new resources as they become available.

Topic 46

Role Playing and Games

Role playing transports students into imaginary situations and requires them to draw on their physical, emotional, and intellectual skills. **Games** can eliminate what would be mundane learning experiences and add excitement to the learning process. This topic explores how each method can be used effectively during social studies instruction.

Teacher's Tip

A **talk by** is a strategy in which the teacher takes on the role of a person from history and gives a presentation as that person. It can include dressing in a period costume.

Role Playing

Role playing has evolved into an important active learning strategy for elementary social studies (Chilcoat, 1996). Unlike theater arts, in which students act out scenes from a play to hone their acting skills, role-playing methods are used in social studies for the express purpose of learning about a topic. Role playing is powerful because it combines the cognitive and affective domains and thus is active learning, not just an activity. In general there are two kinds of role playing, **Simulations** and **Reenactments**. In the literature and searching the Internet, you will not always find the distinction between reenactments, role playing, and simulations. The more basic attributes of role playing are as follows.

1. Role-playing activities require all or some of the students to assume roles.
2. Roles may be based on real or imaginary and contemporary or historical figures.
3. Role-playing activities may be simple and somewhat spontaneous or complex and extensively orchestrated by the teacher.

Reenactments

Reenactments are a form of role playing that focus on people and events in history, recent history included. It can take on many forms, the teacher can role play a character from history, a group activity can be a reenactment, and it can be tied to self directed learning activity where students investigate a historical character and role play the character for their peers. Students are expected to reflect and project emotions as well as develop an appreciation of the people involved and of the time period. For an example of an upper elementary reenactment lesson, you can access through the National Archives a lesson, *Teaching with Documents: Observing Constitution Day,* in which students take up roles of the authors of the U.S. Constitution. For excellent examples of student reenactments of historical figures as a self-directed learning activity, go to the Indiana Prairie School District to see a number of reenactments that have been made available as video downloads.

Teacher-created reenactments can be based on pictures in textbooks, magazines, or the Internet. At Early America's Digital Library you can download an image of the famous engraving of the Boston Massacre by Paul Revere, *The Bloody Massacre Perpetrated in King Street.* Primary documents and background information can be collected from the same website, simplified for children, and used as part of a lesson that includes a reenactment of the events. There are numerous classical paintings of other historical events as well. A painting of Columbus and Indians from the Caribbean reporting to Ferdinand and Isabella can be found in a textbook or at an Internet site. Students could reenact what they think the participants might have thought and said about each other. A website called Museums of the World is a gateway site to the world's museums, many of which have images that can be used in classrooms to create a focal point for a reenactment.

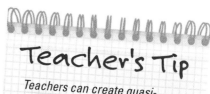

Teacher's Tip

One of the best approaches to reenactments is to place the overhead projector on the floor pointing at a white wall and to keep the image at ground level. Have students stand in front of the images projected on the wall to begin the reenactment. This creates a theater-like sense of a bright light and a backdrop.

At the Premium Website, you can download copies of the Core Knowledge Series Reading 22, "Give Me Liberty or Give me Death," and Reading 24, the Gettysburg Address. Both can serve as material for reenactments.

Simulations

Simulations, another form of role playing, are different from *reenactments.* Rather than depicting a person or an event, simulations provide a simplified representation of a real experience. An example of a simulation would be the teacher introduces the topic such as shopping and elementary school children can pretend to buy something with a student as a cashier and another student as a customer. Another example would be a student making a phone call about an emergency in a lesson about community workers. As part of a lesson on technology, an assembly line could be created. A more elaborate role-playing activity in a law-related lesson would put

Teacher's Tip

Teachers can create quasi-reenactments for dramatic readings. If you are reading a story of Abraham Lincoln aloud, darken the room and light a single candle to demonstrate Lincoln's persistence in learning.

Goldilocks on trial, with scripts for the prosecutor, defendant, and jurors. Because of the dynamic nature of role playing, special care must be taken to ensure that it is a significant learning experience. At the Premium Website, you can download Houghton Mifflin Reading 11, "Community Resources," which includes a role-playing script. Some ideas for simulations are:

1. Archeological digs in the schoolyard
2. Legislation being passed
3. Mock trials
4. Parents deciding on household budget priorities
5. Planning a trip across the United States
6. Playground disagreements
7. City Hall hearings
8. Small claims court trials

Hazards of Role Playing

It is important to remember that all role playing is a representation and, therefore, imperfect. Teachers can find themselves embroiled in controversy if they do not take care to structure such activities with clear, articulated objectives. One of the best-known computer-based simulations is *The Oregon Trail*, a program that lets students go on a wagon train through the Northwest and experience the trials and tribulations of the difficult journey. Academicians (Bigelow, 1996), parents, women's organizations, and Native Americans have expressed concerns about its content, including the portrayal of Indians and the violence. According to a newspaper article (Wilson, 1995) about a lesson using a simulation from *The Oregon Trail*:

> *Van Tassel [the parent] objected to a scenario in which students, while simulating a wagon trip out West, run out of water and are given the options of buying water, forgoing water, or attacking guards at a well and taking the water.*
>
> *Van Tassel said her 11-year-old son wanted to buy water but had to go along with a group decision to rush the guards . . .*
>
> *Consequences are sometimes determined by coin tosses, rolling dice, and pitching checkers into a bucket. If students choose to attack the guards, for example, they're asked to flip a coin five times and for each incorrect call they lose one person in the fight and one "energy point" in their efforts to speed along the wagon trail. Other scenarios have students flipping a checker into a wastebasket to determine whether their pretend child who died of a fever can have a decent burial and tossing a coin to see if their spouse will get killed by an Indian arrow.*

What is your opinion of the parent's perspective? What can you learn from this example about the potential pitfalls of role-playing activities?

Role-Playing Best Practices

Role playing should be part of a comprehensive lesson rather than a gimmick or an afterthought. Based on ideas from Morris (2001) and McDaniel (2000), the following ideas should assist you in setting up successful role-playing experiences.

1. Allow students to select from a menu of topics and then roles to give them ownership.
2. Explain the limitations of role playing to the students: Students must suspend disbelief and accept the limits of the scenario.
3. Ensure that the reenactment or simulation is authentic and purposeful. Make sure the content is accurate and that the ideas it conveys are best delivered by role playing.
4. Start with an introduction explaining the task and goals of the lesson.
5. Prepare the role players by explaining their roles and responsibilities.
6. Provide the observers with ideas about what to look for or questions to answer if there are not roles for all students.
7. Keep all students focused while the role playing is taking place.
8. Guard against trivialization during the simulation.
9. Develop the content by having a briefing and debriefing.
10. Debrief the role playing by pointing out or having students point out motives and actions.
11. Allow students to share ideas and relate the reenactment or simulation to their own lives.
12. Ensure that all students have an opportunity to role play over a period of time: Each simulation or reenactment can provide more opportunities by having one team pick up the situation from another team at a pivotal point or by having a second or third team replay the situation.

Games

Games can add enthusiasm and energy to learning experiences and offer a change of pace from the daily routine. However, even games should have an academic purpose. Some games that may be adapted for integration into a meaningful social studies learning experience are:

1. Bees (spelling bee, geography bee, history bee)
2. Bingo
3. Trivia games
4. Map puzzles
5. Charades
6. Tic-tac-toe
7. Commercial board games

8. Detectives (finding a missing person by making educated guesses to name a person, place, or thing based on clues from the teacher)
9. Stump the teacher (the reverse of detectives, with the students giving the clues and the teacher making the educated guesses)

The Internet offers a number of games and activities that can be used in social studies. The following games found on the Internet could be included in a learning center or could be part of whole class instruction with a large TV monitor.

Assignment 46.1

INTASC Standards 1, 2, 3, 4, 5, 7, and 8

Search the Internet for a Simulation or Reenactment

Conduct a search of the Internet for a simulation, reenactment, or role-playing activity that you could use to teach social studies. Print out a copy of the activity and plan to share your idea with the class and submit the assignment to your professor.

Assignment 46.2

INTASC Standards 1, 2, 3, 4, 5, 7, and 8

Create a Crossword Puzzle Lesson

Based on one of the basal text chapters at the Premium Website, develop a list of vocabulary words. Then go to Puzzlemaker and use your list of vocabulary words to generate one of the puzzle formats that are provided. Plan to share your idea with the class and submit the list and puzzle to your professor.

Learner.org	*Making Bread Together* is a simulation that depicts an assembly line of bread making in a lower elementary school classroom.
Lesson Plans	**ERIC Online** *ED424167 and ED424166,* Adventures in Law and History (1997). *American Bar Association* This site has case studies and simulations for legal education. *National Council for Economic Education.* *Educator's Reference Desk Reenactment of the American Revolution.*
Games	*Fun School.com* *Scholastic.com This site has a comprehensive lesson plan on Thanksgiving that has a game with a virtual tour of Plymouth Plantation.*
	All linked websites (designated by the green color) and those listed here are available as clickable links at the book's Premium Website, www.cengage .com/login, for ease of access. These links will be updated periodically to reflect changes and new resources as they become available.

Topic 47

Discussion and Case Studies

Social studies educators advocate **discussion** as one of the primary forms of instruction because the strategy requires students to think critically and logically and promotes the skills needed for civic engagement (Henning, et al, 2008; Blatt & Kohlberg, 1975; Wilen, 2004b). The **case study method** is a structured approach to using discussion to explore the kind of complex and value-laden issues found in social studies.

"Leading an effective discussion can be one of the most difficult tasks of teaching," according to Barton (1995, p. 346). It requires a commitment to a shared dialogue with students and great restraint from the teacher, who naturally wants to work through his or her planned lesson (Wilen, 2004a, b). And since students' ideas (sometimes poorly conceived, tentative, or opinionated) become public through their communication, discussions can be both intimidating and gratifying on a personal level for the student.

This topic is not about the serendipitous discussions that occur in the classroom but the **planned discussions** that are part of a lesson or focused with a case. In both instances, the teacher has knowledge that he or she has decided students need to know but believes the best approach is to have students come to the new understanding through a dialogue with the teacher and other students. A discussion approach can be the entire content presentation, part of a lecture, or planned as small-group activities (Muller, 2000). But in all cases, your class notes should clearly delineate the knowledge that will be conveyed and the kinds of propositions or topics you may need to interject should the students not be as spontaneous as anticipated.

Discussions

A well-designed discussion requires that the topic have more than one possible perspective, students have a sufficient baseline of information to at least begin the discussion, and there are concepts or big ideas that make it worth pursuing. Heming, et al. (2008) identify 4 kinds of approaches:

1. **Responding to a problem:** "How can the same government allow cars to speed at 70 miles per hour but require airbags?"
2. **Responding to an observation:** Display a picture of parents and their young children with a caption, "a homeless family."
3. **Responding to a narrative:** Read from Dolly Madison's diary while evacuating Washington D.C. during the War of 1812.
4. **Reflecting on classroom activities:** Students discuss a previous activity such as a simulation or reenactment.

In **whole-class discussions**, the teacher typically serves as the guide, using a communication style that is informal and conversational. The substance of discussions should be propositions delivered in a casual environment rather than the kinds of questions used in the Socratic method (see Topic 40). This casualness requires a high degree of self-control in the teacher, who can become impatient and too quickly bring closure to the dialogue. Teachers have been shown to wait less than a second after a student's last syllable is uttered before interjecting something (Rowe, 1974). Poorly managed discussions can take on the form of a quiz show, with the teacher as inquisitor at one end of the spectrum, or a bull session at the other end (Roby, 1981). Therefore, even though the teacher has planned the outcome (the destination, if you will) by choosing a discussion approach, he or she must accept that the trip to this knowledge will not be the most direct route and will take longer than a traditional lecture.

Best Practices for Discussions

There are a number of best practices to consider in planning and conducting discussions, some of which are drawn from Parker (2001) and Johannessen (2002).

1. To prepare students for general discussion, at the beginning of the year have students discuss the nature of a good discussion.
2. Create a set of guidelines or rules for discussions that ensure civility, and review those at the beginning of the year and periodically.
3. Plan the discussion. What topics do you want to cover? In what order? What will you do if nobody says anything?
4. Create a stimulus, what Larry Johannessen (1984) calls "controversy," to begin the discussion. This is usually a provocative question, an emotionally laced statement, a proposition that on the surface appears to be a contradiction ("The sun doesn't rise in the east!"), a crux, a dilemma, a problem, a paradox, or something similar.

Teacher's Tip

Don't always think just because they are in elementary school that discussions need to be teacher centered. Even elementary students, with a little background information, can be effectively put in groups to hold thoughtful discussions.

5. The focus is not on what you will say, but on how you will respond to students' propositions and questions.

6. Use students' comments as points at which you insert your planned agenda rather than laying out an agenda, as in a lecture, and entertaining questions from students.

7. Use a combination of group and whole-class discussions, even on one topic. As an example, provide the stimulus, put the students in groups, and then debrief through a whole-class discussion.

8. Guide participation by rephrasing a statement made by one student into a question for another.

9. If a class discussion is not going well because of lack of energy or enthusiasm, stop and discuss the situation with the students.

10. Because discussion must be based on substantial knowledge, the teacher needs to consistently ask the students to relate their comments to the content that they read, viewed, or heard in a lecture.

11. Use silence, your own! If you are silent, they will speak. Studies show that teachers dominate what are characterized as discussions almost as much as lectures (Bellack et al., 1966).

12. Deliberately slow the pace so that students sense they have time to reflect.

13. Remember that you are modeling for your students how to listen while being involved in a class discussion, so you are teaching both content and an academic disposition (Borg et al., 1970).

14. Instead of responding, ask another student what he or she thinks.

Discussion Versus Questioning by the Teacher

Teachers are often inclined to use questions to promote discussion. However, the kind of structured and rigorous questioning described in Topic 40 can detract from the more casual, reflective strategy of leading discussions if students sense that they are being quizzed or evaluated by the teacher. And too many questions tend to disrupt the flow of a discussion. In addition, we know that students' responses are longer and more complex when they are (1) responses to statements by the teacher rather than to a question (Colby, 1961; Dillon, 1981a), and (2) responses to fellow students' statements or questions rather than to the teacher's questions (Mishler, 1978). You can use a number of alternatives to questions to maintain momentum in the discussion (Dillon, 1981b, 1981c).

1. Express your own thought.
2. Summarize your interpretation of what the last speaker just said.
3. If you are confused by the last statement, express your feeling and invite the student to elaborate.
4. Invite a student to comment on the last statement.

5. If a student has difficulty making him or herself understood, suggest that he or she turn the thought into a question for the class.
6. Be silent—someone will speak.

The Case Study Method

The case study is an effective method of structuring discussions and shifting the class from a teacher-centered classroom to a dialogue. The typical case study is a written account, but it can also be presented verbally. A written case study can begin as a homework assignment or, if it is short, classroom reading. When the case is assigned as homework, students can be required to bring their solutions to class for discussion; that way all students are prepared to be participants.

Like the situations faced by real policymakers or in personal life decisions, information provided in a case is ambiguous, complex, or incomplete. The case describes a problem that has been generalized to disguise the outcome and circumstances, particularly if there is a chance that students would already know of the case or if they are likely to be familiar with the problem. A case is always constructed to have more than one possible outcome. It must be sufficiently difficult, relevant, and interesting to engage students' interest.

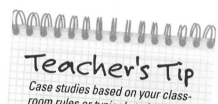

Teacher's Tip

Case studies based on your classroom rules or typical student problems that you have encountered can preempt unwanted behaviors and lead to a more thoughtful classroom if taught each day during the first two weeks of school.

After the teacher "briefs" the case, students—in groups or as a whole class—participate in a collective analysis and decision-making discussion. Facts, concepts, and solutions emerge interactively through the case study process. At the end, the teacher debriefs the class, restating and clarifying the concepts and solutions students have developed rather than teaching them directly.

Preparing for a Case Study

Teachers need to prepare students for a case study. One of the first steps is to model how to read a case. The following suggestions are adapted from the Political Science Department at Florida Atlantic University (2008).

1. Read the case quickly the first time to get a sense of it.
2. Identify the decisions that have to be made.
3. Reread the case, noting facts.
4. Identify and list the problems, constraints, and opportunities.
5. Identify alternative actions along with good and bad short-term and long-term consequences.
6. Be prepared to present your ideas forcefully and to support them with as much care and persuasion as you can.
7. Listen to other students' ideas.

8. Ask questions and admit confusion.
9. Keep on track; don't raise another issue until the current topic is exhausted.
10. Build on the ideas of others.

The Advantages of Case Studies

There are a number of benefits to using the case study method.

1. Students are taken out of a passive role and become active agents in the learning process.
2. Students are typically required to analyze information and develop solutions to problems.
3. Students develop skills that allow them to think clearly about unstructured, ambiguous situations using incomplete information.
4. Students must decipher underlying motivations of the characters or causes of events in the case.
5. Students must deduce assumptions and principles because cases do not explicitly denote the underlying problems.
6. Some students are natural listeners and some are natural talkers; a case study, with appropriate teacher supervision, should ensure that students learn to do both, regardless of their temperaments.
7. Students develop skills in articulating ideas to influence and persuade others.

Organization of Cases

There are a number of ways to organize cases to produce different effects.

The Full Case

In a **full case**, all the narrative and background information is provided at the beginning. A teacher could start a lesson on government by converting the events of the American Constitutional Convention into a generalized description for a case on forming a new nation. The hypothetical case could start with a group of delegates from five countries in Africa that are thinking of joining together to become a new nation. Students would be given statistics on population, wealth, geography, and other factors of each country: Some countries would have large populations, some would have small populations, some would be wealthy, some would not. The students could be consultants hired by the United Nations to help the new country by deciding on and writing a constitution for a democratic nation, or they could be grouped to be representatives from the countries. The case would pit the countries with large populations against the countries with small populations, and the students would be charged to create a "fair" system of government.

The Sequential Case

In a **sequential case**, the narrative and background information is given out in installments so that the case changes over time. After the discussions have begun in the case about the formation of a new nation, the teacher could announce that two of the states with smaller populations don't think they will join because they will always be outvoted.

The Research Case

In a **research case**, students are expected to research and gather information before making a decision. For example, students could be asked to research the governments of Minnesota (which has a unicameral legislature) and two other states and of countries with different types of executive, legislative, and judicial organizations. To facilitate a research case at the elementary level, different groups of students are often given information packets containing different data.

The Unsifted Case

In an **unsifted case**, narrative and background information are handed out, but some of the background information is irrelevant. This forces students to make a judgment about the relevance of the data. For example, the background material for the new nation case could point out that one nation is landlocked and another has a border on the ocean. While this is interesting information, it does not directly bear on decisions about how to organize the government of the new nation.

Types of Cases

In addition to deciding how to organize the case, the teacher must decide on the content.

Live Case Study

A **live case study** is often based on an ongoing event; students are asked to make decisions while the real decision makers are doing the same. The case could be a current court case in the local news, a national event like the Hurricane Katrina flood of 2005, or a local newspaper report on an environmental problem. Often, all that is needed to precipitate the learning experience is a video of a news broadcast or a magazine or newspaper account.

Historical Case Study

A **historical case study** can be drawn from history and may or may not be disguised, depending on students' prior knowledge. The decision to buy the Louisiana Territory, to relocate the Seminole Indians, or to send federal troops to integrate the Little Rock public schools could be crafted into a case study. The Indian rain dance case in the "Lewis and Clark Class Notes" at the Premium Website is a fictionalized historical case study.

Social Issues Case Studies

Social issues case studies lend themselves to policy decisions and lawmaking cases. "Goldilocks and the Three Bears" can be presented as a case for students to decide issues of breaking and entering, destruction of property, and so on.

Economics Case Study

Economics case studies focus on economic issues. A case could tell students that a group of children can go on a field trip to Disneyland, but only if they can pay $50 each. The students would have to come up with strategies to raise money so that all the children could go on the trip. Economics case studies developed by the Indiana State Department of Education can be found at ERIC Online and entering "ED378057" for *Energy Economics and the Environment: Case Studies and Teaching Activities for Elementary School.*

Teacher's Tip

Sometimes a student quietly brings you a problem of teasing, cheating, or foul language. A strategy for dealing with this kind of problem is to create a case based on the scenario rather than to directly confront students.

Student-Developed Case Study

A **student-developed case study** involves asking students to develop case studies based on something they experienced or observed and would like to have the class discuss. Students can present conflicts with classmates, neighborhood problems, or relations with siblings as cases for other students to help solve.

Assignment 47.1

INTASC Standards 1, 2, 3, 4, 5, 7, and 8

Create a Case Study Lesson
Using the steps in leading value analysis from Topic 37 and the ideas contained in this topic, construct a grade-appropriate social studies case study lesson plan based on one of the Houghton Mifflin readings at the Premium Website. Be prepared to share your ideas with the class and to submit your assignment to the professor.

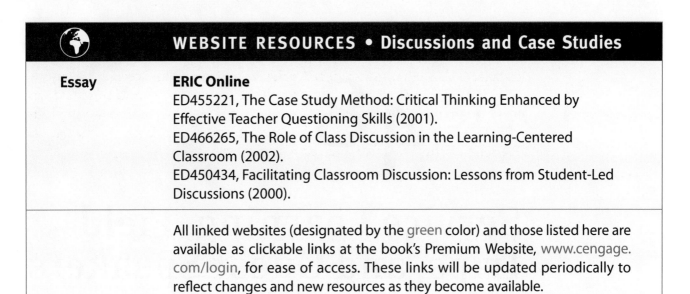

Essay	**ERIC Online**
	ED455221, The Case Study Method: Critical Thinking Enhanced by Effective Teacher Questioning Skills (2001). ED466265, The Role of Class Discussion in the Learning-Centered Classroom (2002). ED450434, Facilitating Classroom Discussion: Lessons from Student-Led Discussions (2000).
	All linked websites (designated by the green color) and those listed here are available as clickable links at the book's Premium Website, www.cengage.com/login, for ease of access. These links will be updated periodically to reflect changes and new resources as they become available.

Topic 48

Service Learning, Field Trips, and Guest Speakers

Service learning, field trips, and **guest speakers** provide a different context, stimulus, and voice than the typical classroom learning experiences. The time commitment can be considerable, so their use should be based on the needs of students and weighed against lost opportunities to teach more efficiently with other methods. So that they do not drift into "fun-only" activities, these experiences should be integrated into a comprehensive lesson plan—that is, they should not be stand-alone events and should serve as a motivating device to stimulate the acquisition of important concepts. What all three of these kinds of learning experiences have in common is the additional and different kind of planning necessary to orchestrate the activity. Teachers must consider issues like parental approvals, extra supervision, quality of an experience that is often not controlled by the teacher, and other logistical issues.

Service Learning

Service learning engages students in meaningful service to their schools and communities by involving them in real-world issues and by linking academic content with civic action. It allows children to act on their beliefs. Service learning that is community based includes opportunities for students to perform community service through such organizations as boy and girl scouts or with their parents. These extracurricular school activities should be encouraged by allowing children to share their individual experiences in class to encourage other students to pursue service activities. Service learning that is organized by a teacher or on a schoolwide basis is the second major approach. These experiences include participating in student government, voluntering at school, and service learning projects (cleanup days; schoolwide food, gift, and fundraising collections; etc.). Service Learning.org is an excellent website to get ideas on how your young students can become active citizens.

Best Practices for Service Learning

There are a number of keys to successful and meaningful service learning experiences.

1. Let students come up with the activity, with the teacher helping structure their plans and introducing the academic content; this ensures that it is meaningful to the students.
2. Let students take the lead, with the teacher as the advisor.
3. Structure the experience so that it requires teamwork, not competition. Cooperative learning models from Topic 43 can be helpful in this regard.
4. Integrate topics into meaningful lessons. As an example, if students had wanted to send food or collect donations for hurricane Katrina victims in New Orleans, a lesson on the city, sea level, global warming, and population density should be part of the service learning, followed by students making posters to motivate students in other classes to bring in donations.
5. Place problem solving at the center of the activity. Using the New Orleans case as an example, you could focus on solutions for New Orleans to prevent such destruction or turn the class's attention to the potential for catastrophic disasters that are typical of their community.

Teacher's Tip

At Learn and Serve America, you can apply for a grant to support service learning at your school or in your classroom.

> **Can you share a good example of a guest speaker or field trip in your local area? Can you recall a good experience from your elementary schooling to share with the class?**

Social Studies Field Trips

A **field trip** should be an integral part of a social studies lesson plan, not an add-on or an afterthought. The field trip can be used as a motivating device prior to classroom instruction, a content segment in the middle of a lesson, or a culminating activity at the end. Regardless of when the trip takes place, specific briefing and debriefing should be part of the instructional pattern.

Many teachers use field trips as rewards that students must earn. While this is a common practice, it implies that the field trip is not an essential part of an important planned learning experience. When a trip is used as a reward for students who are achieving or who do not have behavior problems, students who might be motivated to improve their behavior or performance by participating in the active learning experience are deprived of the opportunity to do so.

Field Trip Venues

The following are some venues that have educational value and should be considered.

- Archeological dig
- Boat or train ride or tour of a plane
- Factory
- Farm historic site
- Municipal building
- Museum

- Military base
- Nature and ecology park
- Newspaper or TV station
- Performance
- Police or fire station
- Reenactment site (such as Colonial Williamsburg)</DCBL>

If you were teaching about communities, a visit to a municipal building and courtroom could be an integral part of the learning experience. If you plan far enough in advance, a city council member, judge, or attorney could also serve as a guest speaker.

Virtual field trips can be taken over the Internet. For example, you can search the database of the Smithsonian Institution or go to the gateway website, Internet4Classrooms for a guide to planning virtual field trips and listing of more than 25 virtual field trips students can take in the classroom or in a computer lab.

Best Practices for Field Trips

You will need to commit a great deal of your time to planning the trip in order to avoid the hazards of a poorly planned field trip. The following are useful guidelines.

1. Make a pretrip visit before deciding to take students.
2. Take the time to meet with your principal and explain your educational goals.
3. Decide if you will run the tour or if a guide from the venue will do so.
4. Verify and confirm all arrangements in writing (transportation, meals, departure and return information, additional supervision).
5. Make arrangements for students with special needs.
6. Create clear rules about conduct and attire for the students.
7. Invite parents to serve as additional supervisors.
8. Create a permission slip that includes a statement of the educational goals.
9. Take roll before, during, and after the trip to keep track of students.
10. Assign partners and place nametags on each child.
11. Preview the trip with students.
12. Provide each student with a guidesheet or questions to answer while on the trip.

13. Provide instruction before and after the trip.
14. Give students specific assignments (additional reading, drawing pictures, projects, mapmaking) to be completed as a result of the trip.

Guest Speakers

Guest speakers can provide powerful learning experiences. For example, when you are teaching about world cultures, a parent from India or China can be asked to talk to the class and share realia, pictures, and music.

Guest speakers can also be disasters. Many are experts on very particularized areas and are unable to simplify the content for elementary students. Others do not have the skill to create a grade-appropriate presentation. Many of the people who want to come to your classroom have biased agendas and will attempt to indoctrinate your students. Some guest speakers are performers with no background in the history or culture they propose to represent. You need to decide if a guest speaker is the best source of information for the students.

Types of Guest Speakers

Some types of guest speakers for social studies lessons are the following.

- Representatives of civic organizations
- Representatives of cultures
- Military personnel, police, or firefighters
- Performers
- Representatives of historical societies or Immigration Associations
- Experts on population, ecology, or local history
- Politicians
- Public figures
- Storytellers
- Representatives of professions and careers

Best Practices for Guest Speakers

To ensure an excellent outcome, teachers should set expectations for their classroom visitors.

1. If at all possible, preview the speaker before extending the invitation. If that is not possible, meet with them or call a reference from a recent presentation. Deciding to invite the speaker based solely on a brief phone conversation is highly risky.
2. Get your principal's approval.
3. Communicate all the arrangements (arrival time, length of presentation, number of children) verbally, and verify and confirm them in writing.

Send the speaker a map, alert the front desk, and have someone meet the person at the entrance to the school.

4. Clearly state the focus of the presentation and your expectations. If you can't reach agreement, don't run the risk; it would better to decline the opportunity. Remember, your credibility is on the line.
5. Limit the time to the children's attention span.
6. Encourage an active presentation with mementos or handouts.
7. Encourage guest speakers to use realia, music, artwork, primary documents, pictures, and period dress if appropriate.
8. Suggest the value of storytelling and anecdotal stories, and warn the speaker to avoid preaching.
9. Prepare students by reviewing etiquette and questioning skills.
10. Provide instruction about the topic as part of a comprehensive lesson before and after the presentation.
11. Require students to prepare questions for the visitor.
12. Give students specific assignments (additional reading, drawing pictures, projects, mapmaking) to be completed as a result of the presentation.
13. Send a thank-you note from the class.

Can you share some examples of outstanding service learning activities that you observed as a student, parent, or teacher on an early field experience?

Assignment 48.1

INTASC Standards 1, 2, 3, 4, 5, 7, and 8

Reflective Journal: Making A Difference

Go to learner.org and view the video lesson *Making A Difference through Giving*. After viewing the video about a fourth grade class becoming invested in a service learning project, identify attributes of the teacher and lesson in an essay that you would want to incorporate into a service learning project in your classroom. Be prepared to submit your assignment to your professor and to discuss your ideas in class.

Essay	*ERIC Online* *ED472974*, Walk around the Block Curriculum (2002). *ED466535*, Community Lessons: Integrating Service-Learning into K–12 Curriculum, A Promising Practices Guide (2001). *NCLC*, Learning That Lasts: How Service-Learning Can Become an Integral Part of Schools, States and Communities.
Websites	*National Service Learning Clearing House.*
	Smithsonian Visit the Smithsonian American Art Museum without leaving your school! *Library of Congress* American Treasure**s.** *Whitehouse for Kids*. All linked websites (designated by the green color) and those listed here are available as clickable links at the book's Premium Website, www.cengage .com/login, for ease of access. These links will be updated periodically to reflect changes and new resources as they become available.

Topic 49

Video and Sound Recordings

Take a moment, close your eyes, let your shoulders relax, try to wash all thoughts out of your head by listening (focusing) on the motion of your breathing. This kind of meditation allows one to bypass (as much as any human can) the constant processing that goes on in our brains and puts an individual more directly in touch with his or her senses and emotions. Video and sound are powerful teaching tools because they have the capacity to reach past your cognition and directly reach your emotions.

Video and sound recordings are so familiar to students that it is almost a given that teachers will use this technology in the classroom. However, classroom video and sound should not be the passive experience of consumers viewing movies in theaters or listening to CDs. In a classroom, video and sound should be an integral part of a learning experience.

In using a video or sound recording, you should follow the same kinds of protocols you use in reading and deciphering images. That is, the video or recording should be previewed, played, and then debriefed so that students acquire a big idea or concept. During the preview, students should be told what to look for and, perhaps, to record their observations on a rubric or in a prescribed note-taking or narrative form as the video or music is being played.

Video

Videos appeal to multiple senses with sound and images, provide cognitive information, and promote powerful emotional responses. **Feature films** (movies), such as key clips, from the recent HBO series on John Adams can give students a sense of a period in history, can graphically depict characters from history, and can dramatize historical events. Tapes of **news broadcasts** can serve as a basis for case studies and depictions of current social issues. **Documentaries** from National Geographic and other series on historical topics can provide vivid details, rich visual images, and background information. **Animated features**, such as a clip from *Pinocchio*, can provide material for a values lesson (versions are available on YouTube).

Misuse of Video

In spite of the merits just listed, video is arguably the most misused technology in the classroom. A growing number of teachers show videos of animated features and shorts and other films as a substitute for teaching, rewards, or as entertainment while they perform other duties. Not only is this a questionable use of valuable instructional time, but it is also a poor use of the unique opportunities for social studies learning that can only take place in a classroom. Some school districts have facilitated the misuse of video by providing an approved list of videos (from Disney's *Cinderella* to *Glory*, the Civil War drama) that teachers can show so that they do not have to preview a video for the administration and get approval. Classrooms are not effective settings for video presentations, but they are ideally suited for discussions, discovery learning, simulations, etc. Teachers should use classroom time to maximize the kind of learning that can only take place in a classroom and school.

Teacher's Tip

The copyright law permits you to rent a video or record a program and show it to a class as long as you do not charge a fee and are using it for an educational purpose. Always have your school administration approve the segment you plan to show.

The Key Clips Approach

The **key clips approach** is the best practice for use of films, newscasts, and documentaries because it is effective, efficient, and appropriate to children's attention spans, and because it ensures that the video is grounded in a lesson. In this approach, the teacher shows only a 5- to 20-minute clip of the video to make a very specific point related to the lesson.

For example, the movie *Glory* (key clips are available at YouTube), starring Matthew Broderick and Denzel Washington, is a compelling dramatization of the Civil War. It would not be a good practice to show the entire movie, either in segments over a number of days or at one sitting to children. It would be a questionable use of valuable instructional time under any circumstance, and certainly at the elementary school level. Children's attention spans would not accommodate a single showing, and the movie provides too much information that is not relevant to a lesson plan on slavery and the Civil War for elementary students.

With the key clips strategy, the following three approaches to using *Glory* in a lesson plan could be used. One or more clips could be chosen to depict:

1. The period dress (hoop skirts, soldiers' uniforms, slaves' ragged clothing) and transportation (carriages, trains), so the students better understand the time period.
2. The bravery of the African American soldiers related to a value lesson using the big idea of duty to a principle or cause.

3. The sacrifice of the character played by Matthew Broderick, who chose to lead the former slaves at risk to his own career and whose loyalty compelled him to lead his men into a situation that meant his own almost-certain death, related to a values lesson on sacrifice.

Sound Recordings

Sound recordings are not used as frequently as they once were because of the relatively inexpensive and convenient access to video. However, they have the advantage of requiring students to create mental images, so when used correctly they can be a far richer learning experience than video. Playing car, train, plane, and harder-to-recognize sounds—like a soccer game or rain—can be a great introduction to a number of social studies topics for lower elementary students. You can download historical and other kinds of recordings from the Internet and play them in the classroom with relative ease.

Best Practices Using Video and Sound Recordings

The following practices should be used when making sound and video part of your instruction in social studies.

1. Sound recordings and video must be integrated into a comprehensive lesson plan.
   - They can be used as an attention-getter to stimulate students' interest and followed by an explanation and examination of the recording. For example, a recording of the Gettysburg Address or a clip of a movie showing Lincoln delivering the Gettysburg Address could be used to gain students' attention and interest in learning about one of the United States' notable figures.
     - They can be used as a content presentation or part of a content presentation. For example, a National Geographic video clip of the Amazon rain forest could be integrated into a lesson on conservation.
     - They can be used as a closing or summary following a content presentation. For example, a clip of the president's State of the Union Address to Congress could be used after a lesson on the organization of the federal government.
2. Only use a clip, no more than about 5 to 20 minutes, to achieve your objective.
3. Do not play whole videos or sound recordings in the elementary classroom because of time constraints, children's attention spans, and the goal of the lesson.

Teacher's Tip

Children come to school familiar with popular music like country and rock-and-roll. Teachers should introduce students to what they do not know. Playing classical music as students enter your class, at transitions, and when students are leaving class can be soothing, can signal a change in activity, and can be engaging.

Can you think of a movie clip that could be effectively used to teach a social studies topic?

	WEBSITE RESOURCES • Video and Sound Resources
Music	*Songs for Teaching* This site has songs and lyrics for sing-alongs online for social studies. *Scout Songs* From the Boy Scouts that are patriotic. *Air Combat Command* Has patriotic and ceremonial songs.
Videos	*History Channel* Has great speeches and video clips. *History and Politics Out Loud* Has video conversations with well-known world leaders. *TeacherTube* Has a number of the Schoolhouse Rock videos like "How a Bill becomes Law" and other video resources that can be used in the classroom.
	All linked websites (designated by the green color) and those listed here are available as clickable links at the book's Premium Website, www.cengage.com/login, for ease of access. These links will be updated periodically to reflect changes and new resources as they become available.

Topic 50

Conclusion: Integrating What You Have Learned

You have reached the end of this book having learned a large number of new concepts about social studies education. To conclude this text, I suggest you need a plan, both to integrate what you have learned thus far and to prepare yourself for your future teaching career. The purpose of this final assignment is to give you an opportunity to prepare a comprehensive plan to show what you can do and, I would suggest, the kind of plan you would want in your **employment portfolio**. You can go to the Premium Website and download a recommended table of contents for an employment portfolio.

Creating a Comprehensive Lesson Plan

In this text, particularly in Unit 4, you had the opportunity to create a number of "Statements of Goals" for lesson plans that cover the breadth of the social studies disciplines. With this final assignment, you will have the chance to put it all together by combining the goals with the methods you have learned.

Assignment 50.1

INTASC Standards 1-8

Comprehensive Topic Lesson Plan

Retrieve one of the "Lesson Plan Statement of Goals" that you may have completed earlier and download the "Lesson Plan Class Notes template" from the Premium Website. Based on your statement of goals, (which you may

(Continued)

Comprehensive Topic Lesson Plan

wish to now revise or to create your first one), create your detailed class notes (or use a model preferred by your professor). While doing so, be sure to:

1. Apply the principles of the instructional sequence from Topics 8 and 9.
2. Incorporate the basal text reading using strategies from Unit 5.
3. Select and apply from instructional strategies found throughout the textbook.
4. Define your teacher tasks, teacher talk, and resources tasks.
5. Create resources like transparencies, handouts, and the like.

Be prepared to turn in the assignment to your professor and to discuss your topic lesson plan ideas in class.

The Ideas for Future Teachers

While you will want to create your own lesson plans and download great lesson plans from the Internet, I would be remiss not to suggest that you join the National Council for the Social Studies (NCSS), which includes with its membership subscription, *Social Studies and the Young Learner*. This is *the* journal for practical ideas for teaching social studies and will allow you to continue to grow professionally as a teacher of social studies. To give you some idea what to expect, here is a sampling of articles from the last couple of years.

"Pirates in Historical Fiction and Nonfiction: A Twin-Text Unit of Study"
"Service-Learning and Nonfiction Texts: Connections for Comprehension"
"Connecting Children to the Bigger World: Reading Newspapers in the Second Grade"
"Using Photography to Tell a Story"
"Advocating for Peace and Justice through Children's Literature"
"The World in Spatial Terms: Mapmaking and Map Reading"

Some Teaching Ideas Not Covered

An author cannot cover all the great ideas that teachers use to engage their elementary students in social studies. The following are some ideas that you might want to research on your own either in ERIC or through a general search of the Internet.

Artifact's Box
Book Clubs
Cemetery Studies
Dioramas
Genealogies
Interactive Bulletin Boards

Museum Exhibits
Oral Histories
Picture Boards
Public and Private Records
Reader's Theatre

A Personal Plan for Transitioning to Life as a Teacher

Your transition to becoming a full-time teacher will be both exhilarating and challenging. To help you cope with one of the most significant changes in your life, the following suggestions are adapted from a class presentation to students in their final internship (Cruz, 2001).

1. Plan to be a better professional.
   a. Continue your education; go to graduate school.
   b. Join a professional organization like NCSS.
   c. Read professional journals, such as *Social Studies and the Young Learner*.
   d. Attend professional development conferences and workshops.
   e. Make a presentation at your regional NCSS conference.
   f. Volunteer for one out-of-class project at school.
2. Plan to be a better teacher.
   a. Take risks, experiment, and adopt new teaching strategies.
   b. Use your summers to recharge your batteries; try to avoid teaching during the summer.
   c. Focus on doing a few things really well by setting a few reasonable goals for improvement each year.
   d. Ask your students for advice on what you can do better.
   e. Ask a colleague to look over some of your lessons and to provide advice.
   f. Always be on the lookout for ideas to improve your lessons.
   g. When you make a mistake, admit it, correct it, and move on.
3. Plan to be a better person.
   a. Keep a perspective on both your successes and failures; rewards are intrinsic and not immediate.
   b. Avoid negative colleagues and friends; choose to be upbeat and positive.
   c. Care about your students, but remember that you are their teacher, not their friend.
   d. Develop a life that is separate from school with friends and loved ones and with exercise, hobbies, and reading.
   e. Learn to laugh at yourself and enjoy the moment.
   f. You can't accomplish everything in a day; learn to pace yourself.

Best wishes to you in your future as a dynamic teacher of social studies!

List of Assignments and INTASC Standards Correlations for
Teaching Elementary Social Studies: Strategies, Standards, and Internet Resources

NCATE Standards (See "Professor's Preface"). Where the assignment and column intersect on the INTASC standards and a letter(s) appear, the assignment could be used to meet the INTASC or NCATE standard.

NCATE A: *Content Knowledge for Teacher Candidates*

NCATE B: *Pedagogical Content Knowledge for Teacher Candidates*

NCATE C: *Professional and Pedagogical Knowledge and Skills for Teacher Candidates*

NCATE D: *Student Learning for Teacher Candidates*

NCATE E: *Professional Disposition for All Candidates*

NCATE Standards (See "Professors Preface"). Where the assignment and column intersect on the INTASC standards and a letter(s) appear, the assignment could be used to meet the INTASC or NCATE standard.

NCATE A: *Content Knowledge for Teacher Candidates*
NCATE B: *Pedagogical Content Knowledge for Teacher Candidates*
NCATE C: *Professional and Pedagogical Knowledge and Skills for Teacher Candidates*
NCATE D: *Student Learning for Teacher Candidates*
NCATE E: *Professional Disposition for All Candidates*

Topic/No.	Pg.	Assignments	Subject Matter Expertise	Learning & Development	Diverse Learners	Multiple Instructional Strategies	Motivation & Classroom Management	Communication Skills	Instructional Planning	Assessment	Professional Commitment & Responsibility	Partnerships
		INTASC STANDARD #	1	2	3	4	5	6	7	8	9	10
1.1	3	What Is Social Studies?	A	D		B			B		E	
1.2	3	Apply the List, Group, and Label Method to Symbols	A	D	C	B	C		B	D		
2.1	12	Text Structures	A	D	C	B	C		B	D		
2.2	16	Web of Social Studies	A			B			B	D		
3.1	27	Self-Discipline Interview		D	C		C					
3.2	28	Character Education: YouTube Lesson Plan	A	D	C	B	C		B	D		
4.1	42	Islands' Critical Attributes	A	D		B			B	D		
4.2	44	Citizenship Education Lesson Plan: Internet Lesson Plan	A	D	C	B	C		B	D		
5.1	52	Multicultural Perspectives: Resources for a Lesson Plan	A	D	C	B	C		B	D		
6.1	59	State Standards Comparison	A	D					B		E	
6.2	59	State Scope and Sequence	A	D					B		E	
6.3	61	Hanna or Hirsch?	A			B			B	D		
7.1	68	TeachSource Video Case: Thematic and Interdisciplinary Instructional Models: Group Activity	A	D	C	B	C		B	D	E	
8.1	78	Download Lesson Planning Templates and Models							B		E	
10.1	90	Search a Multidiscipline Website	A			B			B	D		
10.2	91	Internet Resources: General Search	A	D	C	B	C		B	D		
11.1	100	Strategies for the Lewis and Clark Lesson Plan	A	D	C	B	C		B	D		
12.1	105	Lesson Planning Based on an Internet Activity	A	D	C	B	C		B	D		
12.2	105	Lesson Planning Based on an Internet Lesson	A	D	C	B	C		B	D		
13.1	115	Grading Plan	A	D	C	B			B	D		

continued

List of Assignments and INTASC Standards Correlations

Topic/ No.	Pg.	Assignments	Subject Matter Expertise	Learning & Development	Diverse Learners	Multiple Instructional Strategies	Motivation & Classroom Management	Communication Skills	Instructional Planning	Assessment	Professional Commitment & Responsibility	Partnerships
		INTASC STANDARD #	1	2	3	4	5	6	7	8	9	10
13.2	116	TeachSource Video Case: Directed Reading Activity Observation Guide	A	D	C	B	C		B	D		
14.1	121	TeachSource Video Case: Portfolio Assessment	A	D	C	B	C		B	D		
14.2	121	Create a Product and an Assessment Rubric	A	D	C				B	D		
15.1	129	Create a Traditional Test	A	D	C				B	D		
16.1	136	State Standards	A						B	D	E	
17.1	155	Needs and Wants: Classifying	A	D	C	B	C		B	D		
17.2	155	Five Types of Questions: Modern History	A	D	C	B	C		B	D		
17.3	156	The WWWWWH Method: Lincoln-Douglas Debates	A	D	C	B	C		B	D		
18.1	167	History Lesson Plan Statement of Goals	A	D	C	B	C		B	D		
18.2	168	History: Modify an Internet Lesson Plan	A	D	C	B	C		B	D		
19.1	177	Economics Lesson Plan: Teacher Created	A	D	C	B	C		B	D		
19.2	178	Economics: Modify an Internet Lesson Plan	A	D	C	B	C		B	D		
20.1	191	Geography Lesson Plan: Teacher Created	A	D	C	B	C		B	D		
20.2	191	Geography: Modify an Internet Lesson Plan	A	D	C	B	C		B	D		
21.1	200	Government Lesson Plan: Teacher Created	A	D	C	B	C		B	D		
21.2	201	Government: Modify an Internet Lesson Plan	A	D	C	B	C		B	D		
22.1	205	The Nacirema	A									
22.2	207	Current Issues Lesson Plan: Teacher Created	A	D	C	B	C		B	D		
22.3	208	Career Education: Modify an Internet Lesson Plan	A	D	C	B	C		B	D		
22.4	209	Environmental Education: Modify an Internet Lesson Plan	A	D	C	B	C		B	D		
22.5	210	Law Related Education: Modify an Internet Lesson Plan	A	D	C	B	C		B	D		

continued

Topic/ No.	Pg.	Assignments	Subject Matter Expertise	Learning & Development	Diverse Learners	Multiple Instructional Strategies	Motivation & Classroom Management	Communication Skills	Instructional Planning	Assessment	Professional Commitment & Responsibility	Partnerships
		INTASC STANDARD #	1	2	3	4	5	6	7	8	9	10
23.1	221	Reading Plan	A	D	C	B	C		B	D		
23.2	222	TeachSource Video Case: Metacognition and Reading	A	D	C	B	C		B	D		
24.1	228	Vocabulary Development	A	D	C	B	C		B	D		
25.1	235	Choreography of Reading and Instruction	A	D	C	B	C	B	B	D		
26.1	243	Trade Book Lesson Plan	A	D	C	B	C		B	D		
27.1	251	ABC Report	A	D	C	B	C		B	D		
28.1	257	Cartoon or Picture Interpretation	A	D	C	B	C		B	D		
28.2	258	Collect Primary Documents or Realia	A	D	C	B	C		B	D		
29.1	268	Teaching a Graph	A	D	C	B	C		B	D		
30.1	272	Integrating History and Geography	A	D	C	B	C		B	D		
30.2	273	Map Skills: Modify an Internet Lesson Plan	A	D	C	B	C		B	D		
31.1	278	Time Periods and Data Organizers	A	D	C	B	C		B	D		
31.2	278	Lower Elementary Timeline	A	D	C	B	C		B	D		
33.1	290	Concept Formation	A	D	C	B	C		B	D		
33.2	295	Concept Formation Lesson	A	D	C	B	C		B	D		
34.1	300	Active Learning Internet History Lesson Plan	A	D	C	B	C		B	D		
35.1	306	Remodeled Lesson Plans	A	D	C	B	C		B	D		
36.1	311	Why Is Juneau, Alaska, Warmer?	A	D	C	B	C		B	D		
36.2	314	Create a Decision-Making Lesson	A	D	C	B	C		B	D		
37.1	324	The Heinz Dilemma	A	D	C	B	C		B	D		

continued

List of Assignments and INTASC Standards Correlations

NCATE Standards (See "Professors Preface"). Where the assignment and column intersect on the INTASC standards and a letter(s) appear, the assignment could be used to meet the INTASC or NCATE standard.

NCATE A: *Content Knowledge for Teacher Candidates*
NCATE B: *Pedagogical Content Knowledge for Teacher Candidates*
NCATE C: *Professional and Pedagogical Knowledge and Skills for Teacher Candidates*
NCATE D: *Student Learning for Teacher Candidates*
NCATE E: *Professional Disposition for All Candidates*

Topic/No.	Pg.	Assignments	Subject Matter Expertise	Learning & Development	Diverse Learners	Multiple Instructional Strategies	Motivation & Classroom Management	Communication Skills	Instructional Planning	Assessment	Professional Commitment & Responsibility	Partnerships
		INTASC STANDARD #	1	2	3	4	5	6	7	8	9	10
37.2	324	Planning a Moral Dilemma Lesson	A	D	C	B	C		B	D		
37.3	325	Planning a Moral Dilemma Internet Lesson	A	D	C	B	C		B	D		
38.1	332	Modeling			C						E	
39.1	338	Create a Lecture Based on Lecture Types	A	D	C	B	C		B	D		
39.2	338	Content for Organization of Lectures	A	D	C	B	C		B	D		
39.3	339	Internet Resources	A	D	C	B	C	B	B	D		
40.1	346	Grounded Questions Lecture	A	D	C	B	C		B	D		
40.2	346	Bloom's Taxonomy Questions	A	D	C	B	C		B	D		
41.1	352	Creating an Analogy for a Controversial Issue	A	D	C	B	C		B	D		
41.2	353	Character Education and Perils of Analogies	A	D	C	B	C		B	D		
42.1	358	Create a Concept Organizer	A	D	C	B	C		B	D		
42.2	360	Create Graphic Organizers	A	D	C	B	C		B	D		
43.1	367	TeachSource Video Case: Cooperative Learning Lesson	A	D	C	B	C		B	D		
44.1	374	Homework Handout	A	D	C	B	C	B	B	D		E
45.1	383	Webquest	A	D	C	B	C		B	D		
46.1	388	Search the Internet for a Simulation or Reenactment	A	D	C	B	C		B	D		
46.2	388	Create a Crossword Puzzle Lesson	A	D	C	B	C		B	D		
47.1	396	Create a Case Study Lesson	A	D	C	B	C		B	D		
48.1	402	Reflective Journal: Making A Difference	A	D	C	B	C		B	D		
50.1	408	Comprehensive Topic Lesson Plan	A	D	C	B	C	B	B	D		

References

Adams, G., & Engelmann, S. (1996). *Research on direct instruction: Twenty years beyond DISTAR*. Seattle, WA: Educational Achievement Systems.

Aikens, N. L., & Barbarin, O. (2008). Socioeconomic differences in reading trajectories: The contribution of family, neighborhood, and school contexts. *Journal of Educational Psychology*, 100 (2): 235–251.

Allan, S. D., & Tomlinson, C. A. (2000). *Leadership for differentiating schools and classrooms*. (ERIC Document Reproduction Service No. ED469218).

Allington, R., & Johnston, P. H. (2000). *What do we know about effective fourth grade teachers and their classrooms?* Albany, NY: National Research Center for English Learning and Achievement. Retrieved July 2, 2001, from http://cela.a.bany.edu/4thgrade/index.html.

Andrade, H., & Valtcheva, A., (2009). Promoting learning and achievement through self-assessment. *Theory Into Practice* 48 (1): 12–19.

Angell, A. V. (2004). Making peace in elementary classrooms: A case for class meetings. *Theory and Research in Social Education* 32 (1): 98–104.

Avery, P., & Graves, M. (1997). Young learners: Reading of social studies text. *Social Studies for the Young Learner* March/April: 10–14.

Baldwin, R. S. et al. (1982). The impact of subschemata on metaphorical processing. *Reading Research Quarterly* 4: 528–543.

Bandura, A. (1979). *Social learning theory*. Englewood Cliffs, NJ: Prentice-Hall.

Banks, J. A. (1997). Multicultural education: Characteristics and goals. In J. A. Banks & C. A. McGee Banks (Eds.), *Multicultural education: Issues and perspectives*. Boston: Allyn & Bacon.

Banks, J. A. et al. (2005). Education and diversity. *Social Education* 69 (51): 36–40.

Barton, J. (1995). Conducting effective classroom discussions. *Journal Reading* 38 (5): 346–350.

Barton, J. (1997a). "I just kinda know": Elementary students' ideas about historical evidence. *Theory and Research in Social Education* 24 (4): 407–430.

Barton, J. (1997b). *Did the devil just run out of juice? Historical perspective taking among elementary school students*. Paper presented at the American Education Research Association, New York. (ERIC Document Reproduction Service No. ED401203).

Barton, J. (1997c). History, it can be elementary: An overview of students' understanding of history. *Social Education* 61 (1): 13–16.

Barton, K. C. (2001). A picture's worth: Analyzing historical photographs in the elementary grades. *Social Education* 65 (5): 278–283.

Basch, N. (1995). From the bonds of empire to the bonds of matrimony. In David T. Konig (Ed.), *Devising liberty: Preserving and creating freedom in the new American republic*. Palo Alto, CA: Stanford University Press.

Bearman, A., Feagin, C., Bottoms, G., & Tanner, B. (2003). *Instructional strategies: How teachers teach matters*. (ERIC Document Reproduction Service No. ED479271).

Beck, I. L., McKeown, M. G., Hamilton, R. L., & Kucan, L. (1998). Getting at the meaning: How to help students *unpack* difficult text. *American Educator* 22 (1–2): 66–71.

Beck, I. L., McKeown, M. G., & Omanson, R. C. (1987). The effects and uses of diverse vocabulary instructional techniques. In M. G. McKeown & M. E. Curtis (Eds.), *The nature of vocabulary acquisition*. Hillsdale, NJ: Lawrence Erlbaum Associates.

Beckner, C. (1995a). *100 African Americans who shaped American history.* San Mateo, CA: Bluewood Books.

Beckner, C. (1995b). *100 great cities of world history.* San Mateo, CA: Bluewood Books.

Beeth, M. E., Ozdemir, O., & Yuruk, N. (2003). *The role of metacognition in facilitating conceptual change.* (ERIC Document Reproduction Service No. ED477315).

Bellack, A. A., Kliebord, H. M., Hyman, R. T., & Smith, F. (1966). *The language of the classroom.* New York: Teachers College Press.

Bennett, W. J. (1996). *Book of virtues: A treasury of great moral stories.* New York: Touchstone Books/Simon & Schuster.

Berk, L., & Winsler, A. (1995). Vygotsky: His life and works, and Vygotsky's approach to development. In *Scaffolding children's learning: Vygotsky and early childhood learning* Washington, D.C.: National Association for the Education of Young Children.

Bernoff, R. (1992). *Teaching thinking skills.* Paper presented at the University of South Florida.

Bevilacqua, L. (1997). Ten years later Developmentally appropriate practice: What Have We Learned? *Common Knowledge* 10 (1/2). Retrieved February 16, 2009 at http://coreknowledge.org/CK/about/print/DevAppPrac.htm.

Beyer, B. K. (1988). *Developing a thinking skills program.* Boston: Allyn & Bacon.

Bigelow, B. (1996). On the road to cultural bias. *Social Studies and the Young Learner* 8 (3): 26–29.

Birkerts, S. (1995). *The Gutenberg elegies: The fate of reading in an electronic age.* Winchester, MA: **Faber and Faber, Inc.**

Bisland, B. M. (2006). *Geographic perspectives with elementary students: The silk road.* Paper presented at the International Assembly of the National Council for the Social Studies Washington, D.C. (ERIC Document Reproduction Service No. ED494334).

Blatt, M., & Kohlberg, L. (1975). The effects of classroom moral discussion upon children's level of moral judgment. *Journal of Moral Education* 4: 129–161.

Block, C. (2001). *Think analogies: Learning to connect words and relationships.* (ERIC Document Reproduction Service No. ED471006).

Bloom, B. (1956). *Taxonomy of educational objectives. Handbook 1: Cognitive domain.* New York: David McKay.

Boehm, R. C., & Peterson, J. F. (1994). An elaboration of the fundamental themes in geography. *Social Education* 58 (4): 211–218.

Bond, N. (2008). Questioning strategies that minimize behavior problems. *Education Digest: Essential Readings Condensed for Quick Review* 73 (6): 41–45.

Bonwell, C. C., & Eison, J. A. (1991). *Active learning: Creating excitement in the classroom.* ASHE-ERIC Higher Education Report No. 1. Washington, DC: George Washington University School of Education and Human Development.

Borg, W. R., Kelley, M. L., Langer, P., & Gall, M. (1970). *The minicourse: A microteaching approach to teacher education.* London: Collier-MacMillan.

Boston, C. (Ed). (2002). *Understanding scoring rubrics: A guide for teachers.* (ERIC Document Reproduction Service No. ED471518).

Boston, C. (2002). *The concept of formative assessment.* (ERIC Document Reproduction Service No. ED470206).

Bourdieu, P. (1986). The forms of capital. In J. Richardson (Ed.), *Handbook of theory and research for the sociology of education* (pp. 241–258). Westport, CT: Greenwood Press.

Boyce, J. S., Alber-Morgan, S. R., & Riley, J. G. (2007). Fearless public Sseaking: Oral presentation activities for the elementary classroom. *Childhood Education* 83 (3): 142.

Boyd, S. L., Lillig, K. A., & Lyon, M. R. (2007). *Increasing student participation and advocacy of primary students through role play, teacher modeling, and direct instruction of communication skills.* (ERIC Document Reproduction Service No. ED498927).

Bradley Commission on History in Schools. (1988). *Building a history curriculum: Guidelines for teaching history in schools.* (ERIC Document Reproduction Service No. 310008). Washington, DC: Educational Excellence Network.

Brandt, R., & Perkins, D. N. (2000). The evolving science of learning. In R. S. Brandt (Ed.), *Education in a new era* (pp. 159–184). Alexandria, VA: ASCD Yearbook, Association for Supervision and Curriculum Development.

Brett, A., Rothlein, R., & Hurley, M. (1996). Vocabulary acquisition from listening to stories and explanations of target words. *The Elementary School Journal* 96 (4): 415–418.

Bridgeland, J. M., DiIulio J. J., Streeter R. T., & Mason J. R., (2008). *One dream, two realities: Perspectives of parents on America's high schools.* A report in association with Peter D. Hart Research Associates for the Bill & Melinda Gates Foundation, Civic Enterprises, Washington, D. C.

Brogan, R. R., & Brogan, W. A. (1995). The Socratic questioner: Teaching and learning in the dialogue classroom. Educational Forum 59 (3): 288–296.

Brookhart, S. M. (2008). Feedback that fits. *Educational Leadership* 65 (4): 54–59.

Brophy, J., & Alleman, J. (2006). Children's thinking about cultral universals. Mahwah, NJ: Lawrence Erlbaum Associates.

Brophy, J., & Alleman, J. (2002). Learning and teaching about cultural universals in primary-grade social studies. *The Elementary Education Journal* 103 (2): 99–114.

Brown, J. (2004, July 25). Teachers, here's yet another challenge. *Tampa Tribune*, p. 6.

Bruner, J.S. (1967). *On knowing: Essays for the left hand.* Cambridge, MA: Harvard University Press.

Bull, A. (2000). *Joan of Arc.* New York: DK Readers.

Carr, D. (2005). On the Contribution of Literature and the Arts to the Educational Cultivation of Moral Virtue, Feeling and Emotion. *Journal of Moral Education* 34 (2): 137–151.

Center on Education Policy (2008). *Instructional time in elementary schools: A closer look at changes for specific subjects.* Washington, D.C., Center on Education Policy.

Chall, J. S., Jacobs, V. A., & Baldwin, L. E. (1990). *The reading crisis: Why poor children fall behind.* Cambridge, MA: Harvard University Press.

Charnier, L. (1988). Employability credentials: A key to successful youth transition to work. *Journal of Career Development* 15 (1): 30–40.

Cheney, L. (2002). *America: A patriotic primer.* New York: Simon & Schuster.

Chick, K. A. (2006). Fostering student collaboration through the use of historical picture books. *Social Studies* 97 (4): 152–157.

Cliché, J., & Wiggins, G. (2004). *Understanding by design professional development workbook.* Alexandria, VA: Association for Supervision & Career Development.

Chilcoat, G. W. (1996). Drama in the social studies classroom: A review of the literature. *Journal of Social Studies Research* 20 (2): 3–17.

Childrey, J. A. (1980). Read a book in an hour. *Reading Horizons* 20: 174–176.

Christie, F. (1998). Science and apprenticeship: The pedagogic discourse. In J. R. Martin & R. Vell (Eds.), *Reading science: Critical and functional perspectives on discourses of science* (pp. 152–177). London: Routledge.

Clay, M. M. (2005). *Literacy lessons designed for individuals: Teaching procedures.* Portsmouth, NH: Heinemann.

Collaborative for Academic, Social, and Emotional Learning (2002). *Safe and sound: An educational leader's guide to evidence-based social and emotional learning programs.* Chicago, IL: University of Illinois at Chicago. Retrieved February 16, 2009 at http://www.casel.org/.

Colby, K. M. (1961). On the greater amplifying power of causal-correlative over interrogative input on free association in an experimental psychoanalytic situation. *Journal of Nervous and Mental Disease* 133: 233–239.

Cooper, H. (1989). Synthesis on research on homework. *Educational Leadership* 47 (3): 85–91.

Cooper, H. (2001). Homework for all—in moderation. *Educational Leadership* 58 (7): 34–38.

Cortes, E. C. (2000). *The children are watching: How the media teach about diversity.* New York: Teachers College Press.

Cortese, A. (2007). Get real: Here's the boost that poor children, their teacher and their school really need. *American Educator* 31 (1): 4–9.

Costa, A. L., & Loveall, R. A. (2002). The legacy of Hilda Taba. *Journal of Curriculum and Supervision* 18 (1): 56–62.

Cox, S. G. (2008). Differentiated instruction in the elementary classroom. *Education Digest: Essential Readings Condensed for Quick Review* 73 (9): 52–54.

Crompton, S. W. (1997). *100 battles that shaped world history.* San Mateo, CA: Bluewood Books.

Crompton, S. W. (1999a). *100 families who shaped world history.* San Mateo, CA: Bluewood Books.

Crompton, S. W. (1999b). *100 military leaders who shaped world history.* San Mateo, CA: Bluewood Books.

Cruz, B & J. Duplass (2009). Making Sense of 'Race' in the History Classroom: A Literary Approach." *The History Teacher* 42 (4): 426–440.

Cruz, B. (1994). Stereotypes of Latin Americans perpetuated in secondary school history textbooks. *Latino Studies Journal* 1 (1): 51–67.

Cruz, B. (2001). Lecture presented to graduating social studies majors, University of South Florida.

Cruz. B., & Duplass, J. (2006). *The elementary teacher's guide to the best Internet resources: Content, lesson plans, activities and materials.* Upper Saddle River, NJ: Pearson Merrill Prentice-Hall.

Cusik, J. (Ed.). (2002). *Innovative techniques for large-group instruction* (An NSTA Press Journals Collection). Arlington, VA: NSTA Press.

Cvetek, S. (2008). Applying chaos theory to lesson planning and delivery. *European Journal of Teacher Education* 31 (3): 247–256 (ERIC Document Reproduction Service No. EJ807784).

DeRoche, E. F. (1999). Character education: A one-act play. *ACTION in Teacher Education.* Virginia: Association of Teacher Educators.

de Tocqueville, A. (2001). *Democracy in America,* edited by R. Heffner. New York: Penguin Putnam.

Devine, T. (1987). *Teaching study skills: A guide for teachers,* 2nd ed. Boston: Allyn & Bacon.

DeVries, R., & Zan, B. (1994). *Moral classrooms, moral children: Creating a constructivist atmosphere in early education.* New York: Teachers College.

Dewey, J. (1916). *Democracy and education.* New York: Macmillan.

Dewey, J. (1915). *The school and society: Being three lectures by John Dewey,*

References

supplemented by a Statement of the University Elementary School (Chicago: University of Chicago Press, 1899; London: P. S. King, 1900; revised and enlarged edition, Chicago: University of Chicago Press, 1915; Cambridge: Cambridge University Press, 1915).

Dillon, J. T. (1981a). Duration of response to teacher question and statement. *Contemporary Educational Psychology* 6: 1–11.

Dillon, J. T. (1981b). To question or not to question during discussion: I. Questioning and discussion. *Journal of Teacher Education* 32 (5): 51–55.

Dillon, J. T. (1981c). To question or not to question during discussion: II. Non-questioning techniques. *Journal of Teacher Education* 32 (6): 15–20.

Dolinski C. (2006). "Social studies demand equal testing," *Tampa Tribune*, May 24, 2006, Tampa, FL.

Dollman, L., Morgan, C., Pergler, J., Russell, W.; & Watts, J. (2007). *Improving social skills through the use of cooperative learning.* (ERIC Document Reproduction Service No ED496112).

Duit, R. (1999). Conceptual change approaches in science education. In W. Schnotz, S. Vosniadou, & M. Carretero (Eds.), New perspectives on conceptual change (pp. 263–282). Oxford: Elsevier.

Dulberg, N. (2002). *Engaging in history: Empathy and perspective taking in children's historical thinking.* AERA New Orleans, April 1–5. (ERIC Document Reproduction Service No ED474135).

Duke, N., Bennett-Armistead, V., & Roberts, E. (2003). Filling the great void: Why we should bring nonfiction into the early-grade classroom. *American Educator* 27 (1): 30–35, 46–48.

Duplass, J. A. (1996a). Charts, tables, graphs and diagrams: An approach for the social studies teacher. *The Social Studies* 87 (1): 32–39.

Duplass, J. A. (1996b). Proposition 187: A metaphors strategy for reflective inquiry. *The Social Studies Review* 35 (2): 8–13.

Duplass, J. A. (2006). *Middle and high school teaching: Methods, standards and best practices.* Boston, MA: Houghton Mifflin.

Duplass, J. (2008). Social studies: In search of a justification. *The Social Studies Record* 47 (2): 45–51.

Duplass, J. (2008). Elementary social studies: Trite, disjointed, and in need of reform. *The Social Studies* 98 (4): 137–144.

Edmunds, K. M.; & Bauserman, K. L. (2006). What teachers can learn about reading motivation through conversations with children. *Reading Teacher* 59 (5): 414–424.

Education Week. (2006). Quality counts at 10: A decade of standards-based reform. *Education Week* 25 (17).

Eggen, P., & Kauchak, D. (2001). *Educational psychology: Windows on classrooms* (5th ed.). Upper Saddle River, NJ: Prentice Hall.

Ekiss, G. O., Trapido-Lurie, B., Phillips, J., & Hinde, E. (2007). The world in spatial terms: Mapmaking and map reading. *Social Studies and the Young Learner* 20 (2): 7–9.

Elias, Maurice J.; Zins, Joseph E.; Weissberg, Roger P., et al. (1997). *Promoting social and emotional learning: Guidelines for educators.* Alexandria, VA: Association for Supervision and Curriculum Development.

Elias, Maurice J.; Arnold, H.; & Hussey, C. S. (Eds.) (2003). *EQ + IQ = Best leadership practices for caring and successful schools.* Thousand Oaks, CA: Corwin Press.

Elkind, D. H., & Sweet, F. (1997). The Socratic approach to character education. *Educational Leadership* 54: 56–59.

Engle, S., & Ochoa, A. (1988). *Education for democratic citizenship: Decision making in the social studies.* New York: Teachers College Press.

Epstein, T., & Shiller, J. (2005). Perspective matters: Social identity and the teaching and learning of national history. *Social Education* 69 (4): 201–204.

Erickson, H. Lynn. (2002). *Concept-based curriculum and instruction teaching beyond the facts.* Thousand Oaks, CA: Corwin Press.

Fertig, G. (2005). Teaching elementary students how to interpret the past. *Social Studies* 96 (1): 2.

Fenstermacher, G. D. (1994). The knower and the known: The nature of knowledge in research on teaching. In L. Darling-Hammond (Ed.), *Review of research in education,* Vol. 20 (pp. 1–54). Washington, DC: American Education Research Association.

Finn, C. E., and Ravitch, D. (Eds.) (2004). *The mad, mad world of textbook adoption.* Thomas B. Fordham Foundation. Retrieved February 16, 2009 at http://www.edexcel-lence.net/institute/publication/publication.cfm?id=335.

Flavell, J. (1979). Metacognition and cognitive monitoring: A new area of cognitive-developmental inquiry. *American Psychologist,* 34: 906–911.

Flood, J., & Lapp, D. (1986). Types of text: The match between what students read in basal and what they encounter in tests. *Reading Research Quarterly* 121: 284–297.

Forni, P.M. (2002). *Choosing civility: The 25 rules of considerate conduct.* New York: St. Martin's Press.

Frazee, B., & Ayers, S. (2003). Garbage in, garbage out: Explaining environments, constructivism, and content knowledge in social studies. In J. Leming, L. Ellington, & K Paroter (Eds.). Where did social studies go wrong? (pp. 111–123). Washington, D.C.: Thomas B. Fordham Foundation.

Fraenkel, J. (1980). *Helping students think and value: Strategies for teaching the social studies,* 2nd ed. Englewood Cliffs, NJ: Prentice-Hall.

Fuchs, J. (2006). History detectives. *Teaching Pre K–8* 37 (2): 56–57.

Gagné, R. M. (1965). *The conditions of learning.* New York: Holt, Rinehart and Winston.

Gagné, R. M., Briggs, L. J., & Wager, W. W. (1992). *Principles of instructional design,* 4th ed. Fort Worth, TX: Harcourt Brace Jovanovich.

Gagnon, G. W., & Collay, M. (2001). *Designing for learning: Six elements in constructivist classrooms.* (ERIC Document Reproduction Service No. ED451136).

Gagnon, Paul. (2003). *Educating democracy: State standards to ensure a civic core.* Washington, DC: Albert Shanker Institute.

Gertig, G., & Silverman, R. (2007). No walking and talking geography: A small-world approach. *Social Studies and the Young Learner* 20 (2): 15–17.

Gitlin, T. (1995). *The twilight of common dreams: Why America is wracked by culture wars.* New York: Henry Holt.

Gilligan, C. (1982). *In a different voice: Psychological theory and women's development.* Cambridge, MA: Harvard University Press.

Glasser, W. (1997). A new look at school failure and school success. *Phi Delta Kappan* 78 (8): 596–602.

Good, T. L., & Brophy, J. E. (1986). School effects. In M. C. Wittrock (Ed.), *Handbook of research on teaching,* 3rd ed. New York: Macmillan.

Grant, S. G. (2007). High-stakes testing: How are social studies teachers responding? *Social Education* 71 (5): 250–254.

Greer, J., Greer, B., & Hawkins, J. (2003). Building a sense of family in the classroom. *Social Studies and the Young Learner* 16 (2): 23–26.

Green, L. (2007)."Teachers want civics added to FCAT." *Palm Beach Post,* Sunday, April 15, 2007.

Grigorenko, E. L., & Sternberg, R. L. (2000). Teaching for successful intelligence to increase student learning and achievement. Arlington Heights, IL: SlyLight Professional Development.

Griswold, P. A., Cotton, K. J., & Hansen, J. B. (with LeTendre, M. J., & Stonehill, R. M.). (1986). *Effective compensatory education sourcebook.* Vol. 1: A review of effective educational practices. Washington, DC: U.S. Department of Education. (ERIC Document Reproduction Service No. ED276787).

Halverson, S. (2004). Teaching ethics: The role of the classroom teacher. *Childhood Education* 80 (3): 157–159.

Hanna, P. R. (1937). Social education for children. *Childhood Education* 14: 74–77.

Hanna, P. R. (1965). *Design for a social studies program: Focus on the social studies.*

Washington, DC: NEA, Department of Elementary School Principals.

Hansen, D. (1994). Teaching and the sense of vocation. *Educational Theory* 44 (3): 259–275.

Harari, H., & McDavid, J. (1973). Name stereotypes and teachers' expectations. *Journal of Educational Psychology* 65 (2): 222–225.

Hart, B., & Risley, T. R. (2003). The early catastrophe: The 30 million word gap. *American Educator* 27 (1): 4–9.

Hauser, M. D. (2006). *Moral minds: How nature designed our universal sense of right and wrong.* New York: Ecco/Harper Collins.

Hawkins J. D., Kosterman, R., Catalano R. F., Karl G. H., & Abbott R. D. (2008). Effects of social development intervention in childhood 15 years later. *Archives of Pediatrics & Adolescent Medicine* 162 (12): 1133–1141.

Heath, C., & Heath, D. (2007). *Made to stick: Why some ideas survive and others die.* NY: Random House.

Helbig, A. K., & Perkins, A. R. (1997). *Myths and hero tales: A cross cultural guide to literature for children and young adults.* Westport, CT: Greenwood Press.

Hendrix, J. C. (1999). Connecting cooperative learning and social studies. *The Clearing House* 73 (1): 57–60.

Henning, J. E., Nielsen, L. E., Henning, M. C., & Schulz, E. (2008). Designing discussions: Four ways to open up a dialogue. *Social Studies* 99 (3): 122–126.

Hertzberg, H. W. (1982). The teaching of history. In M. Kammen (Ed.), *The past before us: Contemporary historical writing in the United States* (pp. 474–504). Ithaca, NY: Cornell University Press.

Hess, D. (2004). Discussion in social studies: Is it worth the trouble? *Social Education* 68 (2): 151–157.

Hess, D. (2005). How do teachers' political views influence teaching about controversial issues? *Social Education* 69 (1): 47–49.

Hest, A. (1997). *When Jessie Came across the Sea.* Cambridge, MA: Candlewick Press.

Hicks, D., Carroll, J., Doolittle, P., Lee, J., & Oliver, B. (2004). Teaching the mystery of history. *Social Studies and the Young Learner* 16 (3): 14–16.

Hinde, E. (2005). Revisiting curriculum integration: A fresh look at an old idea. *Social Education* 96: 105–111.

Hirsch, E. D. (1987). *Cultural literacy: What every American needs to know.* New York: Houghton Mifflin.

Hirsch, E. D. (1996). *The schools we need and why we don't have them.* New York: Doubleday.

Hirsch, E. D. (2001). Seeking breadth and depth in the curriculum. *Education Leadership* 59 (2): 22–25.

Hirsch, E. D. (2006). Building knowledge: The case for bringing content into the language arts bloc and for a knowledge-rich

References

curriculum core for all children. *American Educator* 30 (1): 8–29.

Hoffman, R. (1983). Recent research on metaphor. *Semiotic Inquiry* 3: 35–62.

Horner, S. L., Bhattacharyya, S., & O'Connor, E. A. (2008). Modeling: It's more than just imitation. *Childhood Education* 84 (4): 219.

Hoyt, L. (2002). *Make it real: Strategies for success with informational texts.* Portsmouth, NH: Heinemann.

Huitt, W. (2004). Moral and character development. *Educational Psychology Interactive.* Valdosta, GA: Valdosta State University. Retrieved March 28, 2006, from http://chiron.valdosta.edu/whuitt/col/ morchr/morchr.html.

Hunter, M. (1984). *Mastery learning.* El Segundo, CA: TIP Publications.

Jacobs, G. M., Power, M. A., & Inn, Loh Wan. (2002). *The teacher's sourcebook for cooperative learning: Practical techniques, basic principles, and frequently asked questions.* Thousand Oaks, CA: Corwin Press.

Jacques, D. (1992). *Learning in groups*, 2nd ed. Houston, TX: Gulf.

Johannessen, L. R. (2002). *Let's get started: Strategies for initiating authentic discussion.* (ERIC Document Reproduction Service No. ED471394).

Johnson, A. P. (2002). *Using thinking skills to enhance learning.* (ERIC Document Reproduction Service No. ED471387).

Johnson, D. W., Johnson, R. T., & Holubec, E. J. (1991). *Circles of learning: Cooperation in the classroom.* Edina, MN: Interaction Book Company.

Jordan, D.W., & Le Metais, J. (1997). Social skilling through co-operative learning. *Educational Research* 39: 3–21.

Kagan, S. (1993). The structural approach to cooperative learning. In D. D. Holt (Ed.), *Cooperative learning: A response to linguistic and cultural diversity.* (ERIC Document Reproduction Service No. ED355813). Bloomington, IN: ERIC Clearinghouse for Social Studies/Social Science Education.

Kalsounis, T. (1987). *Teaching social studies in the elementary school: The basics for citizenship*, 2nd ed. Englewood Cliffs, NJ: Prentice-Hall.

Kelley, T. E. (1986). Discussing controversial issues: Four perspectives on the teacher's role. *Theory and Research in Social Education* 14 (2): 112–138.

Kennedy, J. F. (2000). *Profiles in courage.* New York: Harper Perennial Library/HarperCollins.

Kist, B. (2001). *Using rubrics: Teacher to teacher.* (ERIC Document Reproduction Service No. ED458392).

Kneip, W. M. (Ed.) (1987). *Next steps in global education: A handbook for curriculum development.* New York: American Forum for Global Education.

Knipper, K. J., & Duggan, T. (2006). Writing to learn across the curriculum: Tools for comprehension in content area classes. *Reading Teacher* 59 (5):462–470.

Knowles, L. (2009). Differentiated instruction in reading: Easier than it looks! *School Library Media Activities Monthly* 25 (5): 26–28.

Kobrin, D. (1996). *Beyond the textbook: Teaching history using documents and primary sources.* Portsmouth, NH: Heinemann.

Kobus, J., Maxwell, T., & Provo, L. (2007). Increasing motivation of elementary and middle school students through positive reinforcement, student self-assessment, and creative engagement (ERIC Document Reproduction Service No. ED498971).

Kohlberg, L. (1969). Stage and sequence: The cognitive-developmental approach to socialization. In D. A. Goslin (Ed.), *Handbook of socialization theory and research.* Chicago: Rand McNally.

Kohlberg, L. (1987). *Child psychology and childhood education: A cognitive-developmental view.* New York: Longman.

Kolbe, K. (1990). *The conative connection.* Reading, MA: Addison-Wesley.

Lamare, J. (1997). *Sacramento start: An evaluation report.* (September, No. BBB34917). Sacramento, CA: Sacramento Neighborhoods Planning and Development Services Department.

Lamber, N. M., & McCombs, B. L. (Eds.). (1965). *How students learn: Reforming schools through learner-centered education.* Washington, DC: American Psychological Association.

Langer, H. (1996). *American Indian quotations.* Westport, CT: Greenwood Press.

Lapham, S. (2001). Time zones in the USA. *Social Studies and the Young Learner* 13 (3): 3–4.

Lapp, Michael S. et al. (2002). *The Nation's Report Card: U.S. History 2001.* (ERIC Document Reproduction Service No. ED464893). Washington, DC: National Center for Education Statistics.

Lattimer, H. (2008). Challenging history: Essential questions in the social studies classroom. *Social Education* 72 (6): 326–329.

Leming, J. S., Ellington, L., & Porter, K. (Eds.) (2003). *Where did social studies go wrong?* Washington, DC: Thomas B. Fordham Foundation.

LeRiche, L.W. (1987). The expanding environments sequence in elementary social studies: The origins. *Theory and Research in Social Studies,* 15 (3): 37–164.

Leu, D., & Kinzer, C. K. (1999). *Effective literacy instruction, K–8*, 4th ed. Upper Saddle River, NJ: Prentice-Hall.

Levstik, L. S., & Barton K. C. (2001). *Doing history: Investigating with children in elementary and middle schools*. Mahwah, NJ: Lawrence Erlbaum Associates.

Lewison, M., & Heffernan, L. (2008). Rewriting writers workshop: Creating safe spaces for disruptive stories. *Research in the Teaching of English* 42 (4):435–465.

Linn, R. L. (2002). *Accountability systems: Implications of requirements of the No Child Left Behind Act of 2001 (CSE Technical Report)*. (ERIC Document Reproduction Service No. ED467440).

Lowery, L. (1998). *Number the stars*. New York: Laure Leafbooks.

Luria, A. R. (1983). *The development of writing in the child*. In M. Martlew (Ed.), The psychology of written language: Developmental and educational perspectives (pp. 237–277). New York: Wiley.

Lyga, A. W. (2006). Graphic novels for (really) young readers: Owly, buzzboy, pinky and stinky. Who are these guys? And why aren't they ever on the shelf? *School Library Journal* 52 (3): 56.

Macken, C. (2008). Artifacts bring Grover Cleveland's presidency to life for first graders. *Social Studies and the Young Learner* 21 (2): 8–11.

Manhood, W. (1987). Metaphors in social studies instruction. *Theory and Research in Social Education* 15: 285–297.

Mann, C. C. (2005). *1491: New Revelations of the Americas Before Columbus*. New York: Knopf.

Martin-Hansen, L. (2004). What to toss and what to keep in your curriculum. *Science Scope* 28 (1): 22–24 Sept.

Marzano, R. J., Gaddy, B. B., & Dean, C. (2000). *What works in classroom instruction*. (ERIC Document Reproduction Service No. ED468434).

Massey, D. D., & Heafner, T. L. (2004). Promoting reading comprehension in social studies. *Journal of Adolescent and Adult Literacy* 48 (1): 26–40.

Maxim, G. (1991). *Social studies and the elementary school child*, 4th ed. New York: Maxwell Macmillan International.

McBee, R. H. (1994). *Living the law by learning the law. A K–12 law-related education curriculum guide*. (ERIC Document Reproduction Service No. ED381482).

McCombs, Barbara L. (2001). The learner-centered psychological principles: A framework for balancing academic and social and emotional learning. *Center on Education in the Inner Cities Review.* 10 (6) 8–9.

McCullough, C. (1958). Context aids in reading. *The Reading Teacher* 11: 225–229.

McDaniel, K. N. (2000). Four elements of successful historical role-playing in the classroom. *The History Teacher* 33 (3): 357–362.

McGowan, T. M., Erickson, L., & Neufeld, J. A. (1996). With reason and rhetoric: Building the case for the literature-social

studies connection. *Social Education* 60 (4): 203–207.

McGuire, M. E., & Cole, B. (2005). Using storypath to give young learners a fair start. *Social Studies and the Young Learner* 18 (2): 20–23.

McLuhan, M. (2001). *The medium is the message*. Madison, WI: Gingko Press.

MacMillan, M (2009) *Dangerous Games: The Uses and Abuses of History*. NewYork: Modern Library.

McTighe, J., & Wiggins, G. (2004). *Understanding by design professional development workbook*. Alexandria, VA: Association for Supervision and Career Development.

Mee, M. (2007) Enough about You, Let's Talk about Me: Student Voice in the Classroom. *Middle Ground* 10 (3) 37-38 (ERIC Document Reproduction Service No. ED497115).

Merryfield, M. M. (2004). Elementary students in substantive culture learning. *Social Education* 68 (4): 270–274.

Merrill, M. D. (2002). First principles of instruction. *Educational Technology Research and Development* 50 (3): 43–59.

Meyer, C. F., & Rhoades, E. (2006). Win multiculturalism: Beyond food, festival, folklore, and fashion. *Kappa Delta Pi Record* 42 (2): 82–87.

Michaelsen, L. K., Fink, L. D., & Knight, A. (1997). Designing effective group activities: Lesson for classroom teaching and faculty development. *To Improve the Academy* 16: 373–398.

Miller, S. L., & Vanfossen, P. J. (2008). Recent research on the teaching and learning of precollegiate economics. In L. S. Levstik, & C. A. Tyson (Eds.) *The handbook of research in social studies education*. New York: Routledge.

Mishler, E. G. (1978). Studies in dialogue and discourse: III. Utterance structure and utterance function in interrogative sequences. *Journal of Psycholinguistic Research* 7: 279–305.

Moje, E., Young, J. P., Readence, J., & Moore, D. (2000). Reinventing adolescent literacy for new times: Perennial and millennial issues. *Journal of Adolescent and Adult Literacy* 43 (5): 400–410.

Morgan, H. (2008). American school textbooks: How they portrayed the Middle East from 1898 to 1994. *American Educational History Journal* 35 (2): 315–330.

Morris, R. V. (2001). Using first-person presentation to encourage student interest in social history. *Gifted Child Today Magazine* 24 (1): 46–53.

Moss, B., and Newton, E. (2002). An examination of the information text genre in basal readers. *Reading Psychology* 23: 1–13.

Muller, H. L. (2000). *Facilitating classroom discussion: Lessons from student-led discussions*. (ERIC Document Reproduction Service No. ED450434).

National Assessment of Education Progress. (2007). 2006 civics assessment. Retrieved February 21, 2009 from http://nces.ed.gov.

Nagel, D. (2008). Partnership for 21st century skills debuts 21st century skills and social studies map. *T.H.E. Journal.* Retrieved February 16, 2008 from http://www.thejournal.com/articles/22973.

Nagy, W., & Scott , J. (2000). Vocabulary processes. In M. Kamil, P. Mosenthal, P. Pearson, & R. Barr (Eds.), *Handbook of reading research* (pp. 269–284). Mahwah, NJ: Lawrence Erlbaum Associates.

Nash, G. B., Crabtree, C., & Dunn, R. E. (1997). *History on trial: Culture wars and the teaching of the past.* New York: Alfred A Knopf.

National Center for History in the Schools. (1994). *National standards for world history: Exploring paths to the present.* Los Angeles: NCHS.

National Center for History in the Schools. (1996). *National standards for history.* Los Angeles: NCHS.

National Council for Geographic Education. (1987). *Geographic Education National Implementation Project: K–6 geography: Themes, key ideas and learning opportunities.* Macomb, IL: Western Illinois University.

National Council for the Social Studies [NCSS]. (1989). In search of a scope and sequence for social studies. *Social Education* 53 (6): 376–385.

National Council for the Social Studies [NCSS]. (1990). *Social studies curriculum planning resources.* Dubuque, IA: Kendal/Hunt.

National Council for the Social Studies [NCSS]. (2008a). *Expectations of excellence: Curriculum standards for social studies.* Draft, retrieved February, 16, 2009 from http://www.socialstudies.org/system/files/StandardsDraft10_08.pdf.

National Council for the Social Studies [NCSS]. (2008b). *Powerful and purposeful teaching in elementary school social studies.* Draft Position Statement for Elementary Education, retrieved February 16, 2009 from http://communities.ncss.org/node/309http.

National Research Center on Education in the Inner Cities. (2000). How small classes help teachers do their best: Recommendations from a national invitational conference. *CEIC Review* 9 (2). (ERIC Document Reproduction Service No. ED440198).

National Research Council. (2000). *Inquiry and the national science education standards: A guide for teaching and learning.* National Research Council: Washington, DC.

Nauta, M., & Kokaly, M. (2001). Assessing role model influences on students' academic and vocational decisions. *Journal of Career Assessment* 9 (1): 81–99.

Naylor, D., & Diem, R. (1987). *Elementary and middle school social studies.* New York: Random House.

Nisbett, Richard E. (2009). *Intelligence and how to get it: Why schools and culture count.* New York: Norton & Company.

Newmann, F. (Ed.). (1988). *Higher order thinking in high school social studies: An analysis of classrooms, teachers, students, and leadership.* Madison, WI: University of Wisconsin, National Center on Effective Secondary Schools.

Noddings N. (1984) *Caring: A Feminine Approach to Ethics and Moral Education.* Berkeley: University of California Press

Noddings N. (1995) *Philosophy of Education.* Dimensions of Philosophy series. Boulder, Colorado: Westview Press.

Noushad, P. P. (2008). Cognitions about cognitions: The theory of metacognition (ERIC Document Reproduction Service No ED502151).

Numeracy Task Force. (2004). *Numeracy matters: Final report, implementation of the national numeracy strategy.* Retrieved January 4, 2004 from http://www.dfes.gov.uk/numeracy/contents.shtml.

Onsko, J. J. (1990). Comparing teachers' instruction to promote students' thinking. *Journal of Curriculum Studies* 22: 443–461.

O'Rourke-Ferra, C. (1998) "Did you complete all your homework tonight, dear?" Washington, DC: U.S. Department of Education. (ERIC Document Reproduction Service No ED425862).

Ortony, A. (1979). *Metaphor and thought.* New York: Cambridge University Press.

Pachtman, A. B., & Wilson, K. A. (2006). What do the kids think? *Reading Teacher* 59 (7): 680–684.

Palincsar, A. S., & Duke, N. K. (2004). The role of text and test-reader interaction in young children's reading development and achievement. *The Elementary School Journal* 105 (2): 183–197.

Pappas, M. L. (2007). Tools for the assessment of learning. *School Library Media Activities Monthly* 23 (9): 21–25.

Pappas, C., Keefer, B., & Levstik, L. (2005). An integrated language perspective (4th ed.). New York: Allyn & Bacon/Longma.

Parker, W. C. (2001). *Social studies in elementary education.* Upper Saddle River, NJ: Prentice-Hall.

Passe, J. (2006). Social studies: The heart of the curriculum, together we need to stop the marginalization of the social studies. *Social Education* 70 (1): 6–8.

Paul, R., & Elder, L. (2006). The thinkers guide to how to read a paragraph: The art of close reading. *The Foundation for Critical Thinking*, Dillon Beach, CA.

Peck, M. S. (1997). *The road less traveled.* New York: Simon & Schuster.

Piaget, J. (1929). *The child's conception of the world.* New York: Harcourt, Brace Jovanovich.

Piaget, J., & Inhelder, B. (1958). *The growth of logical thinking from childhood to adolescence: An essay on the construction of formal operational structures*, trans. A. Parsons & S. Milgram. New York: Basic Books.

Pica, R. (2008). In defense of active learning. *Young Children*, 63 (6): 52–53.

Political Science Department at Florida Atlantic University (2007), *Case Study Method*. Retrieved April, 20 2008, from http://www.fau.edu/polsci/1930/cases.html.

Prescott, J., & Chikes, T. (1996). *100 explorers who shaped world history*. San Mateo, CA: Bluewood Books.

Raths, L. E., Harmin, M., & Simon, S. B. (1978). *Values and teaching*, 2nd ed. Columbus, OH: Merrill.

Ravitch, D. (2003a). *The language police: How pressure groups restrict what students learn*. New York: Knopf.

Ravitch, D. (2003b). Thin gruel: How the language police drain the life and content from our texts. *American Educator* 27 (3): 6–19.

Readence, J. E., Baldwin, R. S., & Rickelman, R. J. (1983). Work knowledge and metaphorical interpretation. *Research in Teaching English* 17: 349–358.

Resnick, L. B., & Klopfer, L. E. (1989). Toward the thinking curriculum: An overview. In L. B. Resnick & L. E. Klopfer (Eds.), *Toward the thinking curriculum: Current cognitive research* (pp. 1–18). Alexandria, VA: Association of Supervision and Curriculum Development.

Richardson, V. (1996). The role of attitudes and beliefs in learning to teach. In J. Sikula (Ed.), *Handbook of research on teacher education*, 2nd ed. (pp. 102–119). New York: Macmillan.

Riecken, T. J., & Miller, M. R. (1990). Introducing children to problem solving and decision making by using children's literature. *The Social Studies* 81 (2): 59–64.

Risinger, C. F. (1987). *Improving writing skills through social studies*. (ERIC Document Reproduction Service No. ED285829). Bloomington, IN: ERIC Clearinghouse for Social Studies/Social Science Education.

Ritchhart, R. (2002). *Intellectual character: What it is, why it matters, and how to get it*. San Francisco, CA: Jossey-Bass.

Roby, T. W. (1981). *Bull sessions, quiz shows and discussions*. Paper presented at the annual meeting of the American Education Research Association, Los Angeles.

Rolka, G. M. (1994). *100 women who shaped world history*. San Mateo, CA: Bluewood Books.

Rothman, R. (2005). Is history . . . history. *Harvard Education Letter*, November/December.

Rowe, M. B. (1972). *Wait-time and rewards as instructional variables, their influence in language, logic, and fate control*. (ERIC Document Reproduction Service No. ED061103). Paper presented at the National Association for Research in Science Teaching, Chicago, IL.

Rowe, M. B. (1974). Pausing phenomena: Influence on quality of instruction. *Journal of Psycholinguistic Research* 3: 203–233.

Rowe, M. B. (1987). Wait time: Slowing down may be a way of speeding up. *American Educator* 11 (spring): 38–43.

Rowe, W. G., & O'Brien, J. (2002). The role of Golem, Pygmalion, and Galatea effects on opportunistic behavior in the classroom. *Journal of Management Education* 26 (6): 612–628.

Rule, A. C. (2007). Mystery boxes: Helping children improve their reasoning. *Early Childhood Education Journal* 35 (1): 13–18.

Salmon, M. (1986). *Women and the law of property in early America*. Chapel Hill, NC: University of North Carolina Press.

Sanchez, T. R. (2005). Facing the challenge of character education. *International Journal of Social Education* 19 (2): 106–111.

Saxe, D. (1992). Solving students' confusion about indefinite time expression. *The Social Studies*, September–October: 188–192.

Scheurman, G., & Newman, F. M. (1998). Authentic intellectual work in social studies: Putting performance before pedagogy. *Social Education* 62 (1): 23–25.

Schnotz, W., Vosniado, S., & Carretero, M. (Eds.) (1999). *New perspectives on conceptual change*. Oxford: Elsevier.

Schurr, S., Thomason, J. T., Thompson, M., & Lounsbury, J. H. (1995). *Teaching at the Middle Level: A Professional's Handbook*. Lexington, MA: D. C. Heath.

Scott, A. (2006). "Activists and lawmakers seek to revive civics in schools," *Herald Tribune*, Sarasota, FL. Retrieved April 10, 2006 at http://www.heraldtribune.com/apps/pbcs.dll/article?AID=/20060410/NEWS/604100446/1023/SPORTS08.

Severgnini, B. (2002). *Ciao, America: An Italian discovers the U.S.* New York: Broadway.

Shaftel, F. R., & Shaftel, G. (1982). *Role-playing in the curriculum*. Englewood Cliffs, NJ: Prentice-Hall.

Shamos, M. H. (1995). *The myth of scientific literacy*. New Brunswick, NJ: Rutgers University Press.

Sheffied, C. & J. Duplass (2009) Creating Effective Citizens: Unique Opportunities for Gifted Education through the Social Studies. *Gifted Education International*, 25: 237–245.

Shores, W., & Michael, A. J. (2007). When the A is for agreement: Factors that affect educators' evaluations of student essays. *Action in Teacher Education* 29 (3): 4–11.

Shuell, T. (1996). Teaching and learning in a classroom context. In D. Berliner &

R. Calfee (Eds.), *Handbook of educational psychology* (pp. 726–764). New York: Simon & Schuster.

Shulman, L. (1986). Those who understand: Knowledge growth in teaching. *Educational Researcher* 15 (2): 4–14.

Shulman, L. (1987). Knowledge and teaching: Foundations of the new reform. *Harvard Educational Review* 57 (1): 1–22.

Shweder, R. (1982). Beyond self-constructing knowledge: The study of culture and morality. *Merrill-Palmer Quarterly* 28: 41–69.

Singer, J., & Singer, A. J. (2004). Creating a museum of family artifacts. *Social Studies and the Young Learner* 17 (1): 5–10.

Slamecka, N. J., & Graf, P. (1978). The generation effect: Delineation of a phenomenon. *Journal of Experimental Psychology: Human Learning & Memory* (4): 592–604.

Slavin, R. E. (1990). *Cooperative learning: Theory, research and practice.* Englewood Cliffs, NJ: Prentice-Hall.

Smagorinsky, P. (2007). Vygotsky and the social dynamic of classrooms. *English Journal* 97(2), 61–66.

Smith, M. (2007). *Improving community involvement and citizenship among elementary school students through service learning experiences.* (Eric Document Reproduction Service No ED497403).

Smutny, J. F. (2003). *Differentiated instruction* (Fastback). (ERIC Document Reproduction Service No. ED477301.)

Snowman, J., & Biehler, R. (2006). *Psychology applied to teaching,* 11th ed. Boston: Houghton Mifflin.

Stahl, R. J. (1980). *Improving the effectiveness of your questions: Some A, B, C's of questioning.* (Eric Document Reproduction Service No. ED198052). Paper presented at Annual Meeting of the National Council for Social Studies, New Orleans, LA.

Stallones, J. R. (2004). Paul Hanna and "Expanding Communities." *International Journal of Social Education* 18 (2): 33–43.

Stanley, W. B. (2005). Research and practice: Social studies and the social order: Transmission or transformation? *Social Education* 69 (5): 282–286.

Starnes, B. A. (2004). Thoughts on teaching: The theory of everything and yada, yada, yada. *Phi Delta Kappan* 86 (4): 329–330.

Stern, S. M. (2003). *Effective State Standards for U.S. History: A 2003 Report Card.* Washington, DC: Thomas B. Fordham Foundation.

Stone, R. (2002). *What! Another new mandate? What award-winning teachers do when school rules change.* (ERIC Document Reproduction Service No. ED471195).

Stuber, G. M. (2007). Centering your classroom: Setting the stage for engaged learners. *Young Children* 62 (4): 58–59.

Suiter, M., & Meszaros, B. (2005). Teaching about saving and investing in the elementary and middle school grades. *Social Education* 69 (2): 92–96.

Symcox, L. (2002). *Whose history? The struggle for national standards in American classrooms.* (ERIC Reproduction Document Service No. ED477893).

Taba, H., Durkin, M., Fraenkel, J., & McNaughton, A. (1971). *A teacher's handbook to elementary social studies,* 2nd ed. Reading, MA: Addison-Wesley.

Teal, T. (2003). *Strategies to enhance vocabulary development.* (ERIC Reproduction Document Service No. ED479128).

Thomas B. Fordham Institute (2005). *The mad, mad world of textbook adoption.* Retrieved February 16, 2009 at http://www.edexce-llence.net/institute/publication/publication.cfm?id=335.

Thornberg, R. (2008). "It's not fair!"—Voicing pupils' criticisms of school rules. *Children & Society* 22 (6) 418–428.

Thornton, S. J. (2007). Integrating geography into American history. *Education Digest: Essential Readings Condensed for Quick Review* 72 (9): 30–36.

Thousand, J., Nevin, A., McNeil, M., & Liston, A. (2006). *Differentiating instruction in inclusive classrooms: Myth or reality?* Paper Presented at TED/TAM, San Diego (ERIC Reproduction Document Service No. ED493953).

Tierney, D. S. (1991). The social studies teacher as analogist. *Social Science Record* 28: 53–57.

Tishman, S., Jay, E., & Perkins, D. N. (1992). *Teach-ing thinking dispositions: From transmission to enculturation.* Harvard University. Paper funded by the John D. and Catherine T. MacArthur Foundation.

Tomlinson, C. (1999). *The differentiated classroom: Responding to the needs of all learners.* ED 429 944. Alexandria VA: Association for Supervision and Curriculum Development.

Tomlinson, C. (2001). *How to differentiate instruction in mixed-ability classrooms* (2nd ed.). Alexandria, VA: Association for Supervision and Curriculum Development (ERIC Document Reproduction Service No. 451902).

Trumbull, E., Rothstein-Fisch, C., Greenfield, P. M., Quiroz, B. (2001). *Bridging cultures between home and school: A guide for teachers—with a special focus on immigrant Latino families.* (ERIC Document Reproduction Service No. ED460094).

Trygestad, J. C. (2001). "Toads on Logs": A mapping mnemonic. *Social Studies and the Young Learner* 13 (3): 1–2.

Turley, E. D., & Gallagher, C. W. (2008). On the "success" of rubrics: Reframing the great rubric debate. *English Journal* 97 (4): 87–92.

University of Illinois (2007). *Lecture.* Retrieved April, 20 2008, from http://wwwoit.uiuc.edu/Did/docs/Lecture/Lecture2.htm.

University of Pittsburg (2007). *Lecture Method.* Retrieved April, 20 2008, from http://www.pitt.edu/~ciddeweb/Faculty-Developlment/FDS/lectumeth.html.

Vanfossen, P. (2005) Economic concepts at the core of civic education. *International Journal of Social Education* 20 (2): 35–66.

Van Hover, S., & Van Horne, M. (2005). Teaching for citizenship in the social studies classroom. *Learning and Leading with Technology* 32 (8): 48–52.

Van Patten, J. (2002). *Hi stakes polarization or accountability.* (ERIC Document Reproduction Service No. ED464151).

Van Sledright, B. A. (2004). What does it mean to think historically and how do you teach it? *Social Education* 68 (3): 230–233.

Vogler, K. E., & Virtue, D. (2007). "Just the facts, ma'am": Teaching social studies in the era of standards and high-stakes testing. *Social Studies* 98 (2): 54–58.

Wakefield, J. F. (2006). Textbook usage in the United States: The case of U.S. history (ERIC Document Reproduction Service No. ED491579).

Walker-Dalhouse, D. (1993). Beginning reading and the African American child at risk. *Young Children* 49 (1): 24–28.

Walsh, B. A. (2008). Quantity, quality, children's characteristics, and vocabulary learning. *Childhood Education* 84 (3): 163.

Walsh, R. (1974). Lectures on sex and reproduction presented at St. Louis University.

Watson, S. B., & Linder, J. L. (2004). The scientific method: Is it still useful? *Science Scope* 28 (3): 37–39.

Weber, F. (1999). *Student assessment that works: A practical approach.* Boston, MA: Allyn & Bacon.

Weems, M. L. (1809). "The fable of George Washington and the cherry tree," *The life of Washington.* Retrieved February 16, 2009 at http://gwpapers.virginia.edu /articles/weems .html.

Welton, D. A. (2002). *Children and their world: Strategies for teaching social studies,* 7th ed. Boston, MA: Houghton Mifflin.

Werner, W. (2004). "What does this picture say?" Reading the Intertextuality of Visual Images. *International Journal of Social Education* 19 (1): 64–77.

West, M. (2007). Problem solving: A sensible approach to children's science and social studies learning—and beyond. *Young Children* 62 (5): 34–41.

WestEd. (2001). *Making time count.* Policy Brief. San Francisco: WestEd. Retrieved April 24, 2004, from http://web.wested.org/online_pubs/making_time_count.pdf.

Whimbey, A., & Lockhead, J. (1980). *Problem solving and comprehension.* Philadelphia: Franklin Institute Press.

White, T. G., Graves, M. F., & Slater, W. H. (1990). Growth of reading in diverse elementary schools: Decoding and word meaning. *Journal of Educational Psychology* 82: 281–290.

Wilen, W. (2004a). Encouraging reticent students' participation in classroom discussions. *Social Education* 68 (1): 51–57.

Wilen, W. (2004b). Refuting misconceptions about classroom discussion. *Social Studies* 95 (1): 33–40.

Wilkens, K. (2003). Lecture presented to graduating social studies majors, University of South Florida.

Will, G. (1998, May 15). Address to the class of 1998, Washington University, St. Louis.

Will, G. (2004, March 11). Whose child shall be left behind? *Tampa Tribune,* p. 19.

Will, G. (2005, October 19). 2005's kind of progress. *Newsweek,* p. 88.

Will, G. (2008, August 12). In praise of paternalism. *St. Pete Times,* p. 11A.

.Willingham, D. T. (2003a). *Cognition: The thinking animal.* Upper Saddle River, NJ: Prentice-Hall.

Willingham, D. T. (2003b). Students remember what they think. *American Educator* 27 (3): 37–41.

Willingham, D. T. (2006). How knowledge helps. *American Education* 30 (1): 30–37.

Willingham, D. T. (2007). Teaching critical thinking. *American Educator* 31 (2): 8–19.

Wilson, J. H. (1976). The illusion of change. In A. F. Young (Ed.), *The American revolution: Explorations in the history of American radicalism.* DeKalb, IL: Northern Illinois University Press.

Wilson, W. (1995, April 29). Golden gate parent objects to school's role-playing exercise. *Naples Daily News.*

Wineburg, S. (2001). *Historical thinking and other unnatural acts: Charting the future of teaching the past: Critical perspectives on the past.* Philadelphia: Temple University Press.

Wood, K. D., & Dickinson, T. S. (Eds.). (2000). *Promoting literacy in grades 4–9: A handbook for teachers and administrators.* Boston: Allyn & Bacon.

Woods, C. S. (1998). Raising literate children: Tips for parents. *Montessori Life* 10 (3): 45.

Wilford, S. (2007). Modeling appropriate behaviors: Helping teachers recognize their position as role models for children. *Early Childhood Today* 21 (5): 8–9.

Wright, I. (2002). *Is that right? Critical thinking and the social world of the young learner.* Toronto, Canada: Pippin.

Yilmax, K. (2007). Historical empathy and its implications for classroom practices in schools. *History Teacher* 40 (3): 331–338.

Yenne, B. (1994). *100 men who shaped world history.* San Mateo, CA: Bluewood Books.

Yenne, B., & Grosser, M. (1993). *100 inventions that shaped world history.* San Mateo, CA: Bluewood Books.

Yenne, B., Perkins, C. N., & Chikes, T. (1996). *100 authors who shaped world history*. San Mateo, CA: Bluewood Books.

Yopp, R. H., & Yopp, H. K. (2000). Sharing informational text with young children. *The Reading Teacher* 53: 410–423.

Young, D., & Behounek, L. M. (2006). Kindergartners use powerpoint to lead their own parent-teacher conferences. *Young Children* 61 (2): 24–26.

Zeidler, D. L., & Duplass, J. (2000). Critical thinking and the role of logical argument in social studies education. *International Journal of Social Education* 15 (1): 113–127.

Zins, Joseph E., Weissberg, Roger P., & Walberg, Herbert (2003). *Building school success on social and emotional Learning*. New York: Teachers College Press.

Zins, Joseph E., Weissberg, Roger P., Wang, Margaret C., & Walberg, Herbert J. (2001). Social and emotional learning and school success: Maximizing children's potential by integrating thinking, feeling and behavior. *Center on Education in the Inner Cities Review* 10 (6): 1–3, 26–27.

Zhao, Y., & Hoge J. D. (2005). What elementary students and teachers say about social studies. *Social Studies* 96 (5): 216–222.

Index

*Websites and **ERIC online documents** cited in the text are listed and are accessible by clickable links at the Premium Website*
***References** include all cited works except ERIC online documents*
***Assignments** are listed on page 411*

Index

Index

440   **Index**